T0350311

Applications of Complex Adaptive Systems

Yin Shan
Medicare Australia, Australia

Ang Yang
CSIRO Land and Water, Australia

IGI PUBLISHING

Hershey • New York

Acquisition Editor:	Kristin Klinger
Senior Managing Editor:	Jennifer Neidig
Managing Editor:	Sara Reed
Development Editor:	Kristin M. Roth
Assistant Development Editor:	Meg Stocking
Editorial Assistant:	Deborah Yahnke
Copy Editor:	Holly Powell
Typesetter:	Amanda Appicello
Cover Design:	Lisa Tosheff
Printed at:	Yurchak Printing Inc.

Published in the United States of America by
    IGI Publishing (an imprint of IGI Global)
    701 E. Chocolate Avenue
    Hershey PA 17033
    Tel: 717-533-8845
    Fax: 717-533-8661
    E-mail: cust@igi-global.com
    Web site: http://www.igi-global.com

and in the United Kingdom by
    IGI Publishing (an imprint of IGI Global)
    3 Henrietta Street
    Covent Garden
    London WC2E 8LU
    Tel: 44 20 7240 0856
    Fax: 44 20 7379 0609
    Web site: http://www.eurospanonline.com

Product or company names used in this book are for identification purposes only. Inclusion of the names of the products or companies does not indicate a claim of ownership by IGI Global of the trademark or registered trademark.

Library of Congress Cataloging-in-Publication Data

Applications of complex adaptive systems / Yin Shan and Ang Yang, editors.
    p. cm.
 Companion volume to: Intelligent complex adaptive systems.
 Summary: "This book provides an estimable global view of the most up-to-date research on the strategies, applications, practice, and implications of complex adaptive systems, to better understand the various critical systems that surround human life. Researchers will find this book an indispensable state-of-art reference"--Provided by publisher.
 Includes bibliographical references and index.
 ISBN-13: 978-1-59904-962-5 (hardcover)
 ISBN-13: 978-1-59904-963-2 (ebook)
 1. Functionalism (Social sciences) 2. System analysis. 3. Biocomplexity--Simulation methods. 4. Social systems--Simulation methods. 5. Economics--Methodology. 6. Organizational sociology--Simulation methods. 7. Modularity (Engineering) 8. Modularity (Psychology) 9. Self-organizaing systems. 10. Adaptive control systems. I. Yang, Ang. II. Shan, Yin.
 HM484.A67 2008
 306.4'2011--dc22
                 2007032060

British Cataloguing in Publication Data
A Cataloguing in Publication record for this book is available from the British Library.

All work contributed to this book is new, previously-unpublished material. The views expressed in this book are those of the authors, but not necessarily of the publisher.

economic behavior. An integrated social science, for so long an impractical notion, now seems a possibility as complex adaptive systems science develops.

The core of this new science lies in agent-based modeling, which enables both natural and social scientists to engage in theorizing that is not deductive and does not require equilibrium solutions. Simulation experiments can be conducted, starting with stylized facts concerning aspects of the real world. The availability of modern computing power combined with a new understanding of how networks operate, developed mainly by sociologists such as Duncan Watts in social science settings, can permit exhaustive explorations of agent interactions. Calibrations on real data can be conducted; although it is fair to say that the methodologies involved remain in the early stages of development in the social sciences.

A large and important research program is now evolving and the contributions in this book provide excellent examples of the advances in understanding that are being made, both within and beyond the social sciences. These contributions are what we expect in the early stages of a scientific revolution: they are wide ranging in focus, they are adventurous in scope, and they reflect the excitement of participating in a frontier field of research. All of the main fields of complex adaptive modeling are represented here and both social and natural science applications are considered. Each author has taken care to introduce his or her field in a way that is comprehensible to the non-expert before offering their particular contribution. For anyone looking to gain an understanding of what the new field of complex adaptive system modeling is about, this book will constitute an excellent starting point. While, at the same time, experts in the field will find perspectives, approaches, techniques, and methodological discussions that are novel and important.

John Foster
Professor, School of Economics, University of Queensland, Australia

Preface

Our world is a large, integrated system of systems. These systems, whether they are ecological, social, or financial are complex and they constantly adapt to their environment. Many of them are essential for our very existence. Because of the intensive interactions among the system components and because they are so complex, they cannot be fully understood by isolating their components or applying simple cause and effect reasoning. These systems, however, can be examined by looking for patterns within their behaviour. Intelligent complex adaptive system (ICAS) research uses systemic inquiry to build multi-disciplinary representations of reality to study such complex systems.

Because the use of ICASs is prevalent across a number of disciplines, papers describing ICAS theory and applications are scattered through different journals and conference proceedings. It is, therefore, important to have a book that broadly covers the state of the art in this highly evolving area. There has been a strong interest among researchers regarding the publication of this book. Forty-nine submissions were received. All papers went through rigid peer review by at least three reviewers and only 23 were accepted for publication, an acceptance rate of just under 50%. Because of size constraints, these papers were published as two volumes. This book focuses on the techniques and applications of ICASs while its sister book *Intelligent Complex Adaptive Systems* emphasises the theoretical side of ICASs. These two volumes cover a broad spectrum of ICAS research from discussion of general theory and foundations to more practical studies of ICASs in various artificial and natural systems. It is important to highlight that a significant portion of contributions come from the social sciences. This will, we believe, provide readers of these books with extremely valuable diverse views of ICASs and also clearly demonstrates the wide applicability of ICAS theories.

Intelligent Complex Adaptive Systems

The study of ICASs draws richly from foundations in several disciplines, perhaps explaining in part why ICAS research is so active and productive. These diverse fields that contributed to the formation of ICASs included the genetic algorithm (Holland, 1975) and cellular automata (Gardner, 1970; Von Neumann, 1966 in computer sciences, evolution, and predator-prey models (Lotka, 1925) in biology and game theory in economics (Von Neumann & Morgenstern, 1944).

Researchers of ICASs are interested in various questions, but these can be summarised as to how to describe complex systems, and how to describe the interactions within these systems that give rise to patterns. Thus, although researchers from different backgrounds may have very different approaches to the study of ICASs, it is the unique properties of ICASs, such as nonlinearity, emergence, adaptivity, and modularity that form the centre of inquiries. Many of these properties will be thoroughly explored in these two volumes. It is the complexity of ICASs which means that although a variety of techniques which have been employed to study ICASs, computer simulations have become important and widely used. These simulations involve several important computing techniques that may interest readers of these books.

- Evolutionary computation (EC) is a highly active field of research inspired by natural evolution. Essentially, EC models the dynamics of a population of distinctive entities such as chromosomes in genetic algorithms or programs in genetic programming. Thus, while EC has been used as a simplified model to study ICASs, it is also an ICAS itself having wide applicability for solving scientific and engineering problems.

- Cellular automata (CA), and related techniques such as Boolean networks, are common techniques in ICASs. The behaviour of entities that respond to the environment is defined as rules or other forms. Each entity can interact with adjacent ones. The topology of adjacency can be defined in various ways depending on the focus of the research. CA and related techniques have been widely used to study important properties of ICASs such as emergence.

- Multi-agent systems (MASs) are systems composed of several autonomous agents. These agents may use a belief-desire-intention model or other mechanisms to guide their behaviour, respond to the environment, or communicate and interact with other agents. The concept of the MASs model can be directly applied to study a number of ICASs. More often, a computer simulation of MASs is used to understand corresponding ICASs.

ICAS research has applications across numerous disciplines. As we are surrounded by complex systems, and indeed are ourselves a complex system, applications are everywhere. In this preface, we have no intention of providing a complete list of applications of ICASs, although some of the chapters do survey ICAS applications in a particular field, but we do wish to highlight the following subjects that are covered by this book and its sister volume.

Because human society is a complex system, comprising a large number of autonomous individuals and entities that are connected by various layers of networks, it has been one of the major fields of applications of ICAS research. As explained in a number of excellent chapters, significant research has been conducted into how disease, information, belief, language, and innovation propagate and diffuse in society.

Economics and finance are also the focuses of applied ICAS research. The economic and financial interactions among the entities of modern society, either at individual or institutional level, are vital to its existence. ICASs have been used to study these interactions and to understand the dynamics that underpin them.

Management can also be understood and further explored with ICAS concepts and methodologies that provide both a novel perspective and an exciting new set of tools. Besides applications to general management, these two books also have chapters dedicated to specific management applications such as military transformation.

And finally, ICASs have been widely used in science and engineering. Complex systems exist almost everywhere in the natural world, from the complex dynamics of the weather to important ecological systems. ICASs play an important role in understanding these systems. Furthermore, it is well known that the robustness and reliability of an ICAS is partially due to the fact that there is usually no centralised control system. This idea has been explored in solving engineering problems.

Audience

Researchers working in the field of ICASs and related fields such as machine learning, artificial intelligence, MASs, economy, finance, management, international relations, and other social sciences should find this book an indispensable state-of-the-art reference. Because of its comprehensive coverage, the book can also be used as complementary reading at the post-graduate level.

Organisation

Papers in this second volume are divided into two sections on techniques (four chapters) and applications (eight chapters). The first techniques chapter by Chiong and Jankovic presents modelling of the economy using agent-based representation and the iterated prisoner's dilemma (IPD). They create a simulated market environment with agents acting as firms to perform transactions among each other with chosen IPD strategies, and investigated strategic interactions between different firms were. Following this, De Luca and Quattrociocchi model context-aware interactions in autonomous systems using an agent-based model, complex dynamic system (CDYS). CDYS uses information from multiple perceptions and provides real-time updates and context-specific guidance to state representation and synthesis. The work includes the design of state and ontology-based interaction and context, a set of representations of perception, and a set of rules.

A third techniques chapter by Bossomaier discusses CA as the quintessential complex system and how they can be used for complex systems modelling. Firstly, he considers various theoretical issues relating to the complexity of CA behaviour before discussing the input entropy as a way of quantifying complex rules. Finally, the author contrasts explicit CA modelling of geophysical systems with heuristic particle-based methods for the visualisation of lava flows.

The final techniques chapter by Negrello and colleagues applies dynamical system theory to the analysis of the structures and functions of recurrent neural networks. This approach is exemplified with the dynamical analysis of an evolved network controller for a small robot that maximises exploration, while controlling its energy reserves by resorting to different periodic attractors.

In the second section of this volume, eight reports are grouped together under the title of applications. These chapters begin with a paper by Ratna, Dray, Perez, Grafton, and Kompas in which they apply agent-based modelling to capture the complexity of the diffusion process in medical innovation and consider the classic study on diffusion of the drug tetracycline. They extend a previous model to heterogenous social agents that vary in terms of their degree of predisposition to knowledge and explore the impact of stage-dependent degrees of external influence from the change agent (the pharmaceutical company). Cumulative diffusion curves suggest that the company plays a weaker role in accelerating diffusion when diffusion dynamics are explored with complex agents. Analysis also reveals that the degree of adoption threshold or individual predisposition to knowledge is crucial for adoption decisions.

In the second applications chapter, Satterfield constructs multi-scale "artificial societies" to examine competing first- and second-language acquisition-based theories of Creole language emergence. Sociohistorical conditions and psycholinguistic capacities are integrated into the model as agents (slaves and slave owners) interact. Linguistic transmissions are tracked and grammar constructions are charted. The study demonstrates how a CAS approach offers clear indications for computational solutions to questions of language change and formation.

In chapter VII, Turrini and colleagues present a theory of reputation. Reputation is the result of evaluation spreading through an MAS, and the capacities of agents that spread reputation are decomposed and analysed. They demonstrate how interdisciplinary research can help understand the complex intelligent phenomena among adaptive social systems. Reschke and Kraus then raise several important issues in the application of economics, psychology, sociology, and evolutionary theories to strategic management. They provide a brief survey from an evolutionary complexity perspective and discus the evolutionary processes of changes and their implications for strategic planing and related organisational issues.

Agent oriented software engineering (AOSE) is the design of distributed software systems as collections of autonomous and proactive agents. Since software applications result from the interaction of agents in MASs, this design approach facilitates the construction of software applications which exhibit self-organising and emergent dynamics. In chapter IX, Sudeikat and Renz examine the relation between self-organising MAS and CAS, highlighting the resulting challenges for engineering approaches. They propose a multi-level analysis to comprehend MAS dynamics and guide agent design, which may relieve development efforts and bridge the gap between top-down engineering and bottom-up emerging phenomena.

Two chapters present information concerning several important real-world examples. In chapter X, Outkin and his colleagues provide an overview of a financial system model (FinSim) created at the Los Alamos National Laboratory. The model aims to understand the impacts of external disruptions to the financial system, and how those impacts are affected by the interactions between the different financial system components and by individual agent's actions and regulatory interventions. In chapter XI, Holloman investigates how the US and others have initiated transformation of their defensive capabilities to take advantage of recent advances in technologies and to meet emerging security challenges. Progress has been mixed. The author examines questions regarding our ability to manage large scale organisational change and suggests that transformational efforts can be viewed through the lens of the agent structure, which posits that social change is the outcome of a complex dialectic between human agents and social structures. It is argued that understanding this dialectic may be significantly enhanced if we examine the theoretical and empirical insights gained from the study of CAS.

In this volume's final chapter, Sycara and colleagues use evolutionary game theory (EGT) to model the dynamics of adaptive opponent strategies for a large population of players. In particular, the effects of information propagation through social networks are investigated. The key underlying phenomenon that the information diffusion aims to capture is that reasoning about the experiences of acquaintances can dramatically impact the dynamics of a society. Results from agent-based simulations show the impact of diffusion through social networks on the player strategies of an evolutionary game, and the sensitivity of the dynamics to features of the social network.

Conclusions

This book, and its sister volume, bring together prominent ICAS researchers from around the globe who provide us with a valuable diverse set of views on ICASs. Their work covers a wide spectrum of cutting-edge ICAS research, from theory to applications in various fields such as computing and social sciences, and provides both comprehensive surveys on some topics and in-depth discussions on others. This offers us a glimpse of the rapidly progressing and extremely active field that is ICAS research. More importantly, because of the interdisciplinary background of the contributors, these books should facilitate communications between researchers from these different fields and thus help to further enhance ICAS research. Thus, we hope that these books may help to raise the profile of the contribution that complex adaptive systems can make toward a better understanding of the various critical systems around us. In doing so, this work should encourage both further research into this area and also the practical implementation of the results derived from this area.

Yin Shan, Ang Yang

Canberra, Australia

June 2007

References

Gardner, M. (1970). Mathematical games: The fantastic combinations of John Conway's new solitaire game "life." *Scientific American, 223,* 120-123.

Holland, J. H. (1975). *Adaptation in natural and artificial systems.* Ann Arbor, MI: University of Michigan Press.

Lotka, A. J. (1925). *The elements of physical biology.* Baltimore, MD: Williams & Williams Co.

Von Neumann, J. (1966). Theory of self-reproducing automata. In A.W. Burks (Ed.), *Lectures on the theory and organization of complicated automata.* Champaign, IL: University of Illinois Press.

Von Neumann, J., & Morgenstern, O. (1994). *Theory of games and economic behavior.* Princeton, NJ: Princeton University Press.

Section I

Techniques

Chapter I

Agent Strategies in Economy Market

Raymond Chiong, Swinburne University of Technology, Sarawak Campus, Malaysia

Lubo Jankovic, InteSys Ltd., University of Birmingham Research Park, UK

Abstract

This chapter presents a method on modelling the economy market using agent-based representation and iterated prisoner's dilemma (IPD). While IPD has been used widely in various economic problems, most of the studies were based on quantitative data which could be deductive and inappropriate. The main objective of this chapter is to present a unique agent-based approach which places lower demand on data using IPD to model the complexity of the economy market. We create a simulated market environment with agents acting as firms to perform transactions among each other with chosen IPD strategy. From empirical results, we investigate strategic interactions among different firms. In the concluding remarks, we present our observations on the qualities of a winning strategy.

Introduction

The economic world is essentially a large multi-agent system. Computer-based simulations are therefore a useful test bed for developing real world economic models to investigate the dynamic and complex behaviour of such systems. As the real world market is normally driven by numerous players going about their business and interacting with each other through financial transactions, computer models that do not follow the same principles are less likely to be successful than those based on agents interacting with each other. Nevertheless, the agent-based approach and their connectivity through market transactions are somehow not sufficient to create a realistic model. The missing ingredient is the strategy that the agent uses when deciding whether or not to perform a transaction.

Much of strategy research have been based on prisoner's dilemma (PD), an elegant model of game theory for studying decision making and self-interest. The existing works on PD have shown that a number of different strategies are possible and that they all lead to known but different outcomes. A particularly interesting version of PD occurs when it is played more than once between a range of agents, as it allows for dynamic development and adjustment of strategies by each individual agent. This iterated PD (IPD) is therefore particularly suitable for investigation of the dynamics of the cooperative and competitive behaviour in an economic environment.

Although the IPD has been studied extensively over the past two decades, most of its literature on economics to date focus mainly on measurement techniques, data collection methodology, prediction, empirical findings, and so forth (Paldam & Svendsen, 2002). According to Gilbert (2005), quantitative data that are used normally come from measurements that are taken at a certain point in time, which could be deductive and inappropriate. As such, the main objective of this chapter is to present a unique agent-based approach which places lower demand on data using IPD to model the complexity of the economy market.

The rest of this chapter is organised as follows: the next section introduces the concept of an agent. Subsequently, we review the development of multi-agent simulations and highlight their implications on economy market. We then explain the background of PD and present an analysis on different kinds of strategies proposed for IPD throughout its history. Ensuing sections describe the economy model we use and a market competition simulation. Finally, we present a discussion on the simulation results and draw conclusions highlighting potential future work.

The Concept of an Agent

The concept of an agent has been common since the 1990s. With the development of new paradigms for computing and technology, various types of agents can be found today, including robot agents in engineering, software agents in computer science, as well as societal agents in economics and social sciences. In all these fields, the adaptive behaviour of agents and their rational reactions towards the dynamic environment they are in are essential for the creation of a realistic computer model.

Before we proceed further, it is necessary to take a look at some of the definitions that have been proposed for the term *agent*. One of the earliest definitions at the beginning of 1990s can be found in the work of Brustoloni (1991), where he stated that agents are simply systems capable of autonomous, purposeful action in the real world. From this brief definition we see that agents are autonomous and goal oriented. Nevertheless, Brustoloni has confined his agents to live and act in the real world, thus excluding software agents in programs, mobile agents on the Internet, or artificial life agents in an artificial environment in general.

In 1995, Maes defined autonomous agents as computational systems that inhabit some complex dynamic environment. The agents sense and act autonomously in the environment and realise a set of goals or tasks for which they are designed. Her definition replaces Brustoloni's "real world" with "an environment" that is complex and dynamic, hence allows more flexibility. Around the same time, Russell and Norvig (1995) proposed that an agent is basically anything that can be viewed as perceiving its environment through sensors and acting upon that environment through effectors. For example, a human agent has eyes, ears, and other organs for sensors, and hands, legs, mouth, and other body parts for effectors. A robotic agent, on the other hand, substitutes cameras and infrared range finders for the sensors and various motors for the effectors. Meanwhile, a software agent has encoded bit strings as its percepts and actions. These two definitions have something in common, but both depend heavily on what we take as the environment, and on what sensing and acting mean. If we define the environment as whatever provides input and receives output and assume receiving input to be sensing and producing output to be acting, then every program can be an agent.

To arrive at a more useful contrast between program and agent, Franklin and Graesser (1996) provided a definition that restricts some of the notions of environment, sensing, and acting. They defined autonomous agent as a system that is situated within an environment that senses that environment and acts on it, over time, in pursuit of its own agenda and so as to affect what it senses in the future (Franklin & Graesser, 1996). Their definition distinguishes the agent and the program from two aspects: First, an ordinary program senses the world via its input and acts on it via its output, but is not an agent because its output would not normally effect what it senses afterward; Second, a program does not act over time, as it usually runs once and then goes into a coma, waiting to be invoked again only at a later time.

Subsequently, Poole, Mackworth, and Goebel (1998) labelled agent as a system that acts intelligently based on circumstances and goals and is flexible to changing environments and changing goals. Apart from that, they emphasised that an agent also learns from experience and makes appropriate choices given perceptual limitations and finite computation. The definition highlights the notion of learning in the agent, where each agent is equipped with the ability to learn based on its experience and interaction within the given environment. This notion has brought forth an important aspect of adaptivity for an agent, and the view is further supported by Weiss (1999) who stated that agent is a computational entity that can be viewed as perceiving and acting upon its environment and that is autonomous in the sense that its behaviour depends on its own experience to some extent. Axelrod and Cohen (2000) reiterated that an agent must have the ability to interact with its environment, including other agents. It can respond to what happens around it and can do things more or less purposefully.

From all the aforementioned definitions we see that an agent exhibits certain behaviours that distinguish it from a mere program. Based on these behaviours, Wright (2001) summed up three important characteristics of an agent:

- **Autonomous:** The agent is capable of carrying out actions on its own.
- **Goal-directed:** Like human, the agent has skills or strategies it can utilise to accomplish its objectives.
- **Social:** The agent can communicate and negotiate with other agents in pursuit of their goals, so in a society of cooperating agents, one may be able to draw on the resources of others to help accomplish its goals.

Soon after, Luck, Ashri and d'Inverno (2004) further expanded the characteristics of an agent. Apart from being autonomous and social, they added two crucial elements to it: reactiveness and proactiveness. The agent is reactive as it is capable of monitoring its environment and responding in such a way that it moves efficiently towards the goal from its current situation. Then again, agent is proactive as it has over-reaching goals that direct its behaviour over relatively long periods of time towards its goals and with complex tasks this means it can instigate actions to move towards those goals.

As the use of the agent ranges across diverse fields, an ultimate definition for it would be difficult. One of the most current definitions can be found in the keynote speech of Luck and McBurney (2006), where they described the agent as an autonomous, problem-solving computational entity capable of effective operation in dynamic and open environments. According to them, agents are often deployed in environments in which they interact, and sometimes cooperate, with other agents that have possibly conflicting aims. Intuitively, based on all the discussion that we have seen previously, the agent in the context of our work must exhibit three essential traits: the ability to communicate, the ability to learn, and the ability to take action within a given environment.

Multi-Agent Modelling and Simulation of Economy Markets

In the previous section, we have reviewed some definitions proposed by various parties on the term agent and made observations on the capabilities and characteristics of an agent. When multiple agents are put together and interact within a given environment, such environment is known as a multi-agent system.

Multi-agent modelling offers strong representation of the real world with a certain degree of complexity and dynamism. It has become a new way of tackling the real world problems especially when experimentation with the real system is expensive or impossible, either due to complexity of processes or information shortage. Markets, which are truly complex systems, are characterised by a large and dynamic population of firms. The behaviour of such systems as a whole cannot be determined and understood from the behaviour of individual parts. As such, in recent years many researchers have used multi-agent systems to simulate markets, with agents representing firms, to deal with this complexity. This section discusses the development of multi-agent based simulation, with a particular focus on simulations that model markets. In such simulations, an agent would represent a firm or some other economic entity, and links between agents would represent the trading between them. In this section, we also discuss reasons for using these models, as well as their advantages and disadvantages.

Fixed Price Markets

A fixed price market is a market in which the price is determined by supply and demand. In a model of a fixed price market, the price will in fact vary between different time steps, but it will be fixed during a single time step. The variation will depend on supply and demand. An example of a fixed price market can be found in the work by Jankovic, Hopwood and Alwan (2005) who used market mechanisms for city simulation and subsequently developed a market model of a city (Jankovic & Hopwood, 2005). A system of four different markets was produced: (1) product

Figure 1. Fixed price market mechanisms (Courtesy of InteSys Ltd. © InteSys Ltd. All rights reserved.)

Supply is higher than demand, suppliers
reduce the supply

Supply is lower than demand, suppliers
increase the supply

(s = suppliers, c = consumers)

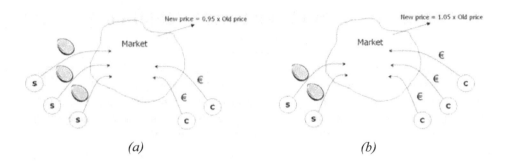

(a)   *(b)*

market, (2) service market, (3) employment market, and (4) property market. In this cellular automata model, agents were cells that represent city land use. There were five economic types of cells: (1) primary production, (2) services, (3) residential, (4) transport, and (5) economically neutral. The agent behaviour stimulated self-regulation, as originally proposed by Adam Smith: "*Provided that consumers limit their purchases and producers increase their output when prices rise, the price…will fluctuate automatically until the number of …(products) produced exactly equals the number of …(products) customers want to purchase*" (cited in Varoufakis, 2005, p.18). This process is illustrated in Figure 1, where suppliers modify their behaviour on the basis of consumer demand, and consumers modify their behaviour on the basis of price. This results in price increase when supply is lower than demand and in price reduction when supply is higher than demand.

Evaluation of transaction costs is also carried out in this model in order to decide whether or not transactions should be performed. This is an application of the equimarginal principle described by Varoufakis (2005). The agent behaviour in the four markets leads to the self-organised behaviour of the city, including its expansion or contraction (Jankovic & Hopwood, 2005).

The main advantage of this model is that it follows the same structure as the object it models: city players are agents; they form links through market transactions; markets are inter-dependent and self-regulated on the basis of behaviour of the players, being them suppliers or consumers; the price fluctuates depending on this self-regulating behaviour. Another advantage of this model is the involvement of the majority of agents in market transactions. At the end of each time step, the number of transactions is

$$T = \min(\ n_c,\ n_s) \tag{1}$$

where

n_c – the number of consumer agents

n_s – the number of supplier agents

and $n_c \sim n_s$

which means that the majority of agents will be linked by market transaction in each time step. This effectively means that this is a parallel processing market model.

A disadvantage of this model is that each agent potentially represents up to 100 people and their economic activities. However, this may simply be described as an appropriate level of detail for the task rather than a disadvantage. Considering that the model has been validated in comparison with geographic data of existing cities/regions, the selected level of detail seems to be appropriate.

Auction Markets

An alternative to the previous model is an auction market model, in which the price of commodity is determined by the highest bid. This is conceptually described in Figure 2, where consumer agents place bids to the supplier of the commodity (property, land, or some other utility) and the price is automatically determined by the highest bid. A minimum reserve price is set to ensure worthwhile transaction. At the end of the auction, the highest bidder and the supplier perform the transaction and the supplier goes away with the money and the highest bidder with the commodity at the end of each time step.

The auction market model is suitable for simulation of a much smaller number of phenomena in comparison with the fixed market model, as the majority of the real world market transactions, excluding the eBay, do not occur through auctions. In a large population of agents, tracking the highest bidder may be computationally expensive, and therefore impractical. As agents can bid in more than one market in order to ensure that the majority of agents acquire the required commodity, there is a potential for an excessive duplication of agent actions, thus affecting the computational intensity of the model.

Figure 2. Auction price market mechanism (Courtesy of InteSys Ltd. © InteSys Ltd. All rights reserved.)

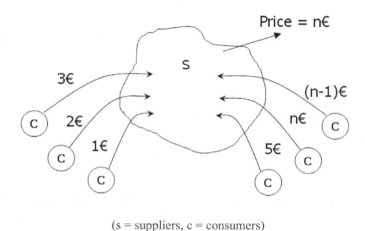

(s = suppliers, c = consumers)

In this type of market, a large number of agents may be bidding for a single commodity, but only the highest bidder will acquire the commodity. Therefore, the number of market transactions is

$$T = n_s \qquad (2)$$

where

$n_s \ll n_c$
n_c – the number of consumer agents
n_s – the number of supplier agents

which means that only a minority of agents will be linked by market transactions in each time step. This effectively means that this is a serial processing market model.

However, in this type of market, the price is determined in a more straightforward manner than in the fixed price market model, by the highest bid.

The Prisoner's Dilemma and Agent Strategies

Game theory has long provided us with powerful tools to understand the possible strategies that agents might use when making a choice. It is mostly concerned with modelling the decision process of rational humans, a fact that should be kept in mind when we consider its applicability to multi-agent systems (Vidal, 2003). In the previous section, we have seen two types of simulation markets, namely the fixed price markets and the auction markets. The success of these types of markets depends heavily on the quantitative data that are used. To this end, game theory offers some advantages—it is simpler and places lower demand on real data to model the complexity of a market.

To date, the applications of game theory have considered many diversified problems, including numerous economic ones. In fact, game theory found its very first practical use in the military field, where Merrill Flood used it to analyse strategic problems at RAND Corporation, such as devising bombing strategies to minimise aircraft losses for the United States of America during war. In January 1950, Merrill Flood worked together with Melvin Dresher on an experiment concerning an equilibrium concept invented by their colleague John Nash. They invited two friends, Armen Alchian and John Williams, to play a game for the experiment. Totally unaware of the potential of their casual experiment, the game Alchian and Williams played was later known as the "Prisoner's Dilemma"—a name given by another RAND Corporation's consultant, Albert Tucker, while he was attending an invitation from the Department of Psychology at Stanford University to give a lecture on game theory (see Poundstone, 1992 for more details).

The Classical Game

The classical PD is a non-zero-sum game that has been studied widely since its inception in the 1950s. It presents a story of two prisoners being interrogated by police in isolation from each other. A confession from any one of the two prisoners and silence from the other would result in a heavy sentence for the latter while the former would walk free. However, if both prisoners remain silent, they would only get a light sentence. Under the circumstance whereby they both confess, they would receive a sentence slightly less severe than the heavy one.

From the previous scenario we see a dilemma among the two prisoners in making their choices on whether to confess or remain silent. It is obvious that the rational choice from the viewpoint of each prisoner would be to confess, because one would be freed if the other remains silent. However, should both of them decide to confess, they are worse off than if they remain silent.

Table 1. The payoff matrix for two-player IPD game

		Player 2	
		Cooperate	Defect
Player 1	Cooperate	R=3, R=3	S=0, T=5
	Defect	T=5, S=0	P=1, P=1

The previous scenario is one-off, as the two prisoners make their choice against each other only once. A renewed interest in PD research in the 1980s has inspired political scientist Robert Axelrod to extend the one-off game into a repeated form, which he called the IPD game (Axelrod, 1984). To formalise the game, we could visualise two players playing simultaneously against each other with the choice of either to cooperate (remain silent) or defect (confess). The notion of four different payoffs resulting from the players' choices has been adopted by Axelrod (1980a, 1980b), namely punishment (P), reward (R), sucker's punishment (S), and tempting reward (T). A reward is given when both players choose to cooperate, whereas punishment will be given if both of them choose to defect. In the situation where one player defects and another player cooperates, the one who defects is awarded a tempting reward but the one who cooperates will be given the sucker's punishment. Table 1 summarises the payoffs of the game.

According to Axelrod (1984), a dilemma will always exist given the rules T > R > P > S and 2R > T + S. Based on these two rules, temptation to defect is always greater than the reward to cooperate since T > R. The highest individual score of T points will be given to the defector and the lowest score of S points to the cooperator. However, T + S is never greater than 2R, which means the total score for a group to cooperate is always greater than the total score for an individual to cooperate and another individual to defect. It could be even more unfortunate for both players to receive the lowest total payoff of P points if both choose to defect.

Axelrod's Computational Tournaments

When the PD game becomes iterated, the players are allowed to form strategies to play the game based on previous moves instead of using mere rationality. The computer-based approach, including the agent-based approach, has been used successfully to simulate various strategies in the game. Axelrod pioneered the attempts in computer simulations of the IPD game by conducting two well-known IPD tournaments in the early 1980s (Axelrod, 1980a, 1980b, 1984). He invited many experts from diverse areas to create and submit strategies to the tournaments.

It is necessary to note that Axelrod had enforced some rules that all the participants must understand and consider before submitting their strategies to the tournaments. Generally, each strategy must decide its moves, which are composed solely with the combination of two actions—cooperate and defect, without knowing the opponent's action until the game takes place. As the only information available in deciding whether to cooperate or defect is the previous moves of other strategies in the game, each strategy has to remember the entire history of the game.

In the first tournament, there were only 14 strategies submitted by game theorists from diverse fields in economics, biology, political science, mathematics, psychology, and sociology (Axelrod, 1980a). Most people produced their strategies by capturing some behavioural assumptions of the sequence of moves for each strategy and specifying them accordingly to generate the current moves. All the strategies were arranged in a round robin format, competing against one another, against itself, and also against an additional Random strategy that randomises its moves. The calculation of the scores for each strategy was based on the payoff shown in Table 1, where the outcome for a particular pair of strategies pitted together was constant.

Based on the payoff structure, all 14 strategies submitted and a Random strategy were pitted against each other and itself for 200 rounds. The tournament was repeated five times, and Axelrod confirmed that the winner was a simple strategy submitted by Anatol Rapoport called Tit-for-Tat (TFT). TFT scored an average of 504 points to win the tournament with simply cooperating on the first move and thereafter repeating the preceding move of the other strategy. In overall, the tournament concluded that cooperative strategies had done better than those non-cooperative strategies, as eight of the top scoring strategies were those called by Axelrod as "nice" strategies, which have never defected on their first move.

Subsequently, a second tournament was carried out by Axelrod after circulating the results of the first tournament publicly. In the second tournament, 62 strategies were submitted from six countries (Axelrod, 1980b), where the participants were more widely ranged from computer hobbyists to professors of various expertises. Instead of playing 200 rounds for each strategy as in the first tournament, this time the game was randomly terminated. As a result, an average of 151 rounds was played for each strategy.

Different tournament, but with the same old story—TFT was again submitted by the same person, and again won the tournament in style. All the "nice" strategies again fared better, except for one strategy called Tit-For-Two-Tat (TFTT). TFTT keeps cooperating unless the other strategy defected twice consecutively. It did well in the first tournament, but did poorly in the second. A thought that comes to mind is be nice, but not too nice (not until opponent defected twice)! Axelrod explained that some participants might have taken into account the lessons learned from the first tournament, and thus capitalised on the weaknesses of some strategies in order to exploit them.

Due to the lack of robustness and dynamics in the simulation of his two tournaments, Axelrod later decided to explore further the evolution of cooperation in IPD using genetic algorithm (GA). The purpose was to variegate the simulated environment and allow new strategies to be discovered based on the genetic operators of GA such as crossover and mutation (Axelrod, 1987). With this new way of implementation, Axelrod again conducted a computational simulation in 1987. In contrast to his previous works, Axelrod imposed fewer restrictions to the game strategies. He considered a set of strategies that were deterministic, where each strategy's decision on its current move was based on the outcome of its previous three moves rather than the entire history.

In this simulation, 20 random strategies had been included, plus another 8 best performing strategies selected from his second tournament. At the conclusion of the simulation, Axelrod found that GA evolved most of the ordinary strategies. However, he specifically highlighted that TFT was one of the strategies that was able to match up with any other strategies in terms of the accumulated payoffs.

Axelrod then removed the 8 specially selected strategies and repeated the simulation with only the 20 random strategies. He noticed that the level of complexity in the simulation intensified due to the concurrent evolution nature of the strategies. The average score accumulated by these evolving strategies gradually increased as the game repeated, hence, it is implied that the strategies were slowly able to differentiate between the cooperators and the defectors.

Axelrod's contribution to the research of IPD has been significant, and the results from his tournaments have been considered by many as a definitive solution to the problem of cooperation in the PD game. In our work, we use Axelrod's research as the framework but build our experiments based on an agent-based economy model we previously developed (Chiong, Wong, & Jankovic, 2006). We believe that only by imposing the IPD strategies to an environment with real-world ingredients, where the agents are selfish and the resources are limited, the nature of IPD can be fully reflected.

Analysis of Strategies

In the early days, the only rational and best strategy for the classical PD was simply to defect all the time, as it was the safest regardless of what action the opponent took. As explained in the previous section, various kinds of strategies only started to emerge after the tournament was organised by Axelrod in the 1980s with an aim to study strategies that would encourage behaviour of cooperation in IPD. When Axelrod initiated his first IPD tournament, only 14 strategies had been proposed.

Today, there are numerous strategies used in the IPD. Among the most common are All-Cooperate (All-C), All-Defect (All-D), TFT, Spiteful, Pavlov, TF2T, and Random. There are also some strategies which are less common, but had been used in several prominent experiments of the IPD in the past, such as soft_majo, per_ddc, per_ccd, mistrust, per_cd, hard_tft, slow_tft, and hard_majo. Table 2 summarises these major strategies.

TFT, a very simple strategy and overall winner of all Axelrod's IPD tournaments, has established its reputation among all other strategies as the most robust strategy available in a PD game on both experimental and theoretical grounds (Axelrod, 1980a, 1980b, 1984; Axelrod & Hamilton, 1981). TFT is simple in the sense that it cooperates on its first move and follows opponent's moves subsequently. According to Axelrod, it has three characteristics that account for its impressive performance:

Table 2. Major strategies in IPD

Strategies	Description
All-C	Always cooperates
All-D	Always defects
TFT	Cooperates on the first move and then plays what its opponent played on the previous move
Spiteful	Cooperates until the opponent defects, then defects all the time
Pavlov	Cooperates on the first move and then cooperates only if the two players made the same move
TF2T	Cooperates except if opponent has defected twice consecutively
Random	Randomly plays, cooperates with probability 1/2
soft_majo	Plays the opponent's most used move and cooperates in case of equality (first move considered as equality)
per_ddc	Plays periodically [defect, defect, cooperate]
per_ccd	Plays periodically [cooperate, cooperate, defect]
mistrust	Defects, and then plays opponent's move
per_cd	Plays periodically [cooperate, defect]
hard_tft	Cooperates except if opponent has defected at least one time in the two previous moves
Slow_tft	Plays [cooperate, cooperate], then if opponent plays two consecutive times the same move plays its move
hard_majo	Plays opponent's majority move and defects in case of equality (first move is considered to be equality)
prober	Begins by playing [cooperate, defect, defect], then if the opponent cooperates on the second and the third move continues to defect, else plays TFT

1.   Nice (cooperates on the first move).

2.   Retaliatory (punishes defection in the prior move with defection).

3.   Forgiving (immediate return to cooperation after the adversary cooperates).

Although TFT has been claimed as the best strategy in IPD for the past 20 years since Axelrod's tournaments, a lot of game theorists in this field have never ceased to depose its status with endless research to investigate more winning strategies. Some researchers even protested that logically speaking TFT can only come to a draw scenario, and it can never win or score more points than its opponent in a single game since its first move is always to cooperate (Sober & Wilson, 1998).

In the late 1980s, Boyd and Lorberbaum (1987) showed that no deterministic strategy is evolutionarily stable in the IPD. Lorberbaum (1994) extended the instability proof to mixed strategies as well. In mixed strategies, the strategies generate moves probabilistically depending on the opponent's previous move.

In early 1990s, Nowak and Sigmund (1992) studied the robustness of TFT in heterogeneous populations, which brought the game into a new dimension with the introduction of noisy environments. They mirrored the noisy environments to real-life situations, and concluded that TFT was prone to making mistakes and did not endure in such environments. Instead, they promoted another strategy that exhibits Win-Stay, Lose-Shift characteristic called Pavlov in their subsequent research (Nowak & Sigmund, 1993). Pavlov cooperates on its first move and then cooperates again only if a previous move is a symmetrical move: either both strategies cooperate or both defect. In summary, Nowak and Sigmund considered Pavlov to have four advantageous attributes from other strategies:

1.   It is nice and is able to maintain cooperation.

2.   It punishes defection with no hesitation.

3.   It restores mutual cooperation but is not exploitable, as it starts to defect if it fails to convey its objective to cooperate with its opponent.

4.   It tends to exploit universal cooperation.

Though Pavlov has the ability to recover from mistakes as we can see in the third attribute, Nowak and Sigmund resigned to the fact that Pavlov fails to All-D, a strategy that defects on every move regardless of what the other player does, due to its objective to maintain cooperation whenever it is possible.

Later in the mid 1990s, Beaufils, Delahaye, and Mathieu (1997) created a new strategy called Gradual, which they claimed to outperform TFT. They carried out their experiments with the same approach based on the tournaments of Axelrod and found that Gradual shares all the good qualities of TFT but by a step further, it is not as simple as TFT. Gradual generally cooperates on its first move, while retaliates upon defection on the subsequent moves. On its opponent's first defection, it reacts in a unique way with a defection and two cooperative moves. On the opponent's second defection, it will defect continuously for two times followed with two cooperative moves. On the opponent's third defection and so forth, it reacts accordingly with a subsequent number of defections but always followed with two cooperations after its defections. Based on this, Beaufils et al. (1997) derived four principles of Gradual from their experiments:

1. Do not be envious.
2. Do not be the first to defect.
3. Reciprocate to not just cooperation, but also defection.
4. Do not be too smart.

As we move into the 21st century, a 20th Anniversary IPD Competition was organised in 2004 based on the original Axelrod's tournaments. The competition attracted 223 entries, and through a round robin setup, a new strategy submitted by a team from the University of Southampton in England proved to be the most successful. This strategy makes a series of moves using agents to recognise each other and act cooperatively. The university submitted 60 strategies to the competition, which were designed to recognise each other through a series of 5 to 10 moves at the start. Once this recognition was made, one strategy would always cooperate and the other would always defect, assuring the maximum number of points for the defector. If the strategy realised that it was playing a non-Southampton strategy, it would continuously defect in an attempt to minimise the score of the competing strategy. As a result, while some strategies from the Southampton team had taken up the top spots in the competition, there were a number of strategies from the team that occupied positions towards the bottom.

Although this strategy is notable in that it proved more effective than TFT, it takes advantage of the fact that multiple entries were allowed in this particular competition. In a competition where one has control of only a single player, TFT is certainly a better strategy. It also relies on circumventing rules about the classical PD in that there is no communication allowed between the two players. When the Southampton strategies engage in an opening "ten moves" to recognise one another, this only reinforces just how valuable communication can be in shifting the balance of the game.

Applications of Prisoner's Dilemma to Economic Problems

Following Axelrod's ground-breaking research, some excellent work has been carried out in the simulations of markets and IPD (Bainbridge et al., 1994). One such example was a new complex tournament staged by Rust, Palmer, and Miller (1993) that simulated a double-auction market, where the winning entries tended to be simple and contained little intelligence. In this section we discuss only a few papers which could have ample contribution to our experiments.

Economic-related PD works have substantially focused on how cooperation may be maintained or disturbed when the game is repeated (Rosser, 1999). In a most common setting, the game in an economic context is usually played with pairs of agents facing one another repeatedly based on a chosen strategy, or in a spatial form, a group of agents adopting different strategies plays against their direct neighbours. Lindgren (1997) studied the interaction among agents who made decisions based on a set of strategies within an economic environment. In his work, agents acquired finite memory and evolved over time with fairly simple strategies such as cooperate, defect, and TFT. He observed that in a finitely repeated game, agents made mistakes from time to time but possessed a self-organising ability to stay in the game. His results showed that strategies were constantly changing and rarely settling down. Therefore, there was no equilibrium in the game.

Another typical work in the same context but with a different background can be found in Arthur, Holland, LeBaron, Palmer, and Tayler (1997). Arthur and his colleagues studied an artificial stock market model developed at Santa Fe Institute. The stock market model was a multi-agent model with numerous market predictors. In their model, agents adopted a random set of expectations rather than strategies and searched among the market predictors. The agents would either adopt or discard the predictors based on their accuracy. The updating process was taking place over time, with approximately 20% of the poorly performed predictors being replaced. The results of this work showed that there were two competing outcomes—the set of expectations adopted by agents evolved either into a stable or unstable way. We see that if the model were given any higher intensity of choice, variety of complex dynamics can emerge.

The oligopoly game is yet another good example of the economic problem studied using the PD game (Diekmann & Mitter, 1986). According to Friedman (1983), oligopoly game focused on the strategic behaviour among a small number of competitors in oligopolistic markets. In Friedman's oligopoly game, a number of firms were offering homogenous products to a market, and the price a single firm set to sell its product would affect other firms' market share. He demonstrated the logic of self-interest behind non-cooperative actions in a one-off game, but showed that cooperation was likely to spread when the game was simulated in a repeated form with unknown length due to the possibility of punishing non-cooperative actions in later rounds. In conclusion, he indicated that firms were likely to go through an adaptive learning process in setting their prices by observing the behaviour of other firms during the build up.

The Economy Model

This section presents the research approach we adopted and the methodology we used. First, we describe the basic elements of our economy model. Subsequently, the implementation of the model and the representation of the agent strategies are explained.

Basic Elements of the Model

The IPD has become a common modelling tool for economic analysis and understanding in recent years. The theory embedded in the game allows us to highlight and exemplify many of the strategic interactions among the trading parties. It thus helps to illuminate the strategic aspects of economics, including market competition which we are interested to explore in this chapter. Based on the work of Morrison and Harrison (1997), we have drawn up the following elements to form the basic structure of our model:

- **The Agents:** An agent is simply a firm that trades with other firms.
- **The Environment:** The environment is a simulated market that consists of many agents where each agent will trade its products or resources with other agents.
- **Actions:** An agent's action is the possible ways it reacts within the simulated environment, which could be trade (cooperate) or do not trade (defect).
- **Strategies:** A strategy is formed by the sequence of actions each agent decides to take under all possible circumstances in the market.
- **Payoffs:** A payoff is the earning an agent gets from each transaction based on its action.
- **Outcomes:** The outcome is resulted from a combination of strategies in the form of total profits since the interaction between agents will generate combinations of actions.
- **An Equilibrium:** The equilibrium concept implies stability that comes when there is a lack of individual incentives for an agent to change from its current action in response to the given actions of others.

- **A Solution:** The solution concept aims to make refinements and eliminate an undesired equilibrium.

With these basic elements, we conduct experiments that simulate a fixed number of firms trading in a single market based on the selection of their own strategies. As each firm aims to maximise its own profit from the trading environment, immense competition will develop and thus the market will exhibit a variety of interesting behaviours or outcomes. The following section describes the model we use which consists of all the elements mentioned previously.

Description of the Model

The main goal of our work is to examine the usefulness of IPD strategies in economic context and investigate the dynamics of behaviour that emerges through the interaction of those strategies. In doing so, we adopt an economy model (Chiong et al., 2006) that simulates a market environment. The economy model uses bit strings to represent natural resources and products created from those natural resources, as described by Kauffman (1996). Each firm in the simulated market can produce its own products from the resources it has and can exchange the products—or even the resources in its original form—with other firms during the trading process.

The firms are modelled as autonomous agents with internally stored state information. The general internal structure of the agent is shown in Figure 3. During the trading process, each firm can either be a buyer or a dealer as the situation in the market warrants. This means that the firms are allowed to trade freely with any other firms without any restriction and from time to time the firms can switch from buying to selling or vice versa.

In the simulated market, it is assumed that there is a binding agreement between firms to a standard market price during the trading process. Therefore, each firm has the choice of selling its products to other firms either at a market price (cooperating) or disregarding the agreement by selling at a higher price (defecting). Although selling products at a high price allows a firm to gain more profit in one single trade, it is necessary that it will yield higher total profit at the conclusion of the entire trading process. This is because some firms that adopt reciprocal strategies will tend to defect in return. When both firms that are involved in a trade interaction decide to defect, the trade between the two firms is halted immediately and thus no profit is distributed between them.

As the aim of each firm is to maximise its own profit, every firm is repeatedly engaged in the market activities in search for the best available strategy that will increase their total profits at the conclusion of each trade cycle. The underlying idea of the simulation is that over time, firms that are unsuccessful tend to look

Figure 3. Internal structure of agents

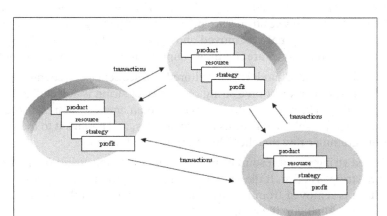

around and probably to imitate strategies of other firms that appeared to be more successful. In other words, unsuccessful firms are likely to copy the strategy of the more successful firms they used to interact with. Therefore when the simulated environment changes, the more successful a firm is, the more likely its strategy is to be copied or imitated by other firms, where the measure of success is simply the profits generated by each firm based on its current strategy. It is necessary to note that this process is not deterministically induced by any mathematical structure of the model or explicitly programmed, but purely based on the strategic interaction among the firms.

Implementation of the Model

As aforementioned, our economy model uses bit strings to represent natural resources and products created from those natural resources. Agents, which represent firms, operate on these strings using grammar rules. A grammar rule consists of an input/output pair of bit strings. When a grammar rule is applied to a given bit string, if the input string is contained within the given string as a substring it will be replaced with the output string. Only one instance of the input string within the given string, which is chosen at random, is replaced if the given string contains more than one copy of the input string.

Each firm, or agent, in the simulated market can produce its own products from the resources it has and exchange the products or even the resources in its original form with other firms during the trading process. As such, the economy model maintains two "pools" of bit strings, the resource pool and the product pool. The resource pool contains a set of randomly generated initial strings that are always available. When a grammar rule acts on a resource string to change it into a new string, the original resource string is still preserved. The product pool is initially empty, and any new strings created from resource strings are placed in it. When a grammar rule acts on a product string, the original is removed and replaced with the new string. Thus resource strings in our model are in infinite supply but product strings are not.

Activities in the simulated model are monitored in a sequence of generations. With a 0.5 probability, either a resource string or a product string is selected at random at each generation. The selected string is passed to an agent, which is also chosen at random. The agent selects one of its grammar rules, and applies it to the selected string. If the grammar rule matches, the string is transformed.

If the selected string was a resource string, it remains in the string pool when the transformed string is added. If the selected string was a product string, however, the original string is removed from the string pool. This makes all the initial resource strings always available in the pool.

The model also adopts a simple graphical user interface (see Figure 4) that helps to visualise the outcomes of market activities during the trading process through real-time animation. The animation allows us to see the simulation dynamics while the agents interact within the market. In addition, an output screen that displays the simulation results is used to report the performance of agents in a graphical form. The graph measures the accumulated profit of each agent during the trading process. The results at the end of the simulation can be saved and read from a text file.

The image in Figure 4 shows the environment of a simulated market where agents are represented as circles. The colour of a firm can vary from brown to dark green. If an agent consumes more resources than products, its colour is brown. As the agent starts to produce more products from the resources it has, its colour changes proportionally from brown to dark green. The size of the agent, which is determined by the radius of the circles, represents how actively an agent is engaged in the market activities. The size increases if the agent is active in its trading but not necessarily representing higher profit. Over time, the size decreases if the agent does not manage to trade its products or resources with other agents for profits, thus signifying that the products or resources have expired after certain period of no trade. Trade interaction between two agents is represented by drawing a line between them. The thickness of the line is proportional to the intensity of trade interaction between corresponding agents. The thicker the line is the more frequent the trade of products between the two agents.

Strategy Representation

As for the agent strategies, we adopt the representation developed by Axelrod (1987). Under this representation, bit strings of 0s and 1s are used to encode dif-

Figure 4. Graphical representation of the simulated market

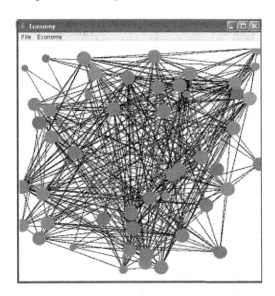

ferent strategies. A 0 is corresponding to a cooperation and 1 to a defection. An agent in the game has to keep the history of the past three rounds of play to decide on a current move. Each of these three rounds is recorded as a bit pair, thus a 6-bit string is produced for a three-round memory. For instance, 11 11 11 means both agents defected for the past three rounds, 00 00 00 means both agents cooperated for the past three rounds, 01 01 01 means the first agent cooperated while the second agent defected for the past three rounds, and so on. In deciding on a current move, a strategy must contain all the possible actions for the previous three rounds, resulting in $2^6 = 64$ possibilities, and thus a 64-bit string is required. Since there is no memory of previous rounds at the beginning of the game, an additional 6-bit is required to be the initial memory. This culminated in a strategy being encoded with the representation of a 70-bit string.

After devising a way to represent the game strategies, an initial population of agents with different strategies needs to be determined. It is almost impossible for us to include all the game strategies from Axelrod's tournaments in our simulation experiments, therefore only six distinctive strategies are chosen, namely All-D, Random, Prober, Mistrust, TFT, and All-C. In addition, Pavlov and Gradual, the two outstanding strategies claimed to be better than TFT, are also included. We are unable to include the winning strategy from Southampton team at the 20th anniversary competition as it is more like a collusion program than a formal strategy.

Table 3. Strategy representation with different colours

Colours	Strategies
Red	All-D
Green	Random
Yellow	Pavlov
Blue	Prober
Magenta	Gradual
Cyan	Mistrust
Gray	TFT
Black	All-C

We incorporate these eight IPD strategies into the model we have just described. Every agent thus has a choice of two actions to either defect or cooperate during each interaction based on the selection of strategies. Various colours are used to represent different strategies selected by different agents. The colours replace the original colours of the agents based on the strategy each agent has chosen. When an agent decides to adopt another strategy from a more successful agent in order to increase its profit during a trading interaction, the colour of the agent will change, thus reflecting the new strategy of its choice. Table 3 shows the representation of colours for different strategies.

Market Competition Simulation

In this section, we present our simulation experiments with our economy model to examine the performance of the eight selected strategies dynamically in order to determine the winning strategy in a market competition. Each agent is allowed to trade freely with any other agents over n generations with the aim to achieve maximum profit. An agent excels above other agents when it acquires a higher profit. We monitor the interactions among firms throughout the trading process and compare the total profits made by all the firms to eventually determine the most profitable strategy within the simulated market. During the trade interactions, all agents are able to learn and improve their profits by either maintaining their current profit-making strategies or shift to adopt the more profitable strategies from among its counterparts.

Fixed-Strategy Market

In our first experiment, we conducted a simulation to examine the performance of the eight selected strategies under the market environment. The assumption is that all the firms are assigned a fixed strategy, and the strategy for each firm will not change from the beginning of the interaction to the end. This experiment is similar to a round-robin simulation, except that each strategy will play against one another more than once.

The experiment is designed for each strategy to play against one another iteratively for 50 generations with the payoffs in Table 1 as their profits. Since there are 50 firms in the simulated market, the eight strategies will be randomly distributed to the 50 firms before the experiment starts. A total profit for each strategy will be calculated after 50 generations. Our hypothesis is that economy does not work in a selfish manner, thus we expect firms with defecting strategies to have lower total profits.

The simulation was repeated for five rounds to ensure the consistency of the results. At the end of the experiment, we measured the strength of each strategy according to the average total profits accumulated over the five rounds. The total profits obtained by each strategy are summarised in Table 4. From Table 4, we see that Pavlov, TFT, and All-C have accumulated comparatively high profits from the trading process, whereas All-D, Prober, and Mistrust did not perform as well as their counterparts. Although it is interesting to see which strategy has accumulated the highest total profit in this experiment, we are, however, more interested to examine why certain strategies performed better than others when they were pitted against each other.

As we examine the sequence of moves of each strategy, we could understand that Pavlov, TFT, and ALL-C did well because they always encourage cooperation. Pavlov and TFT always cooperate at their first move and defect only when the opponent first defected. In situations where every firm uses Pavlov or TFT, these two

Table 4. The results of fixed-strategy simulation

Strategies	Total Profit
Pavlov	2484
TFT	2130
All-C	1821
Random	1730
Gradual	1062
Prober	663
Mistrust	642
All-D	627

strategies simply act like All-C. We presume that the variation between the total profits yielded by the three strategies was due to the frequency of interactions they have had with other firms during the trading process.

On the other hand, strategies such as All-D and Mistrust did poorly because they defected on their first move. In the situation when every firm uses All-D or Mistrust, we could imagine a market scenario where everybody is defecting throughout the trading process and thus the profits they could raise were minimal. Prober, which could turn out to be a TFT if the opponent cooperates on the second and third moves, performed poorly mainly due to the self-destructive nature that emerged from playing [Cooperate, Defect, Defect] on its first three moves. When Prober encounters an opponent who defects on the second and third moves such as itself, it eventually becomes an All-D.

The performance of Random could vary from one simulation to another, thus we will not spend time discussing it here. Gradual could have done better if it had not had the tendency to occasionally defect, hence compromising the chance to raise more profit.

From our first experiment we see that although theoretically the use of defecting strategies always yields higher earnings regardless of what others do given the IPD payoffs, the results have shown that cooperating strategies yield a much better total profits when group interest takes precedence over individual interests.

Mixed-Strategy Market

We have so far dealt with simulation, that was static in our first experiment. In our second experiment, we examine the performance of the eight selected strategies dynamically to determine the winning strategy in a market competition. In this experiment, each firm trades freely with any other firms for 100 generations with the aim to achieve maximum profit. The firms are allowed to choose their own strategy at any given generation, and thus the environment becomes quite complex. Figure 5 shows the initial distribution of firms with different strategies.

A firm will excel above others when it acquires the highest profit. We monitor the interactions among firms throughout the trading process and compare the total profits made by all the firms to eventually determine the most profitable strategy within the simulated market. During the trade interactions, all firms are able to learn and improve their profits by either maintaining their current profit-making strategies or shift to adopt the more profitable strategies from among its counterparts.

After a period of simulation run, the distribution of strategies changed from one generation to another. We noticed that the less cooperative strategies had a higher distribution rate at the initial stage as compared to the more cooperative strategies. However, once those more cooperative firms that have adopted reciprocal strate-

Figure 5. Initial distribution of firms with different strategies

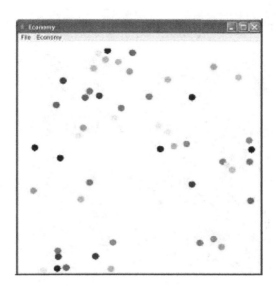

gies such as TFT and Pavlov started to punish against defection, firms who have adopted less cooperative strategies began to realise that their strategies were not going to bring them more profits. Thus, to ensure their continual survival within the market, more and more firms gradually decided to forego their less cooperative or selfish strategies and started to work more cooperatively. We observed this scenario after 15 generations. The simulation of over 100 generations had displayed a very interesting pattern, as shown in Figures 6 through 8.

We repeated the same simulation for another five times. From these subsequent simulations, TFT has shown to be robust and excel under different situations, except on two occasions. In these two occasions, All-C and Prober emerged to be the respective dominant strategies.

In the simulation when All-C became the dominant strategy, the initial distribution of the strategies showed that 11 out of the 50 firms had adopted TFT, which was more than 1/5 of the overall population. We believe that the popularity of TFT strategies at the initial stage caused an early extinction of defecting strategies such as All-D or Mistrust, while All-C was able to maintain a fairly constant representation and eventually overturn TFT to become the overall winning strategy.

In another simulation, Prober, a fairly unpopular strategy that had performed so badly in previous simulations, sprung a big surprise to emerge as the dominant strategy at the conclusion of the 100 generations. This result showed us that a strategy that performs poorly against non-cooperative strategies might have the potential to

Figure 6. Distribution of strategies after 25 generations

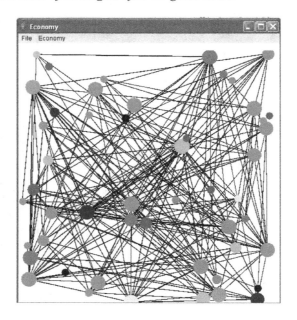

Figure 7. Distribution of strategies after 50 generations

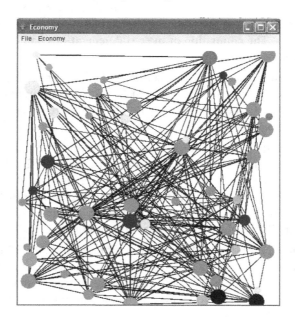

Figure 8. Distribution of strategies after 90 generations

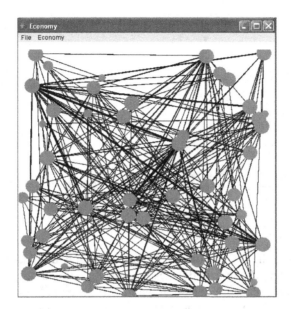

excel while competing against the more cooperative strategies. We observed that the poor performance of TFT had encouraged the emergence of Prober to become the winning strategy. Under these circumstances, TFT's failure had also created a negative impact on the success of All-C.

The results from our second experiment showed that TFT proved to be robust in a new way, though the emerging patterns of the simulated market varied from simulation to simulation. In fact, the behaviour of our model is equally unpredictable as to the real-world economy. We have seen how each strategy reacts to different market environments, and how each strategy is affected by other strategies. We observed that whenever the profit declines, the market becomes more cooperative. Figure 9 shows the percentage of the evolving strategies over 100 generations.

Discussion

Our experimental results demonstrated that the outcome of the entire trading process is determined by the combination of actions of firms. When strategies stop evolving to better ones, the market is considered to be in an equilibrium state. We have shown that there was always a dominant strategy at the end of the market competition.

Figure 9. Percentage of evolving strategies over 100 generations

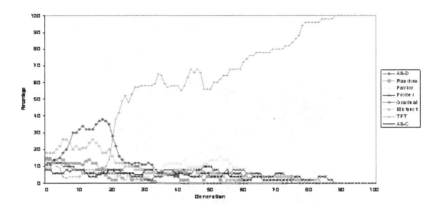

Theoretically, given the IPD payoffs, defecting is the only dominant strategy equilibrium. For instance, if one firm decides to cooperate, it is in the best interest for another firm to defect because defection maximises its gain. However, the experiments showed that if both firms cooperate, their joint profits should exceed the sum of any possible individual profit under the circumstances where one or both defect. The best solution is therefore for firms to cooperate.

Our results have also demonstrated that the performance of some strategies could effectively be enhanced in the competition with the influence of other strategies. Since the performance of a particular strategy adopted by a firm strongly depends on the choice of other firms, it is very difficult to draw a conclusion as to which strategy works the best. Although TFT has proven to be a dominant strategy most of the time, occasionally it could be defeated by other strategies that share similar traits, such as Pavlov in the first experiment and Prober in the second experiment. Based on these results, we believe that a winning strategy in a real-world environment exhibits three qualities: (1) the ability to cooperate with cooperating strategies; (2) the ability to reciprocate against defecting strategies; and (3) the ability to exploit cooperating strategies during mutual cooperation.

Conclusion and Future Work

In this chapter, we investigated the application of the IPD game to economic modelling and provided experimental evidence to demonstrate the usefulness of IPD in simulating the dynamics of market behaviour in an economic environment. Our work showed that cooperation is the optimal solution in economics, and that a winning strategy must exhibit three qualities: (1) cooperate with those who cooperate; (2) reciprocate against defectors; and (3) exploit during cooperation those who cooperate.

We believe that our study could provide an alternative way of thinking about certain aspects of economics and learning how to understand some real and practical economic problems. Though our work cannot predict the outcomes of many real-world transaction scenarios, it enables us to model a certain market condition and envisage what this condition will grow into after a set period of time.

Before we end the chapter, we would like to stress that our experimental model and methodology are not without limitations. We therefore wish to put forth some recommendations for future work. In fact, there are still many possibilities for our model to be expanded further. For instance, instead of considering profits earned from trading both natural resources and products, it would be interesting to make the experiment more structured by distinguishing between profits earned from the natural resources and the products. It will be fascinating to see how the game strategies can differentiate between the resources and products, with an aim to allow the firms to maximise their profits by trading more products than resources.

Meanwhile, another possible extension to the model is to use GA to evolve a new population of agent strategies from the existing population. GA could be very useful for optimising the outcome of the economy market. A preliminary result can be found in Chiong (2007), where different parameters of GA had been investigated for the purpose of fine-tuning the market condition. More information on the possible uses of GA within economics can be found in the work by Sargent (1993).

Following the seminal work of Axelrod (1984, 1987), most of the studies on IPD have assumed that individual agents have no control over whom they interact with. This, however, is not so true in socio-economic interactions that are often characterised by the preferential choice and refusal of partners. As such, Stanley, Ashlock, and Tesfatsion (1994) extended the traditional IPD game with the feature of choice and refusal. The analytical and simulation findings by Stanley et al. (1994), Ashlock, Smucker, Stanley, and Tesfatsion (1996) and Hauk (2001) indicated that the overall emergence of cooperation can be accelerated in evolutionary IPD with this extension. A natural next step, of course, is then for us to investigate whether cooperative behaviour would be effectively enhanced when agents in an economic environment are given the chance to choose and refuse their trading partners.

Ethnocentrism is another enthralling idea that can be considered as the future work for our model. It is one of the latest studies carried out by Axelrod in his relentless efforts on IPD. Together with Hammond, they studied the ethnocentric behaviour that can emerge from a simple evolutionary model of local competition between individuals (Axelrod & Hammond, 2003). They defined ethnocentric behaviour as cooperation with members of one's own group, and non-cooperation towards members of other groups. Their results showed that ethnocentric behaviour could evolve even when direct reciprocity is impossible. Therefore, it would be interesting to observe how ethnocentrism can help the agents that are engaged in market competition to form a coherent group among themselves in order to maintain cooperation within the group, when cooperation seems to be far and impossible outside the group.

To close, we would like to reiterate that complexity and uncertainty are closely related to a great part of economic problems. An analytical solution of these problems may be hard or even impossible to obtain. This chapter presented an artificial adaptive agent approach which we believe can provide more freedom for testing hypotheses and give powerful insights into strategic behaviour of firms and optimal business strategies, thus offering more flexibility and ability to experiment on issues from the real world.

References

Arthur, W. B., Holland, J., LeBaron, B., Palmer, R., & Tayler, P. (1997). Asset pricing under endogenous expectations in an artificial stock market. In W. B. Arthur, S. N. Durlauf, & D. A. Lane (Eds.), *The economy as an evolving complex system II* (pp. 15-44). Reading, MA: Addison-Wesley.

Ashlock, D., Smucker, M. D., Stanley, E. A., & Tesfatsion, L. (1996). Preferential partner selection in an evolutionary study of prisoner's dilemma. *BioSystems, 37(1-2),* 99-125.

Axelrod, R. (1980a). Effective choice in the prisoner's dilemma. *Journal of Conflict Resolution, 24,* 3-25.

Axelrod, R. (1980b). More effective choice in the prisoner's dilemma. *Journal of Conflict Resolution, 24,* 379-403.

Axelrod, R. (1984). *The evolution of cooperation.* New York: Basic Books.

Axelrod, R. (1987). The evolution of strategies in the iterated prisoner's dilemma. In L. Davis (Ed.), *Genetic algorithms and simulated annealing.* Los Altos, CA: Morgan Kaufmann.

Axelrod, R., & Cohen, M. D. (2000). *Harnessing complexity: Organizational implications of a scientific frontier.* New York: Basic Books.

Axelrod, R., & Hamilton, W. D. (1981). The evolution of cooperation. *Science, 211,* 1390-1396.

Axelrod, R., & Hammond, R. (2003). *Evolution of ethnocentric behavior.* Paper presented at the Midwest Political Science Convention, Chicago, IL.

Bainbridge, W., Brent, E., Carley, K., Heise, D., Macy, M., Markovsky, B., et al. (1994). Artificial social intelligence. *Annual Review of Sociology, 20,* 407-436.

Beaufils, B., Delahaye, J. P., & Mathieu, P. (1997). Our meeting with gradual: A good strategy for the iterated prisoner's dilemma. In *Artificial Life V, Proceedings of the 5th International Workshop on the Synthesis and Simulation of Living Systems* (pp. 202-209). Nara, Japan: MIT Press.

Boyd, R., & Lorberbaum, J. P. (1987). No pure strategy is evolutionary stable in the repeated prisoner's dilemma game. *Nature, 327,* 58-59.

Brustoloni, J. C. (1991). *Autonomous agents: Characterization and requirements* (Technical Report CMU-CS-91-204). Pittsburgh, PA: Carnegie Mellon University.

Chiong, R. (2007). Applying genetic algorithms to economy market using iterated prisoner's dilemma. In *Proceedings of the 22nd Annual ACM Symposium on Applied Computing* (pp. 733-737). Seoul, Korea: ACM Press.

Chiong, R., Wong, D. M. L., & Jankovic, L. (2006). Agent-based economic modelling with iterated prisoner's dilemma. In *Proceedings of the IEEE International Conference on Computing and Informatics* (CD-ROM). Kuala Lumpur, Malaysia: Universiti Utara Malaysia.

Diekmann, A., & Mitter, P. (Eds.). (1986). *Paradoxical effects of social Behaviour: Essays in honor of Anatol Rapoport.* Heidelberg, Germany: Physica-Verlag.

Franklin, S., & Graesser, A. (1996). Is it an agent, or just a program? A taxonomy for autonomous agents. In *Proceedings of the 3rd International Workshop on Agent Theories, Architectures, and Languages* (pp. 21-35). Berlin, Germany: Springer-Verlag.

Friedman, J. W. (1983). *Oligopoly theory.* Cambridge, England: Cambridge University Press.

Gilbert, N. (2005). *Agent-based social simulation: Dealing with complexity.* Retrieved from The Complex Systems Network of Excellence Web site: http://www.complexityscience.org/NoE/ABSS-dealing%20with%20complexity-1-1.pdf

Hauk, E. (2001). Leaving the prison: Permitting partner choice and refusal in prisoner's dilemma games. *Computational Economics, 18,* 65-87.

Jankovic, L., & Hopwood, W. (2005). *CAST–A market model of a city* (InteSys Working Paper No. 20060131). Birmingham, England: InteSys Ltd.

Jankovic, L., Hopwood, W., & Alwan, Z. (2005). CAST–City analysis simulation tool: An integrated model of land use, population, transport, and economics. In *Proceedings of the 9th International Conference on Computers in Urban Planning and Urban Management* (Paper 241). University College London.

Kauffman, S. (1996). *At home in the universe–The search for laws of complexity*. London: Penguin Books.

Lindgren, K. (1997). Evolutionary dynamics in game-theoretic models. In W. B. Arthur, S. N. Durlauf, & D. A. Lane (Eds.), *The economy as an evolving complex system II* (pp. 337-367). Reading, MA: Addison-Wesley.

Lorberbaum, J. P. (1994). No strategy is evolutionary stable in the repeated prisoner's dilemma. *Journal of Theoretical Biology, 168,* 117-130.

Luck, M., Ashri, R., & d'Inverno, M. (2004). *Agent-based software development*. Norwood, MA: Artech House.

Luck, M., & McBurney, P. (2006). Computing as interaction: Agent technologies and future progress. In *Proceedings of the 3rd International Conference on Artificial Intelligence in Engineering & Technology* (pp. K17-K26). Kota Kinabalu, Malaysia: Universiti Malaysia Sabah.

Maes, P. (1995). Artificial life meets entertainment: Life like autonomous agents. *Communications of the ACM, 38(11),* 108-114.

Morrison, W. G., & Harrison, G. W. (1997). International coordination in a global trading system: Strategies and standards. In F. Flatters & D. Gillen (Eds.), *Competition and regulation: Implications of globalization for Malaysia and Thailand*. Kingston, Canada: Queens University.

Nowak, M. A., & Sigmund, K. (1992). Tit-for-tat in heterogeneous populations. *Nature, 355,* 250-252.

Nowak, M. A., & Sigmund, K. (1993). A strategy for win-stay, lose-shift that outperforms tit-for-tat in the prisoner's dilemma game. *Nature, 364,* 56-58.

Paldam, M., & Svendsen, G. T. (2002). Missing social capital and the transition in Eastern Europe. *Journal of Institutional Innovation, Development and Transition, 5,* 21-34.

Poole, D., Mackworth, A., & Goebel, R. (1998). *Computational intelligence–A logical approach*. New York: Oxford University Press.

Poundstone, W. (1992). *Prisoner's dilemma*. New York: Doubleday.

Rosser, J. B. (1999). On the complexities of complex economic dynamics. *Journal of Economic Perspectives, 13*(4), 169-192.

Russell, S. J., & Norvig, P. (1995). *Artificial intelligence: A modern approach*. Englewood Cliffs, NJ: Prentice Hall.

Rust, J., Palmer, R., & Miller, J. H. (1993). Behavior of trading automata in a computerized double auction market. In J. Friedman & J. Rust (Eds.), *The double auction market: Institutions, theories, and evidence* (pp. 155-198). New York: Addison-Wesley.

Sargent, T. (1993). *Bounded rationality in macroeconomics*. Clarendon: Oxford University Press.

Sober, E., & Wilson, D. S. (1998). *Unto others: The evolution and psychology of unselfish behavior*. Cambridge, MA: Harvard University Press.

Stanley, E. A., Ashlock, D., & Tesfatsion, L. (1994). Iterated prisoner's dilemma with choice and refusal of partners. In C. Langton (Ed.), *Artificial life III, Proceedings Volume 17, Santa Fe Institute Studies in the Sciences of Complexity* (pp. 131-175). Reading, MA: Addison-Wesley.

Varoufakis, Y. (2005). *Foundations of economics*. London: Routledge.

Vidal, J. M. (2003). Learning in multiagent systems: An introduction from a game-theoretic perspective. In E. Alonso (Ed.), *Adaptive agents: LNAI 2636*. Berlin, Germany: Springer Verlag.

Weiss, G. (Ed.). (1999). *Multiagent system: A modern approach to distributed artificial intelligence*. Cambridge, MA: The MIT Press.

Wright, W. (2001). Agent-based computing in Java. *Java Developer's Journal, 6(1)*. Retrieved from http://java.sys-con.com/read/36191.htm

Chapter II

Dynamic Contexts and Concepts as a Set of State Variations Under Emerging Functions:
A Logical Model for Evolving Ontologies and Autopoietic Multi-Agent Systems

Stefano De Luca, Evodevo srl., Italy

Walter Quattrociocchi, Italian National Research Council (CNR), Italy

Abstract

In this chapter we present a new agent-based model, complex dynamic system (CDYS), for intelligent, flexible, and context-aware, multi-modal interaction on autonomous systems. This model is focused on context models which facilitate the communication and the knowledge representation with a highly customized and adaptable representation and distribution of the entities composing the environment. CDYS uses information from multiple perceptions and provides proactive real-time updates and context-specific guidance in the state representation and synthesis. Our work includes the design of interaction, evolution, context definition by states and ontologies; communication, context, task models based on these ontologies, a set of representations of perception to drive agent behavior, communication, and a compatible integration of rules and machine learning aimed to improve information retrieval and the Semantic web. Currently, we have completed the first stage of our research, producing first pass ontologies, models, and the interaction to apply genetic algorithm to improve the global ontology, by local ontology representation, tested with an initial prototype of a small-scale test-bed on clustering for self-improvement of the agent's knowledge base. Our approach is based on social systems in context-aware applications, informed by autopoietic systems, to use a system (an agent) that is able to describe and manage the evolution of its environment and of the knowledge base in the autopoietic-based model.

Introduction

An agent is defined as a computational program or a problem-solving entity for accomplishing a specific task. It is situated in an environment to employ some knowledge or representation of the users' goal or desires (Jennings, 2000; Liu, 1998). A multi-agent system (MAS) is defined as a software system—a loosely coupled network composed of multiple agents (problem-solver entities) competing, cooperating, and working together as a society aiming at finding answers, solving some problems, or delivering certain services that would exceed the capabilities or knowledge of any individual agent (Durfee et al., 1989). A MAS is an approach to distributed artificial intelligence, especially important in open environments, where agents are not developed by the same organization. In a MAS, multiple agents contain different domain knowledge, have different responsibilities, and can have different internal agent architectures.

The agents are explicitly designed to cooperatively achieve a given goal in a benevolent fashion, so that MASs can be thought of as distributed problem-solving systems (Zambonelli et al., 2000). This is also the reason why the agents are intrinsically prone to integrate (although the agents can be *egoistics* and not cooperating, for example, selling and buying an object on the Internet). Unlike objects, the agents embody a stronger notion of autonomy. Wooldridge and Jennings (1995), Nwana (1996), and Singh and Huhns (1999) identify an agent with the following major properties and attributes: autonomous, adaptability, cooperation, reactivity, social ability, and learning. Not only limited to the aforementioned attributes, the characteristics of a single agent and the whole MAS can be extended by learning.

Especially when the current agent technology combines with Web technologies, a number of researchers have applied this approach by bringing together concepts and ideas from multidisciplinary areas, including computer science, telecommunication, organization, management science, and so forth. Furthermore, nowadays the agent systems are growing to combine with other disciplines such as Semantic Web, grid computing, and Web services in order to improve the functionalities and to be more efficient in problem solving and decision making.

In the agent classification by Brenner et al. (1998), by the degree of intelligence and mobility, MASs can be divided into *task agents* and *information agents* at the lower level and *cooperation agents* at the higher level, because in order to reach coordination and cooperation in a distributed environment the system must have multiple agents to be more mobile and even to be more knowledgeable. The rationale to obtain agent collaboration is to "create a system that interconnects separately developed collaborative agents, thus, enabling the ensemble to function beyond the capabilities of any of its members" (Huhns & Singh, 1994). Moreover, agent interconnections can lead to agents that work in parallel on common problems; solve problems together; share expertise being developed and implemented via modules; and perform a process more synergistically (Huhns & Stephens, 2000).

The essential character of an agent collaborative system is to embed all the components and all the functions in the system consistently and properly reducing user involvement, so that the agents can autonomously and cooperatively carry out tasks by following predefined rules to decrease the manual or semi-manual task preparation.

The term *context* has been loosely defined and used in interactive systems design practice to represent various factors and conditions surrounding and influencing the use of the system. The *performance* of interactive systems is determined in relation to the context in which the system performs its intended roles. The system that correctly performs in one context may not necessarily correctly perform in other contexts. While the context changes dynamically, the systems are usually designed to remain the same and to be operated within a very limited range of the context. For example, the user interface of an existing mobile information system cannot respond to a change from business use in the office to personal use in the automobile to achieve effectiveness of interaction and qualities of user experience. In order to maximize the system performance, therefore, the system needs to be sensitive to the context change and the resulting difference in the goal execution. The agent needs to acknowledge the change in the *task environment* (the goal that the agent is carrying on and the environment in which the agent lives) by a dynamic reconfiguration. Although intelligence is not a mandatory facet of the agents, in a context changing task the agents must be intelligent and adaptive, exploiting that the system has rewards for the correct goal execution (incentives). That is, the rules should be defined (or found) such that as individual agents learn to optimize their own reward, the system as a whole should work with increasing efficiency. Our work shows that the combination of intelligent software agents and well-designed mechanisms can lead to the desired behavior of the system as a whole, a kind of emerging "collective intelligence."

Autopoietic Systems

An autopoietic system is "a machine organized (defined as a unity) as a network of processes production, transformation and destruction of components that produces the components which: i) through their interactions and transformations and regenerate and realize the network of processes (relations) that produced them; and ii) constitute it as a concrete unity in the space in which they exist by specifying the topological domain of its realization as such a network" (Maturana & Varela, 1979, p. 78). Maturana and Varela have developed a concept of cognition consistent with the autopoietic nature of living systems (Maturana, 1987, 1988; Maturana & Varela, 1980, 1988). This approach has been somewhat developed for computational applications by Winograd and Flores (1986), in the language action theory (Winograd, 2006), although limited to agent communication. Maturana and Varela argue that cognition takes place whenever an organism behaves in a manner consistent with its *maintenance* and *without loss of identity*, that is, without loss of any of its defining characteristics. This form of cognition does not imply or require representation and therefore provides a basis for developing agents, which do not include representative structures. Varela, Thompson, and Rosch (1992), in their "The Embodied Mind," relate cognitivism (i.e., representationalist approaches to understanding cognition) to cybernetics, suggesting that the latter is an outgrowth and extension of the former, with application to the understanding of mind.

While this approach represents a more useful (for computer scientists) theory than the behaviorist psychology, which adopts a simple systems view inputs (stimuli) trigger outputs (i.e., behaviors) and think of the mind as a "black box," it is still problematic. Indeed, cognitivism is based on a duality: the environment is experienced as a fact and directly acted upon, but is also conceived and symbolically represented in the mind. Mind and behavior are linked as hypothesis and experiment. The mind looks for patterns in representations and tests the degree at which these patterns accord with the outside world.

Attempts to incorporate this approach into artificial intelligence (AI) have proven computationally costly and difficult to implement (Brooks 1991a, 1991b). On the other side, in the autopoietic model no symbols are invoked or required. The meaning is embodied in fine-grained structure and patterns throughout the world objects network. Representational approaches require a mapping between the external objects and their symbols. In other words, representational systems require a tangible referent, or at least a referent that can be mapped with minimal ambiguity. Most social phenomena emerge in the interaction, so they have not the chance to be linked to an existing symbol or, at least, it is unrealistic to think to these emerging properties before starting the system. Connectionism can derive pattern and meaning by mapping a referent situation in many different (and context dependent) ways. "Meaning" in connectionism is embodied by the overall state of the system in its context—it is implicit in the overall "performance in some domain."

Varela, Thompson, and Rosch (1992) place Minsky's "society of mind" somewhere between connectionist and cognitivist approaches. Here, the cognition arises from networks (societies) of smaller abstract functional capacities. "Emergence is a classical concept in system theory, where it denotes the principle that the global properties defining higher order systems or 'wholes' (e.g. boundaries, organization, control, …) can in general not be reduced to the properties of the lower order subsystems or 'parts'. Such irreducible properties are called emergent" (Heylighen 1989, p. 121). "Agents can become more complex in two ways. First, a designer (or more generally a designing agency) can identify a functionality that the agent needs to achieve, then investigate possible behaviors that could realize the functionality, and then introduce various mechanisms that sometimes give rise to the behavior. Second, existing behavior systems in interaction with each other and the environment can show side effects, in other words, emergent behavior. This behavior may sometimes yield new useful capabilities for the agent, in which case we talk about emergent functionality. In engineering, increased complexity through side effects is usually regarded as negative and avoided, particularly in computer programming. But it seems that in nature, this form of complexity buildup is preferred" (Steels, 1994, p. 283). This notion is highly exploited by the new approach to AI characterized as embodied AI, bottom-up AI, or behavior-based robotics.

However, one has to be careful not to mistake the exchanging emergence for the unexpected effects produced by a lack of understanding of the system: "We are often told that certain wholes are 'more than the sum of their parts.' We hear this expressed with reverent words like 'holistic' and 'gestalt,' whose academic tones suggest that they refer to clear and definite ideas. But I suspect the actual function of such terms is to anesthetize a sense of ignorance. We say 'gestalt' when things combine to act in ways we can't explain, 'holistic' when we are caught off guard by unexpected happenings and realize we understand less than we thought we did" (Minsky, 1986, p. 27). The implicit background to the following blunt and bare sketch of such a taxonomy of domains, dimensions, and methods includes a promiscuous range of variously labelled and subtly differing approaches. Kirsh (2006) offers us a succinct statement of the overall domain: "The study of distributed cognition is very substantially the study of the variety and subtlety of coordination. One key question which the theory of distributed cognition endeavors to answer is how the elements and components in a distributed system—people, tools, forms, equipment, maps and less obvious resources—can be coordinated well enough to allow the system to accomplish its tasks" (p. 94).

Our remarks apply most centrally to two related frameworks: distributed cognition (DC) as practiced by Kirsh and, for example, by Zhang and Norman (1994) and Hutchins (1995); and Clark's (1997) extended mind (EM) hypothesis (Clark & Chalmers, 1998). But they should apply in broad outline also to core examples of research under the tags "situated" or "enactive" or "embedded" or "embodied" or "dynamical" cognition, "active externalism," or "vehicle externalism" (Dennett, 2000; Haugeland, 1998; Hurley, 1998; Rowlands, 1999; Tribble, 2005; Van Gelder, 1995; Varela, Thompson, & Rosch, 1991; Wheeler, 2005; Wilson, 2004), as well as to related work arising more from independent developments in science studies than from within the cognitive sciences (Latour, 1996, 1999; Suchman, 1998). As Kirsh (2006, p. 44) notes, because "coordination is the glue of distributed cognition and it occurs at all levels of analysis," particular explanatory projects must aim at system-level approaches to the idiosyncratic interactivity of distributed cognitive systems. But he also acknowledges the occasional utility of artificial analytical separation of even tightly coupled components, in order to make comparisons and seek generalizations across contexts and allow the possibility of transferring lessons from any one case study. Thinking, remembering, feeling, counting, and the like may sometimes involve embodied activities in ways that transform the cognitive task and sculpt its process.

Embodied interactions with artifacts, gesturing in characteristic ways in a social situation, or following certain bodily procedures and rituals can (on the DC/EM account) themselves be forms of cognizing, rather than the mere expressions of prior internal cognitive processing (Anderson, 2003; Connerton, 1989, chapter 3; Cowart, 2004; Dreyfus, 2002; Sheets-Johnstone, 2003). These embodied cognitive capacities are interwoven in complex ways with our use of the technological, natural, and social resources.

Autopoietic Agents

The system dynamics are expressed by relations and connection between actors. Connections give to any actor a context where to execute some action under a well-defined state of mind. The context is a set of states/situations that changes following the values of a perception function $\wp$: The environment perceptions match the exact state of the entities in relation with other elements of the same domain. Everything is (strongly) connected and any variation of a single value makes different the environment systems; the same is for a knowledge base that describes a particular situation. We can percept the environment via statement description way or via neural network representation.

Transaction between states is possible for two causes: (1) variations in $\wp$ function create a different situation with different requirements; and (2) some events in the interaction between agents could cause a state/situation variation.

To form a knowledge value chain, the system must cooperate with heterogeneous data sources, integrate information, and have spatial and contextual semantic interaction among agents. The agent interaction with ontology assistance would elicit relevant information; provide semantic rich communication and accurate services; and share data, information, and knowledge with other agents.

The problem of action (or behavior) selection for an autonomous agent consists in deciding which behavior to execute in order to fulfill several time-dependent, conflicting goals. It opposes to the more analytic, functional, high-level, decision-making problem, which optimizes the behavioral choice using mathematical modeling of both agent and environment. An action selection mechanism provides a low-level arbitration between behavioral alternatives, following the synthetic approach to AI of behavior-based robotics and embodied AI.

If we think to the social distribution of the intelligence often in some tight complementary fit with technological resources, other people are more-or-less stably and reliably involved in an individual's cognitive-affective processing. This may occur in some respects among other animals, but the variety and centrality of the interpersonal resources which are integrated into human cognition is one of our most characteristic psychological features. In the case of autobiographical memory, to take a key example, we do on occasion remember alone—in some current neural, emotional, psychological, bodily, and circumstantial context—but the sharing of memories with others is also an ordinary human activity with great psychological and social significance. Sometimes such sharing of memories—like other small-group cognitive activities—is merely additive or aggregative, with each individual bringing fully formed intact items to the collective arena, communicating them, and taking them away again unaltered: But more often perhaps, the social manifestation of memories brings into being a new emergent form and content through the transactive nature of collaborative recall (Campbell, 2006; Sutton, 2004, 2006a; Wilson, 2005).

Thinking, remembering, feeling, counting, and the like may sometimes involve embodied activities in ways which transform the cognitive task and sculpt its process. Embodied interactions with artifacts, gesturing in characteristic ways in a social situation, or following certain bodily procedures and rituals can (on the DC/EM account) themselves be forms of cognizing, rather than the mere expressions of prior internal cognitive processing (Anderson, 2003; Connerton, 1989, chapter 3; Cowart, 2004; Dreyfus, 2002; Sheets-Johnstone, 2003). These embodied cognitive capacities are interwoven in complex ways with our use of the technological, natural, and social resources mentioned previously. Although analytically distinguishable, we can also include here the kinds of thinking-in-action apparent in the exercise of certain learned skills in sports, music, and dance (Sheets-Johnstone, 1999; Stevens, Malloch, McKechnie, & Steven, 2003; Sudnow, 2001; Sutton, in press). In these cases occurrent cognitive activity can—in the right circumstances—be distributed across whole patterned sequences of allowable bodily response repertoires, coupling and coalescing dynamically in real time with complex and simultaneous changing physical, technological, and social parameters. For these reasons, expert embodied performance in these domains and the interactions between kinaesthetic and episodic memory, is a rich and barely tapped domain of investigation for both ethnographic and cognitive wings of the distributed cognition movements.

There are also a range of possible dimensions of difference in the nature of the resulting extended cognitive system. As a remembering, planning, reasoning, feeling, or navigating creature, we may gain quite different capacities and idiosyncrasies (and patterns of breakdown) when we hook up with other specific people, objects, or environments, or when we train ourselves in and rely on specific learned bodily or cognitive techniques. In many cases we just could not perform in the same way if we could lean on the unsupported capacities of only our brain; and even when we *could* perform the relevant tasks "on our own" (accessing only the internalized surrogates of these external resources), the way in which this potential performance is actualized will often shift as our openness is altered from influences of various kinds.

The Model

A finite state machine defined in a virtual environment is called *virtual finite state machine* (VFSM). The VFSM method introduces an execution model and facilitates the idea of an executable specification. This technology is mainly used in complex machine control. A variable in the VFSM environment may have one or more values which are relevant for the control—in such a case it is an input variable. Those values are the control properties of this variable. Control properties are not necessarily specific data values but are rather certain states of the variable. For instance, a digital variable could provide three control properties: TRUE, FALSE, and UNKNOWN according to its possible Boolean values. A numerical (analog) input variable has control properties such as: LOW, HIGH, OK, BAD, or UNKNOWN according to its range of desired values. A subset of all defined input names, which can exist only in a certain situation, is called *virtual input* (VI). For instance, temperature can be either "too low," "good" or "too high." Although there are three input names defined, only one of them can exist in a real situation. This one builds the VI. A subset of all defined output names, which can exist only in a certain situation is called *virtual output* (VO). VO is built by the current action(s) of the VFSM. The behavior specification is built by a state table which describes all details of a single state of the VFSM. The VFSM executor is triggered by VI and the current state of the VFSM.

In consideration of the behavior specification of the current state, the VO is set. A state table (Table 1) defines all details of the behavior of a state of a VFSM. It consists of three columns: (1) in the first column, *state names* are used, (2) in the second *the virtual conditions* built out of input names using the positive logic algebra are placed, and (3) in the third column *the output names* appear.

A *finite state machine* (FSM) or *finite automaton* is a model of behavior composed of states, transitions, and actions. A state may or may not store information about the past, that is, a state is just a set of coordinates when all possible coordinate values are considered. A transition indicates a state change and is described by a condition that would need to be fulfilled to enable the transition. An action is a description of an activity that is to be performed at a given moment. There are several action types:

- Entry action

  execute the action *after* entering the state

- Exit action

  execute the action *before* exiting the state

- Input action

  execute the action dependent on present state and input conditions

- Transition action

  execute the action when performing a certain transition

Table 1.

State Name	Condition(s)	Actions(s)
Current state	Entry action	Output name(s)
	Exit action	Output name(s)
	Virtual condition	Output name(s)
	...	...
Next state name	Virtual condition	Output name(s)
Next state name	Virtual condition	Output name(s)
...	...	...

Perception and Variation

Depending on the type of the context, there are several definitions. A perception in our model is a quintuple $(\Sigma, S, s_0, \delta, F)$, where:

- Σ is the input from the world(a finite non-empty set of symbols).
- S is a finite non-empty set of states, in which state there is a set of actions
- s_0 is an initial state, an element of S. In a Non-deterministic finite state machine, s_0 is a set of initial states.
- δ is the state transition function: $\delta: S \times \Sigma \to S$.
- F is the set of final states, a (possibly empty) subset of S.

A transaction in CDYS is a sextuple $(\Sigma, \Gamma, S, s_0, \delta, \omega)$, where:

- Σ is the input alphabet (a finite non-empty set of symbols).
- Γ is the output alphabet (a finite non-empty set of symbols).
- S is a finite non-empty set of states.
- s_0 is the initial state, an element of S. In a Non-deterministic finite state machine, s_0 is a set of initial states.
- δ is the state transition function: $\delta: S \times \Sigma \to S \times \Gamma$.
- ω is the output function.

System Evolutions

A machine organized (defined as a unity) as a network of processes production, transformation, and destruction of components that produces the components which: (1) through their interactions and transformations regenerate and realize the network of processes (relations) that produced them; and (2) constitute it as a concrete unity in the space in which they exist by specifying the topological domain of its realization as such a network (Maturana & Varela, 1979).

An agent is called autonomous if it operates completely autonomously, that is, if it decides itself how to relate its sensor data to motor commands in such a way that its goals are attended to be successful. An agent is said to be adaptive if it is able to improve over time, that is, if the agent becomes better at achieving its goals with experience. It is to be noticed that there is a continuum of ways in which an agent can be adaptive, from being able to adapt flexibly to short-term, smaller changes in the environment, to dealing with more significant and long-term (lasting) changes in the environment, that is "being able to change and improve behavior over time" (Maes, 1995, p. 136).

Constructing a language from a stream of dynamical system states, we wish to produce the minimal representation that consists in sets of states mapped onto discrete symbols, together with rules specifying the allowable transitions between sequences of those symbols.

In the process of producing a discrete symbolic description from a continuous stream of analogue system states, we must make an initial discrete partition of the data stream by dividing the state space of the dynamical system into a number of regions and then recording which of those regions the system is in at regular intervals. The aim of the language reconstruction is then *to reduce* long sequences of these discretely partitioned system states into individual symbols, which nevertheless still predict the subsequent behavior of the system at the symbolic level. If the stream of states was in fact produced by a formal language (you can think to the one of the Searle's Chinese Room) then any sufficiently long sequence of states could be modeled by a reduced set of symbols and deterministic transition rules between those symbols, that is, by a deterministic grammar (see e.g., Aho, Sethi, and Ullman [1986] for methods of achieving this). This is not the case when the stream of partitioned states is produced by a nonlinear dynamical system.

A static environment consists of unchanging surroundings in which the agent navigates. The agent, then, does not need to adapt to new situations, nor do its designers need to concern themselves with the issue of inconsistencies of the world model within the agent itself. Although this is an ideal environment for an agent to navigate in, the actual world is not at all static, and hence the goal is to create an agent that can navigate in the "real" world, which usually is highly dynamic. The usual model where an agent perception of the world is followed by interpretation and organization, in facts, is required.

A fundamental aspect of interpreting sensory observations is grouping observations to define *entities*. Entities may generally be understood as corresponding to physical objects. However, from the perspective of the system, an entity is an association of correlated observable variables. This association is commonly provided by an observational process that groups variables based on spatial co-location. Correlation may also be based on temporal location or other, more abstract, relations.

Thus, an entity is a predicate function of one or more observable variables:

Entity-process(v1, v2, ..., vm) => Entity(Entity-Class, ID, CF, p1, p 2,..., pn)

Entities may be observed by an entity grouping.

The input to an entity grouping process is typically a set of streams of numerical or symbolic data. The output of the transformation is a stream including a symbolic token to identify the kind of the entity, accompanied by a set of numerical or symbolic prop-

Figure 1.

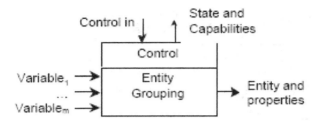

erties given from them relations and connections. These properties allow the system to define relations between entities. The detection or disappearance of an entity may, in some cases, also generate asynchronous symbolic signals that are used as events by other processes.

A fundamental aspect of interpreting sensory observations is determining relations between entities. Relations can be formally defined as a predicate function of the properties of entities with a certain numerical weight. We propose to observe relations between entities using observational processes. Such relation-observation processes are defined to transform entities into relations based on their properties

The concept of *role* is perhaps the most subtle concept of this model. Entities may be assigned to roles based on their properties. Thus roles may be seen as a sort of "variable" placeholder for entities. Formally roles are defined as entities that enable changes in situations. Such a change corresponds to one event. When an entity enables an event, it is said to be able to "play" the role. An entity is judged to be capable of playing a role if it passes an acceptance test based on its properties. For example, a horizontal surface may serve as a seat if it is sufficiently large and solid to support the user, and is located at a suitable height above the floor. An object may serve as a pointer if it is of a graspable size and appropriately elongated. In the user's environment, pens, remote controls, and even a wooden stick may all meet this test and be potentially used by the user to serve the role of a pointer.

The set of entities that can provide a role may be open ended. In the users' context, the user determines if an entity can satisfy a role for a task by applying the acceptance test. The system may anticipate (and monitor) such entities based on their properties. In the system's context, the system may assign entities to roles. Such assignment is provided by a process that applies a predicate function defined over entities and their properties.

Role(E1, E2, ..., Em) =>(Role-Class, ID, CF, E1, E2,..., En)

Figure 2.

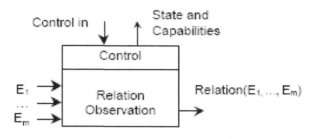

The situation is a particular assignment of entities to roles completed by a set of relations between the entities.

Situation may be seen as the "state" of the user with respect to his task. The predicates that make up this state space are the roles and relations determined by the context. If the relation between entities changes, or if the binding of entities to roles changes, then the situation within the context has changed. The context and the state space remains the same.

For the system's observation of the world, the situation is the assignment of observed entities to roles, and the relations between these entities. However, this idea may be extended to the system's reflexive description of its internal state. In a reflexive description of the system, the entities are the observational processes, and the relations are the connections between processes.

Thus a context can be seen as a network of situations and relations defined in a common state space. A change in the relation between entities, or a change in the assignment of entities to roles is represented as a change of situation. Such changes of situation constitute an important class of events that we call Situation-Events. Situation-Events are data driven. The system is able to interpret and respond to them using the context model via the state variation.

Dynamic Context Variation

This is a way to define a context variation in state/situation under a function that follows the fact that the knowledge representation can change in the context. A variation of value in the context gives different meanings of information.

A whole range of non-deterministic symbol systems representing a single underlying continuous processes can be produced at different levels of detail. Symbols in these representations are not indivisible, if the contents of a symbol in one level of representation are known then the subsequent behavior of that symbol system may be interpreted in terms of a more detailed representation in which non-determinism acts at a finer scale. Knowing the contents of symbols, therefore, affects our ability to interpret system's behavior. Symbols only have contents in a grounded system so these multiple levels of interpretation are only possible if stimuli are grounded in a finely detailed world.

One possibility is to exploit the notion of epistemological knowledge level: A KB is system dependent and may not explicitly contain statements about which objects exist and what their relevant properties and relationships are. An ontology, on the other hand, is a formal specification, done using a language for the publication and communication of knowledge at the epistemological level of a simplified view of the world in terms of entities assumed to exist, their essential properties and the most important relationships that hold them together. This is done using a language for the publication and communication of knowledge at the epistemological level (Gruber, 1993a; McCarthy & Hayes, 1969)

According to this distinction, ontologies are static constructions, either designed by a human being and then imposed from above to the system, or somehow obtained as the final result of the clustering of more primitive attribute-value data representations. Static ontologies are the visible sign of the achievement of an agreement on the meaning of terms (the non-logical vocabulary of a language, its lexicon.) The main problem of this static view is that it leaves completely implicit the fact that every agreement on meaning is always only a partial result in a process of meaning formation and negotiation, which is in principle indefinitely open. Moreover, it leaves unexplained how ontologies are discovered, how they are tested, how they are modified and improved, which architectural aspects in the design of an agent enables the agent to develop an ontology, and so forth.

In order to capture ontologies as dynamic structures, we will draw the distinction between a KB and an ontology in a different way. The idea is to distinguish between modifying a KB and modifying its underlying ontology: when the KB is modified, the language must not be changed, only new facts are added or deleted; when the ontology is modified, the language may need to be changed, since, for example, new terms (corresponding to new concepts) may need to be added.

This distinction between a knowledge base and its ontological core parallels the distinction between knowledge of facts (as the ability to produce and use sentences describing what is the case) and knowledge of objects or knowledge of a domain (as the ability to categorize a domain, to recognize objects, and to apply names). The knowledge of facts is grounded on the knowledge of objects (in the sense that facts always concern a certain particular domain). The knowledge process must be

compositional. The structure must be able to balance the structured a priori representations of entities and their liked concept and properties in a hierarchical way.
A recognition of an event and its categorization is given from the conceptual/hier-
archical associations of concepts in the knowledge base.

The description of the entities start from their relation with their environment in
term of measurable interactions (CONTEXT), to have a description of the dual
system WORLD-MAS based on its evolution, set of relations, set of events that
gives both the entire system descpription and the partial view in a reflexive way.
All the information describing a single entity is bound together as a result of the
synchronous firing of the various nodes. Description of entities in a state like a set

Figure 3.

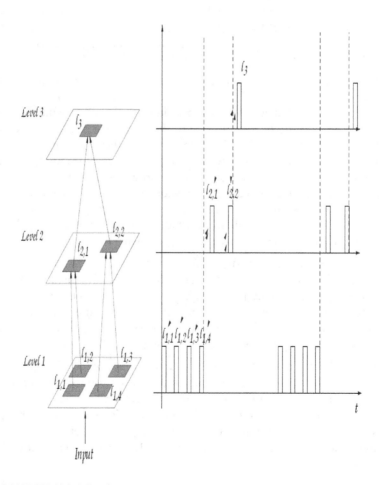

of dynamic relations and temporal pattern processing are interrelated and play an essential role in the interactive evolutions of the KB.

The dynamism of an ontology depends on an agent's ability to modify its conceptual structure, and it's normally triggered by the detection of anomalous situations. An *anomalous situation* is a state of the actual world that is not explicitly considered by the internal world model of an agent. It is often detectable in the form of unusual or unexpected sensor values, and it is perceived by the agent as an anomaly because of the discrepancy between the world and its model of the world.

Anomalous situations can occur at the perceptual level or during a linguistic interaction between two or more agents, in the form of a communication failure. A communication failure is a situation in which an agent sends a query from a certain point of view (and therefore has some expectations about the possible answers) and obtains a completely unexpected (sometimes incomprehensible, often useless) answer.

The objects definitions at the symbolic level L constitute the agent's ontology. The sub-symbolic levels are agent's sensors and effectors.

L and I are the set of internal representations of the agent, and can be viewed as the agent's internal model of the world. The only requirement is that L is an abstraction over I, in some sense. L is partitioned into three subsets:

- LT: A set of object type
- LC: A set of world states
- LA: A set of actions; actions are defined according to their effects, that is, there is a function do: LA X LC
- LC which takes an action and a state as inputs and returns a state as output

At the sub-symbolic level we have:

- IC a set of sub-symbolic definitions of relations; relations are represented as sensor-value pairs; the idea is that each sensor-value pair implements a world state that can be used as a condition for actions;
- IA a set of sub-symbolic definitions of actions; an action _ is represented as a pair <m,p> where m is a sequence of effectors activations and p is a prediction function for m that is p: $IC \rightarrow IC$
- IT: a set of sub-symbolic definitions of objects types; if something is recognized as an object of a certain type by means of applicable motor actions on it and their predicate sensory effects the IT can be defined as IA X IC.

An *action* is an activity that accomplishes something like an evaluation or a move-ment, and a state is a collection of actions that are used while in a particular mode. A *state* is the circumstance of a thing, its condition, and the actions are the attributes of that state. It provides the ability to limit the scope of actions or the amount of knowledge to only the one required for the current state.

Context is a crucial factor in communication. Just consider the confusion that results from a lack of contextual information when, for example, you join a scheduled meeting half an hour late: without the clues of the original context, you might find it hard to make sense of the ongoing discussion. In any case, the discussants would realize this and try to give you a quick rundown of the conversations so far. This is essentially the view of Clark and Carlson (1981) regarding context as informa-tion that is available to a person for the interaction with a particular process on a given occasion. Their "intrinsic context" is an attempt to capture the information available to a process that is potentially necessary for it to succeed. The intrinsic context for grasping what an actor means on some occasion is the (limited) totality of the knowledge, beliefs, and suppositions shared by the speaker and the listener. This is also known as "common ground." Categorization is one of the basic mental processes in cognition (Rosch, 1978). Human beings can categorize various types of objects, events, and states of affairs, where categorizations depend on the cir-cumstance. In order to control the interpretation process, the intermediate results have to be judged so that the best valuated interpretation can be investigated first. A judgment method compares the expectations derived from the concept with the values measured in the signal and stores the result in the slot judgment.

A service agent specialized for a certain context needs only particular focused aspects of the whole ontology. Besides, the nature of the problems found in a distributed environment is normally dynamic and multi-disciplinary. This calls for the agent's capability to be able to extract from a large ontology specific portions and keep evolving them to form a self-organized model.

Here follows the detailed process of the proposed sub-ontology evolution approach for service composition via planning:

1. First, a Service identifies focusing concepts in ontology according to the problem context.

2. Relevant SubOntologies are selected and extracted from the Knowledge Base by matching it with the focusing concepts.

3. If no appropriate SubOntologies in the Knowledge Base can be selected, the Service will turn to its adjacent Service1 agents to look for relevant domain knowledge.

4. If the aforementioned knowledge search succeeds, it means that there exists at least one adjacent P-Service that is specialized in the current context.

5. If the search fails, it hints lacking relevant domain knowledge in the agent's proximity. The Service will try to identify a relevant Ontology directly to support the semantic service matching. SubOntologies potentially needed will be extracted from the DO.

6. The composed service plan/flow obtained will then be executed. If the execution performance is positive, the P-Service will evolve its Local-KB by integrating the new SubOntologies. During the integration, new-coming SubOntologies are compared with the existing ones to check if there exist closely relevant SubOntologies for merging. The part of SubOntologies that is not used for the planning will be pruned or augmented. The SubOntologies not used at all will simply be discarded.

Future Works

The majority of the current agent applications work with fixed ontologies limited to the particular domain and the task within it. This approach reduce the possibility to have high flexibility in a changing environment and high effectiveness in system operation: the agent applications cannot be applied to the new, broader context.

We proposed here a way to overpass this limitation, with a mechanism for transforming the sensory stream into symbolic information enriching the initial ontology, depending on the new agent tasks, and therefore transforming the ontology passive use in a more robust, dynamic architecture aimed to context representation and task achievement.

However, our solution is suited to expert developers skilled in MAS modeling and programming, because there are no tools to easy develop these ever changing non-deterministic automata. So a line of future work is a visual environment to aid developers.

Working in a MAS, switching to open ontologies opens up some problems on the performance of the communication, such as:

*   How to model the situational problems in an MAS and how to build the agent coordination mechanism based on the identified problems

*   Describing in detail domain task descriptions, given that a task is different in different contexts

*   Integration of single agent (and then the single agent automata) with other agents, and the collaboration mechanism, in particular the revision of game theory approach (e.g., Nash equilibria, the monotonic concession protocol) when a new context can change utility function at run time

- The legacy software integration problem, in particular the way to test this new type of agents, and the system evaluation on the quality of the performance and of the underlying ontology

Ultimately, to operate in open environments, change management of the context and adaptability through ontology mapping, merging, and aligning are also the top concerns for system developers that would be further investigated.

References

Aho, A. V., Sethi, R., & Ullman, J. D. (1986). *Compilers: principles, techniques, and tools.* Boston: Addison-Wesley Longman.

Anderson, T. (2003). Modes of interaction in distance education: Recent developments and research questions. In M. Moore (Ed.), *Handbook of distance education* (pp. 129-144). Mahwah, NJ: Erlbaum.

Brooks, R. A. (1991). Intelligence without representation. *Artificial Intelligence, 47*, 139-159

Campbell, S. (2006). Our faithfulness to the past: Reconstructing memory value. *Philosophical Psychology, 19*.

Charniak, E. (1993). *Statistical language learning.* Cambridge, MA: MIT Press.

Clark, A. (1997). *Being there: Putting brain, body, and world together again.* Cambridge, MA: MIT Press.

Clark, A., & Chalmers, D. (1998). The extended mind. *Analysis, 58*, 7-19.

Connerton, P. (1989). *How societies remember.* Cambridge: Cambridge University Press.

Cowart, M. (2004). Embodied cognition. *The Internet Encyclopedia of Philosophy.* Retrieved from http://www.iep.utm.edu/e/embodcog.htm

De Luca, S., & Quattrociocchi, W. (2006). *Dynamic contexts and concepts as a set of state variations under a δ function.*

Dennett, D. C. (2000). Making tools for thinking. In D. Sperber (Ed.), *Metarepresentations: A multidisciplinary perspective* (pp. 17-29). Oxford: Oxford University Press.

Dreyfus, H. L. (2002). Intelligence without representation: The relevance of phenomenology to scientific explanation. *Phenomenology and the Cognitive Sciences, 1*, 367-383.

Durfee, E. H., Lesser, V. R., & Corkill, D. D. (1989). Trends in cooperative distributed problem solving. *IEEE Transactions on Knowledge and Data Engineering, 1*(1), 63-83.

Gruber, T. R. (1993). Towards principles for the design of ontologies used for knowledge sharing. In N. Guarino & R. Poli (Eds.), *Formal ontology in conceptual analysis and knowledge representation*. Kluwer.

Haugeland, J. (1998). Mind embodied and embedded. In *Having thought: Essays in the metaphysics of mind* (pp. 207-237). Cambridge, MA: Harvard University Press.

Heylighen, F. (1989). Coping with complexity: Concepts and principles for a support system. In R. Glanville & G. de Zeeuw (Eds.), *Proceedings of the Conference Support, Society and Culture*. University of Amsterdam.

Huhns, M. N., & Stephens, L. M. (2000). Multiagent system and societies of agents. In W. Gerhard (Ed.), Multiagent systems: *A modern approach to distributed artificial intelligence* (pp. 79-120). Cambridge, UK: MIT Press.

Hurley, S.E. (1998). *Consciousness in action*. Cambridge, MA: Harvard University Press.

Hutchins, E. (1995). *Cognition in the wild*. Cambridge, MA: MIT Press.

Jennings, N. R. (2000). On agent-based software engineering. *Artificial Intelligence, 117*(2), 277-296.

Kaufman, L., & Rousueeuw, P. (1990). *Finding groups in data: An Introduction to cluster analysis*. John Wiley and Sons.

Kirsh, D. (2006). Distributed cognition: A methodological note. *Pragmatics & Cognition, 14.*

Latour, B. (1996). Cogito ergo sumus! Or, psychology swept inside out by the fresh air of the upper deck: Review of Hutchins 1995. *Mind, Culture, and Activity, 3*, 54-63.

Latour, B. (1999). A collective of humans and nonhumans. In Pandora's Hope: Essays on the reality of science studies (pp. 174-215). Cambridge, MA: Harvard University Press.

Liu, S. H. (1998). Strategic scanning and interpretation revisiting: Foundations for an intelligent software agent support system—Part 2: Scanning the business environment with software agent. *Industrial Management and Data System, 98*(8), 362-372.

Maes. (1995). Agents that reduce work and information overload. *Communications of the ACM, 37*(7), 31–40. Retrieved from http://www.acm.org/

Martin, E., Kriegel, H. P., Sander, J., & Xu, X. (1996). A density-based algorithm for discovering clusters in large spatial databases with noise. In *Proceedings of KDD.*

Maturana, H.R. (1987). Everything is said by an observer. In W. I. Thompson (Ed.), *Gaia: A way of knowing* (pp. 65-82). Barrington, MA: Lindisfarne Press.

Maturana H.R., & Varela F. (1980). *Autopoiesis and cognition.* Reidel.

Maturana H.R., & Varela F. (1988). *The tree of knowledge—The biological roots of human understanding.* Shambhala.

Maturana, F. P., Tichy, P., Söecjta, P., Discenzo, F., Staron, R. J., & Hall, K. (2004). Distributedmulti-agent architecture for automation systems. *Expert Systems with Applications, 26.*

Maturana, H., & Varela, F. (1980). Autopoiesis and cognition: The realization of the living. In R. S. Cohen & M. W. Wartofsky (Eds.), *Boston studies in the philosophy of science 42* (Rev. ed.). Dordecht, The Netherlands: D. Reidel.

Mayberry, Marshall R and Miikkulainen, Dr. Risto, (1994). Lexical disambiguation based on distributed representations of context frequency. In *Proceedings Proceedings of the 16th Annual Conference of the Cognitive Science Society.*

McCarthy, J., & Hayes, P. J. (1969). Some philosophical problems from the standpoint of artificial intelligence. In B. Meltzer and D. Michie (Eds.), *Machine intelligence.* Edinburgh: Edinburgh University Press.

Minsky, M. (1987). *The society of mind.* London: Picador.

Nassar, S., Sander, J., & Cheng, C. (2004). Incremental and effective data summarization for dynamic hierarchical clustering. In *Proceedings of ACM SIGMOD* (pp. 467-478).

Ng, R. T., & Han, J. (1994). Efficient and effective clustering methods for spatial data mining. In *Proceedings of VLDB.*

Nwana, H. S. (1996). Software agents: An overview. *Knowledge Engineering Review, 11.*

Nwana, H. S., & Ndumu, D. T. (1999). A perspective on software agents research. *Knowledge Engineering Review, 14*(2).

Pulkki, V. (1995). *Data averaging inside categories with the self-organizing map* (Report A27). Helsinki University of Technology, Laboratory of Computer and Information Science, Espoo, Finland.

Roberts, T. S. (2004). Online collaborative learning: Theory and practice. *Information Management, 17*(1/2).

Rosch, E. (1977). Principles of categorization. In E. Rosch & B. Lloyd (Eds.), *Cognition and categorization.* Hillsdale, NJ: Erlbaum.

Rowlands, M. (1999). *The body in mind: Understanding cognitive processes.* Cambridge: Cambridge University Press.

Schooler, E. M. (1999). Conferencing and collaborative computing. In B. Furht (Ed.), *Handbook of Internet and multimedia systems and applications.* Boca Raton, FL: CRC Press.

Shardanand, U., & Maes, P. (1995). Social information filtering: Algorithms for automating "word of mouth." In *Proceedings of Human Factors in Computing Systems.*

Sheets-Johnstone, M. (1999). *The primacy of movement.* Amsterdam: John Benjamins.

Sheets-Johnstone, M. (2003). Kinesthetic memory. *Theoria et Historia Scientiarum, 7*, 69-92.

Singh, M., & Huhns, M. N. (1999). Social abstraction for information agents. In M. Klusch (Ed.), *Intelligent information agent: Agent-based information discovery and management on the Internet* (pp. 37–52). Berlin, Germany: Springer.

Steels, L. (1994). The artificial life roots to artificial intelligence. *Artificial Life Journal*, 1(1). MIT Press.

Stevens, C. Malloch, S., McKechnie, S., & Steven, N. (2003). Choreographic cognition: The time-course and phenomenology of creating a dance. *Pragmatics and Cognition, 11*, 299-329.

Suchman, L. (1998). Human/machine reconsidered. *Cognitive Studies*, *5*, 5-13.

Sudnow, D. (2001). *Ways of the hand: A rewritten account.* Cambridge, MA: MIT Press.

Sutton, J. 2004. Representation, reduction, and interdisciplinarity in the sciences of memory. In H. Clapin, P. Staines & P. Slezak (Eds.), *Representation in mind: New approaches to mental representation* (pp. 187-216). Amsterdam: Elsevier.

Sutton, J. (2006a). *Pragmatics & cognition.* Amsterdam: Benjamins.

Sutton, J. (2006b). Exograms and interdisciplinarity: History, the extended mind, and the civilizing process. In R. Menary (Ed.), *The extended mind.* Aldershot: Ashgate.

Tribble, E. (2005). Distributing cognition in the globe. *Shakespeare Quarterly, 56*, 135-155.

van Gelder, T. (1995). What could cognition be, if not computation? *Journal of Philosophy, 92*, 345-381.

Varela, F., Thompson, E., & Rosch, E. (1991). *The embodied mind.* Cambridge, MA: MIT Press.

Wheeler, M. (2005). *Reconstructing the cognitive world: The next step.* Cambridge, MA: MIT Press.

Wilson, R.A. (2005). Collective memory, group minds, and the extended mind thesis. *Cognitive Processing 6*, 227-236.

Winograd T., & Flores F. (1986). *Understanding computers and cognition: A new foundation for design*. Norwood, NJ: Ablex.

Winograd, T. (2006). Designing a new foundation for design. *Communications of the ACM, 49*(5).

Wooldridge, M., & Jennings, N. R. (1995). Intelligent agents: Theory and practice. *The Knowledge Engineering Review*, *10*(2), 115-152.

Zambonelli, F., Jennings, N. R., & Wooldridge, M. (2000). Organisational abstractions for the analysis and design of multi-agent systems. In *Proceedings of the First International Workshop on Agent-oriented Software Engineering* (pp. 127-141). Limerick, Ireland.

Zhang, J., & Norman, D.A. (1994). Representations in distributed cognitive tasks. *Cognitive Science 18*, 87-122.

Chapter III

Cellular Automata

Terry Bossomaier, Charles Sturt University, Australia

Abstract

In this chapter we present a view of cellular automata (CAs) as the quintessential complex system and how they can be used for complex systems modelling. First we consider theoretical issues of the complexity of their behaviour, discussing the Wolfram Classification, the Langton, lambda parameter, and the edge of chaos. Then we consider the input entropy as a way of quantifying complex rules. Finally we contrast explicit CAs modelling of geophysical systems with heuristic particle-based methods for the visualisation of lava flows.

List of Key Symbols

r   radius

R   Neighbourhood

S   Input entropy

T   Transition function

H   Entropy

I   Mutual Information

Σ   Alphabet of states

u   number of occurrences of a state

Introduction

The delights and fascination of complex systems arise through *emergence*. Unexpected patterns and dynamics appear, often starting from seemingly simple repetitive behaviours. Complex systems naturally appear when numerous intelligent or adaptive agents interact with one another, as in ecologies or societies. More surprising is that complexity can emerge from the interaction of ultra simple entities, which have no adaptive properties at all. Mathematician John Conway became fascinated by one such system. He called it the Game of Life, and in a sort of meta-emergence it became popular throughout the world, has had entire books written about it, research projects devoted to it and it has drifted throughout cyberspace. It is a CA.

In the Game of Life, each cell occupies a point on a two-dimensional grid, has two states alive or dead, and connects to four neighbours along the grid lines. The update rule is the same for all cells and follows a simple intuitive guess at ecological dynamics. A live cell dies if it is has one or zero neighbours (isolation) or four neighbours (overcrowding). If it has two or three neighbours it survives. A dead cell comes alive if it is surrounded by precisely three live neighbours. The fun of the Game of Life lies in its evolution in time, not easily captured by static diagrams. Some patterns oscillate; gliders are patterns which move steadily across the grid, while glider guns stay in one place but emit gliders.

The originator of *cellular automata theory* was not John Conway, but another great mathematician, John von Neumann. Alan Turing also studied CAs. He and Von Neumann are the unchallenged pioneers of computer science, and CAs are capable of universal computation. Since the purpose of this article is really to enable the reader to see the widespread potential applications of CAs these formal aspects will receive only brief attention. Formal theory tends to work with the simplest lattices and behavioural rules. Yet, as we shall see, many applications extend the original frameworks to rules which are derived from physics or biology and are often quite a lot more complicated.

The section *Definitions* defines CAs in their various guises, but to start with, it is enough to think of them of as a set of interacting cells. Each cell has a *rule* by which it updates its *state* dependent upon the states of the other cell to which it connects; the *connectivity graph.*

CAs as the Canonical Complex System

CAs are intriguing in many ways. They support universal computation but are inherently unpredictable. They exhibit a range of qualitatively different behaviours, easy to classify at the behaviour level but not so easy at the level of the cellular rules and connectivity graph. The section *Cellular Automata Theory* examines these theoretical issues at a fairly qualitative level.

But if it were just for theory, CAs would remain a very minority interest. But for some considerable time they have been a very valuable modelling tool. The essence of a good model is simplicity, the ruthless wielding of Occam's razor. There are many emergent phenomena of interest to us from the spread of bushfires and epidemics to fluid dynamics. Capturing the simplest possible behaviour of system elements and their interactions, which give the observed emergent behaviour, is a key strategy to modelling and predicting complex systems. CAs are thus an excellent modelling tool. But there is another way to view this. By abstracting down complex systems to the simplest elements, we can see how disparate systems are isomorphic and subject to the same large-scale dynamical effects.

CAs have another intrinsic advantage—they are usually defined such that the cells interact only locally. Thus, they are amenable to fast simulation on vector and parallel supercomputers. The locality captures an important physical and social property—flux across local boundaries, leading to the propagation of arbitrary quantities across a global space.

Modelling strategies take two opposite approaches

1.   The emergent behaviour is known and the rules are optimised, often using soft computing techniques such as evolutionary computation to match this emergent behaviour. The section *Evolutionary Strategies* discusses some canonical examples.

2.   The CA states and connectivity are modelled on the behaviour of the elements of a real system. The simulation is then run to determine the emergent behaviour.

In general, the first is very difficult and still an active area of research. The second is a common application strategy. But hybrid methods, where CA parameters are tuned to fit some given data sets and then validated against others also occur.

CAs and Agent-Based Modelling

CAs are an effective modelling tool for a variety of reasons

- They are simple to define and parametrise, enabling us to shave our models to the bone with Occam's razor.

- They are essentially local which also facilitates model description—it is much easier to imagine modelling city traffic flows if each car has only to consider cars immediately adjacent to it.

- They can be implemented directly in hardware, allowing for the scale-up to very large models. One of the largest such CA machines was CAM brain created by Hugo de Garis intended to have the same computational capacity as the brain of a kitten. At the other extreme is a CA hardware building block—the Firefly machine (Sipper, 1997).

- They are very suitable for parallel computation. Because each cell updates every cycle, it is easy to load balance.[1] The local behaviour and often small neighbourhoods imply that the information to be exchanged at boundaries is minimal.

But the space of CA rules is enormous, 2^{512} for a binary CA with just eight nearest neighbours. From a modelling point of view, it is thus desirable to have some theoretical constraints, helping us to choose rules which can give us the right behaviour.

CAs have received a great deal of attention from physicists and mathematicians and we give the briefest of pointers in this paper. But one might ask why the theory is important at all. It turns out that CA dynamics are quite sensitive. It is easy to flip from chaotic behaviour to stable dynamics with small rule changes. But worse, the interesting rules lie at the *edge of chaos* and are hard to find. Since many of the systems we might want to model, such as ecologies, epidemics, and bushfires, may lie in this region, being able to locate and identify these complex rules is of considerable practical importance.

CAs also integrate with other modelling tools. On top of a background or spatial environment defined by a CA, it is possible to put mobile intelligent agents, representing people or animals in an ecosystem or society.

A Very Simple Example

As an illustration of the philosophy of CA simulations, we describe a simple model to demonstrate criticality effects in bank closures within small communities. In effect, this is a Game of Life like simulation, with a social context grafted on. The dynamics are thus things we know about already, but may not be known in the application domain.

Consumer preference is based on two factors

- The proximity of the bank, B.
- A sufficient number of close neighbours who use the new alternative, say, a supermarket bank S, which is always close at hand, offers slight cost savings, but is new and perceived to be slightly risky or suspect.

The initial configuration has most customers using the bank, with some supermarket uses in local clusters. There is a supermarket for every Moore neighbourhood (the grid and diagonal nearest neighbours (9 including the centre)).

The customers can have several states, reflecting how far away their bank is, T_0, T_1, T_2,..., where T_n indicates a bank n steps removed from the local neighbourhood. We now have a series of thresholds, θ_0, θ_1, θ_2... determining whether to switch. This models the willingness of customers to travel to remote banks. The probability of finding a bank goes up as n^2, so we probably do not want to go much beyond T_3.

The rule takes the form:

- If there is a bank in the local neighbourhood, then stay with it, unless the number of local supermarket users, N_s, is greater than some threshold, η_0. - no change.
- If there is no local bank, but there is one within the extended neighbourhood, T_k, then if N_s is greater than some threshold, θ_k, switch to the supermarket.
- If the switch to S does not occur, then set customer state to T_{k+1} where k is the minimum of the neighbourhood.

Now we can look for some starting configurations and bank densities, which create a flash point, where most or all customers switch over, or perhaps where the customers fluctuate wildly in their preferences.

Formally, this is analogous to the sort of CA models which have been used for simulating bushfires and epidemics.

The first use of a simple model of this kind is to look for criticality effects—points at which the bank passes the point of no return. The second is as a template upon which real data may be grafted—realistic consumer choice models, profitability of bank as function of number of customers and so on.

Although the positive feedback effects in a model of this kind are not hard to see, in practice they are easily overlooked. *The Economist* in a special report in April this year described how a new wave of banks is taking over the United States—banks which relish in their local branches, offer extended opening hours more suitable to retail customers, provide toys for kids, and in general dispel the formal/hostile nature of many traditional banks.

Cellular Automata Theory

Definitions

Since the initial work by Von Neumann (1966) and Ulam (1974), many extensions and varieties of CAs have appeared. It is possible to create general (and therefore abstract definitions) and derive each variety as a special case. But with the applications emphasis of the present paper, we adopt an alternative approach of starting with some basic definitions and add to them as necessary.

The simplest CA is a string of cells, each of which may contain a zero or one, that is, has one of two states. Each cell behaves in exactly the same way. At each iteration or time step each and every cell examines its neighbours, looks up the neighbourhood pattern in a table, usually referred to as the CA rule, and determines what state it will take at the next step. There are two principal ways of dealing with the edges: aperiodic, where the cells off the edge are set to some arbitrary value, typically zero; periodic, where the edge cells wrap around to the cells on the opposite side.

In a slightly more formal way, a CA consists of a set of cells $\{c_i\}$, the nodes of a graph, G, which have a number of possible states, drawn from a set, or *alphabet*, $\sum$. Each and every c_i has a neighbourhood, R_i (including c_i). Associated with c_i is a transition function, or rule, T_i. The state of c_i is updated by application of T_i to c_i within its neighbourhood R_i.

$$c_i(t + 1) = T_i(R_i)$$

Usually the graph G is a regular grid, in not more than three dimensions, the neighbourhoods, R are the same for each cell (e.g., the nearest neighbours along grid lines) and the transition functions, T are the same for every cell. Interesting patterns develop with even the simplest set of states, the binary values 0 and 1. Note that state admits of two interpretations: the state of a single cell (0 or 1 in the Game of Life) or a single combination of states for all the cells at any given time. To avoid confusion we refer to this aggregate state as a *configuration*.

The neighbourhood is usually small relative to the total size of the string. So the decisions occur based on *local* information, but *global* patterns can emerge. Many neighbourhoods are possible. Two of the most common, which we encounter herein, are the *Von Neumann neighbourhood*, which has four neighbours on a 2D grid, along the grid lines (North, South, East, and West) and the *Moore neighbourhood*, which adds the diagonals to give eight neighbours.

The transition function may be expressible in algorithmic terms, but it is more often just a table of $|R|^{|\Sigma|}$, referred to as the *lookup table* or just LUT or the *rule* table.

Our concern is usually with finite configurations, whose size we denote by N in one dimension. The key features of CAs then necessary for practical applications are:

- Locality
- Rule
- Set of states
- Configurations
- Boundary conditions

Most work on CAs is *synchronous* but the dynamics are different for asynchronous systems (see the section *Synchronicity*). In a synchronous CA time is discrete, and has no real meaning other than just the number of iterations the CA has executed since some start point.

The most general form of CA is usually called a *Random Boolean Network*, popularised by Kauffman (1993) for genetic regulation. Such a network usually has a finite number of cells connected together by a random graph with a random update rule for each cell. RBNs have a variety of applications, including genetic regulatory models, and their dynamics are extremely interesting. The section *Synchronicity* touches upon them briefly, but they fall outside the scope of this article.

One final distinction, useful in modelling, is between fully deterministic rules, and those which allow some stochastic elements. There are many variations in connectivity, dynamics, and the level of determinism. We shall not attempt to describe or classify them, but some will appear in our discussion of applications.

The Wolfram Classification

Stephen Wolfram, inventor of the software package Mathematica, has had a long interest in CAs and recently published a gigantic book proselytising them in all their guises. He is best known, though, for an early and enduring classification of behaviour.

Four distinct types of behaviour can occur. The CAs are one dimensional with the states of the cells at a given time forming each row of the figure and with increasing row number going downwards showing the evolution in time.

- **Class 1** are the least interesting type. They just stop, or in other words reach a point attractor.
- **Class 2** are not much better. They settle into an oscillatory attractor.
- **Class 3** are the chaotic attractors. They look like noise with no obvious patterns are periodicity.
- **Class 4** are the really interesting ones. They display complex patterns, structured, but endlessly changing. The Game of Life is one such Class 4 CA. Numerous examples will be found in Bilotta, Lafusa, and Pantano (2003).

One of the surprising things to come out of theoretical studies is that the Class 4 CAs are very rare in the space of all possible rules. Thus finding rules to represent complex phenomena is intrinsically difficult. See the sections on *Input Entropy and Complex Rules* and *Evolutionary Strategies* for description of the techniques for reducing the search space.

Maps

It is sometimes useful to think of CAs in terms of maps, akin to dynamical processes (Toffoli & Margolus, 1990). The *local map*, λ, is the pair:

$$\lambda = \langle R, T \rangle$$

mapping the neighbourhood to a new state via the LUT.

The local map also implies a *global map*, τ, from any configuration q to a new configuration q'. The evolution of a CA is the series of configurations q_0, q_1, q_2... of the global map.

Universal Computation and Physics

As alluded to earlier, a CA with a Moore neighbourhood is capable of universal computation. But to simulate physics we need to consider something else as well, reversibility.

Invertible CAs, Reversibility, and Modelling Physics

If CAs are to model many physical systems, they need to be *reversible*. Any configuration of a deterministic CA has one and only one *successor configuration*. But it may have had any number of possible *predecessors*. To be *invertible* and hence reversible, or to model reversible systems, it needs one and only one predecessor.

The mathematical challenge of identifying invertible CAs proved non-trivial. An empirical search is hopeless, because one would have to search the entire gigantic configuration space to be absolutely sure that all predecessors had been found. After a great deal of analysis the following key theorems were proved (Toffoli & Margolus, 1990)

1.   If a CA *is* invertible, then the inverse is itself a CA. In other words there is a local map to go backwards, if the inverse exists. In practice determining that a CA is invertible has always involved determining the inverse (Toffoli & Margolus, 1990).

2.   There is an effective procedure for determining if a 1D CA is invertible. This result is also encouraging.

3.   But the story is bad otherwise—no effective procedure for determining if a 2D CA is invertible. So, akin to the halting of Turing machines, in general invertibility is undecidable.

4.   Although invertible CAs exist, they are infrequent. In fact like Wolfram's Class IV, they form a very tiny subset of the rule space.

Digital Physics

Fredkin (1990) takes the CA agendas of reversibility and universal computation to a whole new level—digital mechanics. The plan is to create a full representation of physical laws, parameters, and constants in a CA world, possibly including quantum mechanics too. This is an exceptionally interesting area with all sorts of philosophical implications.

One especially interesting result which bears, at least philosophically, on the simulation of physics is coarse graining. When we throw a cricket ball, we can rely on macroscopic laws of motion to determine its travel. We do not need to consider the motion of each individual atom with the ball. So we *coarse grain* all the individual components into one macro component, the ball. Israeli and Goldenfeld (2006) showed that CAs are often (and possibly generally) coarse grainable. So, imagine that we have a CA evolving in time, from state s_0 at t_0 to state s_1 at t_1. At time t_0 we aggregate the cells in some way to an aggregate state, S_0 and define a new rule which determines how this new spatially averaged CA will evolve from state, and see what state, S_1 has emerged at t_1. Now, for this coarse-graining aggregation to have worked, if we aggregate the state, s_1, of the original CA at t_1, then this should give the same aggregate state as S_1. They found that for most of the binary 1D CAs of neighbourhood size 3, this was indeed possible, a philosophically very appealing result!

Computation at the Edge of Chaos

The trouble with classifications of the emergent dynamics is that they give us no indication of what sort of rule table characteristics give rise to one form of dynamics or another. From a practical point of view, using CAs to model real systems, such indications would be rather useful.

Langton (1990) looked at dynamical properties as a function of a single parameter λ, which essentially captures the mix of possible result states in the rule table. If every neighbourhood gives the same state, the dynamics will not be very interesting! So, λ is defined according to equation below, where $K = |\sum|$ is the number of states, $L = |R|$ the size of the neighbourhood, and n is the number of transitions to an arbitrary state, the *quiescent state*.

$$\lambda = \frac{K^L - n}{K^L}$$

In the case of a binary CA, then λ would be just the number of zeros or ones in the LUT and is obviously symmetric about 0.5. Langton (1990) found that the least interesting behaviour occurs at the extreme values of zero or one as expected.

At intermediate values, two characteristics appear. Firstly the transients, before the CA settles down to long-term behaviour (its attractor) get dramatically longer, characteristic of phase transitions. Secondly, the long-term behaviour gets more interesting, with various propagating structures appearing. In other words, Wolfram's class IV seems to occur at these values, with classes I and II at lower lambda values and class III above.

Mean Field Theory

Another way of looking at the correlations in configurations as a CA evolves, developed by Harold Gutowitz, is through Markov fields. In brief, for a 1D binary CA, the probability, $P^{t+1}(b)$ of a block of length b occurring at time $t+1$ is (Gutowitz, 1990)

$$P^{t+1}(b) = \sum_{B_{|b|+2r}} \delta(\tau(B), b) P^t(B)$$

where r is the radius of the rule, $B_{|b|+2r}$ the set of blocks of size $|b|+2r$ and $\delta(\tau(B), b)$ is one if application of the rule to block B gives $\mathbf{b}$ and zero otherwise. In general, knowledge of these probabilities is impractical, since the set of configurations even for quite small blocks is gigantic. Thus the challenge is to find ways of approximating P.

Markov fields provide a solution. As the block size increases, more and more correlations in behaviour can be accounted for. The algebraic complexity increases dramatically too, and we shall not pursue this metric in any detail. The zeroth order approximation (block is just a single cell) reduces to Langton's (1990) λ parameter

$$P^{t+1}(b) = \sum_{B_{|b|+2r}} \frac{\delta(\tau(B), b)}{2^{|R|}} = \lambda$$

The next order, referred to as the mean-field approximation, essentially assumes adjacent cells are uncorrelated, and the probability of a block, B is given by simply by the probability of the number of ones $\#1(B)$ and zeros, $\#0(B)$.

$$P(B) = P_1^{\#1(B)} P_0^{\#0(B)}$$

Attractor Basins

For any CA configuration, there is some set of configurations, each of which will eventually lead to this configuration. Just as in dynamics there is *basin of attraction* for any attractor, so this set of precursor configurations is also called the basin of attraction. It turns out, though, that most configurations do not have precursors. They are called the *Garden of Eden* (GoE) configurations.

For almost half a century after Von Neumann, the basin of attraction of a given configuration was thought incomputable. But it just needed a breakthrough. Many creative people feel that learning what has already happened in a field precludes them in doing anything truly original. So it was with Andy Wuensche, a successful architect, who began playing with CA patterns purely out of interest. He subsequently discovered an algorithm which would run a CA backwards, hence discovering all the precursor states. His software DDLab encapsulates the algorithm along with superb graphics for display of the attractor basins.

The reverse algorithm is quite complicated, but not difficult to grasp in principle. Starting at one end of the CA, the possible precursor states form the beginning of a tree of possible precursors. Each of these possible states is now checked for possible states and so on through the whole configuration. The algorithm either yields a tree of configurations or stops at some point where there is no suitable precursor state—in other words a GoE configuration.

So, to take a concrete example of a 1D CA with a neighbourhood of 5. Suppose the algorithm has got k-1 bits along the N bit target configuration and has built a stack of all the configurations up to k-1 bits in length, which could lead to the target configuration. The algorithm now builds a new stack of proto-configurations of length k bits and continues until N. The output of the rule at this position is the k'th bit which is known. The left hand side of the neighbourhood is known, so, there are only $\frac{32}{4} = 8$ elements of the LUT which could be used at this point, not all of which will necessarily give the correct output. This reduced set may contain ones only, zeros and ones, zeros only, or maybe null. Thus the putative configuration is now extended by one bit and possibly split into two (with a new zero or one) and the new k length configurations are added to a new stack, or the configuration is abandoned and the next one from the stack is taken.

Synchronicity

In the previous descriptions synchronisation is implicit—all cells update at the same time. But many natural systems are not synchronous at all. It transpires that the behaviour of CAs is radically different between synchronous and asynchronous update. Harvey and Bossomaier (1997), for example, found a big difference in the number and size of RBNs depending on the update method.

Some systems exhibit mixtures of synchronous and asynchronous updates, as recently described by Cornforth, Green, Newth, and Kirley (2005). In practice synchronous update is common as much for practical convenience as anything else. It is always important to ask, however, if any strong emergent patterns are an artefact of the update procedure.

From Emergence to Rules

In general the problem of working backwards from some given emergent behaviour to a rule set which will create it is intractable. Thus rule design methods are heuristic and are essentially optimisation processes.

Input Entropy and Complex Rules

It seems rather frustrating that the set of rules with interesting behaviour is infinitesimally small. So, finding such rules might be something of a problem. Bilotta et al. (2003) found a clever solution using the idea of *input entropy*.

Input entropy, S, was introduced by Wuensche (1998) for characterising CA behaviour. The idea is to capture the variability across a configuration at any given time, Q_t in terms of the number of times each neighbourhood appears. If this variation is very high, then the behaviour is likely to be chaotic. If it is very low, then the dynamics are likely to be fairly static. Thus the input entropy is defined by

$$S(t) = \sum_{i=1}^{|R|} (\frac{u_i(t)}{N}) \log(\frac{u_i(t)}{N})$$

where $u_i(t)$ is the number of times state i occurs in the configuration of size N.

For a point or low period cyclic attractor, the input entropy will not change very much at all. But for a chaotic attractor it will be high and stay high. The interesting situation is when the input entropy has a high variability, which we can measure by calculating its variance. It turns out that high variability characterises the complex rules. Thus they evolve CA rules using the *variance* of the input entropy as the fitness function (Bilotta et al., 2003).

Canonical Problems

To test methods for creating rules to match emergent behaviour some canonical problems are necessary. One such extremely simple, but powerful example is the *density problem*. Stated in its simplest form, given a configuration, q of a 1D binary state CA, if q has more ones than zeros, then the CA should go to a point attractor of all ones. Conversely, if it has more zeros than ones, the opposite occurs, all zeros result. In other words there are two and only two attractors (all zeros and all ones) with basins equal in size to half the configuration space, corresponding to densities of ones and zeros above and below 50%.[2]

There is no solution! Land and Belew (1995) showed that there are cases which no local rule can solve—but there are only very, very few of them. Performance should be able to reach 99.99% and above just excluding Belew's pathological cases. The first attempts at finding rules performed much worse than this.

The earliest attempts using evolutionary computing gave results in the 70-80% region for a neighbourhood of 7 and a CA length of 149 using circular boundary conditions. This (7,149) setup became the main canonical problem, but the issue of scaling with N will come up later. It is fairly easy to set up the problem for evolutionary optimisation. The LUT has 128 binary entries, so this forms a natural chromosome. The fitness function is simply the performance, obtained by testing the CA rules on a (large) number of random starting configurations. For the better rules, discrimination between the best individuals requires testing on upwards of a million configurations, and our own work required supercomputing facilities (ANU and ac3).

Das (1995) and subsequently Gacs, Kurdymunov, and Levin (GKL) (1978), improved on these early results, the so-called GKL rule, which was for some time top of the league table. The next step forward by Andre Bennet and Koza used genetic programming in a fairly sophisticated way. Jordan and Pollack (JP) advanced further with the current best rules for (7,149) using coevolutionary algorithms.

The co-evolutionary approach is an interesting one, with much more general applicability. The key idea is to co-evolve a pathological training set alongside the solution. Thus the cost of testing each rule is never very great since the number of test examples is always small (but viscous). At present the JP rule is at the top of the league table for (7,149), but it is not clear whether it scales to the best performance as *N* gets bigger. At *N=999* it falls behind the GKL rule.

This sequence of procedures essentially involves even more sophisticated search. Cranny and Bossomaier took a different approach by essentially asking if we can limit the search space a priori and then use simple (even exhaustive) search within this limited subspace. Hence we ask where the best rules really live and conjecture that they live in a space of low algorithmic complexity for describing the rule. There is no mathematical proof of this conjecture, but the heuristic argument is simple. The best rules should have structure that enables them to rapidly handle structural fragments in the input configurations, in a similar way to the way that the generalisation in neural networks is best served by the smallest networks which fit the data reasonably well. For the density problem it seems to work and more mathematical precision can be given.

Monotonicity and Bicameral Rules

Since the goal of the CA rule is to take sparse configurations to zero and dense configurations to one, then the various elements of the LUT should not go in the reverse direction. In other words if a given neighbourhood goes to one, then adding more ones to the neighbourhood should also give LUT entries which go to one. Cranny (1999) called this the *monotonicity* constraint as follows:

A mapping K of strings $\in \{0,1\}^N$ into $\{0,1\}$ is said to be *monotonic* if both of the following hold:

1. $K(s) = 1$ implies $K(s^+) = 1$ for any $s^+ \in \{0,1\}^N$ derived from s by changing one or more 0's to 1's.

2. $K(s) = 0$ implies $K(s^-) = 0$ for any $s^- \in \{0,1\}^N$ derived from by changing one or more 1's to 0's.

Satisfying the monotonicity constraint is easy—it is just equivalent to a linear weighting function. Creating two such weighting functions, one for the current state being a zero, and the other a one, leads to *bicameral* rules. A linear weighting function of this kind is a hyperplane dividing the hypercube of states. We can define two such hypercubes, S^0 and S^1 corresponding to whether the current state is a zero or one.

To specify such a division is sufficient to specify the hyperplane and which side is which, and since we are looking here at the density classification problem, where we want 0 and 1 to be stable, we can simply prescribe $2r+1$ real numbers $w_{-r}, w_{-r+1}, ..., w_{r-1}, w_r$ such that the output-assignment rule for the S_1 input configurations is:

$$x_i^{t+1} = \begin{cases} 0 & if \quad \sum_{j=-r}^{r} w_j x_{i+j}^t < 1 \\ 1 & if \quad \sum_{j=-r}^{r} w_j x_{i+j}^t \geq 1 \end{cases}$$

keeping in mind that by definition, the 'central bit' $x_i^t = 1$ for configurations in S_1. We call $w_{-r}, w_{-r+1}, ..., w_{r-1}, w_r$ a *weighting vector* for the output assignment on S_1, and say that the CA rule is *linearly separable* on S_1.

Obviously only *2r* weights (not *2r+1*) are needed to define the hyperplane, but we may scale the weighting vector so as to have $\sum_{j=-r}^{r} w_j = 2$ by means of the mapping:

$$w_j \to w_j(\Sigma w_j - 1)^{-1} \quad for\, all \quad j \neq 0$$
$$w_0 \to (\Sigma w_j + w_0 - 2)(\Sigma w_j - 1)^{-1}$$

where we note that we may assume $\Sigma w_j > 1$ since we require 1 to be stable.

We many also perform a perturbation so as to ensure that no combination of weights has sum precisely 1 while keeping $\Sigma w_j = 2$. This corresponds to the condition that the hyperplane not pass through any vertex. A rule which is linearly separable on both S_1 and S_0 will be said to be *bicameral*.

The bicameral rules form an *extremely* small subset of the total space of CA rules.

Simple genetic algorithms can now evolve these weight functions instead of the LUT, thus automatically restricting the solution to the bicameral subspace. Cranny was thus able to exhaustively search the bicameral space.

The Neural Network Approximation and Cellular Neural Networks

The bicameral solution represents a tiny subset of the search space. To search the space with gradually increasing complexity requires some generalisation. This comes from recognising that the bicameral rule can be generalised to a simple feed-forward neural network (Bossomaier, Cranny, & Schneider, 1999) as shown in Figure 1.

Figure 1. The GKL rule represented as a feed forward neural network

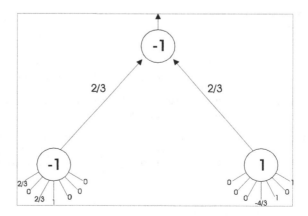

It is now possible to use the evolutionary methods for neural networks and to use the network size as the complexity metric. Quantitative metrics for complexity have been proposed via the Vapnik-Chernovenkis dimension (Anthony & Biggs, 1992).

Methodology of Applied Cellular Automata

The idea of using CAs rests on the assumption that the important patterns arise from interactions between simple elements. Often this involves encapsulating a range of properties and behaviours into simple rules. In the case of physical systems, such as the lava flow, we discuss later, these rules map closely to the differential equations which describe the phenomena and may follow simply from a discretisation. In other situations, particularly involving biological or social systems, the rule may have a more intuitive character.

Take for example the *flocking of boids* model introduced by Reynolds. The flight of a flock of birds in formation, and as they flow around obstacles, can be captured by just three rules of interaction. The model is sufficiently persuasive, that it has passed into the biological community. But there is not any necessarily direct relationship between the actual way the bird's brain takes in information about other birds and determines its flight path.

CAs usually assume that connectivity between elements is local, often over a very small scale relative to system size. Many systems are now recognised as having small-world or scale-free connectivity, which invalidates this assumption. However, the more general random Boolean networks do not suffer from such restrictions.

A particularly interesting issue is asynchronous update which we discuss in the section *Synchronicity*. Distinctive and complex patterns seem to occur more often with synchronous than asynchronous update. It is thus important to determine firstly if synchronous update is justified. If not, and it is used for computational convenience, that the emergent phenomena are not destroyed by asynchronicity.

Mathematical Requirements

Applying CA at a simple level requires very little mathematics. The algorithms rest on LUTs for determining state changes. As one delves into the theory some metrics become useful:

- Entropy is widely used to describe the properties of the configurations generated. It serves to describe the disorder or level of randomness and is important in selecting rules with complex (as opposed to chaotic or simple) behaviour.

- Stochastic methods such as Markov random fields can be useful in attempting to characterise the emergent properties.

- Graph theory is useful in two ways: in understanding the edge of chaos as it applies to CAs and in describing non-grid topologies.

- Some familiarity with nonlinear dynamics is useful at a qualitative level.

- Statistical techniques are useful for cross validation—to determine if a given pattern obtained by CA matches actual data.

- Optimisation techniques, particularly from soft computing methods such as evolutionary programming, are useful to tune parameters (see the urban spread example in the section *Modelling the Spread of Urban Development*).

Data Requirements

Data requirements are very problem dependent, but might be split into two categories

- The characteristics of each cell, the number of states and perhaps internal transitions within the cell which are not affected by its neighbours.
- The connectivity relationships and data flow dynamics between cells.

This division is apparent in the lava example discussed in the section *Modelling Geological Flows.*

Types of Outcome of CA Modelling

Broadly speaking there are two types of output:

1. Criticality, phase transitions, percolation phenomena are the really exciting things to come out of CA models. They are the emergent behaviours, the global patterns not apparent from the local rules. Visualisation is often the primary method of interpretation, but summary statistics (such as spread of an epidemic through time) can be useful.

2. CAs may also be used in a more prosaic fashion to provide an environment upon which a more diverse agent model sits. So, one might use CAs to model environmental characteristics (water flow, vegetation, nutrients, etc.) on which adaptive agents (animals, people) might move.

For spatial models, particularly in the geographic information system (GIS) arena, *spatial metrics* have proved useful (McGarigal, Cushman, Neel, & Ene, 2002). In the Clarke model for Santa Barbara discussed previously they consist of fractal metrics, clustering coefficients, and edge and patch counts.

Just as with soft computing methodologies such as neural networks, and other machine learning techniques, the principle approach is cross validation—measuring the performance against known real examples. This could be the records of the spread of an epidemic or bushfires, the spread of mud and debris following an earthquake. So, the CA parameters would be tuned on part of the dataset, say part of a time series, and then test (validated) on the remaining part. The division into tuning and testing sets is usually repeated a number of times with different divisions on each occasion.[3]

In most cases cross-validation (Witten & Frank, 2000) is necessary, where optimisation techniques are employed to determine parameters within the rule set. This will give some assessment of how well the existing data are fitted and how well the model will generalise.

Success and Limitations of CA Modelling

CAs are useful for abstraction, for getting at global patterns of behaviour, and sometimes for simplifying the computational complexity of a large scale model. Evolutionary (and other soft computing methods) for finding CA rules to fit particular emergent behaviour are a very active area of research. But the study of strongly heterogeneous systems, or making precise numerical predications, may be better pursued elsewhere.

CA theory still has some way to go. The issue of asynchronicity is still being actively studied, while other less regular connectivity patterns are becoming interesting. As a tool for modelling real systems, the challenges are not so much in the CA framework, which is quite mature, but in encapsulating the system properties into a simple rule system.

Applications

There are many applications of CA, particularly in computational physics. We have selected just a few diverse examples. But at the present time, the growth in agent-based modelling is also stimulating renewed interest in CA modelling of social systems, particularly in hybrid form with intelligent agents.

Geographic Modelling

CAs are very popular in modelling spatial systems. In fact some groups, such as Batty's (2007) Centre for Advanced Spatial Analysis (CASA) at the University College London, and Clarke, Hoppen, and Gaydos' (1997) group at Santa Barbara have specialised in this area.

One very appealing application is in the determination of land use. The states of the CA become the different land use categories: residential, agricultural, parkland, and so on. As one might imagine, change in land use, such as urban sprawl, spreads gradually and local rules work well.

Geographical and social knowledge inspires the rule sets, but extensive optimisation and validation is required. Typically, the growth patterns over some period are used to fine tune parameters, and validation occurs over some other period. Thus these models are rooted in real-world data.

Modelling the Spread of Urban Development

Clarke and his group (Clarke et al. 1997; Herold, Goldstein, & Clarke, 2003; Goldstein, Candau, & Clarke, 2004) have looked at the spread of urban development of Santa Barbara from 1930 and projected out until 2030. This idyllic part of the world sits between the Pacific Ocean and the Santa Ynez Mountains. Originally citrus and avocado orchards dominated the region, but since in the 1960s and 1970s the growth of the university, the aerospace industry, and other development increased the level of urban development.

The CA model used for the growth model is Slope, Land-use, Exclusion, Urban, Transportation, and Hillshade (SLEUTH) consisting of four general rules and five parameters. The principle here is to be able to parametrise the model for different urban settings. The rules are (Goldstein et al., 2004)

1.   Selection of locations for new urban settlements out of town.

2.   Selection of new urban centres as growth centres.

3.   Propagation of growth centres for edge spreading and in-fill.

4.   Generation of new growth centres next to transportation routes.

The variable parameters are optimised by soft computing techniques such as genetic algorithms. The performance is assessed by various spatial metrics as defined for example McGarigal and used in the package FRAGSTATS.

Physics

In the section *Invertible CAs, Reversibility, and Modelling Physics* we discussed some of the theoretical challenges in using CAs to model physics. It is now time to look at some examples. A good place to start are *lattice gases* in which particles move along only the axes of a multidimensional grid (and thus can be represented by CAs). It might be thought that the directions would make isotropic behaviour impossible. In other words, the grid directions would always show and there would not be smooth motion in any other direction. But this is not so, if we make the grid sufficiently fine. At a sufficiently large scale view containing many cells, it turns out that only $\frac{p}{2}$ rotational invariance is enough for fully isotropic diffusive phenonema (Toffoli & Margolus, 1990). In other words a rectangular grid suffices to get effectively smooth behaviour in all directions.

But there is a different problem. Fourfold particle directions can create spurious conservation effects, removed by allowing six directions. Lattice gases provide a framework for studying numerous problems in physics, described in some detail by Toffoli and Margolus (1988). The section *Modelling Geological Flows* discusses a fully geologically informed model of lava flow. The section *Lattice Gas Cellular Automata* describes a lattice gas model of lava flows, developed to simulate the overall behaviour as fast as possible for use in real-time applications such as computer games (Van Raay, 2005).

Modelling Geological Flows

CAs have found many applications in modelling flow systems, from fluid dynamics to plasma. Residents of Naples in Italy are only too familiar with the dangers of volcanos—many tourists every year visit the entombed town of Pompeii, a victim of Vesuius which towers above Naples. Thus volcanic activity is likely to be especially interesting in Italian universities. One interesting application is studying large scale geological phenomena (D'Ambrosio, Di Gregorio, Gabriele, & Gaudio, 2001; Di Gregorio, Serra, & Villani, 1999) such as the flow of lava from volcanos and landslides from Salvatore in Calabria in southern Italy (Di Gregorio & Serra, 1999). In these applications a lot of work goes into the detailed physics to determine rules of behaviour for each cell and the local interaction. CA evolution is then used to determine the spatial spread.

Their SCIARA model gives a fairly successful prediction of the flow and the spread of lava from a volcanic eruption. Although the CA is simple the underlying details are quite complicated. Essentially the lava flows along 2D grid axes using a Von Neumann neighbourhood.

- The altitude of the cell, S_a.
- The thickness of the lava, S_{th}.
- The lava temperature, S_θ.

The first stage of the CA update is to model internal changes of the previous variables, independently of the neighbours. As the lava cools, it solidifies, so changing the altitude of the cell and the thickness of the molten lava. These updates follow standard geophysical models. The cell size and time step in real time for the CA is linked to the internal state dynamics.

The rule for the altitude change is a mapping from the altitude, thickness, and temperature. The thickness depends on the thickness and temperature and the temperature on the thickness (affecting rate of cooling) and the temperature itself.

The second stage is to model the lava flows in and out of a Von Neumann neighbourhood. The altitude and the thickness in the five cells and the temperature in the centre cell determine the flow. The net flow in and out for each cell is determined using an algorithm referred to as the *minimisation of the differences*, which serves to conserve the flow quantities (in this case the lava). In a similar, slightly more complicated model, the same group looked at the flow of mud and debris following a landslide caused by an earthquake in Japan. The same basic approach applies, but now the water content, S_w and a run up height, S_R, which determines the extent to which the flow will go over the top of obstacles, replace the temperature.

Lattice Gas Cellular Automata

Lattice gas methods are widely used in fluid flow simulations (Rothman & Zeleski, 1997). Van Raay' real-time simulation of lava flows uses the Lattice Boltzmann

Figure 2. Lattice Boltzmann velocity vectors

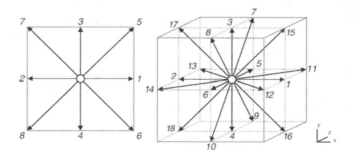

method (Bussemaker & Ernst, 1994; Thurey, Rude & Korner, 2005). A summary can be found in Van Raay and Bossomaier (2006). In this model each cell contains a collection of particles which flow in a number of discrete directions (in this case 19) as shown in Figure 2. A model for cell-to-cell to flow and intra-cell particle collisions enables the Navier-Stokes equations to be simulated with arbitrary precision. The cells are now updated synchronously as in a standard CA.

Traffic

Traffic is one of the great bugbears of modern life. In England traffic jams are now an art form. It is very reassuring to hear on the radio that the traffic jam you are stuck in is in fact 12 miles long and due to an overturned truck at the junction of the A41 and the M6.

Thus understanding and controlling traffic flow is important in much of the developed and developing world. Projects such as TRANSIMS at the Los Alamos National Lab (LANL) are concerned with building sophisticated traffic models on extensive real data. But at the same time, it is useful to build simple models that can uncover emergent and critical behaviours—in other words congestion and traffic jams.

Steen Rasmussen at LANL has been one of the leaders of CA models of traffic flow (Nagel & Rasmussen, 1994). The basic CA framework is slightly different to the CA models discussed previously: It has stochastic elements and implicit movement of entities from cell to cell.

The simplest example, to some extent soluble analytically, is just a single freeway loop, in other words a ring of cells. Each cell has seven states. It may be empty, or containing a vehicle with integer speeds, v, from 0 to 5. The results are not overly sensitive to the maximum value of 5. Each cell has a gap with respect to the vehicle in front. Then at each step each vehicle moves v steps. The rules require the vehicle to speed up or slow down according to the size of the gap. Cars do not collide in the first order model! One additional, stochastic element allows cars to randomly slow down. This stochastic element effects the emergent behaviour, making the critical points less well defined.

The results are surprising. The maximum flow along the road is surprisingly small, around a third of the maximum, but the density of traffic is very low at less than 10%; thereafter the maximum flow decreases. Near the maximum, critical behaviour occurs with a very wide variation in travel times. The results follow analytical results, but the model generalises easily to networks of roads, which are intractable otherwise.

Thus some of the key elements, particularly the problem of criticality, are apparent from such simple CA models and possible remedies (control flow, tolls, etc.) can be studied. It is interesting, though, from a fundamental point of view, how we see critical behaviour emerging at the edge of chaos, much as we saw for the canonical CAs.

Crown of Thorns Starfish on the Great Barrier Reef

The Crown of Thorns starfish is one of the major hazards of the Great Barrier Reef. CA modelling beginning with work by Roger Bradbury and others has a long history in studying reef damage and recovery. Preece and Johnson (1992), for example, describe a model in which cells represent coral reef or deep water. Reef cells generate various levels of coral larvae which are dispersed by water currents.

Conclusion

CAs are fascinating in numerous ways. They exhibit the full gamut of complex behaviours starting from the simplest possible operations. Very simple examples are capable of universal computation.

As a modelling tool, CAs offer the advantages of speed and conceptual clarity, often being able to capture the essential emergent behaviour of many systems from bushfires to economics. The finding of CA rules to describe any given natural or artificial system is a challenging open research question.

Sources of More Information

Key References

There is a reprint of Physica D volume 45, edited by Gutowitz (1990) which has a number of key papers.

Stephen Wolfram's earlier book will be found in many libraries and his new book contains a wealth of detail (Wolfram, 2002)

The book by Toffoli and Margolus is a little dated in software terms but contains solid information (Toffoli & Margolus, 1988).

Useful Web Sites

The following Web sites are useful CA resources at the time of writing:

http://www.santafe.edu/~hag/

http://www.alife.org/

http://www.santafe.edu/projects/evca/

http://www.santafe.edu/projects/CompMech/papers/ECA54TitlePage.html

http://math.hws.edu/xJava/CA/

http://www.stephenwolfram.com/publications/articles/ca/

http://cell-auto.com/

http://www.cogs.susx.ac.uk/users/andywu/index.html

http://www.csc.fi/math_topics/Movies/CA.html

Stephen Wolfram is also the inventor of Mathematica and there is a wealth of software written for this package.

Some of the early work on CA evolution, particularly the density problems may also be found via the Web sites of Melanie Mitchell, Moshe Sipper, and Doyne Farmer. Toffoli and Margolus (1988, 1990) and Fredkin (1990) referred to in the text also have Web sites given below.

Wolfram: http://mathworld.wolfram.com/CellularAutomaton.html

Mitchell: http://www.cse.ogi.edu/~mm/

Farmer: http://www.santafe.edu/~jdf/

Toffoli: http://pm1.bu.edu/~tt/

Margolus: http://pm1.bu.edu/~tt/

Sipper: http://www.moshesipper.com/

Wuensche: http://www.ddlab.com/

Fredkin: http://www.digitalphilosophy.org/index.htm

References

Anthony, M., & Biggs, N. (1992). *Computational learning theory*. Cambridge University Press.

Batty, M. (2007). *CASA: Centre for Advanced Spatial Analysis.* Retrieved from www.casa.ucl.ac.uk

Bilotta, A., Lafusa, A., & Pantano, P. (2003). Searching for complex CA rules with GAs. *Complexity, 8*(3), 56-67.

Bossomaier, T. R. J., Cranny, T. R., & Schneider, D. (1999). A new paradigm for evolving cellular automata rules. In *Proceedings of the Congress on Evolutionary Computation* (pp. 169-176). Washington, DC.

Bussemaker, H. J., & Ernst, M. H. (1994). *Generalized Boltzmann equation for lattice gas automata.* Arxiv preprint comp-gas/9404002

Clarke, K. C., Hoppen, S., & Gaydos, L. J. (1997). A self-modifying cellular automata model of historical urbanization in the San Francisco Bay Area. *Environment and Planning B-Planning and Design, 24*(2), 247-261.

Cornforth, D., Green, D. G., Newth, D., & Kirley, M. R. (2005). Ordered asynchronous processes in multi-agent systems. *Physica D, 204,* 70-82.

Cranny, T. R. (1999). *On the role of symmetry, structure and simplicity in emergent computation* (Tech. Rep. No. RGAI-99-02). Research Group for Complex Systems, Charles Sturt University, NSW, Australia.

D'Ambrosio, D., Di Gregorio, S., Gabriele, S., & Gaudio, R. (2001). A cellular automata model for soil erosioin by water. *Phys. Chem. Earth (B), 26*(1), 33-39.

Das, R. (1995). Unpublished.

Di Gregorio, S., & Serra, R. (1999). An empirical method for modelling and simulating some complex macroscopic phenomena by cellular automata. *Future Generation Computer Science, 16,* 259-271.

Di Gregorio, S., Serra, R., & Villani, M. (1999) Applying cellular automata in complex environmental problems: tThe simulation of the bioremediation of contaminated soils. *Theoretical Computer Science, 217,* 131-156.

Fredkin, E. (1990). Digital mechanics. *Physica D, 45,* 254-270.

Gacs, P., Kurdymunov, G. L., & Levin, L. (1978). One dimensional uniform arrays that wash out finite islands. *Problemy Peredachi Informatsii, 12,* 92-98.

Goldstein, N. C., Candau, J. T., & Clarke, K. C. (2004). Approaches to simulating the march of bricks and mortar. *Computers, Environment and Urban Systems, 28,* 125-147.

Gutowitz, H. A. (1990). A hierarchical classification of cellular automata. *Physica D, 45,* 136-156.

Harvey, I., & Bossomaier, T. R. J. (1997). Time out of joint: Attractors in random Boolean networks. In P. Husbands & I. Harvey (Eds.), *Fourth European Conference on Artificial Life* (pp. 67-75). Cambridge, MA: MIT Press.

Herold, M., Goldstein, N. C., & Clarke, K. C. (2003). The spatiotemporal form of urban growth: Measurement, analysis and modelling. *Remote Sensing and Environment, 86,* 286-302.

Israeli, N., & Goldenfeld, D. (2006). On computational irreducibility and the predictability of complex physical systems. *Journal of Physics E, 73.*

Kauffman, S. A. (1993). *The origins of order.* Oxford University Press.

Land, M., & Belew, R. K. (1995). No two-state ca for density classification exists. *Physical Review Letters, 74*(25), 5148-5150.

Langton, C. G. (1990). Computation at the edge of chaos: Phase transitions and emergent computation. *Physica D, 42,* 12-37.

McGarigal, S. A., Cushman, N. M., Neel, M., & Ene, E. (2002). *FRAGSTATS: Spatial pattern analysis program for categorical maps.* Retrieved from www. umass.edu/landeco/research/fragstats/fragstats.html

Nagel, K., & Rasmussen, S. (1994). Traffic at the edge of chaos. In R. A. Brooks & P. Maes (Eds.), *Proceedings of ALife IV* (pp. 222-235). Cambridge, MA: MIT Press.

Preece, A. L., & Johnson, C. R. (1992). Recovery of model coral communities: Complex behaviours from interaction of parameters operating at different spatial scales. In *Complex systems: From biology to computation* (pp. 69-81). Amsterdam: IOS Press.

Rothman, D. H., & Zeleski, S. (1997). A simple model of fluid mechanics. In *Lattice-gas cellular automata: Simple models of complex hydrodynamics* (chapter 1). Cambridge University Press.

Sipper, M. (1997). *Evolution of parallel cellular machines.* Springer.

Thurey, N., Rude, U., & Korner, C. (2005). *Interactive free surface fluids with the lattice Boltzmann method.* Technical report, Department of Computer Science 10, University of Erlangen-Nuremberg, Germany.

Toffoli, T., & Margolus, N. (1988). *Cellular automata machines.* Cambridge, MA: MIT Press.

Toffoli, T., & Margolus, N. (1990). Invertible cellular automata: A review. *Physica D, 45,* 229-253.

Ulam, S. (1974). Some ideas and prospects in biomathematics. *Annual Review of Biophysics and Bioengineering, 1,* 277-291.

Van Raay, D. (2005). *Real-time simulation and rendering of a free-surface viscous liquid.* Honours thesis, Charles Sturt University, NSW, Australia.

Van Raay, D., & Bossomaier, T. R. J. (2006). Lattice Boltzmann method for real-time simulation of lava flows. In *Proceedings of Geometrical Modelling and Imaging06.*

Von Neumann, J. (1966). Theory of self-reproducing automata. In A. W. Burks (Ed.), *Lectures on the theory and organization of complicated automata*. Champaign, IL: University of Illinois Press.

Witten, I. H., & Frank, E. (2000). *Data mining*. Morgan Kaufmann.

Wolfram, S. (2002). *Cellular automata and complexity*. Perseus.

Wuensche, A. (1998). Discrete dynamical networks and their attractor basins. In R. Standish, B. Henry, S. Watt, R. Marks, R. Stocker, D. G. Green, S. Keen, & T. Bossomaier (Eds.), *Complex systems '98* (pp. 3-22). Complexity Online Network.

Endnotes

[1]   This is a bit of an oversimplification, because there may be configurations containing large areas of empty space where nothing much happens.

[2]   The problem in its more general form allows the density to assume any value.

[3]   In traditional cross-validation, the dataset would be split into a number of folds and each fold would in turn become the test set with the remainder used to determine parameters. Thus this could be applied to spatial subdivisions of a CA evolving in time.

Chapter IV

Adaptive Neurodynamics

Mario Negrello, Fraunhofer IAIS, Germany, & University of Osnabrueck,
Germany

Martin Huelse, University of Wales, UK

Frank Pasemann, Fraunhofer IAIS, Germany, & University of Osnabrueck,
Germany

Abstract

Neurodynamics is the application of dynamical systems theory (DST) to the analysis of the structure and function of recurrent neural networks (RNNs). In this chapter, we present RNNs artificially evolved for the control of autonomous robots (evolutionary robotics [ER]) and further analyzed within dynamical systems tenets (neurodynamics). We search for the characteristic dynamical entities (e.g., attractor landscapes) that arise from being-environment interactions that underpin the adaptation of animat's (biologically inspired robots). In that way, when an efficient controller is evolved, we are able to pinpoint the reasons for its success in terms of the dynamical characteristics of the evolved networks. The approach is exemplified with the dynamical analysis of an evolved network controller for a small robot that maximizes exploration, while controlling its energy reserves, by resorting to different periodic attractors. Contrasted to other approaches to the study of neural function, neurodynamics' edge results from causally traceable explanations of behavior, contraposed to just correlations. We conclude with a short discussion about other approaches for artificial brain design, challenges, and future perspectives for neurodynamics.

Introduction

Life in 4D imposes at least one problem for beings whose solution is general: Beings have to live their lives sequentially, in linear time, through unwinding cause-effect loops. Surely, the impact that the being causes by changing its relations to the world, by moving itself or something in the world, are returned as coherent effects through its perceptual apparatus. Current researchers in robotics, biology, and cognition are acutely aware of this property, to the exclusion of older naive realist views that believed in an objective existence of the world and a separation of the being and its environment. This had its acumen in robots that tried to cope with the world via symbolic search, constantly stumbling on the frame problem (Minsky, 1975). Many philosophers have gone on at lengths to argue for this (not new) embedded view, which goes as far back as Democritus, has not escaped the keenness of Poincaré (1914), is seen in the heideggerian Dasein (Heidegger, 1962), or the cyberneticists (Von Foerster, 1993; Wiener, 1956) being-environment feedback loop, which has also been called structural coupling (Varela & Maturana, 1987), enaction (Varela, Thompson, & Rosch, 1991), and in its latest incarnation, sensorimotor contingencies (Noë & Philipona, 2003). This recurrent structural coupling (as I choose to call it, following the irreplaceable philosopher of biology Francisco Varela) is in intimate relation to the internal states of beings, given that the being has a construction that equips it with ways to interact with the world. To understand how this interaction-being environment is organized from the perspective of the being, should be the gross aim of the cognition researcher.

Despite the embedding of the being in the world, the structures that control the beings are inside the beings, and despite the momentous input, everything the being perceives results from internal activity and processes, as in Varela and Maturana (1987) "[...] for the internal dynamics of the system, the environment does not exist; it is irrelevant" (p. 135). The input to the internal dynamics is nonetheless coherent, as a result of the physical structure of the world. So that changes in relations between the being and environment are likewise lawful, structured, and coherent. Therefore, the study of cognition is the study of how these changes of the output (behavior) manifest themselves as transformations of input (stimuli).

DST lends itself nicely to the job of understanding the being in the world, by providing a formal manner to analyze the behavior generated by evolved network controllers. The subset of DST that studies neural networks is called neurodynamics. The framework is especially useful if the system under study operates according to mathematically formalizable principles or laws, simple in the core, where outputs are also inputs (feedbacks) to the system. This is also the case in neural systems controlling behavior, where interactions in the nanosecond-nanometer (e.g., neurotransmitter release) and smoothly scale up in size and time (e.g., observable behavior). Therefore DST is a theory that is adequate for the description and predictions across spatial and temporal scales, providing both quantitative and qualitative depth. Neurodynamics inherits DST's terminology, which satisfies in explanatory terms, because it acknowledges the core properties of the physical substrate, instead of mere abduction of correlations. At its best neurodynamics provides both quantification and qualification of a system and can show *how* and *under what conditions* simple rules beget complex phenomena (see the *Basic DST* and *Attractor Analysis: Study of Tendency* sections). Particularly, we employ a simple neural model with a sigmoid activation function (see the *The Simple Neuron* section) and show how complex phenomena can appear even in very small artificial recurrent neural networks.

We already vented the proposition that it is necessary to put the *net-in-a-bot*, and as in Brooks' (1991) famous aphorism "the world is its own best model." So, neural networks embedded in the sensorimotor loop provide the beings with the capacity to perceive and act in the world—a wondrously complex place—and through their behavior we learn about the adequacy of the control structures and unforeseen difficulties that the being must robustly overcome. Robots in the real world then are our best bet to advance understanding in the solution of cognitive problems. Neurodynamics provides us with a manner to tackle how the dynamics of embedded neural networks solve problems. To generate those networks we employ ER.

The following argument will take to ER (see the *Form and Control: Structure and Dynamics* section), in four steps. First, we outline some core facts about neurons and nervous systems about connectivity, morphology, and neuronal behavior. Second, we will argue that despite the apparent intractability, due to the sheer magnitude of neuronal numbers in the biological brains, it is possible to reduce it and study it as a bottom-up approach, starting minimal. Third, we show how to start from the bottom: define your *functional units*, define the *relations* between the units and the *functions* updating the system, and finally, fourth, *situate your model* in an orderly interaction with the world/environment.

Succinctly summarizing the approach: first, evolve networks to solve embedded problems, then, analyze it through neurodynamics' lenses. At this point we present results that illustrate the approach. More specifically, we show how *attractor switches* (see the *Modularity and Neurodynamics* section) might govern the behavior of an evolved robot network controller that solves two contraposed tasks, to (1) maximize exploration while (2) keeping its energy source aplenty. Dynamical phenomena such as chaos and oscillations of different periods appear, which allow robust behavior in many different robot morphologies (Hülse et Al., 2002). We will provide the parameter sets wherein for the complex behavior and how these parameter sets promoted adaptation, resulting from exploiting both internal dynamics and environment.

In conclusion, we expose the similarities and dissimilarities with other approaches that attempt to explain behavior with resort to neural models. Brain researchers have a lifelong set of challenges; neurodynamics provides us with an entry point in understanding cognition and behavior in terms of simpler yet powerful models.

Neurons and Dynamics

Outline

This section is composed of three subsections. The first presents core facts about natural neurons and how their properties are abstracted to the artificial neurons in our models. In the second we outline the basics of DST and provide some vocabulary for the subsequent explorations. Thirdly, we exemplify the richness of the behavior with some example RNNs.

The Simple Neuron

The biological neuron is a wonderful piece of evolution. In its astounding multifaceted character it provides the being with information regarding its body and the world, in multifarious ways. Sensory neurons are transducers of reality while motor neurons cause changes by activating muscles. Those in between provide the organization that coordinates these two stances. In the brain their quantity has being estimated in the hundred billions (10^{11}) with up to tens of thousands of synapses (i.e., connections between neurons. The variability on connectivity is very large, depending on function, location, etc.). Surely enough it is impossible to work out an explanation with all their numbers at once, therefore we must understand the putative functionality of their activities, a flow in operation of the sensorimotor loop, where system history intertwines with internal dynamics to output actions. It is here that the simpler models come to the rescue.

There is no such thing as a simple neuron, but the behavior of the neuron can be simplified by smart abstraction, thereby keeping a very decent portion of its true character, and more importantly, enabling dynamical analysis which is otherwise either difficult (Hugues, 2006; Maass & Markram, 2002, 2003) or often intractable. So, to begin with, a real neuron usually receives electric signals, in the form of action potentials (or spikes), from many others. The first modeling measure for knowing how a neuron will respond is summing over its weighted inputs. Weights represent the different spatial overlaps of the dendritic trees and may be negative, standing for possible inhibitory connections. Moreover, no matter how great (or small) the input, the output of the neuron has upper (and lower bounds), that is, the neurons have a firing rate with an intensity between maximal frequency, given by the refractory period and minimum, when it is silent. Early models applied on all or none operation, output being 1 or 0, with respect to a given threshold, analogizing with the membrane potential. Another way to see it is in applying a sigmoidal function (such as the logistic sigmoid and the hyperbolic tangent) on the summed inputs. As bounded functions, the sigmoidals have the desirable properties of saturating non-linearity and of differentiability over all their domain, therefore, a standard choice for a transfer (activation) function. Last, to each neuronal unit (unit for short) in the network a bias term is assumed, representing individual differences of biological neurons, as well as a possible constant background input. This analysis produces the neuron model for discrete time networks given by the formula:

$$\begin{cases} a_1(t+1) = \theta_1 + w_{11}\tau(a_1(t)) + w_{12}\tau(a_2(t)) \\ a_2(t+1) = \theta_2 + w_{21}\tau(a_2(t)) + w_{22}\tau(a_2(t)) \end{cases}$$

Where a_i is the activity of the i_{th} unit of the network, sigma represents a sigmoid function, w_{ij} reads i receives from j with weight ditto, and θ_i is the bias of the i_{th} unit. One notes that this equation implies discrete time steps (t) (Poincaré maps, e.g., in Alligood et al., 1998). Indeed, for the qualitative analysis we are interested in, and for short timesteps, the dynamic aspects of continuous case are present (Pasemann, 1995).

Other neuronal phenomena can be modeled for increased complexity, such as spikes (in contrast to rates), delays (Izhikevich, 1996), decays (Pasemann, 1997), or even biochemical context (cite gas networks). Nevertheless, this model has a tractability that only simple models have, making it a standard choice. Examples of the difficulties we avoid are listed for instance in Izhikevich (2006) for spiking networks and Maass and Markram (2003) for liquid state machines, about which we will have more to say in the discussion. Other complex dynamical properties include (as reported by Izhikevich, Gally, & Edelman, 2004) phasic and tonic firing, bursts, resonance (the neuron fires only when given a certain frequency of its input), adaptation, latency, and bi-stability (these have all been modeled to high detail as dynamical systems, supporting the claim on the introduction of the adequacy of dynamical system's methods across levels). Even so, the study of the dynamic properties of a discrete time network when used in simple units presents an incredible variability of behavior already with simple models (Pasemann, 1995a, 1998b). Besides, and for the despair of the brain modeler, there is always another degree of complexity to be introduced, be it with transmitter release, population coding, epicellular potentials, secondary synapses, synaptic plasticities, and the list grows. Nonetheless we will see that a wide range of interesting systemic phenomena emerges from this simplicity (see the *Modularity and Neurodynamics* section).

Basic DST

In this subsection we explain and exemplify the basic entities of DST as orbits, fixed points, basins of attraction, bifurcations, transients, and chaos and refer in the succeeding section about their significance for behavior. Recurrent connectivity is the linchpin of neurodynamics, in which the output at time t is either a part or the totality of the input of time t+1. In the first case, the latter are called closed systems, and the former are dissipative. As mentioned previously, we defer using continuous time dynamics and employ discrete times, through the Poincaré map, which has been shown to keep all the spectrum of qualitative behavior of the (harder to tackle) continuous case (Pasemann, 1998). In fact as the time step tends to zero, discrete becomes continuous (and necessitates a treatment with differential equations). Using discrete dynamics has an added advantage: It lends itself nicely to computational simulations, and becomes easier to grasp.

RNNs

Before though, a little thought about the dynamics of recurrent neural networks. Perhaps it is useful to remind ourselves of Hopfield (1982) and his seminal work on the attractor dynamics of symmetric networks, which demonstrated how patterns may be stored and retrieved from recurrent neural networks. By imprinting the patterns as attractors in the network, fragmented cues were able to retrieve complete patterns. More recent work has also used it for the coding of temporal patterns. Hopfield's is undeniably a major breakthrough and aroused the interest in RNNs. Nonetheless, from the dynamical perspective, the Hopfield network is rather trivial, where patterns are stored as fixed points. It is not clear how that relates to more complex memory formation, which is happening in transients (Beer, 1993, 2000). That is, when beings are living their lives, their set of inputs is ever-changing, and the behavior emerges from a myriad of dynamic interactions between the being and the environment ("structural coupling"). In the following it will be useful to bear in mind, that in this kind of complex dynamic interaction between being and environment we set now to understand, as the RNNs are given a role in time, and in the *Discussion* section, through embodiment.

Overview of the DST Terminology

Because of space constraints, we propose an unusually visual exposition of DST terms. Examples of these terms will appear in one, two, and three neuron recurrent networks as samples of the putative dynamical wealth. We believe that although rigor is indispensable for making the analysis, it is both more appealing and more intuitive to present it in pictures. So, for the sake of the gist of the approach, the plots to follow will provide a quick entry point. We apologize to those readers with a taste for the mathematics and recommend the thorough and formal treatments in Aligood et al. (1998) and Strogatz (1984) respectively.

Orbits and Transients

So then, the simplest entity in the theory is the orbit. An orbit is, given an initial condition, a sequence of states obtained by the iteration of the network equation. The set of the possible states defines the space. In the case of the neuron with the standard sigmoid[1] as an activation function, the state space has the domain $(-inf., +inf.)^2$ and ranges between $(0,1)$. One possible way to visualize the behavior of the orbits is to plot the mean output of the units, one segment per time step, to visualize the shape of the orbit in phase space (of outputs). So, in Figure 1 (parameters in legend), one sees the depiction of an orbit dwelling on a *chaotic attractor* (in Figure 2) and transients of an asymptotically stable *period 4 attractor*. The portion of the orbit before the attractor is reached is called a transient, and it is in fact the most common state in RNNs that control artificial agents. That is the case because, as the sensors are fed with varying and noisy information through behavior, the activations traverse the parameter space and are influenced by different attractors.

Fixed Points and Periodic Points

Fixed-points and periodic points are perhaps the most prominent entity in the analysis of dynamical systems. Orbits falling in a fixed point (a^*) will satisfy $F^n(a^*) = a^*$ for all n (if it satisfies for n=1 than it does for all n. Where superscript n is the nth iterate of the equation). Fixed points fall into two gross categories, stable or unstable, depending on the fate of orbits under their influence. The analogy is, being at the top of the mountain (unstable) or in the valley (stable). Their taxonomy is given by the behavior of orbits close to them. In one dimension, they may either attract close-by orbits (called attractors) or repel them (repellors). By induction, when more dimensions are involved they might be attracted in one and repelled in other, in which case they are called saddles nodes. Periodic attractors are those to which the network returns after a fixed number of iterates (the orbit). So $F^k(p^*) = p^*$, where k is some whole number. These are called period k attractors. An example of an orbit of a period 4 periodic attractors is seen in Figure 4A. The first-return map indicates the stepwise activity of the network, in that it displays the activity at time t+1 as a function of activity at time t. (or output as a function of input, or the influence of one unit on another). It is particularly useful to visualize periodic attractors, because as eventually o(t) becomes o(t+k). This means that tracing the edges between the points representing the states will reveal the periodic orbits as k-polygons (as in Figure 4A).

Chaotic Attractors

The intuitive definition of chaos is widely known. Chaotic orbits are those that are highly sensitive to initial conditions. That means that two orbits, with arbitrarily close starting points, will diverge with time. Note that this previous statement should not be taken at face value. Chaos presents a rich phenomenology, and there are many instances where the intuitive definition is weak.[3] Here we avoid the discussion and stick to the intuitive definition, which suffices for the present purposes. The example in Figure 1 appears in previous research (Pasemann, 1998a), in the context of a 3-chain neural network (see footnote 4). Another example is given in Figure 4B, for the 2-period attractor.

Figure 1. 3D phase plot (each axis is the output of one unit, each dot is one state in the orbit) of a chaotic attractor of the network (given by the following weight matrix 3 ring with inhibitory neuron[4]). Only one orbit of 35,000 states appear. We see how the orbit densely covers the complex surface of the attractor (in light gray, the 2D projections). Small variations of the initial state of the orbit will impact strongly on the form of the trajectory, although the shape of the attractor being stable for one parameter set.

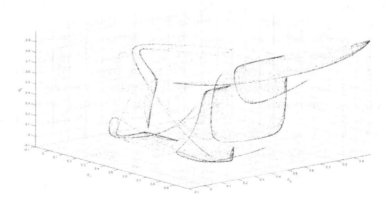

Complex Bifurcation Scenarios in Two Neuron RNNs

One way to approach the analysis of networks is by looking at how parameter changes lead to changes in the dynamical landscape. Parameters are the coefficients of the network equation (the bias and weights). Therefore this analysis is the study of *parametrized dynamical systems*. As we observed previously, it is the fixed points that determine the shape of the transients. One might start by looking for them, as the parameters change smoothly (representing either disturbances/input or changes in synaptic weights). In this case our network is described by the following system of equations (sigma stands for the standard sigmoid[5]):

In order to visualize the changes that attractors undergo as the parameters change, we use the bifurcation diagram. It depicts the long term behavior of the network as a function of one parameter (in Figure 1, θ_1, in Figure 2, w_{11} - the self connection of unit 1). *Bifurcation*[6] is the term referring to the parameter locus of a *qualitative change* of the behavior of the dynamical system, where for example, a system goes from a fixed-point domain to an oscillation domain.

Figure 2. Bifurcation for θ_2 in the network $w_{11} = 16$, $w_{12} = -8$, $w_{21} = 9$, $w_{22} = 0$, $\theta_1 = -.45$. In this case 400 steps in each orbit are plotted as the mean output of the network ($\bar{o} = o_1 + o_2)/2$). Each 100 steps are shaded with a darker gray to indicate how the transients set in the attractors. Figure 3 shows the detail of a period doubling route to chaos (the red rectangle: $3.96 < \theta_2 < 4.08$).

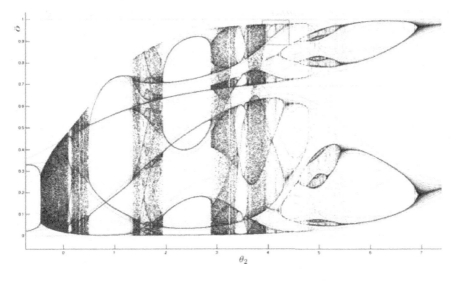

Qualitative changes in dynamics are extremely interesting in the study of behavior, because that is the point in which "something new happens." In a bifurcation diagram one parameter (Figure 1. theta 2) is varied as the others are kept fixed. A number of points in one orbit (here 400), for one random initial condition are calculated. Initial points are plotted in light gray (first 30), for showing the transient activity. In blue, the last 20 states in the network are plotted. One notes that they outline the shapes of the existing attractors.[7] That helps describe the tendency of an orbit as a function of a parameter value. Underneath, a detail showing a period doubling cascade, a clear indication of the existence of chaos. In Figure 2 we have samples of the shapes of the orbits for a particular value of θ in the first return map. When embedded, a network such as this, with varying input (for example, an infrared, represented here by θ_1), will be taken through distinct regions (see Figure 2).

The bifurcation diagram in Figure 2 is somewhat atypical for bifurcation studies, but its peculiarities serve specific purposes. Three features that are usually cleansed from the "final" plots were kept for their intuitive appeal. First, note that near the bifurcations points are smeared. This indicates that the transients are longer in the proximity of bifurcation points (in the case of asymptotically stability). The second unusual feature shown is the scattering of some of the attractors, some discontinuity in their lines (theta 2 ~[4,5]), when two attractors coexist (period 4 in Figure 4A and chaos in Figure 4B). That is because the initial conditions for each parameter in the ordinate axis are randomly chosen. This indicates that there are different *basins of attraction*.[8] In other words, the orbit will be contained in one or another

Figure 3. Detail of above, showing the period doubling route to chaos as theta 2 is varied (remark: in the detail, initial conditions were chosen such that all the orbits fall are in the same basin, to show the attractor fully outlined).

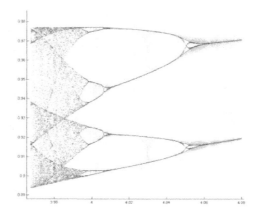

Figure 4. First return map (mean output x mean input) of two orbits, ending in two different attractors, coexisting for one and the same set of parameters of Figure 2 (fixed θ_2 = 3.98). In both plots, the orbits have the same number of time steps (80). In (A) the orbit sets in few passes on the stable period 4 attractor. The gray gradient indicates how the transients are taking the orbit to the attractor. In (B) the orbit indicates much longer transients and chaos.

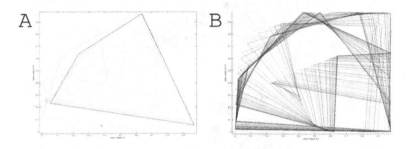

attractor depending on the initial condition (think about a boat navigating through maelstroms). In a system with smoothly changing parameters, switching will occur smoothly or violently, depending on the particular topology on the vicinity of the attractors, history, and sensory input. A third feature appearing in the figure are the lines in lighter gray (for example, o=1). They appear in the early states of the orbits, but disappear in time, indicating that they are unstable. The subplots underneath, show orbit samples of the coexisting period 4 attractor and a chaotic attractor, for the same parameter set (θ_1 = 3.9), on the first-return map.

Isoperiodic Plots

A principal method of finding the domains of parameters for interesting dynamical phenomena of RNNs is by analytical derivations (e.g., Pasemann, 1998b). But, after acquiring some guidelines another fertile method is to explore the parameter spaces empirically. An isoperiodic plot shows the periods of different attractors in parameter space. In Figure 5 we see the outlines of the boundaries between areas of qualitatively different network behavior, as a function of the parameters (in here, the weights w_{11} and w_{12}). It is possible to see the regions in which fixed-point attractors exist for a set of parameters, as well as different periodic attractors and chaos. One observes the impact of a change of parameters in the behavior of the network, in terms of fixed points, oscillations of different periods, and chaos. It is perhaps the clearest instance of the profound impact that even small changes in parameters might have on the overall activity. One observes as well regions with coexisting

Figure 5. Isoperiodic plot showing the range of dynamical phenomena in the two neuron recurrent network as a function of w_{11} *and* w_{12}. *Black regions and dots around 1, 2, 4, and 8 indicate very long transients. By increasing the amount of iterations, these regions shrink.*

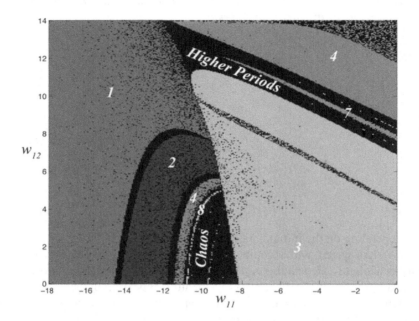

attractors, that can be visualized as some scattered points in what otherwise is a region colored uniformly (signifying that there are different basins for different initial conditions).

Attractor Analysis: Study of Tendency

The reader might argue that, up to this point, the analysis of dynamics offered focused on long-term behavior of the disembodied networks (e.g., the bifurcation diagrams), which might seem as countering what we have evinced before. It is to some extent true, for the attractor analysis shows the final *tendency* of the network given an initial condition. They show where the activations of the network are going, depending on where they are; if the parameters were frozen. As we know, the parameter values change according to external disturbances (stimuli), and previous internal states (history). The transients are under the influence of the attractors. So, in knowing the fixed points and the basins of attraction, one knows where one is going to end. Inasmuch as time never stops for an embedded being, thus the input never ceases to change. To understand the behavior, then, is to understand how parameter changes impact on the tendency of the network.

As one sees from this very short introduction, although the terse vocabulary of dynamical systems might conceal the beauty and variability of the dynamical portfolio, we hope to have dismissed this spurious notion. Already in the single neuron, we find the hysteresis and oscillations; and in the two neuron networks, we saw oscillations of many periods, fractal boundaries, as well as period doubling routes to chaos. Other interesting phenomena have been studied, as synchronous chaos, the single neurons with decay or hysteresis (Pasemann, 1998b, 1999a, 1999b; Pasemann & Steinmetz, 2001). As the networks grow bigger by adding neurons and synapses, the possibilities for dynamical interactions escalate, as a result from the complex nonlinear interactions between units. One possible way to restrain the search space of the possible structures is to let them evolve, selecting them by their ability to coordinate model organisms robots (or animats), in biologically inspired experimental designs. By building artifacts that emphasize the requirements for continued existence the artifact (animat/robot) is able to consistently solve the problems posed by the environment, we thereby discover how function arises from the dynamics of evolved control structures.

Form and Control: Structure and Dynamics

Outline

We have seen now the complexity in dynamics arising from even very simple neuron networks. ER fills the role of finding control networks through evolution with genetic algorithms. Modularity considerations support the evolutionary process, by exploring specific dynamical functionality of RNN modules. After evolving agents that convincingly solve the posed problems, we are able to select networks that produce interesting behavior (or have high fitness values) and analyze them from the neurodynamics stance.

Artificial Evolution of RNNs for Control of Robots (Evolutionary Robotics)

Nature shows us that Darwin's ratchet (variability, fitness, inheritance) is useful to probe huge search spaces, such as brain design. Genetic algorithms emulate these evolutionary principles to try to benefit from what seems to have worked so well in nature. A review of ER and applications thereof is found in Harvey, Paolo, Wood, Quinn, and Tuci (2005). The listing of examples where the application of evolutionary algorithms has been productive includes, but is not exhausted by: central pattern generators (Pasemann, Hild, & Zahedi, 2003), robust object avoidance and light seeking (Hülse, Zahedi, & Pasemann, 2003), inverted pendulum balancers (Pasemann, 1998), walkers (Twickel et al., 2003), as well as communication in multi-agent systems (Wischmannn, Hulse, Knabe, & Pasemann, 2006),[9,10] building of internal models (Lipson et al., 2007), and flying robots (Floreano, Zufferey, & Nicoud, 2005). We encourage the interested reader to consult the individual papers referred to here for further explorations.

In here, the algorithm employed for these evolutions is the ENS,[3] described in Paseman et al. (2000). The genome of the evolution algorithm is the structure of the networks themselves. The variation operator adds or deletes units (neurons) and synapses, as well as changing weights according to on-the-fly specified probabilities (e.g., probability of adding a synapse of N%). The selection of the agents that generates offspring is rank based, which is controlled by the shape of the distribution (gamma function). The distribution represents the probability of an agent with rank r having n offspring, where n is estimated according to a Poisson process. The stochastic character of offspring production is meant to avoid niche exploitation by minimizing opportunism and keeping diversity of the networks, as is argued in Dieckman (1995).

Moreover, the fitness is tested on a simulation environment, which can be 2D or 3D (Zahedi, in press). Then a population of RNNs is generated and embodied in the simulated agent. After the trial, fitness values are attributed to each of the RNNs controlling the agents. The networks are then ranked and the best are selected to generate offspring. The process runs across many generations, while the parameters of the evolution are being changed by the experimenter. During the process the experimenter might select an agent with interesting behavior for dynamical analysis.

Modularity and Neurodynamics

Four principles of brain organization to guide our evolutionary search for RNNs are found in Table 1. Table 1 reads from left to right, starting with facts about the biological brains, the implication of that fact, and how the evolution copes with it.

One particularly nice example of these principles seen in biology is found in Menzel and Giurfa (2003). They describe the vertical organization of some behavior modules of the honey bee (as in 1). By vertical it is meant that one stimulus leads to one response (as in 2,3). The remarkable thing is that the behavior of the bee is not exhausted by simple reflex mechanisms: There are situations in which modules interact horizontally, through the environment. These horizontal interactions are

Table 1. Principles of brain organization related to artificial evolution

Brains	Therefore	Evolution of RNNs
Have a lot of neurons, but those are not randomly connected	Connectivity and structure of networks are important for function.	Parameters alterable in evolution are number of units, synaptic connections, synaptic weights, transfer function, and mean number of offspring.
In simple organisms function is often innate	Only small or no online synaptic weight change	No synaptic change rules (e.g., no Hebbian learning, no SDTP)
Different areas of the brain are responsible for different tasks.	Function is often modular.	Different fitness functions are used at different times. It is possible to fixate a structure or module.
These modules interact in nonlinear ways.	Emergence of behavior from interaction within areas and with the environment	Simulated embodied agents as well as real robots receive the control networks.

nonlinear, and enrich the bees' behavior (as in 4), endowing it with more behavioral breadth (Sterelny, 2001) and more robust problem solving.

One of the benefits of endorsing a modular approach towards cognition is in retrieving the modes of interaction of simple parallel control structures. Modular neurodynamics (Pasemann, Steinmetz, Hülse, & Lara, 2001) approaches the problem of understanding cognition by evolving these control structures in a modular manner, which buttresses the understanding of how the previously known control structures interact in generating overall behavior. Functions arise from this interaction. Hülse et al. (2006) provide us with an example of modular thinking and their underpinnings in behavior. In the following example, two modules were evolved separately and merged into one control structure. The underlying modular neurodynamics is thereby analyzed in terms of visited attractors.

Behavior Transition by Attractor Switches

The *Artificial Evolution of RNNs for Control of Robots (Evolutionary Robotics)* section indicates that ER is a rapidly growing field. The reason for this might be that research groups have been convinced by promising results of behavioral control by RNNs with non-trivial dynamics. However, adaptability is more than behavior control. It is also the control of behaviors, that is, to (1) adequately choose the proper behavior for a given context, and (2) to be able to switch smoothly between different behaviors. Behavior switches of animals are correlated with changes in the internal dynamics (perhaps driven by external disturbances). Therefore, it was our hypothesis that models of behavioral switches were dependent on characteristic dynamics. In fact, we found that behavioral switches depended on switches on the attractor landscape and on slow time scales. We further discuss this finding.

The robot system (Khepera—two-wheeled differential drive mini robot) that we discuss in the following section is equipped with seven sensors. These sensors measure three types of data: (1) distance data (two sensors), (2) light data (four sensors), and (3) one sensor indicating the level of a simulated inner energy reservoir. The latter can be interpreted as the charge of the battery that keeps a robot moving. This reservoir (IE) has a permanent leakage, representing its energy consumption. The replenishing of the batteries can only be compensated by standing in front of a light source—light bathing. Or in other words, by high activations of the front light sensor I_L:

$$I_E(t + 1) := I_E(t) + c_1 * I_L(t) - c_2; c_1, c_2 > 0$$

The RNN robot controllers evolved under these constraints displayed a context-sensitive behavior, which is dependent both on the position of the light sources and on its energy reservoir. The overall behavior could be described as such: as its batteries start to wane it purposefully approaches a light source, staying in front of it until its energy tank is replenished. Once its energy tank is refilled, it resumes exploration.

The result of the simulations of a Khepera is shown in Figure 6A.

Note how the robot switches between exploring the environment and the approaching of light sources. The latter pattern is what we call reactive light-seeking behavior. The diagram in Figure 6B indicates that the behavior switches are determined by the level of energy. At a certain intensity of $I_E \sim 0.7$ the robot leaves the light source. Hence, the output I_E is monotonically increasing or decreasing, depending on the current state of the robot-environment interaction.

Figure 6

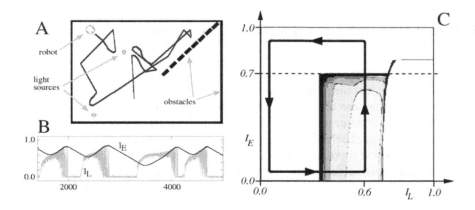

Moreover, the time scale on which I_E is operating is much slower than that of I_L. In other words while the light intensity measured by the frontal light sensor is rapidly changing, the level of the energy is much slower to follow these changes.

In order to explore dynamical underpinnings of switching between exploration light-seeking behavior we calculate the iso-periodic plot of the parameter space I_L and I_E (Figure 6C). The white regions contain the asymptotically stable fixed points, and gray shaded ones indicate periodic attractors of different periods.

The behavioral transitions are indicated via the outlined cycle in the iso-periodic plot of the parameter space $I_L \times I_E$. We therefore see how the behavior is influenced by smooth changes in the parameters, as a function of light perception and energy reservoir. The cycle traverses the region of periodic attractors, as well as the regions of asymptotic fixed points. We see for example that halting in front of the light is based on periodic attractors, because $I_L = 0.6$ and $I_E < 0.7$. Conversely, standing in front of the light refills the energy tank, so IE goes up. Hence, after a certain time interval $I_E > 0.7$, meaning that the parameter configuration is one of asymptotically stable fixed points. In other words, while refilling the reservoir the inner dynamics change qualitatively. Thus, as the internal dynamics traverse the attractor landscape, corresponding qualitative changes in behavior (i.e., switches) occur, which are due to differences in the attractor topology. Thence this phenomenon goes by the name of "attractor switches." We hope this cursory exposition exemplifies how the network structures evolved to solve agent-environment interactions and are analyzed according to its dynamical implementation. The underlying assumption is that all behavior can be explained by strolls in parameter space, as the dynamical entities support the controlling outputs.

Internal Dynamics and Evolutionary Robotics

It is perhaps of interest to underline the distinction between the approach described here and other similar ones. It is indeed the case that if the experiments are subsumed by ER methods, they can all belong to the same cluster. However, the approach we take differs in the attempt to understand the role of internal dynamics as a window to the underpinnings of behavior, contrasting to pure behavioral problem solving. In that sense, the closest approach to ours is the one of Beer (1995), where the temporal analysis of attractor structure permits an insight into the dynamics of gait of a walking machine to perceptual discrimination (Beer, 2003). See also the discussions in the *Journal of Adaptive Behavior*, special issue on Dynamical Approaches to Cognition (2005). In the neurodynamics approach it is necessary to emphasize the evolution of network structures along with weights (connectivity, number of neurons, hierarchical structures. See also Nolfi (1996) and Harvey (1994). The reason for this is that the structure of the networks are known to be crucial for the possible attractor landscapes, and therefore appropriately tackled by neurodynamics.

Discussion

Other Approaches and Perspectives

Large Neural Networks, Detailed Neural Models

Many have seen the limitations in the explanatory power of the Hopfield attractor network as an analogue to cognition, in that it possesses only trivial fixed-point dynamics, resulting in symmetric connections. Given an input, it juggles a bit and settles stably in the answer. As we have seen, cognitive abilities should be seen as a dynamic process that never really "stays." So, one way to reconcile this is by building networks that are constantly active. In the two paragraphs following, we discuss two examples of brain theories similar to ours in that the networks are constantly active, but that differ in that they require many more neurons, rendering attractor analysis infeasible. Without attractor analysis as a tool, they rely on higher level mechanisms, such as statistical correlations and group search, for explaining behavior. That turns out to eschew the simplicity of neurodynamics.

The first example of the very detailed neural models is given by Nachtschläger, Maass, and Markram (2002); Maass and Markram (2003, 2004); and Maas (2002). They suggest that in order to understand the way brains function, one should employ large scale networks with very detailed spiking neuronal models. They have proven that the activities of one neuron at time t is a function of all the history of its inputs, and therefore each and every neuron can be seen as an information processing unit. The approach, baptized as a liquid state machine (as in opposition to finite state machine), should provide insights on how the information in the history may be retrieved from the activations of the single unit, and much more complicated processing might be achieved with coalitions of the same. Alas, it is not clear how structure leads to function.

One difficulty lies in finding the building blocks for functionality. In this work, functionality is expected to be a product of self-organization with learning. That leaves aside the precise way the functionality is achieved. Or in other words, what is it in the self-organized structure that gives rise to a particular function? Although nonlinear filters certainly have an important role in the brain, how to put them together to work is a difficult challenge. Another difficulty is the forceful exclusion of the agent environment interaction, as large scale networks require immense processing power, not on par with today's computational power. Moreover, we suggest that a theory of function should underlie the model and not vice versa. Simpler neural networks, such as ours, because they are easier to generate and to analyze, might be more productive for understanding the connection between structure, function, and dynamics by providing the possibility of embodiment along with a larger possible experimental profile. The growth in number of neuronal units should follow a deeper understanding of their operation, and not the other way around.

Theory of Neuronal Group Selection

Another theory that relies heavily on the presence of massive neuronal networks is the neuronal group theory selection (Edelman, 1984, 1987), which is primarily concerned with the effective underworkings of the biological neurons of the human brain in relation to psychological events. The theory employs a version of Darwin's argument to explain how mechanisms of selection yield the formation of neuronal coalitions. Those coalitions are the explanatory entity of the theory, the neuronal groups. They are suited for explaining perceptual categorization; learning and association; and consciousness phenomena.

Most recent models of this theory have the detailed spiking neuron models and axonal delays (Izhikevich & Edelman, 2006). Some very interesting results regarding perceptual categorization have been achieved (Edelman, 1987). Given perceptual stimuli, structures very similar to topological maps of perception have been observed, and robots also were therewith controlled (Edelman et al., 1992).

Nevertheless, particularly on the question of how the groups are formed, the approach runs into analysis difficulties, because the networks are big, the search space for group retrieval is magnific, due to combinatorial explosion. How to achieve more sophisticated functions is also a question of order, because it is not clear how to build the networks. Three problems arise for them: (1) how to build the initial structure, (2) which modules to choose, and (3) how to find the groups. For problem 1, they assume architecture "similar" (in quantity and connectivity) to the anatomy of the human brain. This has two main difficulties: first, even if the histological data were complete, it is infeasible to simulate the whole brain. Therefore problem 2 arises, of how to choose particular areas for the simulation. The choice for areas for simulation has to be done considerably ad hoc. As a result, at this stage the models are necessarily partial, so it is difficult to unbraid truth from artifact. Problem 3 is how to find the groups that formed in the simulations. To find the neurons that fire in chains, the problem is combinatorial explosion and the astounding search space. The proponents are aware of such challenges and current research will require better analysis methods (Izhikevich et al., 2006).

These attempts should not be seen as competing, but as complementary to ours, everyone of them faces arduous terrain, whether of conceptual (gaps in knowledge), technical (computational requirements), or analytical (tools). Our contribution, an imminently bottom-up approach, might provide understanding of simpler principles that could guide and complement approaches as the previous two in the search for their (necessarily bigger and more complex—not necessarily more capable of behaving) functional structures. It is possible to avoid the problems of sizable networks by keeping the networks sleek. Examples are given by the role of hysteresis in obstacle avoidance, chaos in inverted pendulum balancing (Pasemann, 1998), behavior switching due to attractor switches (Hülse, 2006), or resetting of pattern generators in communication (Wischmann, Hülse, & Pasemann, 2006). We believe that many principles of processing will be inherited by bigger structures in similar forms, and in fact, there is reason to believe that some of this exists in the cortex as pattern generators (Webb, 2000), limit cycles for smell recognition (Freeman, 1998), as well as chaos in conscious processing (Goodwin, 2001).

Learning

Some might rightfully wonder why there has been no reference to learning so far. Learning is a very general word, usually understood as self-organizing changes of nervous systems due to stimuli that underlie behavioral changes. Under "learning," a very broad class of phenomena is subsumed (Edelman, 1989). Learning varies in biochemical implementation (e.g., transmitter concentration, protein formation) and temporal scales (e.g., long-term potentiation [LTP], long term structural changes). Learning also ranges from facilitation in simple organisms (Aplysia), through operant conditioning (from insects [Menzel, 2001] to mammals), up to long term declarative knowledge. It is because of this polymorphous character that we consider learning to be a subject of its own, to be treated carefully elsewhere. Nonetheless, one thing is clear. Whatever it is, learning operates on prior existing structures (with smaller or higher degrees of innateness). So being, it is also necessarily a function of the prior structures that are subject to the synaptic changes. Therefore, the study of learning is posterior to the study of neural function from network topology structure. Neurodynamics hints on how to extend itself to the study of learning, by exploring possible ways to parametrize the dynamical system, on-the-fly. In that, learning is a vast and promising field for future research. Learning framed from the neurodynamics' perspective poses the following question: how do the structures for control of the behaving agent change as a function of the internal dynamics and external disturbances (stimuli)?

Conclusion

Wrap

We motivated the chapter with some fundamentals on how organisms can only behave and perceive through their actuators and sensors, and how the physical implementation of the organisms constrains the possible parametrizations. Views from biology (Maturana & Varela, 1987; Von Üexkull, 1934) lead us to an understanding of the worlds of animals in tighter relation to what their sensors inform them about the world (Merkwelt/Input) and the actuators that implement changes, both in the world and in the being (Wirkwelt/Output), resolving the animal's world (Umwelt). It is clear that the Umwelt is not an independent concept, rather being the product of how the animal connects sensors and actuators and deals with changes in itself and in the world.

Autopoiesis (Maturana, 1977; Varela, 1978) is the property of beings to function in such a way as to continue functioning. The limits that permit the persistence of beings to continue existing in the world is given by the bounds of materials and reactions that the being is and that it encounters. We analogized to these observations and offered neurodynamics as a theory to analyze the influences parameter changes have in behavior.

Evolution works by trial, error, and eventual success, and so does ER, which analogically to Darwin provides a tool as to how these control structures and parameter sets might evolve to generate adapted beings. Structural evolution of neural networks beget those possible parameter sets that allow the animat to better itself.

We explained the approach while providing a fleeting review of fruitful evolution (and co-evolutions) controllers of embodied agents, relying on sprouting research conducted at the Fraunhofer Institute. We detailed one example with a modular approach to the development of behavior of phototactic khepera robots that keep an eye on their energy reservoir and change their behavior accordingly.

Nevertheless, we did not content ourselves with observing the robots behaving with evolved controllers. Rather, this is the moment when we apply the dynamical system's concepts developed in the *Form and Control: Structure and Dynamics* section to understand the causes and dynamical underpinnings of what brings about the desirable features of the controllers. We delved into the role of switches between attractors of different periods that control the mode of behavior of a being trying to maximize exploration while keeping its energy resources aplenty. Much more could be said, but hopefully this illustrates neurodynamics as an analysis method.

Final Remarks

Are we saying that neurodynamics is what life is about? No. Rather, we are saying that the living work *like* that. We are saying that neurodynamics is an adequate model of the behavior of the living, in that our animats are evolved to cope with problems that are analogous to those of animals. With the study of neurodynamics of embedded systems we provide an abstraction layer, where function is solely dependent on a modeled structure, instead of having to go down and disentangle the entwined reality of brain wiring. The theory of neurodynamics delivers concrete ways to define function out of structure. Moreover, the breadth of evolvable functions and modules is wide. By designing the experiments wisely, meaning, by keen observation on the kind of interactions going on between an environment and a perceiver, we level comprehension on how structural couplings lead to adaptation in function and thereby structure. Contrary to some skepticism (e.g., Edelman, 2003), we and members of the *Form and Control: Structure and Dynamics* section (citations in the *Artificial Evolution of RNNs for Control of Robots (Evolutionary Robotics)* section) believe that the approach scales up. We acknowledge the fact that the behavior of our robots is purely reflexive, but suspect that more can be delivered by experiments exploring the rich dynamics as behaviors are modularly assembled. Sterelny (2004) has argued that cognition arises when the beings increase their behavioral portfolio, so as to manage and organize wider *behavioral breadth,* it becomes necessary to evolve sophisticated abilities, such as prediction, evaluation, and curiosity. Modular neurodynamics guided by minimal cognition paradigms (Barandiaran & Moreno, 2006) gives a go at assembling dynamical modules whose abilities interact nonlinearly. The ultimate goal is to provide a vocabulary of behavioral modules and pinpoint their manners of interaction in the embodied agent. If it should be possible to find an understanding on the basics of modularity and nonlinear interactions, then it is in principle possible to construct ever more intelligent and adaptive systems and to incrementally unveil the dynamical underpinnings of cognition.

Acknowledgments

Mario would like to gratefully acknowledge the opinions of one blind reviewer, whose insightful critiques greatly increased the transparency of the message of the chapter.

References

Alligood, A. (1998). *Chaos—An introduction to dynamical systems.* Cambridge, MA: MIT Press.

Barandiaran, X., & Moreno, A. (2006). On what makes certain dynamical systems cognitive: A minimally cognitive organization program. *Adaptive Behavior, 14*(2), 171-185.

Beer, R. (1995). A dynamical systems perspective on agent-environment interaction. *Artificial Intelligence, 72,*173-215.

Beer, R. (2000). Dynamical approaches to cognitive science. *Trends in Cognitive Science, 4*(3), 91-99.

Beer, R. (2004). Autopoiesis and cognition in the game of life. *Artificial Life, 10*(3), 309-326.

Brooks, R. (1991). Intelligence without representation. *Artificial Intelligence, 47,* 139-159.

Channon, A. (1996). *The evolutionary emergence route to artificial intelligence.* Unpublished PhD thesis. UK: University of Sussex, School of Cognitive and Computing Science.

Costa, F. A. E., & Rocha, L. M. (2005). Introduction to the special issue: Embodied and situated cognition. *Artificial Life, 11*(1-2), 5-11.

Di Paolo, E. A. (2004). Unbinding biological autonomy: Francisco Varela's contributions to artificial life. *Artificial Life, 10*(3), 231-233.

Edelman, G. M. (1987). *Neural Darwinism.* Basic Books.

Edelman, G. M. (1989). *The remembered present.* Basic Books.

Edelman, G. M., Reeke, G. N., Gall, W. E., Tononi, G., Williams, D., & Sporns, O. (1992). Synthetic neural modeling applied to a real-world artifact. *Proceedings of the National Academy of Sciences, 89,* 7267-7271.

Edelman, S. (2003). But will it scale up? Not without representation. *Adaptive Behavior, 11*(4), 273-276.

Floreano, D., Zufferey, J.-C., & Nicoud, J.-D. (2005). From wheels to wings with evolutionary spiking circuits. *Artificial Life, 11*(1-2), 121-138.

Freemann, W. J., & Barrie, J. M. (2000). Analysis of spatial patterns of phase in neocortical gamma EEGs in rabbit. *Journal of Neurophysiologie, 84,* 1266-1278.

Harvey, I., Paolo, E. D., Wood, R., Quinn, M., & Tuci, E. (2005). Evolutionary robotics: A new scientific tool for studying cognition. *Artificial Life, 11*(1-2), 79-98.

Heidegger, M. (1962). *Being and time.* London: SCM Press.

Hülse, M. (2006). *Multifunktionalität rekurrenter neuronaler Netye—Synthese und Analyse nichtklinearer Kontrolle autonomer Roboter.* Unpublished PhD thesis, Universitat Osnabrück, Germany.

Izhikevich, E. M. (2006). Polychronization: Computation with spikes. *Neural Computation, 18,* 245-282.

Izhikevich, E. M., Gally, J. A., & Edelman, G. M. (2004). Spike-timing dynamics of neuronal groups. *Cerebral Cortex, 14*(8), 933-944.

Jaeger, H. (2001). *The "echo state" approach to analysing and training recurrent neural networks* (Tech. Rep. GMD Report 148). Darmstadt, Germany: German National Research Center for Information Technology.

Li, Z., & Hopfield, J. (1989). Modeling the olfactory bulb and its neural oscillatory processings. *Biological Cybernetics, 61*(5), 379-392.

Maass, W., & Markram, H. (2002). Temporal integration in recurrent microcircuits. In M. A. Arbib (Ed.), *The handbook of brain theory and neural networks* (2nd ed.). Cambridge, MA: MIT Press.

Maas, W., & Markram, H. (2003). Temporal integration in recurrent microcircuits. *The handbook of brain theory and neural networks.* Cambridge, MA: MIT Press.

Maass, W., & Markram, H. (2004). On the computational power of recurrent circuits of spiking neurons. *Journal of Computer and System Sciences, 69*(4), 593-616.

Maass, W., Natschläger, T., & Markram, H. (in press). *A fresh look at real-time computation in generic recurrent neural circuits.*

McMullin, B. (2004). Thirty years of computational autopoiesis: A review. *Artificial Life, 10*(3), 277-295.

Menzel, R., & Giurfa, M. (2001). Cognitive architecture of a mini-brain: The honeybee. *Trends in Cognitive Science, 5*(2), 62-71.

Natschläger, T., Maass, W., & Markram, H. (2002). The "liquid computer": A novel strategy for real-time computing on time series [Special issue]. *Foundations of Information Processing of TELEMATIK, 8*(1), 39-43.

Neumann, J. V. (1958). *Computer and the brain.* New Haven, CT: Yale University Press.

Paolo, E. D. (2003). Organismically-inspired robotics: Homeostatic adaptation and teleology beyond the closed sensorimotor loop.

Pasemann, F. (1995a). Characterization of periodic attractors in neural ring networks. *Neural Networks, 8,* 421-441.

Pasemann, F. (1995b). Neuromodules: A dynamical systems approach to brain modeling. In *Supercomputing in brain research* (pp. 331-347). World Scientific.

Pasemann, F. (1996). Interne repräsentationen—Neue Konzepte der Hirnforschung, chapter Repräsentation ohne Repräsentation Überlegungen zu einer Neurodynamik modularer kognitiver Systeme. Frankfurt, Germany: Suhrkamp.

Pasemann, F. (1997). A simple chaotic neuron. *Physica D, 104,* 205-211.

Pasemann, F. (1998a). Evolving neurocontrollers for balancing an inverted pendulum. *Computation in Neural Systems, 9.*

Pasemann, F. (1998b). Structure and dynamics of recurrent neuromodules. *Theory in Biosciences, 117,* 1-17.

Pasemann, F., & Ulrich Steinmetz, M. H. B. L. (2001). Evolving brain structures for robot control. In J. Mira, & A. Prieto (Eds.), *Bio-inspired applications of connectionism* (pp. 410-417).

Pfeifer, R., & Gómez, G. (2005). Interacting with the real world: Design principles for intelligent systems. *International Symposium on Artificial Life Robotics, 9,* 1-6.

Pfeifer, R., Iida, F., & Bongard, J. (2005). New robotics: Design principles for intelligent systems. *Artificial Life, 11*(1-2), 99-120.

Philipona, D., & O'Regan, J. (2004). Philosophie de la nature aujourd'hui? , chapter Perception multimodale de l'espace. MSH.

Philipona, D., O'Regan, J., & Nadal, J. (2003). Is there something out there? Inferring space from sensorimotor dependencies. *Neural Computation, 15*(9).

Sterelny, K. (2005). *Thought in a hostile world.* Cambridge, MA: MIT Press.

Strogatz, S. H. (1994). *Nonlinear dynamics and chaos.* Addison-Wesley.

Thom, R. (1975). *Structural stability and morphogenesis.* W.A. Benjamin.

Varela, F. (1978). *Principles of biological autonomy.*

Varela, F., & Maturana, H. (1998). *The tree of knowledge.* Boston: Shambala. (Original work published 1987)

Varela, F., Thompson, E., & Rosch, E. (1991). *The embodied mind: Cognitive science and human experience.* Cambridge, MA: MIT Press.

Von Foerster, H. (1993). *Kybernethik.* Merve Verlag.

Von Uexküll, J. (1934). Bedeutungslehre/Streifzüge durch die Umwelten von Tieren und Menschen. Rowohlt Hamburg, 1956 edition.

Watson, R. A., & Pollack, J. B. (2005). Modular interdependency in complex dynamical systems. *Artificial Life, 11*(4).

Webb, B. (2000). What does robotics offer animal behavior. *Animal Behavior, 60,* 545-558.

Wheeler, M., Bullock, S., Di Paolo, E., Noble, J., Bedau, M. A., Husbands, P., et al. (2002). The view from elsewhere: Perspectives on alife modeling. *Artificial Life.*

Wiener, N. (1961). *Cybernetics: Or the control and communication in the animal and the machine* (2nd ed.). Cambridge, MA: MIT Press.

Wischmannn, S., H. M. P. F. (2005). (Co)evolution of (de)centralized neural control for a gravitationally driven machine. In *ECAL 2005* (pp. 179-188).

Wischmannn, S., Hulse, M., Knabe, J. F., & Pasemann, F. (2006). Synchronization of internal neural rhythms in multi-robotic systems. *Adaptive Behavior, 14*(2), 117-127.

Endnotes

[1]   It can be shown that the standard sigmoid and the hyperbolic tangents have topologically conjugate dynamics, meaning that there exists a homomorphic transformation that transforms one into the other. As a result their dynamics are homomorphic, meaning the qualitative behavior of the dynamics is the same. The proof of topological conjugacy is an important mathematical shorthand that allows the analysis of networks with one type of transfer function to be extended to the other.

[2]   Practically, though, the domain depends on the order of the maximum weights of incoming connections in one unit.

[3]   The definition based on Lyapunov exponents also occasionally fails. For some examples see Alligood et al. (1998).

[4]   parameters for the chaotic ring: w11=w22=w33=0; w12 = w13 = w32 = 8; w21=w31= -8; and theta = [-1.75 0 5.5]

5   $\sigma(x) = \frac{1}{1+e^{-x}}$; the standard logistic sigmoid.

6   The theory of bifurcations examines the possible types of bifurcations for different systems in terms of the equations describing the system. A thorough treatment is found in Kuznetsov (1995).

7   Each slice in the bifurcation diagram is like a long exposure photograph, where we accumulate the points of the orbits during a certain duration (number of steps).

8   It is possible to visualize the basins of attraction, by fixing the parameters and identifying the attractor as a function of the initial condition. Which attractor the orbit will fall into is dependent on the initial conditions. With chaotic attractors one often faces basins with fractal boundaries. That means that there is no sharp line dividing the basin of one from the other attractor. The phenomenon persists as the resolution is increased and neighboring initial conditions might end up in any of the attractors and this extends to arbitrary degrees of precision (Pasemann, 2002).

9   These have been evolved with a software suite (ISEE, Zahedi [2006]) developed in house, consisting of three basic components: an evolution manager that generates neuronal structures able to regulate evolution parameters online (e.g., birth rate, number of synapses, number of neurons in the RNN, connectivity. The implementation is based on the evolutionary algorithm ENS[3] (Dieckman, 1995), which have a test bed of 3D virtual environments (YARS, Zahedi [2006]), and further analyzed with a dynamical systems analysis suite (Brightwell). The main reason for the 3D environment (ODE) is to model as adequately as possible the physical world, to make the transition of the networks to the real robots. This comprehensive set of tools allows flexibility in environment and robot design. Many of the networks are also further tested in real robots.

10   An extensive list of publications relating to work on neurodynamics and evolutionary robotics done at the Fraunhofer Institute for Autonomous Robots is found here: http://alex.ais.fraunhofer.de/zeno/web?action=content&journal=15390&rootid=14741

Section II

Applications

Chapter V

Innovation Diffusion Among Heterogeneous Agents:
Exploring Complexity with Agent-Based Modelling (ABM)

Nazmun N. Ratna, The Australian National University (ANU), Australia

Anne Dray, The Australian National University (ANU), Australia

Pascal Perez, The Australian National University (ANU), Australia

R. Quentin Grafton, The Australian National University (ANU), Australia

Tom Kompas, The Australian National University (ANU), Australia

Abstract

In this chapter we apply agent-based modelling (ABM) to capture the complexity of the diffusion process depicted in Medical Innovation, the classic study on diffu-

sion of a new drug tetracycline byColeman, Katz, and Menzel (1966). Based on our previous model with homogenous social agents, Gammanym (Ratna et al., 2007), in this chapter we further our analysis with heterogeneous social agents who vary in terms of their degree of predisposition to knowledge. We also explore the impact of stage-dependent degrees of external influence from the change agent, pharmaceutical company in this case. Cumulative diffusion curves suggest that the pharmaceutical company plays a much weaker role in accelerating the speed of diffusion when a diffusion dynamics is explored with complex agents, defined as heterogeneous agents under stage-dependent degrees of external influence. Although our exploration with groups of doctors with different combination of social and professional integration signifies the importance of interpersonal ties, our analysis also reveals that degree of adoption threshold or individual predisposition to knowledge is crucial for adoption decisions. Overall, our approach brings in fresh insights to the burgeoning policy literature exploring complexity, by providing necessary framework for research translation to policy and practice.

Introduction

This chapter examines how interpersonal interactions influence the diffusion of a new product. The approach uses ABM to capture the complexity of the diffusion process and the importance of social networks. It builds upon previous work (Ratna et al., 2007) and examines the classic study on the diffusion of a new drug, tetracycline by Coleman et al. (1966). This paper, elaborating on extended version of Gammanym, that is, *Gammanym1*, investigates the diffusion process by incorporating: (1) heterogeneity of adoption thresholds among principal social agents, that is, doctors; and (2) stage-dependent degrees of influence from the pharmaceutical company, a communicating social agent creating external influence for the doctors by providing information through various marketing strategies. We then proceed to capture the complexities of adoption decisions for heterogeneous agents under stage-dependent degrees of external influence. Our principal objective in this exploration with *Gammanym1* is to offer fresh insights into the dynamics of interpersonal relations and the resultant group outcomes in terms of aggregate adoption, and also to provide a comprehensive framework for research translation into policy and practice.

The chapter is structured as follows. We first review the literature and provide a motivation for the current study. The third section summarises our modelling approach while the fourth explores two major and, hitherto ignored, concepts: heterogeneity of adoption threshold among social agents and stage-dependent degrees of external influence. Results of the modelling and simulation with complex agents are provided in the fifth section while the last section offers concluding remarks.

Background

In this section, first, we briefly discuss the central concepts like diffusion, social networks, and also the first major study on diffusion of agricultural innovation. *Medical Innovation*, the original study and the reanalyses using the same dataset are then described in the *Medical Innovation and its Re-analyses* section. We elaborate the rationale for our investigation in the *Rationale for our Study* section.

Social Networks and Diffusion

Diffusion is essentially a social process. By definition, "diffusion of innovations is the process by which a new idea or product is communicated through certain channels over time among members of a social system" (Rogers, 1995). A central premise of *social network analysis* is that individuals have relational ties to other individuals, where each individual may also be tied to another one or a web of social connections. Consequently, any social interactions, such as working with colleagues or meeting in a social organisation like a club, frequently act as a medium of exchanging knowledge and information. Relational ties affect knowledge interactions as trust and norms of reciprocity built within social or community structures encourage the sharing of knowledge and information. Given the uncertainty attached to the new product or practice, the interpersonal exchanges contribute significantly in validating the personal opinions and thus provide the basis for complementarity between diffusion research and social network analysis.

The diffusion paradigm emphasising the role of social network analysis emerged in *Rural Sociology* with the Ryan & Gross (1943) study on diffusion of hybrid corn in Iowa. Hybrid corn was a high-yielding variety, more drought resistant, and more suitable for mechanical corn-pickers (Rogers, 1995). In two small Iowa communities, 345 farmers[1] were asked to recall their adoption process by answering: (1) when the adoption decisions were made; (2) the communication channels used in the decision making process; and (3) how much of the farmers' corn acreage were allocated to hybrid seed. The study findings reveal that the salesmen were most influential for early adopters and neighbours were more important for late adopters. The interpersonal exchanges of experience with the new seed, thus, were the major determinant for diffusion of hybrid corn. Although the study falls short of not having sociometric data, the Ryan and Gross study is considered as one of the cornerstones for classic diffusion paradigm.

Medical Innovation and Its Re-Analyses

The study by Coleman et al. (1966) on diffusion of the then new drug called tetracy-cline, was the first major study to comprise the sociometric data for diffusion. The sociometric data was collected for 126 doctors[2] outlining their three close associ-ates-friends, colleagues, and advisors—in the medical community. Their adoption behaviours were evaluated through a prescription audit in the local pharmacies over a 16-month period following the release of tetracycline for general sale. The original study revealed that relational ties of doctors, either social or professional, influenced their decisions to adopt tetracycline very strongly. In other words, the "integrated" doctors differed very little from their "isolated" colleagues at the beginning of the diffusion process, but with time their rate of adoption produced an increasing gap between "integrated" and "isolated" doctors. The diffusion among integrated doc-tors actually follows a snowball or chain reaction process (Coleman et. al., 1966, p. 96), as the probability of introduction to the new drug increases with more and more doctors adopting the new drug.

Given the availability of the sociometric dataset, a number of re-analyses followed this study. Burt (1987) opines that contagion occurred as a result of structural equivalence,[3] not through social cohesion. A structural equivalence model of diffu-sion postulates that individuals are influenced to adopt an innovation by imitating the behaviour of others to whom they are structurally equivalent. Strang and Tuma (1993, p. 638), on the other hand, emphasise the role of "cohesive ties based on advice giving and discussion" in diffusion of the new drug, in addition to the influ-ence generated through "structurally equivalent" peers.

Valente (1995) and Van den Bulte and Lilien (2001), however, emphasise the role of factors other than social ties or network structure. Applying a threshold/critical mass (T/CM) model (Valente, 1995) on the *Medical Innovation* dataset, Valente indicates that opinion leaders who have greater exposure to external influence, play a dominant role in the diffusion process and thus confirmed the two-step flow hy-pothesis.[4] Van den Bulte and Lilien (2001) analysed the diffusion of tetracycline by combining the *Medical Innovation* dataset and an advertisement dataset to evaluate the marketing effort of major drug companies. Their analysis provides support that doctors' decisions were primarily driven by the various marketing tools from the pharmaceutical companies. As the empirical results show no statistically significant contagion effect once marketing efforts are controlled for, the authors contradicted the social contagion process depicted in the Coleman et al. (1966) study.

Rationale for Our Study

Our principal motivation for re-analysing *Medical Innovation* was to capture the dynamics of network structure and the complexity embedded in the diffusion process, which were not addressed by either by the *Medical Innovation* study or the subsequent re-analyses of the original dataset. Our previous work (Ratna et al., 2007) addresses the dynamic features like topology and evolution of interaction networks generated by *Gammanym* with homogenous agents. In this paper, we address the issue of complexity of actual adoption by incorporating heterogeneity of adoption thresholds among social agents and stage-dependent degrees of external influence from the pharmaceutical company. The application of ABM actually facilitates us, for the first time, to address the complexity depicted in *Medical Innovation* in a better manner.

Our investigation has a strong policy component as it provides the necessary comprehensive framework for research translation to policy and practice. All actors in policy-making, government agencies; international and national nongovernmental organisation (NGOs); and development partners have long utilised the knowledge on local communities for successful implementations of policies regarding introduction of new product or practice. Despite the existence of this research-policy-practice nexus, our work brings fresh insights given the dearth of policy literature exploring complexity with the application of ABM.

Modelling Framework

We develop *Gammanym* with *Cormas*, a programming environment dedicated to the creation of multi-agent systems. In this section we will go over the principal components of each major objects/agents depicted in *Gammanym* and also outline the changes in *Gammanym1* to facilitate the understanding of the dynamics of adoption decisions in this paper. A detailed description of modelling framework and modelling sequence is provided in our previous work (Ratna et. al., 2007). The UML diagrams and the codes for Gammanym are available in the CORMAS Web site (http://cormas.cirad.fr/en/applica/gammanym.htm). To facilitate the understanding of the coding and the UML diagrams, we have also attached a description of different entities in *Gammanym* as Appendix1.

Spatial Distribution

In this model we investigate a medical community of 990 doctors, a 10-fold increase in the number of doctors in *Gammanym* model. Doctors are the principal agents in the diffusion process. The spatial environment, a 17x30 spatial grid, provides three different locations for professional interactions among doctors—hospitals, practices, and conference centre. Based on the findings in the original study on office partnership, three practice types are specified: *Private* (alone in office), *Centre* (sharing office with two colleagues), and *Clinic* (sharing office with four colleagues). The doctors are uniformly distributed in terms of their professional integration with 330 doctors in 330 private practices, 330 doctors in 110 centres, and 330 doctors in 66 clinics.

Two hospitals and a conference centre, similar to *Gammanym*, are incorporated with the notion of depicting diffusion of information among the members of a larger group. Though most of the interactions among doctors take place at their practices, professional interaction also takes place through a monthly visit to hospital and visit to conference centre by the invited doctors (Ratna et al., 2007). These visits enable them to gather information on new drugs from other members in the community. Important to note, however, that the hospitals and the conference centre are randomly allocated over the spatial grid and hence the spatial representation is not sensitive to distance. Figure 1 (a) and (b) represent the activity diagram for doctors' visit to hospital and conference centre respectively.

Figure 1a. Activity diagram for hospital visit

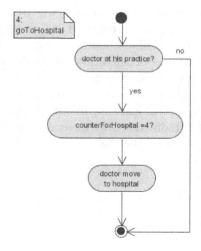

Figure 1b. Activity diagram for conference centre visit

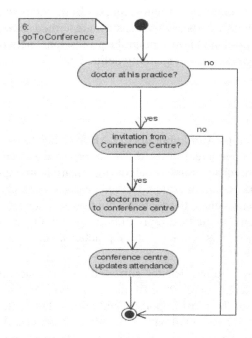

Social Agents

Gammanym1 incorporates two types of social agents: doctors and a pharmaceutical laboratory. Doctors are specified as located and communicating agents; Lab, on the other hand, has been specified as communicating agent.

Doctors

Doctors, the principal social agents in *Gammanym,* are integrated to the community through two networks—friendship and professional networks. Professional networks are spatially defined in the sense that the doctors situated in the same unit cell are specified as discussion partners. This specification is aimed at capturing the central idea of diffusing tacit or non-codified knowledge, a vital part of diffusion process (Ratna et al., 2007). In *Gammanym1*, the doctors are initially situated at their practices and they return to their respective practices after each visit to hospital or conference centre. A friendship network, on the other hand, is random[5] in nature. Each doctor is initiated with a random number of friends ranging from 0 to 3, and communicates with the friends on a monthly basis when the attribute termed as *counterForFriends* (Appendix 1) is 4. Important to note that unlike professional networks, interactions within friendship networks are not spatially defined.

Labs

The pharmaceutical company or Laboratory (LAB from here on), a communicating social agent, is the change agent in the diffusion process. Rogers (1995) defines, "a change agent is termed as an individual or organization attempting to influence clients' adoption decision in a direction deemed desirable by a change agency." In *Gammanym*, the LAB influences the doctors' adoption decisions through three channels of communication: (1) medical representative or detailman visiting practices, (2) advertisement in journals sent to doctors' practices, and (3) commercial flyers available during conferences.

Diffusion literature and policy debates surrounding pharmaceuticals' marketing strategies (Andaleeb & Tallman, 1996; Blumenthal, 2004; Moynihan, 2003) identify detailman as one of the most important and quite often as the first sources of information. In *Gammanym*, detailman visits all the practices. At each time step LAB keeps records of the practices visited by the detailmen and in the next time step sends them to the remaining unvisited practices or available practices, if at least one doctor is present. Advertisement in the medical journals is considered as another marketing tool. Journals are sent to all the practices and thereby ensure a blanket exposure to all doctors at the same time step. The model specifies issuance of quarterly journals.[6] Unlike detailman or journals, the notion of blanket exposure to all doctors is skipped in case of flyers. We specify that LAB, after receiving invitation from conference centre, sends flyers based on the number of previous conference participants. In case of flyers, depending on the number of available flyers, the participating doctors are likely to receive information.

Adoption Decision

Diffusion scholars have long recognised that an individual's decision about adoption is a process that occurs over time, consisting of several stages (Abrahamson & Rosenkopf, 1997; Coleman et al., 1966; Rogers, 1995; Valente, 1995). Based on the literature, we define *readiness* as the attribute signifying five stages of adoption: (1) awareness or knowledge, (2) interest, (3) evaluation/mental trial, (4) trial, and (5) adoption/acceptance. The homogenous doctors in *Gammanym* are thus initialised

Figure 2a. Activity diagram for alert generation from professional networks

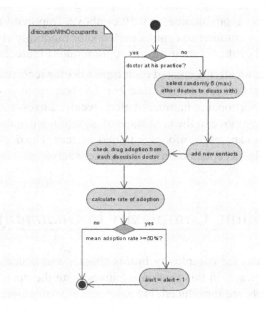

Figure 2b. Activity diagram for alert generation from lab

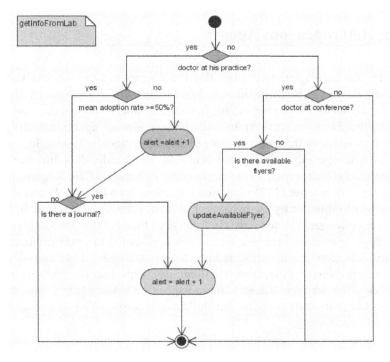

with a readiness of 4 (Appendix1). Discussions with other doctors, either friends or colleagues at practices, conferences, or hospitals generate an alert when the mean adoption rate of the acquaintances is 0.50 or above. Important to note that, while visiting hospitals or conference centres each doctor randomly chooses five of their acquaintances and evaluates their mean adoption rate (Figure 2a).

On the other hand, an alert is created each time a doctor receives information from the detailman, flyers, or journals (Figure 2b). For homogenous doctors, reduction in readiness is proportional to number of alerts received irrespective of the sources. In other words, they move to the next stage of adoption when they receive a single alert (or more) from any of the aforementioned sources. The doctors adopt the drug when they reach the acceptance stage or readiness zero.

Defining Complexity in *Gammanym1*

To provide the basis for complexity in this chapter and hence, defining complex agents in *Gammanym1*, in this section we investigate the diffusion process when two major concepts are introduced: (1) heterogeneity of adoption thresholds, and (2) non-homogenous alert generation process defined by stage-dependent degrees of external influence.

Defining Heterogeneous Agents

In our model, the heterogeneity implies that the doctors in *Gammanym1* vary in terms of their degree of predisposition to knowledge. In *Gammanym* an alert is generated for all doctors when 50% of his/her acquaintances adopted the new drug (see the *Adoption Decision* section). In case of heterogeneous agents, an alert generation criterion is drawn from the rationale of threshold models. Threshold models postulate that heterogeneity of individual threshold causes individual differences in times of adoption (Granovetter, 1978; Granovetter & Soong, 1986; Rogers, 1995; Valente, 1995). Granovetter (1978) initiated the research on thresholds and argues that the degree of influence by the behaviour of some relevant group (i.e., friends, neighbours, or colleagues) varies across individuals. Different versions of threshold models are developed in the literature with a wide application in empirical literature for analysing diffusion of innovation and practices (see Rogers, 1995 and Valente, 1995 for a comprehensive review of this literature). Based on the findings in the literature review that an agent's degree of predisposition to knowledge, is inversely related to his/her individual adoption threshold, we incorporate an additional variable called *innovativeness*.

The rationale for specification with innovativeness in *Gammanym1* has been drawn from the re-analyses of *Medical Innovation*. The re-analyses provide evidence for two statistically significant individual attributes influencing diffusion: *scientific orientation* and *journal subscription* (Burt, 1987; Valente, 1995; Van den Bulte & Lilien, 1999). In the original study, the *index for scientific orientation* was developed on the basis of their answers to a set of questions indicative of their level of concern for medical research, exchange of information, and scientific reliability of reading matter (Coleman et al., 1966, pp. 207-208). As the impact of journal subscription is somewhat reflected in scientific orientation,[7] we include *scientific orientation* only, as a measure for degree of predisposition to knowledge.

Innovativeness in *Gammanym1* signifies doctors' predisposition to knowledge. Based on the findings in the Coleman et al. (1966, pp. 183-185) study, 42%, 18%, and 40% of doctors are specified with three categories of innovativeness—high, intermediate, and low innovativeness respectively. For doctors with high, intermediate, and low innovativeness respectively, an alert is generated when 20%, 30%, and 90% of their acquaintances have adopted the new drug. The previous specification for threshold levels ensures that given the distribution of population, average threshold at the system level for heterogeneous and homogenous doctors are the same. The resultant cumulative diffusion curves under baseline scenario (ten initial adopters, eight detailmen, and four quarterly journals) for heterogeneous and homogenous agents are presented in Figure 3. Important to note that in case of baseline scenario for homogenous agents in *Gammanym*, all practices are visited by the one detailman within 61 time steps. In *Gammanym1* 990 doctors are distributed among 506 practices. To have the same level of exposure within 61 time steps, in this paper, we specify eight detailman for baseline scenario in *Gammanym1*.

To address the randomness incorporated in the algorithm, the cumulative diffusion curves are derived as the average of 100 simulations. All initial adopters (innovators) were selected from medical centres (practices with 3 doctors).

The simulation results in Figure 3 indicate that heterogeneity matters for diffusion. In other words, with the same average threshold, the cumulative diffusion curve with heterogeneous agents is steeper than that of homogenous agents. In comparison to the case when the medical community is defined by the homogeneous doctors, the adoption is quicker when the doctors vary in terms of their adoption threshold. For example, the highly innovative doctors move to the next stage of adoption when only 20% of their acquaintances have adopted the new drug, in comparison to the required mean adoption rate of 50% for homogeneous agents.

Nevertheless, as the average threshold of 0.5 is set arbitrarily, we experiment with another level of average threshold with the same distribution of population. In this case, for doctors with high, intermediate, and low innovativeness respectively, an alert is generated when 10%, 30%, and 60% of their acquaintances has adopted the new drug. The cumulative diffusion curves in Figure 4 depict the same diffusion

Figure 3. Comparison of cumulative diffusion curves with homogenous and hetero-geneous agents for the same average threshold (with 100 simulations)

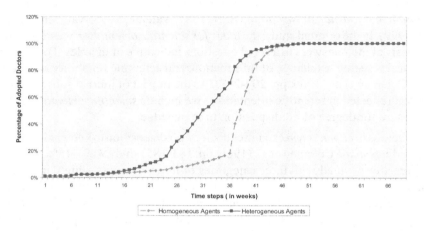

process with a small difference in terms of speed of diffusion. The curve representing average threshold of 0.5 is flatter than the curve representing average threshold of 0.33, and hence signifies a slower diffusion.

The cumulative diffusion curves in Figure 2 and Figure 3 reveal that varied levels of individual adoption thresholds across the population and the average threshold at the system level influence the diffusion process.

Figure 4. Cumulative diffusion curves for heterogeneous agents with different levels of average thresholds(with 100 simulations)

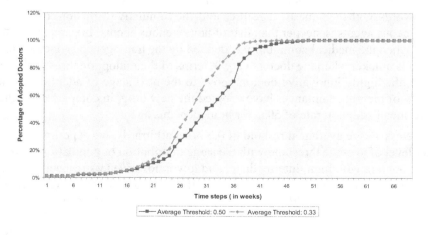

Impact on Diffusion: Innovativeness vs. Integration

In this section, we analyse the significance of individual attributes from the perspective of devising policies for speedier innovation diffusion. First, we investigate the diffusion process for doctors with different combinations of social and professional integration. We then examine groups of doctors with different integration and innovativeness status.

Impact of Integration

Which networks matter more adoption: social or professional? To address the previous, we select the most connected and least connected groups for comparison: (1) both socially and professionally integrated, (2) integrated professionally, but socially isolated, (3) isolated professionally, but socially integrated, and (4) both professionally and socially isolated. Given three types of office partnership and four types of friendship status, a range of definitions for professional or social integration or isolation is comprehensible. First, we define professionally integrated doctors as those with the maximum number of colleagues, or have four colleagues in a clinic; and socially integrated[8] doctors with two or more friends. Isolates—social or professional—are the ones practising alone or without any friend. In Figure 5, the diffusion curves for the aforementioned four groups of doctors are derived after averaging over 100 simulations for the benchmark scenario (with 10 initial adopter, 8 detailmen, and 4 quarterly journals).

The cumulative diffusion curves in Figure 5 indicate that diffusion proceeds exactly the same way, for all groups of doctors, up to the formation of the giant cluster (Ratna et al., 2007) and after that, integration to different networks generates different impacts. Our results show that integration is crucial for initial uptake as the number of doctors, who are both socially and professionally integrated, is higher than for the rest of the groups. Although the speed of diffusion is not significantly different from the rest of the groups, diffusion among the least connected doctors, both socially and professionally isolated, is the slowest at the initial stage (Figure 5). It is important to note that the simulation results for the two groups of doctors, where their integration status in two different networks is mutually reinforcing each other, replicate the findings in the original study (Coleman et al., 1966, pp. 90-91).

Our results are interesting for two groups of doctors with contrasting integration status: integrated professionally, but socially isolated; and isolated professionally, but socially integrated. Figure 5 implies that the degree of professional integration has a stronger impact. The similarity of adoption rates for group one (doctors with four colleagues and two or more friends) and group two (doctors with four colleagues, but with one or no friends) implies that, even if doctors are socially isolated, professional integration enables them to adopt quickly (Figure 5). Never-

Figure 5. Cumulative diffusion curves for groups of doctors defined by integration status (with 100 simulation)

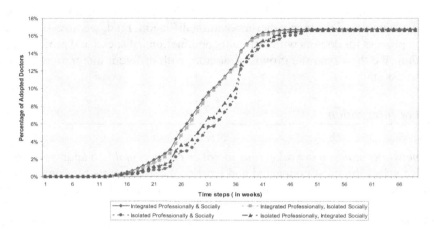

theless, integration to a friendship network is more significant for doctors who are professionally isolated. Given the differences in the adoption rates between group three and group four doctors, the results imply that, to some extent, integration to friendship networks can make up for professional isolation. In other words, even if a doctor is practising alone, social connections can work as an effective source of information.

Impact of Innovativeness

Based on the previous findings, we define four groups of doctors to separate the impacts of innovativeness and status of professional integration: (1) professionally integrated doctors with high innovativeness, (2) professionally integrated doctors with low innovativeness, (3) professionally isolated doctors with high innovativeness, and (4) professionally isolated doctors with low innovativeness. The diffusion curves for the above groups of doctors are depicted in Figure 6.

We observe interesting results in Figure 6 for two groups of doctors with contrasting specifications in terms of innovativeness and integration: professionally integrated doctors with low innovativeness, and professionally isolated doctors with high innovativeness. The difference in the speed of diffusion between the groups reveals that the individual trait or *innovativeness* is more significant for adoption decisions. In other words, the groups of isolated doctors with high innovativeness or lower adoption threshold have a quicker diffusion compared to integrated doctors with higher threshold or low innovativeness.

Figure 6. Cumulative diffusion curves for groups of doctors defined by innovativeness (with 100 simulations)

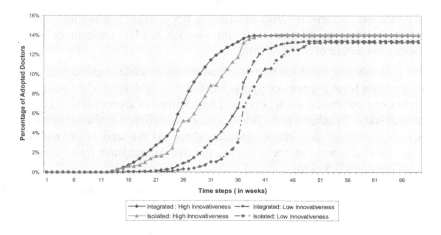

Stage-Dependant Degrees of External Influence

In *Gammanym*, we specify that an alert is created for the doctors whenever they receive information from LAB, irrespective of sources, and of their stages of adoption (*Adoption Decision* section). The diffusion literature, however, provides evidence that degrees of influence from different sources are dependent on the stages of adoption. These studies, primarily conducted with farmers, indicate that mass media channels are relatively more important at the knowledge stage, and interpersonal channels are relatively more important at the persuasion stage in the innovation decision process (Rogers, 1995, p. 195). In this section, therefore, we explore with different criteria for generating alert depending on source of information and the stages of adoption.

Assuming that the doctors do not distinguish among different sources of information when they are unaware of the new drug, we test with three different specifications for alert generation:

1. *Test 1:* Differences between passive and interpersonal communication in terms of alert generation is experimented in this test. Because interpersonal communication allows individuals to clarify their doubts, interaction with acquaintances (friends or colleagues) or detailman at any stage creates one alert and doctors move to the next stage of adoption. Despite being the representative of the LAB, we consider the detailman is important at any stage

of the adoption decision because the interpersonal communication enables doctors to satisfy their queries.[9] Information from journals or flyers, on the other hand, creates one alert only when the doctors are at the awareness stage and decreases afterwards, that is, creating 0.5 alert if their readiness is three or less. In other words, passive communication has less importance once the doctors are aware of the new drug.

2. *Test 2*: In this test, the doctors are comparatively flexible in evaluating passive information from journals or flyers. Thus, the same degree of influence as interpersonal communication is created by journals or flyers till they reach the interest stage. In other words, doctors make no difference among the sources of information till they reach readiness three. At the start of the evaluation stage, that is, when readiness is two, passive information from journals or flyers creates a 0.5 alert.

3. *Test 3*: In this test, we experiment with different notions attached with the motive of the information providers. Given the inherent interest in selling the new drug, the doctors evaluate information from the LAB with reservation in comparison with information from friends or colleagues. Thus, information from the LAB, either through detailman, journals, or flyers creates one alert only when the doctors are at their awareness stage. In other words, when the doctors are unaware of the drug, they make no difference between information from their peers and information from the LAB. However, the influence from the LAB decreases afterwards, that is, creating 0.5 alert if their readiness is three or less.

The specifications for each of the previous tests are described in Table 1 where the number represents the alert value at different stages of adoption process. Figure 7 shows that the cumulative diffusion curves for each of the specifications along with a baseline scenario with identical impact from all sources of information, that is, alert generation irrespective of stage or communication channel. Each scenario is initialised with 10 initial adopters, 1 detailman, and 4 quarterly journals for a medical community of 990 doctors.

The diffusion curves in Figure 7 evolve in predictable ways in the sense that flexibility in terms of weighing passive and interpersonal communication equally ensures more coverage of the new drug (baseline scenario). The almost identical diffusion curves for test 1 and test 3 provides support for our argument. At the end of 68 time steps, 45% and 43% of the doctors have adopted the new drug in case of test 1 and test 3 respectively. Test 2, implying more flexibility towards evaluating passive information, generates a markedly different result with 97% of the doctors adopting the new drug at the end of simulation. The similarity between test 1 and test 3 diffusion curves also reveals that as we specify a single detailman covering all 506 practices, detailman is not the first source of information for the doctors. Overall,

Table 1. Alert generation criteria under stage-dependent degrees of external influence

Stages of Adoption/ Readiness	TEST 1			TEST 2			TEST 3		
	Colleague Friend	Detail man	Journal Flyer	Colleague Friend	Detail man	Journal Flyer	Colleague Friends	Detail man	Journal Flyer
Awareness *Readiness 4*	1	1	1	1	1	1	1	1	1
Interest *Readiness 3*	1	1	0.5	1	1	1	1	0.5	0.5
Evaluation *Readiness 2*	1	1	0.5	1	1	0.5	1	0.5	0.5
Trial *Readiness 1*	1	1	0.5	1	1	0.5	1	0.5	0.5
Adoption *Readiness 0*	Adoption of the new drug								

Figure 7. Experimenting with stage-dependant degrees of external influence (with 100 simulations)

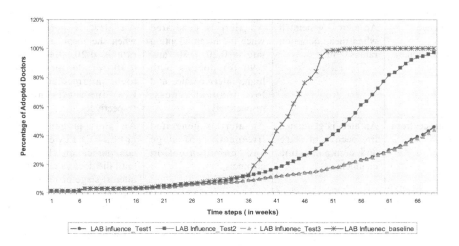

the differences among cumulative diffusion curves depicted in Figure 7 indicate that the system is sensitive to stage-dependant degrees of external influence.

Exploring Diffusion with Complex Agents

In this section, we analyse the diffusion process with complex agents. On the basis of the findings in the pervious section, complex agents are defined as the heterogeneous agents who follow a non-homogenous alert-generation process dependent on stages of adoption and sources of information. This exploration is aimed at evaluating if the complex settings for diffusion with heterogeneous agents under stage-dependant degrees of external influence are significantly different than those with homogenous agents. Table 2 provides the comparison of principal attributes of three social agents: homogeneous agents, heterogeneous agents, and complex agents.

To compare with the diffusion process for homogenous agents in *Gammanym* (Ratna et al., 2007), we evaluate the significance of external influence by changing the number of detailman for diffusion with complex agents in *Gammanym1* for the following three scenarios (Figure 8):

Table 2. Defining three types of located and communicating social agents

Attributes/ Methods	Homogeneous Agents	Heterogeneous Agents	Complex Agents
Initial readiness for doctors	4	4	4
Influence from acquaintances	An alert is generated when mean adoption rate is 0.50.	An alert is generated when the mean adoption rate is 0.20, 0.30, and 0.90 for doctors with high, intermediate, and low innovativeness, respectively.	An alert is generated when the mean adoption rate is 0.20, 0.30, and 0.90 for doctors with high, intermediate, and low innovativeness, respectively.
Influences from LAB	An alert is generated irrespective of stage and communication channels.	An alert is generated irrespective of stage and communication channels.	An alert is generated irrespective of communication channels until the doctors reach the interest stage or readiness 3. Passive information from journals or flyers creates 0.5 alert afterwards.[10]

1.   Baseline scenario with 8 detailman;

2.   Heavy media scenario with 32 detailman;

3.   Integration scenario; without any influence from the LAB

All scenarios are run for the same time length, that is, 68 weeks. For each of the cases, 10 initial adopters have been chosen among the doctors who are in centres, that is, with two colleagues. All three curves are derived after averaging over 100 simulations. Important to note that, in case of heavy media scenario for homogenous agents in *Gammanym*, all practices are visited by the four detailmen within 16 time steps. With 506 practices in *Gammanym1*, to have the same level of exposure within 16 time steps, we specify 32 detailmen for heavy media scenario in this paper.

For a better understanding of the comparison among the cumulative diffusion curves, we have reproduced diffusion curves with homogenous agents (Figure 9) as in our previous work (Ratna et al., 2007).

In Figure 8, the cumulative diffusion curves generated under three scenarios support our earlier findings about media influence in determining the speed of diffusion in case of homogenous agents (Figure 9). The extent of influence, however, is much less in case of these agents. In case of homogenous agents, all the agents adopt the new drug within 25 time steps under heavy media scenario in comparison to 49 time steps for baseline scenario, as shown in Figure 9. For diffusion with complex agents, the system reaches the saturation point at 45 time steps under heavy media scenario and at 68 time steps under baseline scenario (Figure 8). The integration scenario for complex agents, despite revealing a slower process, is significantly

Figure 8. Cumulative diffusion curves for diffusion with complex agents in Gammanym1 (with 100 simulations)

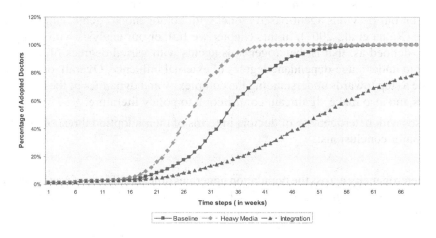

Figure 9. Cumulative diffusion curves for diffusion with homogenous agents in Gammanym (with 100 simulations)

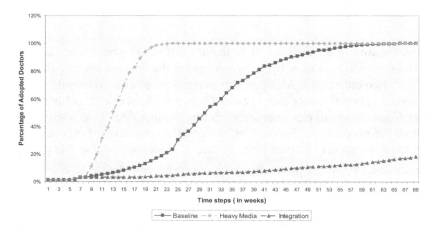

different in terms of coverage of population. At the end of 68 time steps, 80% of the complex agents have adopted the new drug (Figure 8) in comparison to only 18% of the homogenous doctors (Figure 9).

Concluding Remarks

In this chapter we explore the complexity of diffusion process depicted in *Medical Innovation*, a classic study on the adoption of tetracycline by Coleman et al. (1966). Based on our previous agent-based model with homogenous agents, called *Gammanym* (Ratna et al., 2007), in this chapter we further our analysis with complex agents, defined as, that is, heterogeneous agents with varied degrees of adoption threshold under stage-dependant degrees of external influence. Overall, our results provide a step towards understanding the complexity and dynamics of the diffusion process and also make significant contribution to policy literature.

Analyses with heterogeneity of doctors in terms of their adoption threshold lead to three major conclusions:

1.   heterogeneity across the population generates quicker diffusion in comparison with the case when the doctors are homogenous, even if the average threshold at the system level remains the same;

2.   although professional integration has a stronger impact for dissemination of information, to some extent, integration to social networks can make up for professional isolation; and

3.   despite the significance of integration or connectedness, individual predisposition to knowledge or degree of adoption threshold proves to be more crucial for the adoption decisions. For example, we find that the group of professionally isolated doctors with high innovativeness or lower adoption threshold has a quicker diffusion compared to professionally integrated doctors with low innovativeness or higher adoption threshold.

Our investigation with stage-dependent degrees of external influence indicate that the criteria practiced by adopters in terms of evaluating different sources of information at different adoption stages are vital for successful diffusion of innovations. In other words, this finding emphasises the need for sociometric data with detail information on communication channels influencing the adoption decisions. We also find that the speed of diffusion is largely defined by media influence; but its degree is weaker for diffusion with complex agents. For complex agents the system reaches saturation at 45 time steps under heavy media scenario, and at 68 time steps under the baseline scenario with one third of media exposure. Our findings in *Gammanym1* reveal that the optimal marketing strategy, therefore, needs to entail more than intensification of marketing instruments.

Our exploration also reveals fresh insights for policy formulation related to diffusion of a new product or practice. Though our study lacks the intricate details of actual events due to unavailability of data, our approach of addressing complexity provides the necessary framework for further investigation with sociometric data, especially in terms of assessing the network structure and its impact on the diffusion process. Further investigation in this direction would be particularly vital for diffusion policies targeting isolated and ethnically divided rural communities in Africa or Pacific islands. Overall, our approach contributes significantly to the emerging policy literature exploring complexity by paving the way for a more effective research-policy-practice nexus for innovation diffusion.

We are currently working on a model, *Gammanym2* that elaborates on the diffusion process with two competing pharmaceutical labs influencing the adoption decisions of doctors in a medical community. Focusing on the strategic interaction between the labs, our motivation is to address, *how, and to what extent, does information on social networks generate higher economic payoff for change agents like pharmaceutical companies?* In *Gammanym2*, we have included a cost function, defined as the summation of fixed costs, that is, research and development (R&D) expenditure plus two drug promotion costs: sampling and cost of advertising in the journals; and the variable cost, that is, the cost of detailing or sending the detailman. Defining

payoff as the ratio of number of adopted doctors and total cost, in *Gammanym2*
the optimality of two alternative *Tit-for-Tat* strategies are analysed under repeated
games framework for two sets of agents: homogenous agents and deliberative agents.
Given the significance of individual traits for adoption decisions, as evidenced in
this paper, and their rigorous explorations with ABM in diffusion models (Deffuant,
Huet, & Amblard, 2005; Edwards, Huet, Goreaud, & Deffuant, 2003) a different
type of decision dynamics is experimented in case of deliberative agents, with the
introduction of threshold function for adoption decisions.

Adaptive behaviour on the part of the pharmaceutical labs is investigated under repeated games scenario as the labs alter the marketing strategy, following a system of
quarterly evaluation. Benchmark scenario in *Gammanym2* examines a simple game
with a theoretical exposition originating form *Prisoners' Dilemma*. The core assumption is that the two competing pharmaceutical labs, despite the high negotiation cost
or monitoring cost, have the incentive to cooperate given the possibility of reducing
their variable cost. Based on the agreement of cooperation defined in *Gammanym2*,
each lab sends their detailmen to an allocated region, and thereby, reduces the cost
of detailing. Under the repeated games framework, after starting with the benchmark
scenario of random marketing with 20 detailman, the cooperating lab assesses the
possibilities for defection at the 12th time step or first quarterly evaluation,[11] and
decides to retaliate when three or more detailman from the other lab is located in
its own zone. The defecting lab assesses the action of the other lab by evaluating
at 24 time steps using the same criterion and retaliates in the same manner, that is,
adopting the same strategy from then on. The retaliating strategies are: (1) random
intensity marketing when doctors are targeted randomly with increased number of
detailman; and (2) segmented marketing by prioritising the groups based on their
professional integration with the same number of detailman.

In *Gammanym2*, the transitions from random marketing to any of the retaliating
strategies are accompanied by a change in trust cost or monitoring cost. Each firm
changes their monitoring cost when their prior beliefs regarding the opponent
changes. The evolving nature of the trust cost or monitoring cost captures the notion
of learning (Osborne, 2004). As part of discussing the formation of players' beliefs,
Osborne (2004) describes learning as a scenario where the same set of participants
repeatedly play a game, each participant changing his/her beliefs about the others'
strategies in response to observations of their actions. Thus the value of monitoring
cost for the committing company decreases to zero when the committing company
becomes aware of the cheating by their opponent. The preliminary results, so far,
provide interesting insights for devising optimal diffusion policies for pharmaceutical laboratories in particular and change agencies in general.

References

Abrahamson, E., & Rosenkopf, L. (1997). Social networks effects on the extent of innovation diffusion: A computer simulation. *Organization Science, 8*(3), 289-309.

Andaleeb, S. S., & Tallman, R. F. (1996). Relationships of physicians with pharmaceutical sales representatives and pharmaceutical companies: An exploratory study. *Health Marketing Quarterly, 13*(4), 79-89.

Blumenthal, D. (2004). Doctors and drug companies. *The New England Journal of Medicine, 351*(18), 1885-1891.

Burt, R. S. (1987). Social contagion and innovation: Cohesion versus structural equivalence. *American Journal of Sociology, 92,* 1287-1335.

Coleman, J. S., Katz, E., & Menzel, H. (1966). *Medical innovation: A diffusion study.* Indianapolis, IN: The Bobbs-Merril Company, Inc.

Deffuant, G., Huet, S., & Amblard, F. (2005). An individual-based model of innovation diffusion mixing social value and individual benefit. *The American Journal of Sociology, 110*(4), 1041-1069.

Edwards, M., Huet, S., Goreaud, F., & Deffuant, G. (2003). Comparing an individual based model of behaviour diffusion with its mean field aggregate approximation. *Journal of Artificial Societies and Social Simulation, 6*(4), 1-16.

Granovetter, M. (1978). Threshold models of collective behaviour. *American Journal of Sociology, 83,* 1420-1443.

Granovetter, M., & Soong, R. (1986). Threshold models of interpersonal effects in consumer demand. *Journal of Economic Behaviour and Organization, 7,* 83-99.

Moynihan, R. (2003). Who pays for the pizza?: Redefining relationship between doctors and drug companies. *British Medical Journal, 326,* 1189-1192.

Osborne, Martin J. (2004). *An introduction to game theory.* New York: Oxford University Press.

Ratna, N. N., Dray, A., Perez, P., Grafton, R. Q., Newth, D., & Kompas, T. (2007). Innovation diffusion, social networks and strategic marketing. In H. Qudrat-Ullah, M. Spector, & P. Davidsen (Eds.), *Complex decision making: Theory and practice.* New York: Springer-Verlag.

Rogers, E. M. (1995). *Diffusion of innovations* (4th ed.). New York: The Free Press.

Ryan, B., & Gross, N. C. (1943). The diffusion of hybrid seed corn in two Iowa communities. *Rural Sociology, 8*(1), 15-24.

Strang, D., & Tuma, N. B. (1993). Spatial and temporal heterogeneity in diffusion. *The American Journal of Sociology, 99*(3), 614-639.

Valente, T. W. (1995). *Network models of the diffusion of innovations*. Cresskil, NJ: Hampton Press, Inc.

Van den Bulte, C., & Lilien, G. (1999). *A two-stage model of innovation adoption with partial observability: Model development and application* (No. ISBM Report 20). University Park, PA: Pennsylvania State University, Institute for the Study of Business Markets.

Van den Bulte, C., & Lilien, G. (2001). *Medical innovation* Revisited: Social contagion versus marketing effort. *American Journal of Sociology, 106*(5), 1409-1435.

Endnotes

[1] Twelve farmers operating less than 20 acres were discarded from the data analysis, as were 74 respondents who had started farming after hybrid corn began to diffuse (Rogers, 1995).

[2] The Coleman et al. (1966) sample constituted 148 general practitioners, internists, and paediatricians in active practice, of which 85% were interviewed (Ratna et al., 2007).

[3] "Structural equivalence is the degree that two individuals occupy the same position in a social system," so defines Valente (1995).

[4] "This pattern of opinion leaders being early adopters and then passing on information about the innovation to opinion followers is called the two-step flow hypothesis" (Valente, 1995, p. 34).

[5] The case for random friendship network for Gammanym is thoroughly discussed in Ratna et al. (2007).

[6] The drug companies do not publish journals, but adding a publisher, sending journal would not add much to the study, as it is hard to articulate other responsibilities for the publisher.

[7] In estimating the index for scientific orientation, "each physician was given a score consisting of the number of scientifically oriented statements made in response to a set of questions" (Coleman et al., 1966, p. 208). The scores were then divided into three categories: high, low, and medium. The following questions, are, indicative of their journal subscription: (1) What do you find useful about house organs?; (2) Does the appearance of information on medicine in lay publications do more harm or more good? In what way?

[8] We experiment with different definitions of social integration. The diffusion curves with *socially integrated* doctors with maximum number of friends or three friends, depicts similar diffusion processes.

[9]   For many practicing physicians, in short, the detailman seem to serve as a kind of travelling consulting specialist (Coleman et al., 1966).

[10] Given the analysis in the *Stage-dependant Degrees of External Influence* section, we decided to include test 2 specifications to avoid biasness in terms of comparing the results with homogenous agents.

[11] In Gammanym2, the rationale for evaluation is drawn from the assumption that after covering 99% of the practices, the defecting lab may well have incentive to move to the opponent's zone.

Appendix 1: Defining Agents in *Gammanym* and *Gammanym1*

Attribute	Type	Definition	Additional Comments
Cell: Spatial Entity Cell			
buildingType	Symbol	Cell on which the passive objects, representing different destinations for professional interaction of the doctors.	
Doctor: Situated and Communicating			
Alert	Integer	At each time step, lab info and discussions with colleagues/friends increment an Alert.	Based on the number of friends or colleagues who have adopted drug, doctors will receive alert and thus update readiness.
conferenceInvitation	Boolean	At the time steps when a conference is held, doctors will receive invitation from conference centre and move to the cell specified as conference centre	
counterForFriends	Integer	Each doctor contacts their friends when their respective counterForFriends is 4.	Doctors are initialised with counterForFriends ranging from 0-3, as chosen randomly by Cormas

continued on following page

Appendix 1. continued

Attribute	Type	Definition	Additional Comments
counterForHospital	Integer	Each doctor goes to the hospitals when their respective counterForHospitals is 4.	Doctors are initialised with counterForHospitals ranging from 0-3, as chosen randomly by Cormas
dicoContacts	Dictionary	Contains the doctors' id and frequency of contacts, as part of professional networks either at practice, hospital, or conference	*At the beginning, dicoContacts contain the id of the practice colleagues with no. of contacts being 1. *Colleagues are defined as the doctors in the same spatial entity.
dicoFriends	Dictionary	Contains the doctors' id and frequency of contacts, as part of friendship networks.	Doctors are initiated with randomly chosen friends with the number of friends ranging from 0-3. Each time a friend is chosen, they will be added in the dicoFriends with 1.
drugAdoption	Boolean	Doctors' status of adoption	All, but innovators, are initialized with drugAdoption as false
flyer	Boolean	At the conference centre, the doctors will pick up a flyer if available	Flyer will generate alert. Initially, none of the doctors will have flyer
memoryAlert	Ordered Collection	Specifications for the source of alert	Alerts are specified as symbol (e.g #detailman)
practicePatch		Specifies location of doctors for interacting with office colleagues	Initially, all are in their practices
Attribute	*Type*	*Definition*	*Additional Comments*
readiness	Integer	Signifies the adoption threshold, which is decremented with alert.	*Initially, all, but innovators have a readiness of 4 (signifying different stages of adoption). *Individuals adopt their readiness when alert >= 1. * When readiness is zero, doctors adopt the new drug and hence drugAdoption is true.

continued on following page

Appendix 1. continued

allConferences allHospitals	Class instance variable	Collection of conference centres or hospitals	Though the model specifies one conference centre, the class variables (same for all the doctors) is created for possible inclusion of more conference centres or hospitals
Lab: Communicating Agent			
adoptionCurve	Ordered Collection	No. of doctors who have adopted new drug	Labs need to keep track of this variable in order to send journals.
allDoctors	Ordered Collection	Lab needs to know all doctors, to calculate adoption	
allPractices	Ordered Collection	Lab needs to know all practices to send detailman or journal in their practices	
allConferences	Ordered Collection	Lab needs to know all conference centres to send flyers	
conferenceAttendance	Integer	Number of doctors attending the conference	Sent flyers based on the conference attendance of the previous conference. The value of conference attendance will change when conference centre updates the number of conference participants
conferenceInvitation	Boolean	Conference centre sends invitation to the lab to make flyers available	Invitation is sent at the same time period as the doctors
detailman	Integer	Detailman is sent to doctors' practices	Presence of detailman at the practices generates alert. Initialized as 1, and can be changed in the interface

continued on following page

Appendix 1. continued

flyer	Integer	Lab sent the flyers at the conference centre	Initially 10 flyers are sent to the conference centre
journalRelease	Ordered Collection	The time steps at which the lab sends journals to doctors' practice	Aspect of interface appears after the simulation
maxArticlesJournal	Integer	Journals sent to the doctors' practices	Initialised as 2, and can be changed in the interface
Attribute	**Type**	**Definition**	**Additional Comments**
visitedPracticesPatch	Ordered Collection	The id for cells/ practices visited by detailman	Based on this variable the labs, detailman will be sent to unvisited practices
memory VisitedPracticePatch	Ordered Collection	Keeps the id of visited practices when the detailman has visited all the practices.	

Practice : Located Passive Object

detailman	Boolean	Specifies visit by detailman	Initially none of the practices are visited by detailman
journal	Boolean	Availability of journals sent by lab	Initially no journals are available at doctors' practices
practiceType	Symbol	The type of practices in which the doctors will be situated	Doctors will come back to their practices each time they have been to hospitals or conferences. Used for creating shortcuts (e.g. myPractice, myConference)

continued on following page

Appendix 1. continued

Conference Centre: Located Passive Object			
conferenceParticipants	Dictionary	Dictionary with the time step at which conference happens as the key.	*The number of conference participants may not be equal to number of doctors invited to conference; some may be in their hospital and hence did not receive conference invitation. *Number of conference participants are updated based on the size of the dictionary and then sent to labs
invitedDoctors	Ordered Collection	Collection of ALL invited doctors at the conference centre for ALL conferences	
planning	Sorted Collection	Collection of time steps For conferences/at which conference invitation is sent to doctors and labs	Interface for conference centre allows to choose the preferred time period for conferences. Otherwise, Cormas can randomly select the time steps.
availableFlyers	Integer	Number of flyers available at the conference centre	Initially, the number of flyers would be zero.

Chapter VI

Unique Applications of Multi-Agent Models in Uncovering Language Learning Processes

Teresa Satterfield, University of Michigan, USA

Abstract

Multi-scale "artificial societies" are constructed to examine competing first- and second-language acquisition-based theories of creole language emergence. Socio-historical conditions and psycho-linguistic capacities are integrated into the model as agents (slaves and slave-owners) interact. Linguistic transmissions are tracked, and grammar constructions are charted. The study demonstrates how a complex adaptive system (CAS) approach offers clear indications for computational solutions to questions of language change and formation.

Introduction

How does a fully operational and accepted linguistic code evolve out of the complexity of multiple languages and cultures in contact? What principles or mechanisms make such language development possible, both at the individual (cognitive) and at the societal level? Various hypotheses offer explanations for how historical creole languages arose under precisely such "chaotic" language contact settings, notably in plantation scenarios. Since creoles are not exactly the same as any of the *first language (L1)* source languages from which they emerge, creolists support the notion of creoles as adult manifestations of unsuccessful or "imperfect" efforts at *second language (L2)* acquisition. These "flawed" attempts are claimed to gradually converge to a new code over the span of several generations of speakers (Arends, 1995; Chaudenson, 1992, 1995; Mufwene, 1996; etc.). The *language bioprogram hypothesis* (Bickerton, 1981, 1984, 1988) is a competing account which suggests that plantation creoles arise within one generation, and only when young children exposed to impoverished or otherwise deficient primary linguistic input "compensate" by creating a novel L1 from their immigrant parents' "defective" L2. A long-standing challenge for creole studies has been how to reliably test the two theories, due to obstacles such as imperfect records of speakers inhabiting historical plantation communities, the extinction of early and intermediate linguistic forms, along with the added questions of creole studies' place within larger disciplinary contexts such as L1 and/or L2 language acquisition theories.

The general purpose of the current research is to shed light on underlying assumptions of language acquisition theories and to serve as a "barometer" for specific proposals concerning creole formation. We start from the premise that language acquisition, with its complex sets of linguistic processes, as mediated by internal and external factors extending across multiple timescales, can be fruitfully analyzed as a CAS (e.g., Satterfield, 1999a,b, 2001, 2005a, 2005b, in press). For the scope of this work, a CAS is defined as a dynamical network whose emergent properties are produced bottom-up by the simple interactions of many individual elements. A CAS is complex in that it is diverse and made up of multiple interconnected units; it is adaptive in that it has the capability to evolve and to "learn" from experience within a changing environment (Bradbury, 2002; Holland, 1998). While the CAS approach has been applied in several linguistic projects concerning human language evolution (Bartlett & Kazakov, 2004; Briscoe, 2000, 2002; Culicover & Nowak, 2002; Kirby, 1999; Steels, 1997), the present study takes model validity as a key feature (Burton & Obel, 1995); focusing on an application that, while a simplification of the system that it is designed to mimic, still adheres to reality. The intent is to provide a principled explanation for real-world linguistic processes and components at a basic level. Phenomena observed in real-world language acquisition fall naturally into the category of CAS, providing a window into linguistic development at several levels of analysis. At the local level, the present model considers how the existing *internal-language*, the grammar within the mind of each individual speaker, is represented. In turn, dynamical interactions of individuals generate collective linguistic representations at a global level, constructing a particular *external-language* as the linguistic convention of the community.

The CAS dynamics generated in the mapping between numerous external (socio-cultural) conditions of the plantation on one hand and the speakers' internal (cognitive) faculties on the other become quite complex because behaviors of the whole cannot be understood by simply observing the behavior of individual components. For example, the linguistic information inputted to a given inhabitant of the plantation depends on what other speakers are transmitting and receiving, how speakers process this input given their state of linguistic knowledge, how different speakers respond to different plantation conditions, and so forth. In short, the behaviors of inhabitants in the plantation **and** the linguistic code(s) that they ultimately adopt are "emergent" properties of interactions among **and** between speakers **and** the spatial layout of the plantation. Rather than using probabilistic techniques **and** purely statistical analysis, modeling the plantation's operations via agent-based computer models (ABMs) is a viable solution to the mapping problem (e.g., Epstein & Axtell, 1996; Ferber, 1998; Fox-Keller, 2002). Agents of the system are endowed with individual behaviors that must be taken into account, such that each agent is responsible for an activity or recognized property of a domain, yet there is no centralizing system coordinating the whole. Large-scale effects are produced in the domain as populations of agents interact and adapt locally in various ways and within a complex environment. Based on micro-specifications with regard to agents, the environment, and rules of behavior in the model, certain macro-structures and collective behaviors are generated in the system. ABMs enable the researcher to tease apart the contributions of each variable. Furthermore, unlike theoretical accounts that paint the "big picture" while glossing over crucial details, ABMs force us—due to the requirements imposed by programming algorithms—to make explicit the concept/process represented, and also the nature of the mechanisms involved in this process.

The objectives framing the current study are entirely practical. The primary goal is to replicate basic demographic and socio-cultural information in *"silico."* To this end, Sranan Tongo, an English-based creole originating in colonial Surinam is adopted as the base case for the ABM. Demographic parameters derive from historical archives on Sranan (Arends, 1992, 1995, 1996; Braun & Plag, 2003; Migge, 1998, 2000; Seuren, 2001; Van den Berg, 2000; Winford, 2000, 2001, 2003). Theory-based linguistic parameters are also encoded into the ABM, as discussed later on. After releasing an initial population of slave and slave owner agents into the environment, the model is examined at regular intervals. The next objective is to analyze any linguistic data generated, in order to determine whether the interaction between multiple agents indirectly results in the emergence of linguistic structures in the communicative context designed, and to determine if these emergent structures are identifiable as creolized forms similar to those of Sranan. The interactions and data in turn serve to explore in detail the L1 and L2 hypotheses related to plantation creole formation.

The behavior of a CAS is not always predictable and the errors a model generates may not be a deterministic function of its parameter values. As the CAS organization is emergent, the agents in the current study might end up with quite different linguistic repertoires than the historically documented human case, yet it is extremely thought provoking to test whether the agents can arrive at the real-world creole solution, based precisely on the terms advanced under specific accounts of creole development. The current study therefore takes no position on whether an L1- or L2-acquisition theory of creole formation is the more plausible hypothesis given the data available. Rather, the preliminary stance is that no "natural" methodology for detailed examination of the impact and contributions of either hypothesis existed previously. The present inquiry represents an effort to implement a methodology that may by-pass some of the barriers which have hindered past creole formation research.

The chapter proceeds as follows: after a brief overview of the topic, a description of the ABM is outlined. The trajectories and outcomes of two experiments are then presented. Subsequent discussion explores the likelihood for creoles to be formed based on the proposed configurations of demographic, social, and psycho-linguistic variables as integrated into the model. Implications and suggestions for further research conclude the chapter.

Background

Theoretical Overview

Linguistically speaking, a *creole* language emerges when speakers of mutually unintelligible languages must communicate with each other (Arends, Muysken, & Smith, 1995; Holm, 2000; Mühlhäusler, 1997; Sebba, 1997; Thomason, 1997, 2001; Winford, 2003). In this context, vocabulary items of the dominant culture's language (the *superstrate*) may be learned; however, the superstrate's grammar is not (completely) mastered. Grammatical features of word order, verbal paradigms, and the like may be retained from the *substrate* (supplanted or recessive) language(s). Frequently a new language comes into being, and in its earliest stages is known as a *jargon* or *pidgin*. *Pidginization* is a process involving (linguistic and functional-communicative) reduction. If a pidgin becomes accepted in the community, as its usage stabilizes and diffuses the resultant language is known as a *creole*. In contrast to pidginization, *creolization* is a process of expansion generating a quite different grammar than previously exhibited by speakers in that particular linguistic surrounding.

Many creolists consider impoverished L2 access to be the major catalyst for creole language development. Under this hypothesis it is proposed that, for example, newly arrived adult slaves from Africa after a time were not exposed to the original European superstrate of French or English, and so forth, but instead learned "approximations" of these L2 targets from already acculturated adult slaves and from other recently imported slaves (Chaudenson, 1995). The approximate versions of the superstrates are argued to be the foundations for creole language varieties used today. In contrast, creole language formation accounts based on the *language bioprogram hypothesis* (LBH) (Bickerton, 1984) place primary importance on young children's inherent predisposition to acquire any human language. The LBH posits the existence of a species-particular and universal biological "blueprint" for L1 acquisition. In chaotic language contact settings, such as institutional slavery, the child's language bioprogram is argued to give abrupt rise to a creole grammar. The LBH is also invoked to explain a range of linguistic properties that are considered to be common to all creole languages.

In the standard psycho-linguistic references, it is widely held that young children attain L1 and L2 competence implicitly and without conscious effort, whereas adults display varying degrees of "impairment" in L2 acquisition (by monolingual native speaker standards), even when possessing considerable motivation and resources. Lenneberg (1967) describes such age-related differences in terms of the *critical period hypothesis*, where a developmental window exists in the linguistic maturation of humans, such that between the age of 2 years and puberty, it is biologically possible to be exposed to primary linguistic input and to acquire any language in a native speaker capacity. Before and after this approximately 10-year period of opportunity, successful language acquisition is claimed to be increasingly more difficult. That a learner's capacities diminish or are not fully attainable over time is richly attested in studies of specific domains of linguistic knowledge (Johnson & Newport, 1989, 1991; Larsen-Freeman & Long, 1991; Miyake & Shah, 1999; Strozer, 1994; Weber-Fox & Neville, 1996; Werker & Desjardins; 1995). However, certain abstract properties of L2 appear to be successfully acquired by the adult learner, even in the absence of transfer of L1 knowledge to the developing L2 system or explicit L2 instruction. For instance, adult learners frequently master complex L2 word orders while simultaneously exhibiting flawed knowledge of L2 tense verb markers or plural noun markers (Lardiere, 1998a, 1998b, 2000; Lightbown, 1983). The totality of studies have led many investigators to claim that adult L2 acquisition differs significantly from both the initial and the end states of L1 acquisition, although the exact reasons for these differences are by no means obvious (Hudson & Newport, 1999; Hudson-Kam & Newport, 2005; Hyltenstam & Abrahamsson, 2003; Ionin & Wexler, 2002; Sorace, 2003) and creolist studies (DeGraff, 1999, 2005; Lumsden, 1999; and comments in Winford, 2003).

Base Case: Sranan Tongo

Due to its relatively well-documented history, Sranan Tongo is adopted as the base case for the ABM. Sranan originated from the language contact situation with English, Dutch, and French settlers utilizing African slave labor on small Surinamese farms from 1600-1650. Roughly half of the European settlers in the community were British. By 1665, approximately 3,000 African-born slaves labored in the region, along with about 1,500 permanently installed European planters. A Dutch coup in 1667 caused a mass exodus of the majority of English colonists from Surinam; however it is not clear whether the slaves acquired by the British remained in the colony. More than 18,000 slaves were imported from 1680-1700, with similar importation rates occurring through the 19th century. The proportion of Africans to Europeans in Surinam rose from 2:1 in 1665 to 20:1 in 1744. Plantation numbers were routinely decimated from the slaves' short life expectancy, low birth rates, and escape. Healthy males were the preferred commodity of slave-traders (Kay, 1967), with males often outnumbering female slaves about 2:1. With such small numbers of females in the population and the high mortality among slaves, the slave populace was sustained through the constant influx of new African labor, rather than from natural growth. Precise information concerning European demographics, in particular non-African offspring, is murky and is absent in most studies on creole formation.

Linguistically, modern Sranan Tongo exhibits several typological properties found in other creoles: namely, highly impoverished verbal (inflectional) markers, such that the verb form is the same for all tenses, moods, and persons; marking of tense, mood, aspect, and negation expressed by pre-verbal particles, and fixed subject-verb-object word order in declarative and interrogative constructions:

1. Mi no ben si en. *"I did not see him."*

2. Psa te unu kaba nanga skoro dan wi o meki pikin nanga den sani dati.

    "Only when we finish with school, then we'll have kids and all those things."

3. Ma yu nelde yu mama dati wi e go prei bal?

    "But have you told your mom that we're going to play basketball?"

4. Dan te mi miti en mi sa aksi en.

    "Then when I see him I will ask him." (Winford, 2001, p. 1)

Sranan Tongo's superstrate language is essentially Early Modern English. Arends (1995) points to language families on the western African coast as forming Sranan's substrate. A primary substrate likely formed from early arrivals (1650-1720) with 50% of imported slaves speaking languages of the Gbe-cluster (Fon, Ewe), and

40% from Bantu languages (e.g., Kikongo). Slaves imported between 1720-1740 spoke mainly Gbe and Kwa from the Nyo-branch. African languages most likely contributing to post-1740 Sranan are Fon (and other closely related Gbe-languages), Kikongo, and Twi (in the Kwa group). The substrate influences were subject to frequent fluctuations, depending on the quantity and regional origins of slaves in the population at any given time. The linguistic environment appears to gradually become more homogeneous within a 75- to 90-year period, reflecting the prominence of the post-1740 African languages (Arends, 1995).

Degrees of social distance existed early on in the plantation, putting into place restricted social networks between various groups. Over time the plantations functioned as increasingly hierarchical organizations (Price & Price, 1992). In 17th and 18th century Surinam, the possibility of gaining access to the linguistic variety with the highest prestige would have been distributed differentially, rather than as an L2 model equally available for all slaves. Social stratification likely occurred along the following boundaries in the plantation: European versus African; older versus younger; elite slaves, including overseers and house slaves, versus field hands; and to a lesser extent, slave elite with diminished manual tasks versus highly skilled African craftsmen (Valdman, 2000).

Model Architecture

Environmental Specifications

The model implements the generic software platform SWARM (Swarm Development Group 1999-2003). The main components of the framework are specifications for the environment and agents, and local rules for the environment and the agents. The environment consists of the physical landscape, or search space, as the spatial boundaries of the model. The space is made up of a 50x50 square lattice that holds 2,500 slots. Agents are color-coded squares representing five different African and European populations, shown in Figure 1.

Environmental parameters informing population make-up are projected from Surinam's historical statistics (Arends, 1995, 1996). As presented in Table 2, a 2,500-person carrying capacity is specified as the *population limit rule*. Per Geggus (1999), no live births occur during the first 12 iterations of the model, as denoted under *delay Years*. Other population parameters represent historical records of social affiliations, such as: *master-to-slave* ratio in the plantation society, *high-status slave (i.e., houseslaves) ratio to low-status slave (fieldslaves)* ratio, *male-to-female slave* ratio, *child-to-adult* ratio in the total society, and the *percentage of fertile adults* in the general population. All adult agents specified as [+ fertile] have the same

Figure 1. World (population of agents) as 50 x 50 square lattice holding 2500 slots. Agents are color-coded squares representing five different African and European populations (Color-coding in this and subsequent figures has been removed for publication).

potential to "procreate" with adult interlocutors of the opposite sex. Reproductive success is then subject to the *newborn survival rate*, which regulates the number of live births in the plantation.

Language variables encoded as part of the agent's internal (cognitive) "environment," are summarized in Table 1. These parameters fall out from notions of the speaker's capacity for generating and analyzing linguistic structure, formally realized as a cognitive faculty for language (Chomsky, 1995, 2000, Chomsky et al., 2002; Jackendoff, 1997, 2002; Sharwood-Smith & Truscott, 2005). European *eWordmorpheme* and African *aWordmorpheme* parameters constitute ratios for word formation via morphemic stems and affixes. These ratios supply the maximum number grammatical affixes, such as verbal inflection or plural markers, permissible with a transmitted word stem. African languages are mapped three grammatical preverbal markers to every one word stem (DeGraff, 2002, 2005; Fabb, 1992). European languages map two grammatical affixes per word stem, based on Early Modern English data. In a linguistic exchange with another agent, newly encountered items are first stored in working memory (temporary memory buffer). (A linguistic exchange is defined as the transmission and receipt of an "utterance [string of words]." All exchanges are agent-to-agent.) The *Morpheme Learning Rates* regulate the maximum number of

Table 1. World parameters (environment profile). Model's parameterizable theoreti-cal and demographic constructs used to describe system. Refer to text for detailed discussion.

WORLD PARAMETER	ACTION	VALUE
WORLD SIZE	dimension of landscape	50
NUMBER OF AGENTS	initial number of inhabitants	750
POPULATION LIMIT	carrying capacity of world	2500
DROP ALLOWED	agents "removed" in 1 time-step	75
E-NEWBORN SURVIVAL	rate of survival for Euro infants	0.75
A-NEWBORN SURVIVAL	rate of survival for Afro infants	0.30
SLAVE HIGH-LOW RATIO	proportion hi to lo status slaves	0.50
MASTER-SLAVE RATIO	proportion slave-owners to slaves	0.05
MALE-FEMALE RATIO	proportion slaves: men to women	0.50
CHILD-ADULT RATIO	proportion children to adults	0.30
DELAY YEARS	time elapsed before childbirth	1.0
FERTILE ADULT %	adults able to procreate	0.56
LEXICON SIZE	elements stored in creole lexicon	1000
E-WORD-MORPHEME RATIO	maximum Euro-affixes transmitted with Euro-wordstem	2.0
A-WORD-MORPHEME RATIO	maximum Afro-affixes transmitted with Afro-wordstem	3.33
E-MORPHEME LEARNING RATE	maximum Euro-affixes put in working memory in 1 exchange	2.0
A-MORPHEME LEARNING RATE	maximum Afro-affixes put in working memory in 1 exchange	2.0
NUMBER OF E-MORPHEMES	maximum available and learnable Euro-affixes	50
NUMBER OF A-MORPHEMES	maximum available and learnable Afro-affixes	100
E-WORDFLOW	maximum items in Euro-utterance	20
A-WORDFLOW	maximum items in Afro-utterance	20
DISTRIBUTION OF AFRO LANGUAGES: RATIO 1	substrate language #1	0.50
DISTRIBUTION OF AFRO LANGUAGES: RATIO 2	substrate language #2	0.30
DISTRIBUTION OF AFRO LANGUAGES: RATIO 3	substrate language #3	0.15
DISTRIBUTION OF AFRO LANGUAGES: RATIO 4	substrate language #4	0.05
LENGTH OF A YEAR	time-steps = chronological year	12
NUMBER OF SLAVE INDICES	'tag' based on slave ethnic, linguistic, occupational features	3 digits: X-Y-Z

African or European grammatical markers deposited in working memory during any given exchange, whereas the *number of Morphemes* provides the upper bounds on the array of respective European and African grammatical markers available and learnable. The *lexiconSize* specifies the size of new word stems and affixes housed in the lexicon (long-term memory). On analogy with the resources posited in the language processing literature, the agents in the model store information in the lexicon only after a specific number of linguistic exchanges, when an item has been encountered repeatedly. *WordFlow* represents the maximum number of forms contained in an utterance in European (*eWordFlow*) or African (*aWordFlow*) languages, according to the word order typology of each language. A string between 1 and 20 items (stems and affixes) is randomly generated in the current ABM, based on the agent's linguistic and social background. Due to space considerations, outputs of *Wordflow* utterances will not be presented. These items are subsequently transmitted as an output string to other speakers during a linguistic exchange. The recipient of the utterance acquires information (i.e., analyzes as an input string whose units may, over time, be stored in the lexicon).

Chronology is included as a feature of the ABM. For each cycle of language interaction, one unit of time elapses. The hypothetical *Length of a Year* parameter is set at 12 iterations in the current program. While these time steps are abstractions, they

Figure 2. Population distribution over time based on documented stages in Surinam. Graph lines, from bottom to top: European population, Child population, Female population and Total plantation population (labels in original color-coded legend in this and subsequent figures are ordered differently than actual graph lines).

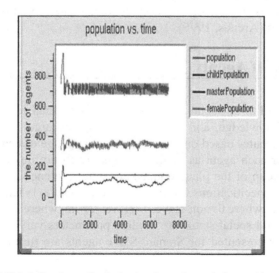

Figure 3. Age distribution at cycle 7000 in the model, based on historical demo-graphic data of Surinam described by Arends (1995).

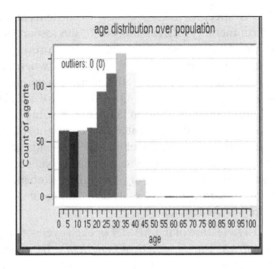

play an important role in identifying historical language contact benchmarks over a specified period. Likewise, Figure 2 illustrates population distribution over time, following the historical demographic range presented previously, as implemented in the model. Periodic oscillations correspond to historically recorded stages of decreased fertility and low birthrates followed by mass slave importation in Surinam. Figure 3 represents age distribution, as documented in real-world Surinam plantation societies (Arends, 1995).

Specifications of Agents

Agents are assumed to be social actors who have individual features, behavioral rules, linguistic knowledge, and language learning resources, as highlighted in Table 2. Fixed attributes based on gender, racial group, age of death, and so forth are designated for each agent as unique profiles. Each profile contributes to the demographic makeup of the plantation. Many states are encoded in binary (0,1) alphabet, based on specifications such as *sex*, where 0=male, 1=female; *dead* 0=no, 1=yes; *social class*, where 0=non-slave, 1=slave; *fertile*, where 0=no, 1=yes; etc.). Cultural identity and social status are flexible parameters varying over time, per historical statistics presented for Sranan. Slave agents are further monitored via

Table 2. Agent Profile parameters of individual features, linguistic knowledge and language learning resources. Attributes based on gender, racial group, age of death, parents, etc., are designated for each agent. Many states are encoded in binary alphabet. Refer to text for further discussion of parameters.

AGENT PARAMETER	ACTION	VALUE
ID	agent identification number	#1018
SEX	gender: 0=male, 1=female	0
SOCIAL CLASS	social status: 0=non-slave, 1=slave	1
AGE	"years of life":12 time-steps = 1 year	3.0
FERTILE	reproductive capability: 0=no, 1=yes	0
DEAD	mortality: 0=no, 1= yes	0
SLAVE INDEX	3 digit tag of ethno + linguistic background + occupation index	1-0-0
X	Agent #1018 location on X-axis	33
Y	Agent #1018 location on Y-axis	4
EURO LEXICON SIZE	items stored as European lexicon	0
AFRO LEXICON SIZE	items stored as African lexicon	0
EURO WORDFLOW	maximum items in Euro-utterance by Agent	20
AFRO WORDFLOW	maximum items in Afro-utterance by Agent	20
MOM CLASS	social status: Agent's mother	0
DAD CLASS	social status: Agent's father	1
MOM INDEX	occupation index: Agent's mother	0
DAD INDEX	occupation index: Agent's father	2
MOM EURO WORDFLOW	maximum items in Euro-utterance by Agent's mother, directed to Agent	0
MOM AFRO WORDFLOW	maximum items in Afro-utterance by Agent's mother, directed to Agent	0
DAD EURO WORDFLOW	maximum items in Euro-utterance by Agent's father, directed to Agent	6
DAD AFRO WORDFLOW	maximum items in Afro-utterance by Agent's father, directed to Agent	6

the *slaveIndex*, ethnolinguistic and social information in the form of a 3-digit "tag" similar to Axelrod's (1997) cultural chromosome. Adult slaves are assigned a status marker as part of the slave index based on their occupational roles in the plantation society. Overseers (index =1) have high occupational status among slaves, whereas house-slaves have an index of 2. Field hands and infirm slaves receive progressively lower indices. Slave-owners are categorized by 0.

Specification of Movement Rules

Movement functions provide the basis for language contact in the plantation. Agents are located in a specific slot, identifiable by ordered pairs of x-y coordinates. Inhabitants never overlap or occupy the same position in the community. Agents seek interlocutors, and thus indirectly "compete" to move through the search space, with agents of higher status having priority for movement over lower status agents. The fact that children receive the second highest movement preference is based on historical accounts (e.g., Blassingame, 1972, p. 96; Ochs, 1996) that (slave) children were typically not as confined as the adult slaves, and until about age 10 were freer to roam about the plantation setting. Movement is executed when an agent moves to the closest unoccupied cell that also has neighboring agents. The current model allows for a maximum of four surrounding neighbors at the north, south, east, and west slots, following the formal conception of Von Neumann neighborhoods. Access is restricted to receiving linguistic information from higher status neighbors, so while an agent can potentially participate in exchanges with four neighbors in a given learning cycle, she may conceivably be limited to one exchange if no other neighbors are "acceptable" in that particular learning cycle.

Specification of Agent-Interaction Rules

Linguistic exchange allows for processing and acquisition of the input languages to which agents are exposed, contingent on individual cognitive resources and social factors. Due to the range of possible linguistic encounters, the agent may form novel linguistic patterns that he/she subsequently transmits to others; alternatively, he/she may transmit their existing L1 or L2 structures. The adaptive nature of the CAS is such that neither the selections made by the agents, nor the overall results are necessarily predictable: the agent's internal-language can undergo drastic changes based on the outcomes of random exchanges. An individual's grammar may eventually be adopted as the external-language of the collective population through multiple, autonomous interactions of individual agents.

Experimental System

Hypothesis

The experimental parameters that make up this particular ABM can be manipulated in many ways; however, the specific purpose of this inquiry is to test two current proposals of creole formation, adhering closely to the criteria advanced in the respective L1 and L2 theories. Regardless of the theory implemented, if a creole grammar emerges in either case, it is predicted to exhibit structures simplistically termed *"prototypical creole effects,"* as observed in modern Sranan. Such properties observable as the output of the ABM should minimally include: subject-verb-object word order, a largely European (English) *superstrate* vocabulary, and African language *substrates* in the form of (limited) inflectional particles and markers.

Experiment I: "Imperfect L2 Hypothesis"

Background

Standard creolist references portray L2 acquisition along a continuum in which creole grammar constitutes "imperfect" L2 learning, as it is considered the outcome of adult L2 acquisition under unusual social circumstances, producing a new L2 grammar over the span of several generations (e.g., Chaudenson, 1995; Gross, 2000; Singler, 1996; Thomason & Kaufman, 1988). Shortcomings in L2 attainment are attributed directly to the quality, quantity, and context of linguistic data available to the learner; and indirectly to the cognitive resources of the adult language learner himself/herself. Due to the non-normative living conditions under which many creoles surface, child populations are assumed peripheral to creole development, even to the degree that they would presumably interact with and affect adult L2 acquisition. Arends (1995, p. 268), among others, calculates that the presence of children was statistically inconsequential (consistently less than 20%) in early Surinam. Consequently, child language is claimed to have no enduring structural effect on emerging creoles such as Sranan, at best contributing only in the subsequent regularization of a formed creole grammar (Winford, 2003, p. 356).

Method

To explore the L2 hypothesis, the basic context of "imperfect" adult L2 acquisition is reconstructed. Monolingual adults exclusively make up the community of language learners, with child language learners (11 years and younger) absent from this contact scenario. A rigid social hierarchy simultaneously constrains African slaves' access to Europeans and to the actual superstrate targets. Adult (age-related) L2 acquisition capabilities such as limited acquisition of L2 inflectional markers are encoded as general specifications, while the population control mechanism extinguishes the possible appearance of locally born children. Population size is stabilized via regular influxes of adult African slaves, randomly appearing every 240-300 time-step intervals, on analogy with historical occurrences. The model's demographic and environmental properties are initialized. Adults receive their specific agent profiles and are distributed into the artificial society. Contacts occur through the movement rule. Regardless of closeness of proximity, the neighbors must be "socially eligible" for linguistic exchange: higher status agents transmit to those of lower status. The following learning algorithm is implemented: agent A transmits an initial utterance to her adult neighbor, agent B. If an item in agent A's utterance is not found in the current lexicon of neighbor agent B, B will then add the new element to her working memory, contingent on the social and linguistic constraints outlined. If agent B receives an utterance from adult agent C and encounters the new word again, agent B will add this new item to her lexicon (long-term memory). Thus, a critical assumption is that statistical frequency plays a role in the language learning process (Hudson-Kam & Newport, 2005; Saffran, Aslin, & Newport, 1996). The initial cycle ends and the algorithm can be repeated for any number of iterations. The outcome of this experiment is based on agent activity spanning 7,000 iterations.

Results

Figures 4 and 5 represent the local level, the internal-language of an average adult inhabitant in the population, where the average speaker is statistically an adult male field slave. "Screenshots" of the average lexicon along any given point in the experiment are shown. Figure 4 illustrates the composite of European- and African-language words across time. (Fon is represented in the key on the right-hand side of the graph as *"average number of A-words"* to denote its high demographic status among African-languages. Words/stems from Kikongo are represented as *"average number of B-words."* The *"average number of C-words,"* represents Twi. The category *"other African-words"* is representative of minority African languages.) After the initial 1-2 generations, the average adult speaker possesses a small amount of L2 vocabulary. This state is represented nearly exclusively by African languages, with little influence from European elements. The average number of European words steadily declines from approximately 50 words/stems in an average lifetime (e.g., t_0 to t_{500} iterations).

Figure 5 highlights the average adult's store of inflectional (grammatical) markers. The top-most line signals the inventory of African-languages markers/particles, shown initially to be slightly less than 100 items across all African languages.

Figure 4. European- and African-language words in average adult's lexicon across time. Fon (top line) is "average number of A-words" to denote its high demographic status among African-languages. Words/stems from Kikongo (second line from top) are "average number of B-words". "Average number of C-words," represents Twi (third line from top). Category 'other African-words' (second line from bottom) represents minority African languages. Number of European words (bottom line) declines over time in average adult lexicon.

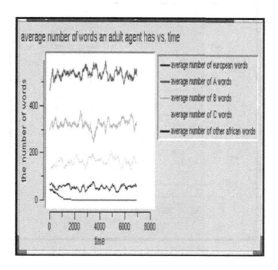

There is evidence that the adult can acquire inflectional information since only after 500-1,000 cycles, the knowledge of African-based markers reaches its maximum, indicating adult L2 acquisition of inflectional affixes. This value remains constant at 100 markers. In the same time span, the number of European (English) inflectional affixes in the internal-language decreases to zero.

Figures 6 and 7 represent external-language within the adult "imperfect L2" context, demonstrating structures acquired across the general population. These graphs also reflect the input to which L2 adults in the environment would be potentially exposed at any given time. Figure 6 shows the quantities of vocabulary acquired across the total population. In the initial time steps, Fon items are acquired with the highest frequency across the community. The global rate is reported at 250-350 words learned per cycle in this experiment, as compared to the average individual inventory (Figure 4) with 400-500 L2 items in Fon. The collective L2 lexicon emerging in the

Figure 5. Average adult's store of inflectional markers. Topmost line signals L2 inventory of African-languages markers, shown initially to be slightly less than 100 items across all African languages. Adult acquires inflectional information for 500-1000 cycles, when knowledge of African-based markers reaches its maximum. Number of European (English) L2 inflectional affixes acquired (lower line) decreases to zero for average adult.

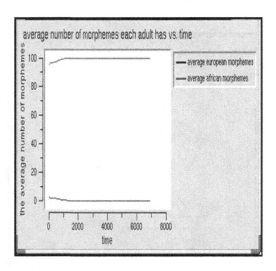

community is smaller, yet all languages in the contact setting initially contribute. After 500 time steps, Fon and Kikongo words/stems are learned at nearly equivalent rates by the general population. At t_{1000}, the frequency of Fon words acquired shows minimal gains, then drops substantially while Kikongo remains stable across all speakers. Fon eventually regains dominance (likely owing to the periodical influx of slaves). European words/stems emerge early within the population, but disappear beginning in cycle 1,500.

Figure 7 charts the population-wide acquisition of English and African language inflection over time. Two lines are actually superimposed, yet appear in the graph as a single "flat" line given their equivalent values. The non-activity of this graph indicates that L2 acquisition of African or European (English) inflectional items into the external-language of the general plantation does not occur, even while certain individual adults may acquire L2 inflection, as demonstrated in Figure 5. A similar pattern has been documented in real world pidgin languages. We will return to further discussion of these points shortly.

Figure 6. Vocabulary items acquired across total adult population. In initial time steps, Fon items (A-words and top range of graph) are acquired with highest frequency. Collective L2 lexicon emerging is small, yet all languages in contact setting initially contribute. European words/stems (bottom left corner of graph only) emerge early within adult-only population, but disappear beginning in cycle 1500.

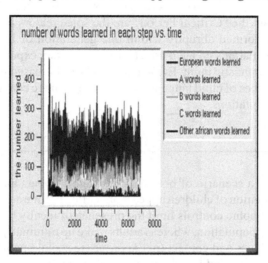

Figure 7. Number of English and African language inflectional morphemes acquired by the total adult population over time. Both lines are at 0, indicating that while some morphemes may be acquired by certain individuals (as shown in Figure 5), there are no African or European (English) inflectional items that are learned through L2 acquisition processes by the entire adult population of the plantation.

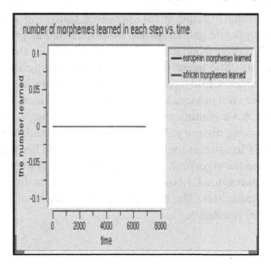

Experiment II: "Language Bioprogram Hypothesis"

Background

The LBH advanced by Bickerton (1984) and others operates under the premise that young children within the "Critical Period" are the sole creators of creoles, and as a result, creoles are formed abruptly within one generation of L1 speakers. The idea is that child populations create a novel L1 system when exposed to chaotic or degenerate primary linguistic input. Evidence for the LBH is based in large measure on synchronic L1 studies of child language and multi-language contact in early 20th century Hawaiian plantations.

Method

The LBH constitutes a scenario of both children (age 11 years and younger) and adults. The first population of children appears only after 12 time steps of interacting adult agents. Demographic controls limit the presence of locally born children to a 16% maximum of the population, whereas adults make up minimally 84%. A regular influx of imported slaves and contact (per appropriate social hierarchies) between neighboring agents further add to the dynamic population properties. Linguistic mechanisms (e.g., processing and acquiring elements for the lexicon) are maximally operative for child L1 acquisition, but are constrained for adults with respect to acquisition of L2 grammatical inflection markers. The language-learning algorithm operates as follows: the model is initialized by generating a diverse population of monolingual European and African adults for the plantation environment. Contact is then instantiated via the movement rule and is carried out in the same manner as in Experiment I. In contrast to Experiment I however, following 12 learning cycles, interacting agents of opposite genders when both specified as [+fertile], may also produce offspring. Children from unions begin to appear in the environment. A surviving child, such as child agent (a), can enter into a linguistic exchange with any agent 5 years or older. Child agent (a) receives an utterance from adult agent AA. Child agent (a) does not possess any items in his/her lexicon and consequently, stores the words from AA's utterance as separate components, as stems and grammatical affixes, in working memory. As vocabulary is accumulated, it will eventually pass to the child's long-term memory of the lexicon. This language-learning cycle is completed, and the algorithm can be repeated for any number of iterations. As the child agent matures, the L1 child acquisition resources diminish and will be replaced by L2 adult capacities. The outcome of this experiment is based on agent activity spanning 7,000 iterations.

Results

Screenshots of the average lexicon are shown in Figures 8 and 9, representing the local level, the internal-language of an average adult inhabitant in the population. The average speaker is statistically a locally born adult male field slave. Figure 8 illustrates the composite of European- and African-language words (stems) in the individual's lexicon over time. At approximately t_{500}, the average internal-language word inventory exhibits an across-the-board increase. While the average adult still maintains an amalgam of African-language items, there is an incremental increase of European-language items. From the onset of contact, Fon (A-language) and Kikongo (B-language) constitute the majority of vocabulary items in the average adult lexicon, with European (English) elements growing to third place over time. The category of *"average number of other African words,"* is gradually overtaken by the rising number of European (English) words.

Figure 9 highlights internal-language over time of an average adult's knowledge of inflectional (grammatical) markers. The average individual shows full knowledge of African-language inflections within the first few time steps. While the strong knowledge of African-based markers remains constant over time, the number of European-inflectional affixes in the internal-language increases rapidly to its near maximal level by approximately 500 cycles. The result is that an average adult in

Figure 8. Composite of European- and African-language words (stems) in average individual's lexicon over time. Incremental increase of European-language items (darkest line, third from the top) occurs, while average individual maintains amalgam of African-language items (all other lines in graph).

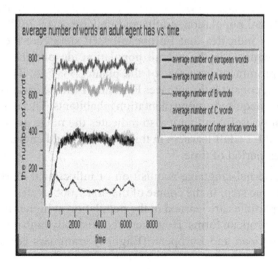

Figure 9. Average individual's knowledge of inflectional markers. Individual shows full knowledge of African-language inflections (top line) within first time-steps. Number of European inflectional affixes (lower line) increases to near maximal level by 500 cycles. Average adult in this setting comes to possess complete knowledge of both African-language- and English-based inflectional verb paradigms, reflecting a feature of bilingualism.

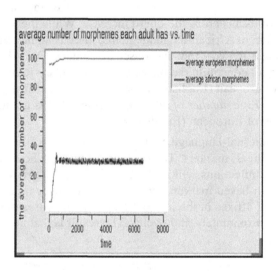

this setting comes to possess an internal-language with complete knowledge of both African-language- and English-based inflectional verb paradigms.

Figure 10 monitors the macro-level, or external-language, vocabulary acquisition process across the total population, adults and children over 7,000 cycles. At t_{500}, robust graph activity indicates that European-based stems are the most frequent vocabulary items acquired in the overall population, despite the presence of the more statistically prominent language of the plantation, Fon. The acquisition of European vocabulary consistently outpaces Fon and all other African-language stems in terms of quantities acquired among plantation inhabitants. This external-language information is doubly useful in that it also indicates the range of vocabulary input that L1 children and L2 adult learners in this context would encounter in the community at any given period of time.

Figure 11 charts external-language acquisition of inflectional markers across the population at each time step. In the course of the first 1,000 cycles, the African-language inflectional particles are learned in the population at higher frequencies than the corresponding European forms. However, a consistently high rate of inflectional learning for both African and European (English) grammars is illustrated in the

Figure 10. Vocabulary acquisition across total population of adults and children over 7000 cycles. At t_{500}, European-based stems (prominent dark area) are most frequent vocabulary items acquired in overall population, and their acquisition consistently outpaces all African-language stems in quantities acquired among plantation inhabitants.

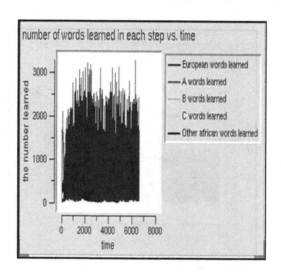

population over time. As an indicator of external-language knowledge of grammatical affixes at any given period in the population, Figure 11 also provides some insight into the type of inflectional features that L1 children and incoming L2 adult learners encounter on average as linguistic input in the plantation setting. From a perspective of language acquisition, the situation is interesting, since a community of speakers equipped with knowledge of two stable inflectional systems can potentially transmit competing or highly redundant grammatical data in communicative encounters. These issues receive further elaboration in the following section.

Discussion

Based on criteria of the "imperfect L2 acquisition" hypothesis in Experiment I, the ABM outcomes did not result in a creole language with the *"prototypical creole effects* (e.g., subject-verb-object word order, a largely European [English] *superstrate,*

Figure11. Acquisition of inflectional markers across total population of adults and children over time. African-language inflectional markers (shown as slightly brighter color on top) initially are learned at higher frequencies than European forms (darker color on bottom). After initial 1000 cycles, a consistently high rate of inflectional learning for both African and European grammars occurs over time, reflecting an aspect of societal bilingualism.

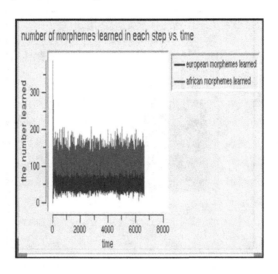

and African language *substrates* in the form of [limited] inflectional particles and markers)" on par with Sranan structures. However, a new L2 form spontaneously surfaces as the external-language in the ABM plantation in this context. Comparing internal- and external-language outcomes in Experiment I, the average individual's L2 lexicon is relatively larger and more "complex (i.e., containing more vocabulary items and inflections)" than that of the general population. For several reasons, however, the internal-language state falls short of being an emergent creole: (1) the number of words stored in the L2 Internal-language lexicon on average is scant; (2) no discernible change in the general pattern of substrate versus superstrate vocabulary storage arises over time; and (3) substantial feature expansion (e.g., further acquisition of grammatical markers) does not materialize. Preliminarily, the resulting internal-language structures most resemble an African-based pidgin, based on the reduced quantity of L2 vocabulary present. However, the availability of L1 inflection may qualify more as a type of stable expanded pidgin that has emerged as the "L2" grammar used by the average plantation inhabitant when he/she is not communicating in their native tongue. The external-language clearly exhibits prototypical pidgin characteristics, since the vocabulary is quite limited and concurrently, no inflection exists. The vocabulary consists of a subset of items shared across the total population. While this pidgin—as most pidgins—emerges abruptly (within 24 cycles), it is quite stable. All told, an interesting dynamic unfolds between the relatively "sophisticated" internal L2 knowledge of the average speaker, which includes a scant acquisition of L2 inflectional markers, and the pared down external L2 repertoire with no inflection which arises in the overall population. Of particular note is the rapid diffusion and stability of the pidgin variety throughout the general population.

Turning to Experiment II, contrary to LBH claims, these outcomes do not demonstrate that children are the lone vehicles of (Sranan) creole formation, with little or no intervention from adults. Nor do Experiment II results uphold any claim that children must have existed in large numbers in the population (per Bickerton, 1984). However, preliminary findings of the ABM do illustrate that when children age 11 years and younger make up between 15%-16% of the total population, plantation outcomes towards creole formation are significantly increased. Both internal- and external-language data indicate that individual and societal vocabularies on average undergo a transformation from a small quantity of knowledge that is purely African language based to knowledge that doubles over time to a robust, yet still unstable, amalgam of European superstrate and African-substrate items. Additional evidence for this conclusion is that the earliest signs of expansion required for creole formation are never attested in the first 12 cycles of the plantation's existence, when adults are the sole inhabitants. Rather, the process begins at a point when locally born children of the plantation have been present for several cycles and a small mass of younger agents is taking root. Despite the child agent's innate and relatively powerful language acquisition resources, the LBH claim that creole languages develop abruptly within a single generation of child speakers is never corroborated in the current agent-based model. The ABM consistently reflects "prototypical creole effects," which emerge at a gradual rate. Moreover, the ABM data suggest that individuals with creolized vocabulary patterns also exhibit complete and stable knowledge of both African and European (English) inflectional systems. Since there is no overlap or impending loss of either inflectional paradigm, this mental state arguably resembles a bilingual acquisition scenario (Bhatia & Ritchie, 1999; Hamers & Blanc, 2001). Following Sebba (1997, p. 179), it is reasonable to assume that children in plantation settings spoke two L1s: one as the evolving creole, and the other that reflects their caregivers' native language. Insofar as individual "bilingual" competence correlates with community-wide creole formation over time, these preliminary findings provide new insights for creole language development in certain contexts. The ABM opens the door for in-depth research on questions of the young child's (inherent) capacity to acquire two or more languages with relative ease. To the extent that a language bioprogram exists, it may best conceptualized as an expansive blueprint toward bilingualism, rather than its present formulation as a "universal" (monolingual) grammar.

Conclusion

The current study represents preliminary stages of research which examine underlying cognitive and social mechanisms in real-world language acquisition by utilizing the CAS approach. This work illustrates that it is possible to reconstruct historical contexts in the investigation of language emergence and development. Large-scale effects were produced in the plantation domain as populations of agents interacted and adapted locally in various ways within a CAS environment. Based on micro-specifications of agents, the environment, and rules of behavior in the model, innovative macro-structures and collective behaviors were generated in the system. Thus, the emergent property of the CAS—in this case, of growing linguistic structures in the computer is achieved in the present study.

Possible criticisms of the CAS framework could include the notion that such models are path dependent, in that the results are shaped by the precise initial conditions chosen. However, this assessment obviously does not hold for experiments carried out in the current study. As demonstrated by the unexpected, yet sound, outcomes of the African-based pidgin in Experiment I and bilingualism in Experiment II, with a CAS it is not trivial, and sometimes it is impossible to determine what behavior will be generated, even with relatively simple CAS such as cellular automata (Wolfram, 2002).

Regarding implementation of ABM, it must be acknowledged that while principled and valid results were obtained with the model, the findings do not closely mirror the base case output of Sranan Tongo. Given that parameters are not inherent properties of the system to be modeled, but rather theoretical constructs used by the researcher to describe the system, it may be the case that the model's parameters require further refinement and manipulation in order to generate a matching outcome that closely corresponds to the real-world system. For instance, the present ABM's moment rule implies that physical distance is directly related to social interaction, such that the rule sets the stage for interaction only between bordering neighbors, as close proximity is viewed as a logical, though no doubt overly simplistic, prerequisite for linguistic encounters. Despite these close encounters, neighbors in the model do not blindly interact as might be predicted; rather, social factors also constrain contact. Secondly, to the extent that identification of the "closest unoccupied cell" is a dynamical process in the model, an agent may randomly cover both large and small distances of the plantation. With each movement, the agent potentially encounters a broad diversity of new neighbors whose distribution in the space may not necessarily be accurate in a historical sense.

Another interpretation is that the results of the experiments do not correspond to the "real system" because fundamental assumptions driving the "imperfect L2 hypothesis" and the LBH themselves may be flawed. In this case, modifications that do not adhere so closely to these particular frameworks could be tested in multiple models and would feasibly yield different results. Specific variations could include:

- making linguistic exchanges have direct effects on agents' movement and its outcomes, instead of indirectly through social contact;
- "importing" other types of agents (e.g., European immigrants rather than exclusively

  African slaves);
- making it possible for individual adult agents to possess variable L2 learning capacities and individualized learning algorithms; or
- allowing the agents to acquire linguistic information from lower-status neighbors under certain circumstances.

Finally, other dimensions of creole formation remain to be addressed in the current model. Future directions can be envisioned regarding both the modeling framework and its extended applications. Linguistically, the current framework was kept relatively simple and abstract to highlight only grammatical aspects of creole formation. The most obvious extensions to the framework concern questions of additional linguistic domains (incorporating sound and meaning modules into the learners' language faculty) to add to the realism of the language acquisition processes. Ideally, the model should also be adaptable to other historic language contact scenarios and language combinations. Lastly, demographic factors must be fine-tuned to include more historical facts of African and European populations and to pinpoint those "critical mass" conditions necessary for triggering individual and population-wide creole emergence over time.

References

Arends, J. (1992). Towards a gradualist model of creolization. In F. Byrne & J. Holm (Eds.), *Atlantic meets Pacific* (pp. 371-380). Amsterdam: John Benjamins.

Arends, J. (1995). The socio-historical background of creoles. In J. Arends, P. Muysken, & N. Smith (Eds.), *Pidgins and creoles: An introduction* (pp. 15-24). Amsterdam: John Benjamins.

Arends, J. (1996). Demographic factors in the formation of Sranan. In J.Arends (Ed.), *The early stages of creolization* (pp. 233-245). Amsterdam: John Benjamins.

Arends, J., Muysken, J., & Smith, N. (Eds.). (1995). *Pidgins and creoles: An introduction*. Amsterdam: John Benjamins.

Axelrod, R. (1997). *The complexity of cooperation*. Princeton, NJ: Princeton University Press.

Bartlett, M., & Kazakov, D. (2004). The role of environmental structure in multi-agent simulations of language evolution. In *Proceedings of the Fourth Symposium on Adaptive Agents and Multi-Agent Systems* (AAMAS-4), AISB convention. Leeds, UK.

Bickerton, D. (1981). *Roots of language*. Ann Arbor, MI: Karoma.

Bickerton, D. (1984). The language bioprogram hypothesis. *Behavioral and Brain Sciences, 7,* 212-218.

Bickerton, D. (1988). Creole languages and the bioprogram. In F. Newmeyer (Ed.), *Linguistics: The Cambridge survey* (pp. 267-284). Cambridge, UK: Cambridge University Press.

Bhatia, T., & Ritchie, W. (1999). The bilingual child: Some issues and perspectives. In W. Ritchie & T. Bhatia (Eds.), *Handbook of child language acquisition* (pp. 569-643). New York: Academic Press.

Blassingame, J. (1972). *The slave community*. New York: Oxford University Press.

Bradbury, R. (2002). Futures, predictions and other foolishness. In M. Janssen (Ed.), *Complexity and ecosystem management: The theory and practice of multi-agentsystems*. Cheltenham, UK: Edward Elgar.

Braun, M., & Plag, I. (2003). How transparent is creole morphology? A study of early Sranan word-formation. In G. Booij & J. Van Marle (Eds.), *Yearbook of morphology 2002* (pp. 81-104). Dordrecht, The Netherlands: Kluwer.

Briscoe, T. (2000). Grammatical acquisition: Inductive bias and coevolution of language and the language acquisition device. *Language, 76*(2), 245-296.

Briscoe, T. (2002). Grammatical acquisition and linguistic selection. In T. Briscoe (Ed.), *Linguistic evolution through language acquisition: Formal and computational models* (pp. 255-300). Cambridge, UK: Cambridge University Press.

Burton, R., & Obel, B. (1995). The validity of computational models in organization science: From model realism to purpose of the model. *Computational and Mathematical Organization Theory, 1*(1), 57-71.

Chaudenson, R. (1992). *Des îles, des hommes, des habues*. Paris: L'Harmattan.

Chaudenson, R. (1995). *Les Créoles*. Paris: Presses Universitaires France.

Chomsky, N. (1995). *The minimalist program*. Cambridge, MA: MIT Press.

Chomsky, N. (2000). Minimalist inquiries: The framework. In R. Martin, D. Michaels, & J. Uriagereka (Eds.), *Step by step: Essays in Minimalist syntax in honor of Howard Lasnik* (pp. 89-155). Cambridge, MA: MIT Press.

Chomsky, N., Belletti, A., & Rizzi, L. (2002). *On nature and language.* Cambridge, UK: Cambridge University Press.

Culicover, P., & Nowak, A. (2002). Markedness, antisymmetry, and complexity of constructions. In P. Pica, & J. Rooryck (Eds.), *Variation yearbook.* Amsterdam: John Benjamins.

DeGraff, M. (1999). Creolization, language change and language acquisition: A Prolegomenon. In M. DeGraff (Ed.), *Language creation and language change* (pp. 1-46). Cambridge, MA: MIT Press.

DeGraff, M. (2002). Relexification: A reevaluation. *Anthropological Linguistics, 44*(4), 321-414.

DeGraff, M. (2005). Morphology and word order in "creolization" and beyond. In G. Cinque & R. Kayne (Eds.), *The Oxford handbook of comparative syntax* (pp. 293-372). Oxford, UK: Oxford University Press.

Epstein, J., & Axtell, R. (1996). *Growing artificial societies.* Cambridge, MA: MIT Press/Brookings Institute.

Fabb, N. (1992). Reduplication and object movement in Ewe and Fon. *Journal of African Languages and Linguistics, 13,* 1-41.

Ferber, J. (1998). *Multi-agent systems.* Harlow, England: Addison-Wesley.

Fox-Keller, E. (2002). *Making sense of life: Explaining biological development with models, metaphors, and machines.* Cambridge, MA: Harvard University Press.

Geggus, D. (1999). The sugar plantation zones of Saint Domingue and the revolution of 1791-1793. *Slavery & Abolition, 20,* 31-46.

Gross, D. (2000). When two become one: Creating a composite grammar in creole formation. *International Journal of Bilingualism, 4*(1), 59-80.

Hamers, J., & Blanc, M. (2001). *Bilinguality and bilingualism* (2nd ed.). Cambridge, UK: Cambridge University Press.

Holland, J. (1998). *Emergence: From chaos to order.* Reading, MA: Addison-Wesley.

Holm, J. (2000). *An introduction to pidgins and creoles.* Cambridge, UK: Cambridge University Press.

Hudson, C., & Newport, E. (1999). Creolization: Could adults really have done it all? In A. Greenhill, H. Littlefield, & C. Tano (Eds.), *Proceedings of the Boston University Conference on Language Development, 23*(1), 265-276. Somerville, MA: Cascadilla Press.

Hudson-Kam, C., & Newport, E. (2005). Regularizing unpredictable variation: The roles of adult and child learners in language formation and change. *Language Learning and Development, 1*(2), 151-195.

Hyltenstam, K., & Abrahamsson, N. (2003). Maturational constraints in second language acquisition. In C. Doughty & M. Long (Eds.), *The handbook of second language acquisition* (pp. 538-588). Oxford, UK: Blackwell.

Ionin, T., & Wexler, K. (2002). Why is "is" easier than "-s"? Acquisition of tense/agreement morphology by child L2-English learners. *Second Language Research, 18*(2), 95-136.

Jackendoff, R. (1997). *The architecture of the language faculty*. Cambridge, MA: MIT Press.

Jackendoff, R. (2002). *Foundations of language*. Oxford, UK: Oxford University Press.

Johnson, J., & Newport, E. (1989). Critical period effects in second language learning: The influence of maturational state on the acquisition of ESL. *Cognitive Psychology, 21,* 60-99.

Johnson, J., & Newport, E. (1991). Critical period effects on universal properties of language: The status of subjacency in the acquisition of a second language. *Cognition, 39,* 215-258.

Kay, F. (1967). *The shameful trade.* NJ: A.S. Barnes & Company.

Kirby, S. (1999). *Function, selection and innateness: The emergence of language universals.* Oxford, UK: Oxford University Press.

Lardiere, D. (1998a). Case and tense in the "fossilized" steady-state. *Second Language Research, 14,* 1-26.

Lardiere, D. (1998b.) Dissociating syntax from morphology in a divergent L2 end-state grammar. *Second Language Research, 14,* 359-375.

Lardiere, D. (2000). Mapping features to forms in second language acquisition. In J. Archibald (Ed.), *Second language acquisition and linguistic theory* (pp. 102-129). Oxford, UK: Blackwell.

Larsen-Freeman, D., & Long, M. (1991). *An introduction to second language acquisition research.* London: Longman.

Lenneberg, E. (1967). *Biological foundation of language.* New York: Wiley Press.

Lightbown, P. (1983). Exploring relationships between developmental and instructional sequences in L2 acquisition. In H. Seliger & M. Long (Eds.), *Classroom oriented research in second language acquisition* (pp. 217-245). Rowley, MA: Newbury House.

Lumsden, J. (1999). Language acquisition and creolization. In M. DeGraff (Ed.), *Language creation and language change* (pp. 129-158). Cambridge, MA: MIT Press.

Migge, B. (1998). Substrate influence on creole formation: The origin of *give*-type serial verb constructions in the Surinamese plantation creole. *Journal of Pidgin and Creole Language, 13*(2), 215-266.

Migge, B. (2000). The origin of the syntax and semantics of property items in Surinamese plantation creole. In J. McWhorter (Ed.), *Language change and language contact in pidgins and creoles* (pp. 201-234). Amsterdam: John Benjamins.

Miyake, A., & Shah, P. (Eds.). (1999). *Models of working memory.* Cambridge, UK: Cambridge University Press.

Mufwene, S. (1996). The founder principle in creole genesis. *Diachronica, 13,* 83-134.

Mühlhäusler, P. (1997). *Pidgin and creole linguistics.* London: University of Westminister Press.

Ochs, E. (1996). Linguistic resources for socializing humanity. In J. Gumperz & S. Levinson (Eds.), *Rethinking linguistic relativity* (pp. 407-438). Cambridge, UK: Cambridge University Press.

Price, R., & Price, S. (1992). *Stedman's Surinam: Life in eighteenth-century slave society.* Baltimore, MD: Johns Hopkins University Press.

Saffran, J., Aslin, R., & Newport, E. (1996). Statistical learning by 8-month old infants. *Science, 274,* 1926-1928.

Satterfield, T. (1999a). The shell game: Why children never lose. *Syntax, 2*(1), 28-37.

Satterfield, T. (1999b). *Bilingual selection of syntactic knowledge.* Dordrecht, The Netherlands: Kluwer.

Satterfield, T. (2001). Toward a sociogenetic solution: Examining language formation processes through SWARM modeling. *Social Science Computer Review, 19*(3), 281-295.

Satterfield, T. (2005a). The bilingual bioprogram: Evidence for child bilingualism in the formation of creoles. In J. Cohen, K. McAlister, K. Rolstad, & J. MacSwan (Eds.), *Proceedings of the 4th International Symposium on Bilingualism* (pp. 1070-1090). Somerville, MA: Cascadilla Press.

Satterfield, T. (2005b). It takes a(n) (agent-based) village: Peer commentary article to Steels & Belpaeme. *Behavioral and Brain Sciences, 28,* 506-507, 522-523.

Satterfield, T. (in press). Back to nature or nurture: Using computer models in creole genesis research. In R. Eckardt, G. Jäger, & T. Veenstra (Eds), *Language evolution: Cognitive and cultural factors.* Amsterdam: Mouton de Gruyter.

Sebba, M. (1997). *Contact languages: Pidgins and creoles*. New York: St. Martin's Press.

Seuren, P. (2001). *A view of language*. Oxford, UK: Oxford University Press.

Sharwood-Smith, M., & Truscott, J. (2005). Stages or continua in second language acquisition: A MOGUL solution. *Applied Linguistics, 26,* 219-240.

Singler, J. (1996). Theories of creole genesis, sociohistorical considerations, and the evaluation of evidence: The case of Haitian creole and the relexification hypothesis. *Journal of Pidgins and Creole Languages, 11,* 185-230.

Sorace, A. (2003). Near-nativeness. In C. Doughty & M. Long (Eds.), *The handbook of second language acquisition* (pp. 130-151). Oxford, UK: Blackwell.

Strozer, J. (1994). *Language acquisition after puberty.* Washington, DC: Georgetown University Press.

Steels, L. (1997). The synthetic modeling of language origins. *Evolution of Communication Journal 1*(1), 1-34. Amsterdam: John Benjamins.

Thomason, S., & Kaufman, T. (1988). *Language contact, creolization, and genetic linguistics*. Berkeley, CA: University of California Press.

Thomason, S. (1997). A typology of contact languages. In A. Spears & D. Winford (Eds.), *The structure and status of pidgins and creoles* (pp. 71-88). Amsterdam: John Benjamins.

Thomason, S. (2001). *Language contact: An introduction.* Washington, DC: Georgetown University Press.

Valdman, A. (2000). Creole, the language of slavery. In D. Kadish (Ed.), *Slavery in the Caribbean francophone world* (pp. 143-163). Athens, GA: University of Georgia Press.

Van den Berg, M. (2000). *"Mi no sal tron tongo": Early Sranan in court records 1667-1767.* Unpublished masters thesis, University of Nijmegen, The Netherlands.

Weber-Fox, C., & Neville, H. (1996). Maturational constraints on functional specializations for language processing: ERP and behavioral evidence in bilingual speakers. *Journal of Cognitive Neuroscience, 8,* 231-256.

Werker, J., & Desjardins, R. (1995). Listening to speech in the first year of life: Experiential influences on phoneme perception. *Current Directions in Psychological Sciences, 4*(3), 76-81.

Winford, D. (2000). Tense and aspect in Sranan and the creole prototype. In J. McWhorter (Ed.), *Language change and language contact in pidgins and creoles* (pp. 383-442). Amsterdam: John Benjamins.

Winford, D. (2001). Workshop at the MLK Linguistics Colloquium, University of Michigan.

Winford, D. (2003). *An introduction to contact linguistics*. Oxford, UK: Black-well.

Wolfram, S. (2002). *A new kind of science*. Wolfram Media.

Chapter VII

The Intelligence of Rumors:
A Cross-Methodological Approach to Social Belief Dynamics

Paolo Turrini, University of Siena, Italy

Mario Paolucci, Institute for Cognitive Science and Technology (ISTC/CNR), Italy

Rosaria Conte, Institute for Cognitive Science and Technology (ISTC), Italy

Abstract

This chapter presents a theory of reputation seen as the result of evaluation spreading in a multi-agent system (MAS). In particular the capacities of agents that spread reputation have been analyzed and decomposed in their atomic parts (pragmatic, memetic, epistemic). For each decision we state and verify several claims, using the methodologies that allowed best to capture the relevant aspects of the theoretical statements. Our major claim is that only when considering agents' architectures and roles it is possible to find out which regulatory patterns cannot emerge. Reputation is argued to be no exception to this rule. Therefore, in order to interact with each other, agents need evaluation concerning which partner to choose. We will describe how by using various kinds of methodologies that account for theory fragments a coherent picture can be observed and how interdisciplinary can help to account for complex intelligent phenomena among adaptive social systems.

Introduction

The topic of our study is social reputation, seen as a fundamental mechanism for the diffusion and evolution of normative behavior in a complex adaptive system (see also Coleman, 1990; Dunbar, 1996; Merry, 1984; Milgrom & Roberts, 1992; Yamagishi & Matsuda , 2002).

We propose a definition of reputation as socially transmitted higher level beliefs concerning properties of agents, namely, their attitudes towards some socially desirable behavior, be it cooperation, reciprocity, or norm-compliance.

Such a definition leads us to investigate reputation as a crucial mechanism in the evolution of these behaviors: Reputation transmission allows cooperation to emerge and persist even with low probability of repeated interaction.

In the first part of the paper, therefore, we will establish the fundamental ingredients needed to describe the action of reputation mechanism in a MAS, by decomposing the notion of reputation and relating it to more basic ones from cognitive and social sciences, like evaluation, belief, goal, ability, and so forth. In particular we will refer to the theoretical discussion in Conte and Paolucci (2002), which considers reputation as the main tool for establishing social order among intelligent agents, and we will analyze the pragmatic, memetic, and epistemic operations that allow reputation to function.

In the second part, instead, we will verify the hypotheses put forward by using a cross-methodological approach. The motivations for the application of each methodology will be justified and results will be analyzed with respect to both their soundness and generalizability. Therefore, we will firstly deal with pragmatic choice—which is the decision to cooperate or not to cooperate with another agent—by showing via computer simulation the effects of overoptimistic and overpessimistic evaluation both in presence and absence of reputation. Secondly, we will deal with memetic choice—which is the decision to pass or not to pass (good or bad) reputation—by showing via natural experiments how different initial experimental condition can lead to the diffusion of different patterns of reputation. Thirdly, we will deal with epistemic choice—which is the decision to accept or not an incoming information concerning reputation—with the instrument of multimodal dynamic epistemic logic, of which the KARO framework (Van der Hoek et al., 1997) represents the richest elaboration from an agent theory perspective, and which is capable to show how agents that communicate social image instead of reputation will tend to take more responsibility than the others. Finally, we will describe how by using various kinds of methodologies that account for theory fragments a coherent picture can be observed and how interdisciplinary can help to account for complex intelligent phenomena among adaptive social systems.

Theoretical Background

The cognitive approach in the study of reputation starts now to be perceived as fundamental. Until very recently, the cognitive nature of reputation was substantially ignored. In Milgrom and Roberts (1992) as well as in many other economic sources, reputation is seen as an automatic mechanism for ensuring the execution of contracts, paying no attention to the consequences that also in economical settings (as it will be shown) richer descriptions can have.

The study of reputation as a reciprocity mechanism resulting from individuals deliberation, has been started by studies of evolutionary psychology (Dunbar, 1996), empirical economics (Camerer & Fehr, 2006), and evolutionary biology (Nowak, 2006).

Reputation has been addressed from the point of view of all five Nowak (2006) mechanisms to ensure fitness: kin selection, direct reciprocity, indirect reciprocity, network reciprocity, and group selection, even though only some theories (indirect reciprocity, network reciprocity, and group selection) have shown more explanatory power in understanding reputation functioning as indirect reward or punishment (cf. Coleman [1990] account of reputation as non-heroic sanction).

Instead, our major claim is that only when considering agents' architectures and roles it is possible to find out which regulatory patterns cannot emerge. Reputation is argued to be no exception to this rule. Therefore, in order to interact with each other, agents need evaluation concerning which partner to choose.

A basic idea on which many authors would converge is that gossip—which is the act for which reputational information circulates—evolved as a means for finding out cheaters and other exploiters, and for penalizing or neutralizing them. The emphasis laid by some authors (Coleman, 1990; Merry, 1984) on the role of gossip in social control seems to indirectly confirm this interpretation.

Social Evaluation

But what is gossip made out of? We argue that the core ingredient of gossip is social evaluation.

The cognitive theory of social behavior (Miceli & Castelfranchi, 2000) defines an evaluation of an entity x as a belief of an evaluating agent e about x's usefulness regard to a goal p. We define a social evaluation as a shared judgment by a set (or community) of agents:

A social evaluation includes:

- an evaluative belief regarding an agent or on a group of agents, that we call the target, believed as GOOD-FOR a goal of the belief holder;
  - ○ regarding the performance of a skill, ability, or capability attributed;
  - ○ regarding the intention or willingness of T to perform some action;
- a set or community of agents (the evaluators) that share the belief.

Image and Reputation

We define the difference between image and reputation as the following: Image is a global or averaged evaluation of a given target by the agent. It consists of a set of evaluative beliefs (Miceli & Castelfranchi, 2000) about the characteristics of the target. It refers to a subset of the target's characteristics, that is, its willingness to comply with socially accepted norms and customs, or its skills.

The key feature of image is that it is a *believed* evaluation. We can define special cases of image, including third-party image, the evaluation that an agent believes a third party has of the target, or even shared social image, that is, an evaluation shared by a group.

We call reputation a transmission of an evaluation without the specification of the evaluator.

Another characteristic of reputation is that on its grounds an agent can "jump to conclusions," that is usually inferences only on the grounds of reputation are made. How to integrate this double functioning? This is part of what will be specified in the formal section of the paper.

Reputation is at last a believed, social, meta-evaluation; it is built upon three distinct but interrelated objects:

- a believed evaluation—this could be somebody's image, but is enough that this consists of a communicated evaluation;
- a population object, that is, a propagating believed evaluation;
- an objective emergent property at the agent level, that is, what the agent is believed to be.

In fact, reputation is a highly dynamic phenomenon in two distinct senses: (1) it is subject to change, especially as an effect of corruption, errors, deception, and so forth; and (2) it emerges as an effect of a multi-level bidirectional process.

A World for Gossip

We will classify an environment in which reputation communication takes place as composed by four types of agents:

- **evaluators**, the set of agents that judges a target to respect to a value;
- **targets**, the set of agents to which the valuation is referred to;
- **gossipers**, the set of agents that spread valuations; and
- **beneficiaries**, the set of agents to which the value is referred.

As an example, the sentence "John is considered a good sailor" refers to a set of evaluators (The people who judge John), a set of targets (the singleton John), a set of gossipers (the people who talked about John), and a set of beneficiaries (the people for which it is useful to have good sailors). Moreover, we will describe the three fundamental decision procedures that enable gossipers to make reputation circulate in such an environment, and verify their added value, according to the best suited methodologies. Following Conte and Paolucci (2002), we classify the three fundamental decision procedures ascribed to agents as pragmatic, memetic, and epistemic.

Pragmatic Decision

In economic and social settings agents often choose whom to interact with: that is what we call pragmatic decision. Our claim is that social evaluation, and in particular reputation, do influence such a choice. But is there any added value of having reputational information in a social system? A preliminary intuitive answer would be that a voice that is extremely imprecise and context-biased as gossip is can help cheaters to prevail. We claim this is not the case, and in order to show it we will construct societies with different available information patterns and look at their evolution by means of computer simulation.

Rather than focusing on cooperation, which is a traditional subject of investigation among social and rational action scientists, we decided to study norm-based social order by means of simulation. In societies of agents competing for scarce resources, we introduced norm-based behavior, defined as being neither immediately nor necessarily advantageous for the individual performer but beneficial for the society as a whole.

We can thus formulate two hypotheses:

- **First hypothesis:** Norm-based social order can be maintained and its costs reduced thanks to distributed social control. But a theory of social control should answer the question of why agents control one another spontaneously.

- **Second hypothesis:** Social cognitive mechanisms are needed to account for distributed social control. In particular, the propagation of social beliefs plays a decisive role in distributing social control at a low or null individual cost and for a high global benefit.

Memetic Decision

If we allow agents to communicate their evaluation, we can study the condition under which a positive or a negative evaluation spreads. For instance, why is gossip usually bad?

The roles distinguished so far may help to test a number of empirical hypotheses about the likelihood of provision and biases in reputation reporting under different structural conditions. By means of role intersections, a proxy of the factors examined previously can be obtained. In fact, the higher the intersect between G and E, the higher G's commitment, and therefore their responsibility and attitude to provision.

On the contrary, the overlapping between G and B (and, what is the same, between E and B) gives rise to a beneficiary-oriented benevolence, with the consequent negative bias. Instead, a higher intersect between G and T (or between E and T) leads to the leniency bias. Finally, the intersection between T and B concerns the perception of effects of gossip on targets; the higher this perception, the stronger the expected responsibility of gossipers.

We claim that a prediction of agents' behavior with respect to memetic decision can be obtained by looking at the agents' types intersections. That is different patterns of reputation spread if we allow gossipers to be intersected with evaluators, rather than with targets or with beneficiaries. In order to test these claims and to add reliability to our results we can classify natural settings and run experiments on top of them.

Epistemic Decision

When agents face incoming information they can decide whether to update or not their epistemic state, according to the information they already have, and the trust they have in the source of this information. They can also transmit information with no reliability: this is what happens with reputation, which is spread by gossipers with no particular commitment to the truth value of the core evaluation.

It is intuitively clear that the agent that spreads a determinate image is assuming some responsibility about it—is indeed its own judgment. Even in the case of a third party image, the agent is somehow endorsing the judgment, even if in this case most of the responsibility may be attributed to the third party itself. The case of reputation is different: The gossiper is referring a de-responsibilized rumor and cannot be held responsible.

But apart from intuition, we will give substantial evidence to the fact that gossipers take less responsibility when transmitting reputation, as claimed in Conte and Paolucci (2002), since they leave epistemic decision to the speakers, while they take more responsibility by transmitting social image. In order to deal with trust and speech act analysis in epistemic decision we will use the well known KARO framework, which has been used for formalized rich kind of multi-agent interaction such as belief revision (Van der Hoek, Van Linder, & Van der Hoek et al., 1997).

Theory Verification

Theory Verification for Pragmatic Decision

The model that we are going to present was worked out in order to investigate how norms control and reduce aggression and what their effect is on global (i.e., societal) and local (i.e., individual) efficiency. In particular, SIM-NORM was designed in the hope of shedding some light on the crucial issue of why self-interested agents may exercise social control. Although we are far from having reached a final conclusion on this issue, the studies based upon the model in question confirmed the importance of reputation in the analysis of social control.

Reputation was found to be the main factor responsible for the survival and reproduction of norm-complying agents interacting with violators (cheaters, or, in Prisoner's Dilemma terms—see Axelrod, 1984—defectors). More precisely, the difference between image and reputation was found to be crucial. Image, that is, individually acquired evaluation of other agents, gave norm executors no significant advantage.

Conversely, reputation, that is, the transmission of information among norm executors, proved to be decisive for leveling the outcomes of these two subpopulations (if they were numerically balanced).

We plan thus to investigate the role of norms as aggression controllers in artificial populations living under conditions of resource scarcity. To this purpose, two different strategies will be compared, namely:

- **normative strategy**, which reduces aggressions but at least in the short run may prove disadvantageous for the agent executing it; and

- **utilitarian strategy** (also called the cheaters strategy), which is always advantageous for the executor but is less efficacious in aggression reduction.

These strategies are compared (see also Conte, Castelfranchi, & Paolucci, 1998) along an efficiency measure, the average strength of the population after *n* periods of simulation, and a fairness measure, the individual deviation from the average strength.

Computer Simulation: The General Setting

The program is implemented in *C* language (a variable-size grid, defaulting at 10x10) with randomly scattered food. The grid is toroidal (opposite edges are connected, so agents may leave on the left and reappear on the right, etc.), and agents cannot move diagonally (i.e., the metric is such that two squares joined by an edge are at distance 2). Each experiment includes a set of runs with a fixed number of turns (2,000 as the default, to be modified in different experiments). Food is self-replenishing but scarce in units at any fixed time.

The program—also re-implemented independently by several authors in published experiments, including Staller and Petta (2001) is written in C and defines agents as objects moving in a two-dimensional common world (a variable-size grid, defaulting at 10x10) with randomly scattered food. The grid is toroidal (opposite edges are connected, so agents may leave on the left and reappear on the right, etc.), and agents cannot move diagonally (i.e., the metric is such that two squares joined by an edge are at distance 2). Each experiment includes a set of runs with a fixed number of turns (2,000 as the default, to be modified in different experiments).

In each turn, all agents choose one action and perform it simultaneously, with specialized routines for conflict resolution. Results are appropriate averages (whole-set or subset-specific) on the set of agents in a single run, further averaged over different runs. Fitness is measured in absolute, arbitrary units; each agent is characterized by a fitness value (strength), which grows with the agent eating food and decreases when the agent moves, attacks, or is attacked. Food units are associated with the (fixed) amount of fitness they provide when eaten.

At the beginning of each run, agents and food items are assigned locations at random. A location is a cell on the grid. The same cell cannot contain more than one object at a time (except when an agent is eating).

Redistributing the Costs of Compliance: Image

In previous batteries of experiments (Conte & Paolucci, 2001; Paolucci, Marsero, & Conte, 2000), we had shown that, in mixed populations, Normative agents perform less well than non-normative, because they are exploited by Utilitarians, who are assisted by an individualistic algorithm. It could be useful for Normative agents to resort to some retaliation strategies against cheaters.

Let us see whether image, here implemented as the capability to record (and reason about) past direct interaction, can mimic the success of standing. The results from a set of experimental runs on a mixed population equally composed of normative and utilitarian agents are reported in Table 2. These results are quite disappointing,

Table 1. Experimental runs between blind, utilitarian, and normative

	Str	stdev	StdP	stdev	Agg	stdev
Experiment Blind-Utilitarian						
Blind	4142	335	1855	156	4686	451
Utilitarian	4890	256	1287	102	2437	210
Experiment Blind-Normative						
Blind	5221	126	1393	86	4911	229
Normative	4124	187	590	80	1856	74
Experiment Utilitarian-Normative						
Utilitarian	5897	85	1219	72	3168	122
Normative	3634	134	651	108	2034	71

Table 2.Experimental runs on mixed populations

	Str	Stdev	StdP	stdev	Agg	stdev
Cheaters	5973	89	1314	96	3142	140
Respectful	3764	158	631	101	1284	59

at least from the point of view of the respectful agents: a slight increase in cheaters' average strength is accompanied by a slight decrease in the average strength of the respectful, providing a globally worse picture than the preceding experiment did.

To our surprise, self-acquired knowledge and punishment did not prove useful in redistributing the costs of norm compliance.

Redistributing the Costs of Compliance: Reputation

To get better results, our normative agents need something more than direct experience. They need to access relevant information while avoiding at least some of the costs (in terms of unwarranted attacks) of the acquisition. A natural candidate for solving this dilemma is communication, allowing agents to exchange their evaluations of cheaters.

Henceforth, we provided the respectful agents with the capacity to exchange with their (believed-to-be) respectful neighbors (at distance 1) images of other agents. With the implementation of a mechanism of transmission of information, we can start speaking of a reputation system. We ran the experiment again with normative agents exchanging information about cheaters. Since, at this stage, information can be incomplete but must be true, the build up of information is incremental. Each agent will add others' information to its own.

The results look very different from those of the previous experiment (Table 3). At the end of all runs, communication brought the average recognition of cheaters by the respectful up to 100%.

The experiments suggest that:

1.   Knowledge about others' behaviors significantly improves normative agents' outcomes in a mixed context only if

2.   Such knowledge circulates among beneficiaries.

Table 3. Experimental runs with informational noise

	Str	stdev	StdP	Stdev	Agg	stdev
Cheaters	4968	309	2130	108	2417	227
Respectful	4734	301	737	136	2031	253

Still, the final results show a slight dominance of cheaters under the current conditions of density of the agents over the grid (50%), concentration of food (1 food item for every 2 agents), and strategy proportions (50% cheaters against 50% respectful).

Dealing with False Information

But what's the threshold for acceptance that agents should have with possibly false incoming information?

Findings showed that the mechanism of propagation is extremely powerful (Table 4).

Table 4. Experimental results under different conditions

	Low Noise	High Noise
Low threshold	Prevalence of cheaters, Leniency (inclusive error)	Prevalence of cheaters, Leniency (inclusive error)
High threshold	Prevalence of respectful, no error	Prevalence of cheaters, Calumny (exclusive error)

Figure 1. Strength of outcomes in different settings, showing the breakdown of calumny and hidden cheaters

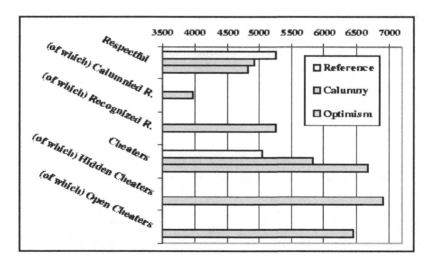

False reputation, whether at the expense of a subset of honest agents (calumny), or to the benefit of hidden cheaters (leniency or optimism), is always convenient for the whole population of cheaters and disadvantageous for the honest if considered as a whole.

False beliefs about reputation always penalize honesty and norm obedience and reinforce cheating.

From a social point of view, the effect of noise is to bring about two different types of social bias:

- **Inclusive error (social optimism or leniency):** A subset of cheaters was erroneously assigned a good reputation (in the recipients' lists, some cheaters were recorded as respectful agents) (Low Threshold, both High and Low Noise)
- **Exclusive error (calumny or social cynicism):** A subset of respectful agents was erroneously believed to be cheaters. (High Threshold, High Noise)

What lessons can we draw from the results presented previously? The conclusion that false good reputation penalizes honest citizens is not surprising. Perhaps, less obvious is that leniency is more detrimental to the honest than calumny is, however socially unattractive or unfair this effect may appear, since gullibility is certainly more acceptable and less blameworthy than calumny. The most counterintuitive outcome is the fate of the underestimated, which are usually (and probably correctly) perceived as the weakest and most unarmed part of the population. This finding deserves some careful consideration.

Strategies for Accepting Noisy Information

To check further these results, we have run a new set of simulations, in a different framework. All original simulation code has been migrated from C language to Java, with the support of the REPAST (http://repast.sourceforge.net/) framework. The sequence of agent's activation has been modified from contemporary moves to randomly scheduled sequential moves.

The indications coming from reference simulations confirm previous results. In this new set of simulations, we model explicitly courtesy and calumny as different algorithms. Instead of adding noise and memory effect, we start by introducing a strength of belief, ranging from 0 to 1, associated with each reputation item.

While checking each other's records, agents must make a decision based on their own record (R or C) and the transmitted information (again, R or C), and an update strategy must specify what happens for each possible combination.

We examine the following strategies:

- **Reference strategy:** Only C are transmitted, and they are accepted with belief 1.0;

- **Courtesy strategy:** RR and CC cause the belief to be set to the maximum of the two beliefs, while RC and CR cause the receiver to subtract the strength of the transmitted belief from its own.

- **Calumny strategy:** Transmission of C on an R is accepted with strength 1.0: RR and CC cause the belief to be set to the maximum of the two beliefs, while transmission of an R over a C is ignored.

Simulations are then run with and without noise, defined here as mistakes resulting in faulty transmission. The numerical value given is the probability of error with respect to the single copy. Taking into account the average volume of information exchanges, a rate of 0.0001 causes on average a single copying error each eight turns, that is, about 250 mistakes per 2,000-turns run.

Data represent averaged strength per population, over 300 runs. The unsuitability of the courtesy algorithm is clear even from the case with no noise: even if still more efficient than the cheaters' group, it qualifies last. Even with a very low amount of noise, cheaters can easily prey on the courtesy algorithm, while calumny needs a more substantial noise to be taken over. The number following N is the probability of a copying mistake multiplied by 10.

With accurate information and no noise, the normative strategy remains more efficient. Moreover, the calumny strategy exhibits higher efficiency than the courtesy strategy.

Figure 2. N-C performance in different conditions

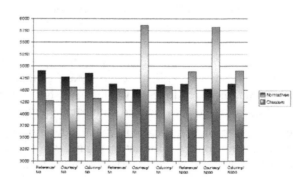

Although intrinsically antisocial and aggressive, calumny cooperates with the diffusion of norm-abiding behavior more than courtesy, which is instead a tolerant, mild, more acceptable behavior.

Asymmetry of Errors about Reputation

In the simulations, bad reputation (whether false or not) proved socially disruptive in two distinct senses. On one hand, it ends up with increasing the number of retaliations and hence of aggressions at the population level. On the other, this effect is due to a non-trivial interactive side-effect.

Calumny acts as a self-fulfilling prophecy. In fact, its targets will be attacked also by their fellows (other norm-abiders). Hence, these unlucky agents will update their own lists, by deliberately turning their attackers, once considered old friends, into believed cheaters (since the old friends now behave as cheaters in their inverted perspective).

In the simulation, that which is perceived to violate the norm is recorded as a cheater. That which does not, instead, is not recorded as a norm-abider, since it might be the case that, that violation was contextually inconvenient. Hence, bad reputation spreads faster than good reputation. Once you get a bad reputation, it will stick to you because:

- others will not revise it immediately even if you do not behave according to your bad reputation (asymmetry); and
- others will have less and less reasons to revise it because you will increasingly behave according to your bad reputation (self-fulfilling prophecy).

Theory Verification for Memetic Decision

As argued in Conte and Paolucci (2002) a weak intersection between evaluators, gossipers, and targets would allow for a bad reputation to widely circulate.

In this section we will present and discuss findings from an experiment with human subjects in a competitive virtual market, that we have called Fantasymarket. In Fantasymarket, a subject can participate by Internet connection to the experiment. They meet at a preestablished time to trade virtual goods showing a fictitious identity. Three experimental conditions are checked, namely, *control condition* (with anonymity), *identity condition* (agents keep nicknames), and *reputation condition* (agents exchange information about others). We show how reputation is related to the average quality of products sold in the market. In particular reputation will be shown to be a factor that avoids the onset of "Lemon Markets." Information asymmetry and identity changes are instead shown to act towards low quality transactions, which are alleviated both by direct and indirect experience communication. The mere possibility to be evaluated seems to have a strong effect on the honesty level of agents.

Fantasymarket: Reputation Online[1]

The study that we have performed has been inspired by the work of Toshio Yamagishi and colleagues, who performed a series of experiments on reputation in online markets (Yamagishi & Matsuda, 2002). They examined the role of reputation for alleviating the problem of lemons, as exemplified in a famous paper from Akerof (1970), where it is argued that asymmetry of information drives honest traders and high quality goods out of the market. The result is a market where only "lemons," or fraudulent commodities, are available—often to the detriment of both sellers and buyers.

The classical example of a lemon market is the used car market, where only sellers have information about problems with the cars they are selling, and most consumers are incapable of discerning these problems. Contemporary online traders such as users of Internet auction sites face the same problem; individuals who purchase a good online can learn about the quality (or condition) of the good only after they have paid for it.

The main results from this work can be summarized as:

- information asymmetry drives the experimental market among anonymous traders into a lemons market in which only the lowest quality goods are traded;

- either experience-based information or reputation about other traders moderately alleviates the lemons problem;

- the power of experience-based information or reputation as a solution to the problem of lemons is substantially reduced when traders can freely change their identities and cancel their reputations; and

- the negative reputation system is particularly vulnerable to identity changes, whereas the positive and mixed reputation systems are not so vulnerable to identity changes.

The objective of our work is to compare these results and to devise specialized settings in order to account for the effects of image vs. reputation.

Our platform, based on Java Server Pages (JSPs), Apache/Jakarta, and a MySQL server to maintain data, is currently ready to host the next stages of the experiments. The platform that we developed has been baptized with the name of Fantasymarket.

The Experiment

In Fantasymarket, subjects can participate by Internet connection to the system. They meet at a predetermined day and hour to trade virtual goods. In all experiments, subjects do not communicate with each other, since they connect to the Internet mostly from their home. On the market, they show (when this option is available) only a fictitious identity, a nickname of their choice.

Every player, after having read a set of instructions, received a login and an amount of virtual money for both producing goods to sell in the market and to buy goods for sale. Products have a real value (the amount paid for its production) which is hidden, and a face value (price), with which they are shown on the market. Asymmetry of information about products traded in this market is obviously present. The true quality of the product is known only to the seller as in the case of (Akerof, 1970) the used car market. The buyer finds out the quality of the product only after he/she has paid for it. Products, depending on the experimental condition, come with either no information at all, or with some information (identity or reputation) on the producer agent. Agents have an obvious rational incentive to produce low-quality goods and sell them at a high price, especially in an anonymous situation.

To avoid the introduction of multiple products with the consequent necessity of analyzing dependence networks, which are not a focus of this experiment, the system presumes the existence of a use value, higher (1.5 times in the original version, 1.3 time in Fantasymarket) than the real value. The use value is immediately converted back into monetary value.

To avoid cluttering the product list, we remove products after a fixed period of time.

We performed three experiments, in different experimental conditions. Each group included about 12 players.[2]

The Experiments

We performed three series of experiments. In the first experiment (Control), we introduced no recognition mechanism. Players could not find out who was the producer of a product in the market. In the second experiment (Identity), explicit identities are shown; producers are so individual and will have less chances of exploiting another agent twice. In the third (Reputation condition) experiment, we allowed agents to post their assessment of transactions. These evaluations were available to other players when deciding which products to buy.

Results

In Table 5 we report a summary of the results for all experimental conditions. As foreseen, in the control condition (anonymity) a lemons market takes place, with large quantities of bad products. Identity improves the quality of products, but also causes a sort of dampening that reduces average wealth.

In the third condition, average wealth reaches again higher levels, but the quality of the products gets much better.

From the results we conclude that the possibilities of giving evaluations and of getting evaluated have a strong effect on the honesty of agents.

In the reputation condition, the production and sale of good quality products gets much larger with respect to the identity condition, and even more with respect to the control condition. From a mere 12 fair products, in the control condition, we obtain 124 fair products in the reputation condition; it looks like the participants are trying to reach at least a neutral reputation. Since, as we noted before, subjects are playing with fictitious identities, the cooperation effect cannot lean upon a pre-existing knowledge network.

It is then very interesting how the effects in the reputation setting are produced by an anticipated, assumed punishment from the other players; this even without the anticipated effect ever happening.

Time Trends

Fantasymarket, time trends. The lines correspond to the three conditions: control, identity, and reputation. In the columns we have, in sequence, number of items pro-

Table 5. Fantasymarket, experiment results: All values except number of players and product quality are per player

	Wealth (\10)	No. Products	Products Sold	No. Good Products	No. Bad Products	Id Chamges	No. Players	Quality	Quality Shown	Quality, L5	Quality Shown, L5
Control	49.50	42.3	18.3	1.2	39.8	0	10	3.01	32.5	2.58	25.29
Identity	39.05	27.5	11.92	4.08	17.83	2.92	12	22.05	71.63	11.47	30.14
Reputation	49.90	34.09	22.45	11.27	12.55	4.91	11	20.09	44.55	42.07	50.07

duced, number of items sold, average quality shown, average actual quality, and the difference between them as an index of dishonesty. Interpolation is made by R supsmu function.

Figure 3. Fantasymarket time trends

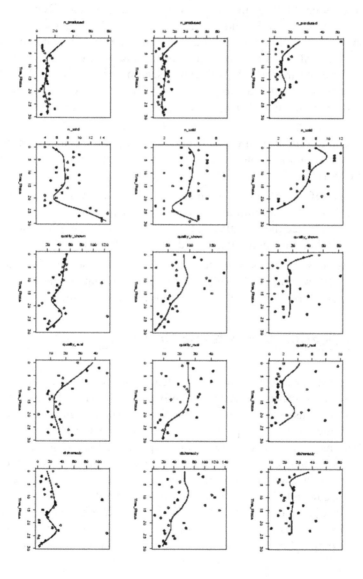

The results are further confirmed by looking, as in (Yamagishi & Matsuda, 2002), at the trend in time of the main indicators. We report, per minute of the run; the number of items produced and sold; the averages of quality declared and real; and their difference as a measure of dishonesty.

For what regards the apparent quality of items, a plateau is reached in the Control condition. The plateau in the Control condition could perhaps be explained by an indifference equilibrium, since the players discover quite fast that there is no relation between announced and actual quality, they start to lose interest in that parameter, using the market default to hide under uniformity. Instead, in both Reputation and Identity conditions the general trend of announced quality is a descending one; a simple reason for that could be, in a more honest market, funding scarcity. While under Identity the quality starts very high and then shows a uniform decline, for Reputation we have what looks like a tentative search—about minute 20 we have a minimum, the players then start to produce with higher prices, but then after 5 minutes they reverse the trend. Note, however, the very low absolute value of this indicator.

In all cases the final quality is quite low, and it is only the Reputation condition that shows a final (unremarkable) increase. This increase should be checked by repeating the experiments.

Finally, as a result of the previous two indicators, the level of dishonesty is more or less constant in Control condition—actual quality is an order of magnitude less than shown quality, hence the variation in the difference is nearly invisible—while decreasing sharply in both Reputation and Identity conditions.

All the previous considerations show that the variety of responses that can arise in experiments with human participants. The hypotheses stated here as proposed explanation should all be tested in future versions of the experiment.

Theory Verification of Epistemic Decision

In the theoretical framework previously presented, agents face the decision whether to believe or not to an incoming pattern of information. Various fields of science have been tackling this issue, above all psychology (i.e., cognitive dissonance resolution; Festinger, 1957), computer science (belief revision; Alchourron, Gardenfors, & Makinson, 1985), and philosophy (epistemic logic; Van der Hoek et al., 1997). In order to analyze the difference in terms of responsibility between the communication of image and the communication of reputation—such as that stated by our theory—we need to have clear notions of responsibility, image, and reputation and to analyze their formal structures. This is the reason why we use modal logic as a tool for rigorous analysis. In particular we anchor our axiomatization to the theory of responsibility by Conte and Paolucci (2004), very well suited to be implemented in temporal reasoning logics, and to the theory of trust in epistemic decision by Castelfranchi and Falcone (2002), which is built on cognitive factors such as beliefs, goals, and abilities.

A Complex World of Cunning Cognitive Agents

In order to model the concepts we discussed in the theoretical part of the paper, and that concern the responsibility gossipers assume in spreading reputation, we call upon the formal tools of rational agents theory.

In particular, we stick to the integrated modal framework KARO byVvan der Hoek et al. (1997) that provides a rigorous specification of agent belief dynamics and communication.

KARO is by large one of the most quoted and used formal architectures, which has recently had applications in areas usually subject of computational studies investigations such as the an agent-based approach to emotions (Dastani & Meyer, 2006). A full introduction to KARO is impossible here, since it is grounded on already complex graph theoretical investigations. The references pointed in this chapter are enough for a reader to have acquaintance with the frame. What we can say here is that KARO is a multimodal epistemic dynamic logic that investigates the dynamics of commitments and belief revision among rational agents. As far as the basic intuitions are concerned, what follows is, from a model theoretic perspective, self-contained. That is, the reader is only required to know set theory and basic propositional logic.

Most features of the KARO framework are kept, but some need to be changed. The most disturbing one, which forbids agents to lie and to gossip ("We demand our agents to be sincere in that they are morally unable to lie or gossip" [p. 23]) will be dealt with in the appendix. Other simple changes will be addressed as the formalization goes on. These changes are the minimal necessary to deal with reputation dynamics.

We drop *realizability* for observation. That is, agents are not always allowed to observe everything. It seems more plausible that an agent can observe only some states of the world, and it is even too intuitive that perfect observers do not need gossip: Agents can always verify in prima persona the correctness of any statement.

We keep *idempotence* and *determinism*, that is, we do not investigate notions like "saying it twice" and we consider an action to lead to unique world state.

Agents are endowed with "informational attitudes" that represent their ways of believing. To operationalize them we use KARO modal operators

$$B_i^k, B_i^o, B_i^c, B_i^t$$

to mean that the agent i knows for sure, believes for observing, believes for being told, believes that something is said. As an acquainted reader will have noticed, we changed the KARO default modality into a new one that in our framework mimics the belief of the existence of a shared voice.

Our domain of discourse is grounded on the language L_0, which is the smallest set that contains the propositional atoms and the canonical truth, closed by negation and conjunction. Propositional calculus connectives are derived as usual.

The full language L is its augmentation by means of the standard dynamic operations of iteration, confirmation, conditioning, and repetition (Harel, Kozen, & Tyurin, 2000) that range over a set $Agt = \{1,...,n\}$ of agents and a set Act of either atomic ($At = \{a,b,...\}$) or composed $(\alpha, \beta...)$ actions.

We interpret formulas in a Kripke structure like $M = <W, \pi, \Delta, I>$, where W is a non-empty set of worlds, π is a classical valuation function, $\{\Delta, I\}$ encode how to interpret the Dynamic and Informational operations.

The dynamic logic semantics for action, that inductively define the action result function (r^*) and the action capacity function (c^*) are inherited from KARO.

From KARO we also inherit the notions of Practical Possibility for an agent to act, which holds when there is a physical opportunity to carry out an action,[3] $<do_i(a)> \varphi$, plus the ability to do so $A_i a$. For a sound and complete axiomatization see Van der Hoek et al. (1993).

The notion that they propose for proper "Can" seems also reasonable: There is Can when there is awareness of Practical Possibility, strictly as defined previously; there is Cannot when there is awareness of not Practical Possibility.

$$Can_i(a, \varphi) = B_i^k PracPoss_i(a, \varphi)$$

In line with Castelfranchi (2003) it could also be said that capability of agents vanishes when there is no *belief* of own capabilities—instead of opposed knowledge—which can be rendered by weakening the definition of Cannot to ignorance or to absence of belief. We are not dealing with this issue now, but it is in principle a possible extension.

Out of these considerations, we have the basic semantics for capabilities:

Definition 1

$M,s \models [do_i(a)] \varphi$ iff $M,t \models \varphi$ for all $M,t \in r^*(M,s)$

$M,s \models A_i a$ iff $c^*(M,s) = true$

$M,s \models PracPoss_i(a, \varphi)$ iff $M,s \models A_i a \wedge <do_i(a)> \varphi$

A Variety of Beliefs

We require the knowledge relation to be an equivalence relation, that is, to describe epistemic indistinguishability in such a way to satisfy the S5 properties. This holds for observational beliefs as well that are assumed to be truthful. Finally, we keep the requirement that for all $i \in Agt$ and $s,s' \in W$:

- $s \in B^k (i,s)$ (same for B^o)
- $s' \in B^k (i,s) \Leftrightarrow B^k (i,s')= B^k (i,s)$ (same for B^o)
- $B^k (i,s) \neq \phi$
- $B^t (i,s) \subseteq B^c (i,s) \subseteq B^o (i,s) \subseteq B^k (i,s)$
- if $s' \in B^o (i,s)$ then $B^c (i,s) = B^c (i,s')$ and $B^t (i,s) = B^t (i,s')$

Taken $X \in \{B_i^k, B_i^o, B_i^c, B_i^t\}$ the following theorems hold:

$$|= (B_i^k \varphi \to \varphi) \wedge (B_i^o \varphi \to \varphi) \qquad (T)$$
$$|= \neg (X \varphi \wedge X \neg \varphi) \qquad (D)$$
$$|= X \varphi \to XX \varphi \qquad (4)$$
$$|= \neg X \varphi \to X \neg X \varphi \qquad (5)$$
$$|= (B_i^k \varphi \to B_i^o \varphi) \wedge (B_i^o \varphi \to B_i^c \varphi) \wedge (B_i^c \varphi \to B_i^t \varphi)$$

From the philosophical point of view the way we built the belief about a voice requires some explanation with respect to the aforementioned validities. We skip the explanation about the other forms of beliefs, widely explained in Van der Hoek et al. (1997). The first item says that beliefs about a voice are not necessarily true (they lack property T), which is in line with the theory. The second says that beliefs about a voice are never inconsistent. This needs some argumentation and it is not to be taken for granted. The intuitive point is that an agent cannot at the same time say, "It is by and large said that p" and "It is by and large said that $\neg p$" without leaving to the hearer a feeling of incoherence. What is stronger from the intuitive point of view is that we require the agent to hold at least a belief about a voice. This is easier to understand if we for instance think of agents holding a belief about a voice about trivialities ("It is by and large said that $\neg (p \wedge \neg p)$"). The third and fourth item strengthen the belief about a voice: in case I hold a belief about a voice that something is true (or false), I also hold the belief about a voice that I hold the belief about a voice about that something is true (or false). These last assumptions sound very strong, but the first of them seems more reasonable if we think that the sentence "it is said that it is said that p" does not differ much from "it is are said that p." Thus we are going to equate them. The negative version instead seems more problematic, since it considers the presence of a voice about what it is not said (If something is not said, then It is said that something is not said), but we will deal with that in further work. The last validity simply says that the belief about a voice is the weakest form of belief with respect to the truth value of the information, and to the relation with the other forms of beliefs.

Basic Concepts Formalized

These ingredients are already enough to build a very simple "good evaluation" of an agent by its considering his or her "can do." We are going to constraint the notion of image to this valuation. Further extensions are possible but are not going to be treated now.

$Good\text{-}Image(i,j,\alpha,\ \varphi,\ x) = B_i^x\ Can_j\ (\alpha,\ \varphi)\ with\ x \in \{t,\ c,\ o,\ k\}.$

In principle we can distinguish an (good or conversely bad) image coming from knowledge, from direct experience, from reliable communication, and from voice. It goes without saying that the most interesting forms of image are not coming from perfect knowledge, but are—like reputation—coming from uncertain and unreliable communication.

The following propositions hold in our logic:

Propositions 1
$\models Good\text{-}Image(i,j,\alpha,\ \varphi,\ k) \to Good\text{-}Image(i,j,\alpha,\ \varphi,\ o)$
$\models Good\text{-}Image(i,j,\alpha,\ \varphi,\ o) \to Good\text{-}Image(i,j,\alpha,\ \varphi,\ c)$
$\models Good\text{-}Image(i,j,\alpha,\ \varphi,\ c) \to Good\text{-}Image(i,j,\alpha,\ \varphi,\ t)$
$\models Good\text{-}Image(i,j,\alpha,\ \varphi,\ k) \to [do_j(\alpha)]\ \varphi \wedge A_j\ \alpha$
$\models Good\text{-}Image(i,j,\alpha,\ \varphi,\ k) \leftrightarrow Can_j\ (\alpha,\ \varphi)$

The first three items state that image coming from knowledge is stronger than image coming from observation, which is in turn stronger than that coming from communication, and in turn from the belief that there is a voice. The fourth states that image coming from knowledge implies the effective capacity of agents to perform the action under consideration. The last item states that self good image comes with the awareness of own capacities, and the believed possession of them results in good image.

They hold as well (with the obvious inversions) for bad image, in the various forms of believing.

We will clarify the difference between these ways of believing by looking at their logics: they are different because they function in a different way, that is, they react differently to the same operation.

Inheriting Informative Actions

In general, as emphasized by Conte and Paolucci (2002), responsibility in reputation concerns the commitment to the truth value of the utterance by a gossiper. This can be rendered formally by saying that in a given group there is a constraint (a moral soft-constraint) to say the truth. The corresponding damage (for the notion of damage in responsibility, see again Conte & Paolucci, 2004) is the violation of such an obligation.

We like the action $inform(\varphi,i,t)$, which allows us to translate, very well, operations like ("I tell somebody that I am told that p"), by means of the tag "t," which refers to the fourth modality one has as belief. But while dropping the no-plain-lie constraint we prefer to change its name into $tell(\varphi,i,t)$.

We also inherit the notion of credibility, $D_{(i,j)}\,\varphi$, very simplistic and self-explanatory. The function $D{:}Agt \times Agt \rightarrow \wp\,(L)$, which describes the authority relation for each agent, can be used for observation and communication as well. Thus the language is expressive enough to describe informative connections among agents. Here for authority relation we mean a relation of strong trust and reliance, not necessarily symmetric, between two agents. All this differentiates our logic from the classical public announcement ones (Kooi, 2004) in which communication is always truthful and broadcast.

Computing Responsibility in Communication

In what case by saying "people say" am I assuming less responsibility than by saying "people believe"? That is, can we prove when (if ever) communicating reputation bears less responsibility-taking than communicating image?

One simple answer can be derived by looking at the theory: All the responsibility I am assuming in the second case I am also assuming in the first case, simply because I cannot infer what one believes by simply observing. I can only infer beliefs if a reliable source informs me about them.

I think here we need to clarify what we mean by assuming responsibility. For the point of Conte and Paolucci (2002) is that gossipers "assume less responsibility" and not that gossipers are "less responsible": assumption is different from preemption.

We are going to translate the fact that a gossiper assumes less responsibility with the intuitive sense that if the information is wrong he/she has less fault. In a nutshell, it is the commitment he/she takes about the truth value of the content of the utterance.

Assuming Responsibility

The claim that "If I tell somebody about something I assume responsibility before him/her concerning its truth value" can be written as follows:

$$Assume\text{-}resp(i,j, \varphi) = \neg\, B_i^k\, \varphi \wedge D_{\{i,j\}}\, \varphi \wedge <do_i\, tell(\varphi,j,x)>\, T,\ with\ x \in \{o,c,t\}$$

That is *i* assumes responsibility with respect to the information φ when he/she is not sure of φ (it rules out trivialities), *i* has to have an authority relation towards *j*, and he/she has the opportunity of communicating with him/her.

The following proposition holds:

Propositions 2

$$\models Assume\text{-}resp(i,j, \varphi) \rightarrow <do_i\, tell(\varphi,j,x)>\, (\neg\, B_j^k\, \varphi \wedge B_j^c\, \varphi)$$

which states that assuming responsibility implies effective capacity to influence the hearer.

What we lack is to state formally the impossibility of direct observation of others' beliefs.

Uncertainty About Others' Minds

One important feature of human communication about others' mental states is their observational inaccessibility. As we already said, in KARO observations are always possible. We need a modification to the core logic of observation in such a way that no one can observationally believe that somebody else believes something. Or better, we cannot observe that somebody else believes something.

That is, if I assume a belief about others' non-trivial beliefs, either I believe it is a voice or I believe it from being told.

One way to do it is to constrain observation to propositional formulas, as in KARO. On the other hand we should be able to allow the agent to observe some opportunities for them and for others, that is, we need to extend the language to which observable formulas belong to the propositional plus the dynamic one. Let us assume for now that this is possible. We will show later on that it is.

Taken $x'' \in \{o,c,t\}$ we can conclude what follows.

Propositions 3

$|= (\varphi \rightarrow \psi) \rightarrow$ *Assume-resp(i,j, φ)* $\rightarrow$ *Assume-resp(i,j, ψ)*

$|= <do_i\ tell(B_j^{x''}\varphi,j,c)>\ T \rightarrow\ <do_i\ tell(B_j^{x''}\varphi,j,t)>\ T$

$|=$ *Assume-resp(i,j, $B_j^c\ B_z^{x''}\ Can_k\ (\alpha,\ \varphi)$)* $\rightarrow$ *Assume-resp(i,j, $B_i^t\ B_z^{x''}\ Can_k\ (\alpha,\ \varphi)$)*

What is resulting as validity in such a system is that social image implies reputation in a very precise sense, that is, if I know that people believe from being told I also know that people say. This is a very strong statement, but it is both consistent with others' belief inobservability and with belief inference only coming from behavior, the only admitted behavior being uttering. We can remove it, but only if we enlarge the meaning of reputation not only to linguistic behavior but to "evaluative behavior in general." This may allow for investigating the difference between shared voice and reputation, by considering the diversity of possible evaluations, but we prefer to leave such complications to further investigations.

Further Considerations

In this part of the chapter we described a multimodal approach to rational agents able to deal with reputation dynamics. We augmented the language to constrain observation and to allow lying, we introduced a belief about a voice as weakest form of agents' informational attitude, and we gave some properties of the system and some relevant validities. The main one proved that assuming responsibility in reputation spreading is at most equal to assuming responsibility in image spreading. One suggestion of the model is that agents are probably more willing to communicate reputation and to accept image.

Technical Modifications to KARO

We can modify the model in such a way to restrict observations, allowing for lies and credibility update.

Observing

The observation has to be limited to some world states. For instance I cannot observe whether another agent has a belief. Moreover observational action should not be endowed with perfect realizability, as argued before.

In the formalism, observations are truthful and overrule any beliefs acquired by other means.

To render them we introduce a function $S{:}A \to W \to \wp(L_l)$ which associates to each agent and each world the propositions (plus the dynamic operations) he/she is able to observe. It has to be noted that in principle we can augment the language to some L_i, such that $L_0 \subseteq L_1 \subseteq L_i \subseteq L$ to allow for observation of important elements like internal abilities, that can render agents even more realistic.

In any case, $M{,}s \models Sees_i\ \varphi \leftrightarrow \varphi \in S(i)(w)$ is the corresponding operator for limiting observation.

Let now for x $\in$ *{k,o,c,d}*, $Bwh_i^x\ \varphi = \neg Ignorant_i^x\ \varphi \leftrightarrow B_i^x\ \varphi \vee B_i^x\ \neg\varphi.$

For all $M \in M^l$ with state s and $\varphi \in L_l$ we define:

$r(i,\ obs\ \varphi)(M{,}s) =$

$$
\begin{cases}
\phi & \text{if } M,s \models \neg Sees_i\ \varphi \\
M,s & \text{if } M,s \models Bwh_i^x\ \varphi \\
revise^\circ\ (i,\varphi\ )(M,s),s & \text{otherwise}
\end{cases}
$$

The functioning of *revise° (i, φ)(M,s)* is described in details in the KARO model and it updates observational beliefs by paying attention to minimal change and leaving the prexistent relations between beliefs intact.

It has to be noted that the following proposition holds:

$$\models Can_j\ (\alpha,\ \varphi) \to B_j^k\ Can_j\ (\alpha,\ \varphi) \wedge \neg Sees_i\ Can_j\ (\alpha,\ \varphi),\ for\ i \neq j$$

That is, if an agent "Can" do something, that agent is aware of that, but no other can be sure of this ability. The explanation is that the "Can" is composed of an external part (the opportunity) which may be accessible to others, and an internal part (moral capacity, willingness, interest) that is not directly observable.

Lying

We redefine the operation *tell* allowing for communicated formulas to range over the whole language.

For all $M \in M^l$ with state s; $i,j \in Agt$; $x \in \{k,s,h,t\}$ and $\varphi, \psi \in L$ we define:
$r(i, tell\ (\varphi, i, x))(M, s) =$

$$
\begin{cases}
revise^{cred-}\ (i, j, \varphi)(M, s), s & \text{if}\quad M, s \models B_i^x\ \neg\varphi \\
revise^c\ (i, \varphi)(M, s), s & \text{if}\quad M, s \models \neg B_i^x\ \varphi \wedge D_{\{i,j\}} \\
M, s & \text{otherwise}
\end{cases}
$$

The behavior of the utterance is very simple: If an untrustworthy agent tells another agent something this second does not share at all, the latter will not revise his/her beliefs. If instead a trustworthy agent shares something some other agent can accept, then that agent will accept this information.

The functioning of *revise^c (i, φ)(M,s)* is described in details in the KARO model and it updates communicational beliefs by paying attention to minimal change and leaving the prexistent relations between beliefs intact.

A more complex case is when an agent I trust tells me something strongly against my beliefs; *revise^{cred-} (i,j, φ)(M,s)* simply updates the authority relation in such a way that if I am convinced that someone I trust is lying, I simply do not trust him/her anymore concerning the statement for which he/she was lying. Of course far more interesting operations can be formalized here. For instance I can extend my mistrust to all the consequences of the statement, to all the statements, or I can even give others a bad image about him/her.

Future Work and Trends

Many follow-up questions that are relevant for complex adaptive systems study may come from our findings.

To what extent, within which limits false reputation is tolerable from a social point of view, and at which point the chain of misperceptions and misbehaviors leads to prejudice, discrimination, and social breakdown? Is this a merely quantitative matter, or is there some interesting qualitative phenomenon we should take into account? Can it be shown that responsibility of gossipers allows spreading of reputation instead of image? What are the consequences of such phenomena for Complex Adaptive Systems? And for regulation of MAS?

All our findings point out the direction for a more sound understanding of a well-known social phenomenon, gossip as the spread of calumny.

Findings are corroborated by the stability they show, even in the face of remodeling: They support our general claim that, in order to tell something about social and cultural phenomena, it is necessary to include in the modeling explicit mental components in the structure of the agent.

Future work will be endorsed in all the three application areas.

In computer simulation, a cognitive architecture is being worked out, and some preliminary results are already available (Paolucci, 2005). The purpose of such architecture is to provide a cognitive basis for understanding reputation in market scenarios.

In natural settings, FantasyMarket experiments are being further investigated in order to understand the role of communication among agents that deal with imperfect and possibly false information. Moreover investigations on the role of reputation in online auction systems are being carried out (Marmo, 2006).

In formal settings the role of responsibility is being further clarified in order to understand the mechanisms allowing this feature to influence belief dynamics (Turrini, Paolucci, & Conte, 2006).

What is missing at this moment in the studying of complex social phenomena is an interdisciplinary integrated approach to reputation, accounting for both evolutionary grounds and cognitive mechanisms and processes. We claim that only such an integrated approach can point to guidelines for managing reputation and for designing technologies of reputation.

Conclusion

This chapter presents a theory of reputation seen as the result of evaluation spreading in a MAS. In particular the capacities of agents that spread reputation have been analyzed and decomposed in their atomic parts (pragmatic, memetic, epistemic). For each decision we stated and verified several claims, using the methodologies that allowed best to capture the relevant aspects of the theoretical statements. For analyzing the evolution of populations that based their pragmatic decisions on reputation we used computer simulation. In order to understand the actual advantage of reputation in social interaction we use experiments in natural settings. And finally, in order to analyze the structure of communicative acts and relating them to the notion of responsibility, we used a formal framework.

The aim of the chapter has been to show how a theoretical framework can be verified using an interdisciplinary approach and which methodologies are best suited for particular settings. In adaptive systems investigation methodologies that deal with evolutionary analysis, real data gathering, and formal specification are shown to be needed in order to have a full comprehension of phenomena structure and change.

The result is a view of reputation as a complex, multifaceted object both at the agent and at the population level. At the agent level, it is a property of the target which emerges from the propagation of social meta-beliefs, that is, beliefs about how the target is evaluated by social surrounders.

An analysis of the cognitive features of such meta-belief allows us to characterize reputation as an evolutionary process, characterized by efficient transmission (descent), supported by low responsibility, quite stable even if contradicted by experience (with limited variation), and under some hypothesis endowed with differential survival. In particular, reputation spreads quite fast but is often inaccurate, and it a common opinion that bad reputation spreads faster.

We propose, as an alternative to the model oversimplification, a multifaceted approach, where modeling and experimenting have the role of fostering theoretical advances.

References

Akerof, G. (1970). The market of lemons: Quality uncertainty and the market mechanisms. *The Quarterly Journal of Economics, 84,* 488-500.

Alchourròn, C. E., Gärdenfors, P., & Makinson, D. (1985). On the logic of theory change: Partial meet contraction and revision functions. *Journal of Symbolic Logic, 50,* 510-530.

Axelrod, R. (1984). *The evolution of cooperation.* New York: Basic Books.

Camerer, C., & Fehr, E. (2006) When does "economic man" dominate social behavior? *Science,* 47-52.

Castelfranchi, C. (2003). The micro-macro constitution of power. *Protosociology, 18*(19), 208-265.

Castelfranchi, C., & Falcone, R. (2002). Issues of trust and control on agent autonomy. *Connect.Sci, 14*(4), 249-263.

Coleman, J. (1990). *Foundations of social theory.* Cambridge, MA: Belknap Harvard.

Conte, R., Castelfranchi, C., & Paolucci, M. (1998). Normative reputation and the cost of compliance. *Journal of Artificial Societies and Social Simulation, 1*(3). Retrieved from http://jasss.soc.surrey.ac.uk/1/3/3.html

Conte, R., & Paolucci, M. (2002). *Reputation in artificial societies. Social beliefs for social order.* Boston: Kluwer.

Conte, R., & Paolucci, M. (2004). Responsibility for societies of agents. *Journal of Artificial Societies and Social Simulation, 7,* 4. Retrieved from http://jasss. soc.surrey.ac.uk/7/4/3.html

Dastani, M., & Meyer, J. J. Ch. (2006). Programming agent with emotions. In G. Brewka, S. Coradeschi, A. Perini, & P. Traverso (Eds.), *Proceedings of the 17th European Conference on Artificial Intelligence (ECAI'06)*. Amsterdam: IOS Press.

Dunbar, R. (1996). *Grooming, gossip and the evolution of language.* Faber Faber and Harvard University Press.

Fagin, R., Halpern, J. Y., Moses, Y., & Vardi, M. Y. (1995). *Reasoning about knowledge.* Cambridge, MA: MIT Press.

Festinger, L. (1957). *A theory of cognitive dissonance.* Stanford, CA: Stanford University Press.

Harel, D., Kozen, D., & Tyurin J. (2000). *Dynamic logic.* Foundations of Computing Series. Cambridge, MA: MIT Press.

Kooi, B. (2004). *Knowledge, chance and change.* Unpublished PhD thesis, University of Amsterdam, Institute for Logic, Language and Computation (ILLC) dissertation series.

Marmo, S. (2006). *L'Uso della Reputazione nelle Applicazioni Internet: Prudenza o Cortesia? L'Approccio Socio-Cognitivo.* 3o Convegno Scienze Cognitive, Genova.

Merry, S. E. (1984). Rethinking gossip and scandal. In D. Black (Ed.), *Toward a general theory of social control* (Vol. II.). New York: Academic Press.

Miceli, M., Castelfranchi, C. (1989). A cognitive approach to values. *Journal for the theory of Social Behavior, 19,* 169-194.

Miceli, M., & Castelfranchi, C. (2000). The role of evaluation in cognition and social interaction. In K. Dautenhahn (Ed.), *Human cognition and social agent technology.*

Milgrom, P., & Roberts, J. (1992). *Economics, organization and management.* Prentice Hall.

Nowak, M. (2006). Five rules for the evolution of cooperation. *Science, 314*(5805), 1560-1563.

Paolucci, M. (2005). *Reputation as a complex cognitive artefact. Theory, simulations, experiments.* Unpublished Phd thesis, University of Firenze.

Paolucci, M., Marsero, M., & Conte, R. (2000). What's the use of gossip? A sensitivity analysis of the spreading of normative reputation. In R. Suleiman, K. Troitzsch, & N. Gilbert (Eds.), *Tools and techniques for social science simulation.* Berlin, Germany.

Staller, A., & Petta, P. (2001). Introducing emotions into a computational study of social norms: A first verification. *Journal of Artificial Societies and Social Simulation, 4*(1).

Turrini, P., Paolucci, M., & Conte, R. (2006). Social responsibility among deliberative agents. In P. Peppas (Ed.), *Proceedings of STAIRS'06* (pp. 38-49). IOS Press.

Van der Hoek, W., Van Linder, B., & Meyer, J. J. Ch. (1997). An integrated modal approach to rational agents. In *Proceedings of PRR97, Practical Reasoning and Rationality.*

Yamagishi, T., & Matsuda, M. (2002). *Improving the lemons market with a reputation system: An experimental study of Internet auctioning.* Retrieved from http://joi.ito.com/archives/papers/Yamagishi_ASQ1.pdf

Endnotes

[1]   The platform for this experiment has been developed in collaboration with Jordi Sabater.

[2]   Some measures can be taken against identity changes, each providing a different level of security. Of course, these are all based on identity consistency in the real world. The more relaxed identification mechanisms depend upon entrance costs, ranging from time-consuming, and hence discouraging, subscription procedures to monetary entrance fees. The main point is that while identity shifts endanger reputation, anonymity favors exchanges and is generally seen as an asset of electronic interaction.

[3]   We remind that action determinism—which is a constraint of our model—means that $\models <do_i(a)> \varphi \rightarrow [do_i(a)] \varphi$, that is, each action leads to, at most, one world state. Strong determinism adds an action unicity condition.

Chapter VIII

Strategic Management, Evolutionary Economics, and Complex Adaptive Systems

Carl Henning Reschke, Institute for Management Research Cologne, Germany

Sascha Kraus, Vienna University of Economics & Business Administration, Austria

Abstract

This chapter sketches a strategic map of a selection of the relevant issues at the intersection of economics, psychology, sociology, and evolutionary theories applied to strategic management. It takes an evolutionary complexity perspective, based on a (manageable) selection of the relevant literature. The discussion focuses on evolutionary processes of change and their implications for strategic planning and related issues of organisation. The chapter concludes by discussing practical and research issues.

Introduction

This chapter argues that the process of *strategic management* is analogous to evolution and learning processes (Alchian, 1950; Dopfer, 2001; Veblen, 1898). We argue that economic evolution based on competition, cooperation (Nash 1953; Von Neumann 1945), innovation, and tradition in organizations (Nelson & Winter, 1982; Schumpeter, 1993) is structurally comparable to evolutionary processes in biology (Goertzel, 1992; Kane, 1996; Smith & Szathmary, 1995; Standish, 2000). Therefore, an evolutionary framework can be used to integrate planning and management processes in strategy making.

The evolutionary approach shows many similarities to complexity perspectives on physical and social phenomena, where complexity perspectives can provide (technical) tools for data analysis, and evolutionary perspectives can provide an integrated conceptualization of the process.

Each of the relevant disciplines offers a specific way of dealing with complex phenomena, with distinctive advantages and disadvantages. Physics supplies the measures for potentially relevant characteristics of social systems. Computer science aims at algorithmic accounts of how complex systems can be artificially constructed. Biology provides more than 200 years of research experience dealing with the history and the consequences of complex interaction, competitive processes, and creation of novelty. Methodologically, the successful integration of these areas requires a transfer of complex adaptive systems methods and evolutionary concepts, as well as development of further methods in the complexity/simulation area. The chapter therefore discusses how these areas intersect conceptually.

In consequence, we suggest integrating evolutionary and complexity approaches for the management of social systems, particularly with respect to long-term strategic issues. Doing so requires using such a perspective in *research* on strategic management issues as well. The aim of this chapter is to sketch a strategic map of some of the relevant issues at the intersection of economics, psychology, sociology, and evolutionary theories applied to strategic management, when seen from an evolutionary complexity perspective. In the section section we discuss the background fields of evolutionary theory, organizational learning, social systems, elements of psychology, and strategy. In the third section we discuss the evolutionary and the complexity view on strategy, and in the fourth section we derive implications for research and practice. The last section presents future issues and concludes.

Background

Evolutionary Theory

Evolutionary thinking shifts attention from a generalized standard optimality criterion to a differentiated account of selection criteria and selection conditions in specific circumstances as it explicitly asks for the adaptive value of specific characteristics (Lorenz, 1977; Mayr, 1982; Riedl, 1978). However, evolutionary theory bears some characteristics of a scientific paradigm and is thus more than just a theoretical system with its associated instruments. This can explain some of the tension between evolutionary approaches and those derived from the so-called "hard sciences." Complexity and reduction approaches are not competitors, but complementary approaches that both have distinctive advantages. Complexity perspectives are especially valuable if used in a "constructive" form, that is, validating the elements that have been found by reduction of systems and phenomena to the bare necessary elements. The question of research thus becomes: how do systems have to be composed and which "development paths" are to be taken to generate the observed real patterns? This offers a way of validating scientific results in social sciences analogous to the experiment of the natural sciences. Applying these results to social systems research allows to identify several research directions: recording and comparing characteristics of complex systems, explaining the existence of complex systems, explaining the history of complex systems, and trying to predict future developments. These questions are of practical importance in the strategic management of organizations.

The distinctive focus of the systemic evolutionary school are selection processes internal to an organism, the constraining and directing force of existing structures (Riedl, 1978), and the functional interaction of (organic) systems and their parts for the evolution of adaptations. It is argued that morphological and hierarchical constraints in the organization of information govern the evolution of biological systems. The emergence of stable "species" requires a balance between traditional structures and variation. At times these constraints are broken, which leads to a realm of opportunity for exploration and (relatively) rapid change (Crutchfield, 2001; Gould & Eldredge, 1977).

Systemic evolutionary theory is closely connected to an epistemological view of evolution. Mutations are like hypotheses that are tested in the biological environment. Successful selection of variants leads to the build up of knowledge about the life-world of a species. From this perspective, selection provides "feedback" effects from "the environment" on the medium that carries information over successive generations. These feedback effects are obvious in social systems, but are usually rejected in standard evolutionary biology (the so called Neo-Darwinian synthesis). It should be noted, however, that systemic evolutionary theory does not argue for a Lamarckian theory of evolution, but for a feedback effect on the level of the population via successfully selected structures. These are built up cumulatively and influence the direction of evolutionary processes. Systemic evolutionary theory therefore does not reject the standard Neo-Darwinian synthesis, but rather claims that this theory needs to be extended (Riedl, 1978).

Strategy and Organizations

The complexity perspectives on strategy and organizations can still be seen as a fledgling field despite some (text)books (e.g., Mittleton-Kelly, 2003; Stacey, 1993) and a growing number of articles (Brown & Eisenhardt, 1997; Gavetti & Levinthal, 2000; Lane & Maxfield, 1997; McKelvey, 1999; Rivkin, 2000; Schilling, 2000; Warglien, 1995) adopting a complexity view. There is a link to the trade-off between exploitation and exploration (March, 1991) or between search and stability (Rivkin & Siggelkow, 2003). Some articles are related to an evolutionary view (e.g., Gavetti & Levinthal, 2000; Levinthal, 1997; Siggelkow, 2002). There are also relations to the configuration school (e.g., Miller & Friesen, 1980) and evolutionary perspectives of organizational change (Tushman & Rosenkopf, 1992). The main argument for adopting a complexity perspective on organizations and strategy usually runs along the following lines: The increasing complexity of markets as well as the speed of the change in the environment requires enterprises to be constantly prepared to use new possibilities and deal with badly calculable risks (Berndt, 1998). Thus, enterprises are often said to face "hypercompetition" (D'Aveni, 1994). Hypercompetition can be described as accelerating competition over price, quality, market position, and perception in the eye of stakeholders, in which some actors manage to attain unimitable positions (cf. Rivkin, 2000).

The increasing dynamics of business requires thinking in the interrelations in and between complex systems considering their constraints and opportunities for change (Stacey, 1993). This requires a sound knowledge of the historical development of organizational and social structures. These structures are successively layered expressions of historical decisions under economic constraints and (historical) actors' views that may be hidden today, but are likely still ingrained into these social systems. Changing these structures affects traditions that need to be considered and may exist for more or other reasons than an organizational efficiency view suggests. Therefore, as Malik (1993) argues, evolutionary thinking is always thinking in systemic contexts.

Strategic management needs to consider organizational culture, that is, the system of shared meaning, values, and beliefs. This system is tremendously important for the development and growth of an organization and the transfer of knowledge within, which results in an evolutionary process (March & Simon, 1958; Nelson & Winter, 1982). Organizational culture is condition and result of the social system. Thereby, the network of values, faith conceptions, cognitive and normative orientation patterns hold the system together on the mental level. A certain culture can never be "ordered" from the inside or "attached" from the outside. Rather, it develops due to a reflexive development process and is thus a result of the dynamics inside the network, for example, in the form of self-organization processes. In times of rapid, unforeseeable change, those processes and structures are likely to be economic successfully, that is, of high adaptive value, which permit experiments and diminish obstacles for the learning processes (cf. Lorenz, 1977; MacKay, 1956). Thinking in networks facilitates the handling of these complex problems. Only an integrated approach that considers a variety of factors—in contrast to an isolated view, followed in many disciplines—can lead to the goal of successfully managing complex systems.

Strategic management depends on managing a dynamically changing network of influences. The task of strategic leaders is to create dynamic equilibrium between the enterprise and its environment (Smith & Tushman, 2005). The principles of evolution and self-organization in natural systems can be applied to innovations and dealing with complexity and uncertainty (Kirsch, 1997). Management needs to be situatively adapted with complexity. This means to reduce complexity when situations and requirements are principally known and to increase complexity in situations of uncertainty and change, such as the development of new products and processes. A reduction of rules and creation of spaces of freedom in networks fosters innovation. A creative environment can be built by reducing inflexible hierarchies and striving for power as well as measures fostering open communication, openness to experimental approaches, and measures for conflict management (Steinbrecher, 1990). Management is thus not so much oriented at optimization, but at balancing, integrating, and synthesizing different factors. Continuous development of the organization can be controlled via conditions and rules, needs to be reflected upon, and needs to be adapted to the requirements of a changing situation (Malik, 1993).

We therefore develop a framework that allows analyzing organizational and competitive processes based on concepts from evolutionary biology, population ecology, and organization theory. It allows seeing the development of economic actors as ecologic-evolutionary process across several levels of aggregation. On this basis, we argue for the integration of strategic management concepts as parts of an evolutionary learning process and the complex adaptive systems perspective.

Complexity, Evolution, and Strategy

The Evolutionary View

Economics can be seen as a learning process that takes place in the form of arbitrage; entrepreneurship; invention and innovation; and strategy. Kirzner (1997) has discussed the equilibrating effects of entrepreneurs that look for price differentials for the same goods in different markets and trade them accordingly. Thus they look for imbalances in information and use it to profit, which transmits information from one market to another. In contrast, Schumpeter (1993) has discussed the dis-equilibrating effects of entrepreneurial behavior based on introducing and commercializing new innovations. Here new hypotheses about products and their chances in market segments are tested with the results being widely transmitted in an economy spawning imitation or demise of product ideas. Nelson and Winter (1982) have modelled Schumpeter's process based on systemic view of organization influenced by the work of Simon and March (1958), and model innovation in differing industrial regimes.

Strategy can be seen as a learning process, partly alongside to, interrelated with, and nested into other learning processes such as innovation and entrepreneurship. Developing and implementing strategies involves deriving and testing hypotheses about potential markets, their growth rates and sizes, the actions competitors take, and expected outcomes of this process. Reschke and Kraus (2007) describe an evolutionary characterization of economic processes with particular attention to innovation, strategy and entrepreneurship in industrial development. The basis for the link between these fields is that in all three areas, business actors build and test hypotheses that lead to learning processes, which can be described and analyzed in evolutionary terms. The use of an evolutionary perspective offers two advantages: (1) it supplies a framework that allows to think about economic processes in a "similar, but different" perspective, which allows to break habits of thinking for the purpose of innovating economic and management theory, and (2) it allows the transfer of modeling approaches and techniques found in (mathematical) biology to economic processes and vice versa.

This view of economics as an instance of a general evolutionary process allows and requires a manifold approach based on the different "foundation pillars" of evolutionary processes in the related social sciences. We can identify the following five evolutionary perspectives that are relevant for strategy:

1. **Complexity perspectives on social systems.** This will require a foundation in a behavioral perspective, just as sociology and economics do. In an evolutionary perspective, it is sensible to found it in the evolutionary heritage of man,

which affects cognition, social psychology, and strategic management. This relates particularly to evolutionary psychology (Tooby & Cosmides, 1989) and behavioral economics (e.g., Camerer & Loewenstein, 2004).

2. **Characterization of the evolutionary process.** It has been shown that economic and evolutionary learning processes can be captured in a Neo-Darwinian way (Hodgson & Knudsen, 2006), where mental representations based on Kelly's (1955) personal constructs seem to form the best alternative to routines (Nelson & Winter, 1982), which suffer from conceptual and operationalization shortcomings (Hodgson & Knudsen, 2006; Reschke, 2003) and delegate them to a role between interactor and replicator (Reschke, 2003, 2005a). The same seems true for Dawkin's (1989) memes, which suffer from similar shortcomings (Edmonds, 2005).

3. **Mathematical formulation of evolutionary processes in economics and strategy.** Inroads into this area have been made Reschke & Kraus, 2007; (Standish, 2000), which show that economic processes of competition and innovation can be dealt with in an ecologic-evolutionary framework, which resembles the modern synthesis of evolutionary biology and is based on (sociological) population ecology (Hannan & Freeman, 1989). Cognition needs to be built more deeply into this framework.

4. **Organization as information processing units.** Daft and Weick's (1984) view of organizations as information processing entities offers a useful starting point, particularly when combined with an evolutionary epistemological view (Lorenz, 1977; Riedl, 2000). The outcome of this information processing can be connected to Mintzberg's (1994) view of strategy as emergent resultant between actors' intentions and environmental influences.

5. **Co-evolutionary perspectives on organizational and industrial change.** Volberda and Lewin (2003) use the concept of co-evolution to describe the interaction between organizations and industries. Complexity and uncertainty lead to imitation in economic actors, which results in similar strategies and actions, among which fate selects (Alchian, 1950). This suggests searching for similar patterns and processes in the evolution of economic entities, for example, industries (McGahan, 2000; Reschke & Kraus, 2007). This line of reasoning leads to the development of typologies or taxonomies of organizations, which have been developed among others by Tung (1979) and McKelvey (1982) and the configuration school (e.g., Miller 1996). For a short overview of open issues in research see Harms, Kraus, and Reschke (in press).

If change is to be explained by an evolutionary model that requires us to explain how change is possible given differences in fitness among innovative and established, young and old products, technologies, or social tools. We can turn to evolutionary biology for an answer to the last question. How does variation and change come about on the level of molecular entities that underlie phenotypic effects? This question is addressed by Eigen and Schuster's (1977) quasi-species model. The quasi-species model presents a mechanism of adaptation to higher fitness based on a distribution of (incremental) variations around a consensus "wild-type" DNA-sequence of a species. A population of variants, which constitutes a species, is characterized by a distribution of variations around the optimal wild-type sequence. This distribution is characterized by decreasing frequencies for an increasing number of changes in DNA sequence away from the wild-type sequence. These variations provide the fuel of the evolutionary process in that they code for changes in the phenotype that might coincidentally be adapted to changing environmental conditions. The "cloud" of small variations in a species allows the "quasi-species" to move around on the landscape defined by environmental conditions enabling adaptation of the species to new circumstances. The speed of environmental change must be slow enough to allow for the generation of mutations producing the required characteristics. Otherwise, environmental change would be disruptive in the sense that new environmental conditions cannot be answered by a matching member of a species' population.

This model explains adaptation to novel circumstances by stating that species characteristics and fitness landscape move in concert with each other such that the adaptation path is smooth and monotonous. It means that fitness landscape move as well and thus allows adaptation if and when troughs in the fitness landscape get filled through co-evolutionary movements of variation distribution and fitness landscape itself. Depending on the degree of selection pressure, variations of (slightly) lower fitness than the wild-type may be viable or not. This element of near-neutral mutations could even explain the move through some fitness valleys.

However, the Eigen and Schuster (1977) model does not explain how new adaptations can be sustained and reach better optima, if they have to move through larger fitness troughs, that is, moving from one local optimum to another one through a trough of lower fitness and that fitness landscape does not move. One solution is to assume macro-mutations (Goldschmidt, 1940) that jump from one favorable position to another, corresponding to large step sizes in variations that immediately lead to complex adaptations. This solution has been ruled out in evolutionary biology. However, the observation of large, comparatively fast phenotypic changes in the paleontologic record did not quite exclude this solution (Gould & Eldredge, 1977). Another solution is presented by the systemic evolutionary school that emphasizes the modular nature of evolutionary adaptation and the codification of these. Larger step sizes of variation are possible if modular elements can be reused for new functions in organisms even if they are not well adapted but "necessary" in its formation from embryo to adult and/or required for the generation of steps that follow in ontological development of an organism (Riedl, 1978).

The Complexity View

As hinted at in the model of Eigen and Schuster (1977), the process of learning in social systems such as economies and organizations can be seen as a process of hill climbing on shifting, co-evolving fitness landscapes in order to find relatively better positions (Anderson, Arrow, & Pines, 1988; Kane, 1996; cf. also Volberda & Lewin, 2003 and the literature in the strategy section). Research into the improvement of technical artifacts by means of simulated random variation (e.g., Rechenberg, 1973) has highlighted the importance of the properties of the fitness function and the variation event in evolutionary optimization processes (cf. also Kauffman, 1993). The fitness function (usually assumed to be constant in such exercises) should be smooth and increasing steadily, points of higher fitness should not be too far away from the starting point. This means for biology that small changes in the genetic code should lead to small changes in associated fitness values. There also should not be too many troughs and peaks in the fitness landscape. Success of variations also depends on the size of a mutation step. The size of an optimal variation step depends in turn on the topology of the fitness landscape, leading to the concept of a window of evolution around this optimal step size. Step sizes larger than this window usually lead to stabilizing selection since the variations created by them are extremely prone to extinction as they usually "land" in farther away and thus more "risky" areas of lower fitness values which likely to be of lower heights than previous achievements.

In social systems (such as organizations), one can use human's ability for foresight and planning to explain how companies or business units may be made to move through periods of "resource drought" and lower fitness levels until profits are made with a new product or service. However, this is only true if the vision is shared among employees, the concept is sponsored by powerful people in the organization, and enough resources are available. For young enterprises, business angels and venture capitalists can provide these resources. However, practice shows that neither in large nor in small organizations this is necessarily a path to successful adaptation. It may get stuck in political fights or foresight and planning may mislead into fata morganas of markets and/or cost positions that do not materialize. On the other hand, venture capitalists, due to their insistence on profitable exits in a foreseeable future, may curtail opportunities that offer higher returns, but are riskier and farer away, corresponding to limited step sizes that allow moving over smaller troughs in fitness landscapes but shying away from the larger chasms.

One way to account for change in social systems may be the interaction between social and physical "realms." These are discussed based on some elements of Beinhocker's (2006) popular book *The Origin of Wealth*. The book has recently drawn some (controversial) attention, and at the same time draws together most relevant elements for a complexity/evolutionary perspective on competition, strategy and growth in economics. It therefore serves as a good starting point for discussing the implications of a complexity perspective on strategy and change. Beinhocker argues for a biological evolutionary view of economic processes on the basis of complexity theory and associated methods (e.g., Anderson et al., 1988, Arthur, Durlauf, & Lane, 1997). He describes the economic process as a special case (just as evolutionary biology) of a general evolutionary process (see also Riedl, 2000), which is based on the re-combinatory generation, variation, and selection of modules of "business plans" (respectively their outcomes in terms of product offerings and services) in organizations, markets, and society at large. In his words, "business plans combine social technologies and physical technologies under a strategy, understood as a goal and way(s) to achieve them" (Beinhocker, 2006, p. 293). Products such as sweaters that can be bought by customers are, just as business plans, however not de-novo variations but strongly influenced by the history of past designs (see also Arthur, 1989; David, 1985, 1992; Mokyr, 2002). Beinhocker's contribution can be criticized on several counts (apart from glitches that popular accounts almost inevitably must have in the eyes of scientists), the most important being the link between model and reality—a point that other complexity based simulations share.

One way to improve the link between complexity model and modeled reality is to define the layers from individual actors up to patterns of social behavior and how they are interlinked. Beinhocker (2006) uses the concept of schemata that stems from evolutionary algorithms (Banzhaf, Nordin, Keller, & Francone, 1998) as model for cognitive elements. While postulation of schemata allows easy transfer of evolutionary algorithm methodology, the question remains what the equivalents to schemata in social psychology are. Similar questions are allowed for the use of NK-models by Gavetti and Levinthal (2000), but see also Gavetti (2005) based on Kauffman (1993). An answer can be provided by the following line of reasoning, which covers the field from individual and group mental representations (Kelly, 1955) as units of information "storage," locus of learning, and controller of actions up to aggregated patterns of social behavior. Thus the complexity view on strategy requires asking: How are the equivalents of Beinhocker's social and physical technologies combined into strategies?

The more or less intuitive answer is that this happens through analytical and creative cognitive processes, which are embedded in and composed of individual and social psychological processes and obviously correlated with effects on and feedbacks from the real world. As Veblen (1898) already has argued a long time ago, institutions such as habits, norms, and cognitive patterns as "frames of mind" are passed on in social systems and shape the actions of actors. Cloak's (1975) model of interaction between cultural instructions and material culture (that serves to propagate its cultural instructions and in turn affects the composition of cultural instructions) seems a useful structure for modeling such social learning processes. The structure is of course modeled on the biological evolutionary process. As we have seen that seems useful for modeling learning also (Hodgson & Knudsen, 2006; Mokyr, 2002).

However, Nelson and Winter's (1982) routines cannot be taken easily as replicators (Hodgson & Knudsen, 2006), rather hierarchically organized mental representations are suitable for this role (Kelly, 1955; Reschke, 2003; 2005a; cf. also Gavetti, 2005 for a similar argument from the point of view of complexity, criticizing the routine concept in evolutionary economics).

To drill further down to the bottom: Cloak (1975) links cultural instructions to interneural instructions, which further links into (evolutionary) psychology (e.g., Tooby & Cosmides, 1989). The link up to aggregated social patterns is provided by the following line of reasoning: Cognition, in turn, is based on individual shaping of beliefs through childhood, youth, adolescence, and maturity respectively later development as well as social psychological processes that shape thought and action (Bandura, 1986; Weick, 1987), which aggregate up into processes of social construction of reality (Berger & Luckmann, 1966).

Thus, cognition, associated actions, and feedback from these on cognitive frames can be seen as the gluing process between the development of new forms of social interactions and inventions in the form of new artifacts. Both, taken together, may be turned into innovations, if cognition of entrepreneurs and business people about markets and product strategy as well as consumers on products fits (relating to the arguments of Schumpeter [1993]), given institutional arrangements [relating to the works of e.g., Veblen (1898), Coase (1937), & Williamson (1981)]—or if strategy, products, and consumer perceptions can be made to fit—via marketing. Thus fit between a company, its strategy, and its environment is mediated through historically shaped "co-evolving" cognition elements expressed in strategy and product image which influence consumer adoption. Therefore strategy and marketing play important roles in the gluing process (Hunt & Morgan, 1995) leading to product life cycles in their various forms (Lambkin & Day, 1989). Epidemiologic diffusion models (Mansfield, 1961; Rogers, 2003) are often used to model this process and should be differentiated for relevant cognitive and sociological factors, which might explain split up of adoption curves in smaller s-curves (Gold, 1989) and deviations from the prototypical product life cycle (Tellis & Crawford, 1981).

Implications

Implications for Research

The link between the complexity perspective-based computer simulations and the modeled mental and physical elements of complexity perspectives such as Beinhocker's is indeed weak. This shortcoming can partly be explained by slow acceptance of computer simulations as a modeling tool in scientific discourse. It will likely proceed largely by the emergence of a new generation of scientists as described by Kuhn (1970). However, also other simulations can still be criticized for lacking an established connection between model and reality.

Therefore complexity perspectives need to establish a link between reality and model through focus on the specification of the model that needs to correspond in characteristics to the real phenomenon. What needs to be shown here is not so much that complexity models are useful modeling tools to capture specific characteristics (we know that), but—turning the direction of thinking around—that reality conforms to assumptions about functional forms, and process characteristics made in complexity models. This is a difficult endeavor, as it requires detailed collection and the testing of large data sets and usually cannot be done by the modeler and certainly not alone. This approach conforms to the strategy used in biology, and less so in economics, for instance. However, economic modeling is after more than 100 years still being criticized for its specific mathematic modeling strategy (e.g., Mirowski, 1989) on the grounds that the characteristics of actors and model do not closely enough match reality—which at least implies there is a link between models and reality, while the complexity perspective still needs to argue about making the link at all. Furthermore, constraints are getting scientists: (1) to engage in cross-disciplinary, long-term projects, (2) to identify suitable fields for data analysis, and (3) to transfer knowledge about complex data analysis to social scientists. However, complexity perspectives can supply a lot of tools for data identification and analysis in large, often unstructured data sets.

Coincidentally, the development of evolutionary biology can show the way here—detailed historical research plus modeling. These issues may be rectified if the complexity perspective is accompanied by an account of how the elements in the complexity view link together. This can be achieved by building on elements of (systemic) evolutionary theory, which is complemented by an epistemological view on evolutionary processes. This epistemological view in turn matches with the idea that there is a general theory of evolution whose instances can be found in biological nature and economic processes. Both share the basic variation/selection/retention nature of evolution processes. However, specific conditions in natural and social evolution lead to differing characteristics of the process (Riedl, 2000).

Practical Implications

On a more practical plane of organization and strategy, the issue is how to jump from one good, established technology, strategy, or organization form to one that is still inferior, but that promises to be superior in the future, given further development. In that respect, the question for managers arises: how to manage the transition between two differing paths of adaptation, particularly when there are diverging interests and opinions on the viability of the new versus old field of business. Thus, strategic management requires answers to whether—and if so when and how—or not to switch strategic paths. It can be assumed that switching—as all change efforts—need additional resources to bridge the path from one trajectory to another one (which is often enough neglected to make the case for change efforts more easily). Economics would prescribe to estimate cost of switching, gains from switching, relative to cost of staying on a path, and gains; strategists would implement that analysis possibly under differing scenarios so as to derive alternative options for alternative futures. That is a straightforward procedure—and often results in wrong estimates, as assumptions must be made. It is certainly not useful to follow an average path, since that is likely inferior to both options.

The planning issue is related to the issue of exploration versus exploitation (Cohen & Levinthal, 1990; Smith & Tushman, 2005), that is, how much to look around and draw in new information, technologies, and organizational forms (and when to stop exploration) versus how much to stick to established programs of action and exploit its proceeds, possibly gaining from efficiency improvements through moving down a learning curve. This requires tools to measure learning effects. These can alert mangers to situations when learning effects (e.g., measured as cost savings with increasing volume) start to decline, in order to take this as a signal to look for new fields. This rationale was moulded into, for example, the Boston Consulting Group matrix with limited success, which is particularly due to rules prescribing too early divestment of ultimately promising projects (Phelan, 2005).

Planning tools should therefore be used to get a grip on future developments. Analysis and planning for future paths should be seen as a sounding and test effort (Hamel & Prahalad, 1994; Reschke & Kraus, 2007) to investigate which options to take under different scenarios. Long-term planning needs to be differentiated from short-term planning focussed on implementing a path towards a specific future. Here also the different views of management with respect to the impact of environmental change need to be considered (Javidan, 1984). However, implementing this kind of planning and differentiating between long-term and implementation-oriented planning requires an adaptable, flexible organization that can withstand the threats of traditionalizing forces ingrained into routines.

One solution to deal with such complex situations is to employ hierarchies and modularization. Strategy can be seen as Lego®-like-strategizing: using modular building blocks to compose complex but adaptable organizations. Management is dealing with a process of interactions between organizational or strategic modules that are usually in turn composed of interactions between further elements. While such a view has been promoted in many books and articles, the focus has been on seeing the elements as relatively simple entities and on stressing that the results of interaction will produce nonlinear and/or holistic outcomes, against earlier views of management as a linear, decomposable process. The linear view had fostered the view that organizations and tasks may be easily cut in parts and dealt with in linear parts.

This usually does not work over longer time horizons and larger systems with many interrelations—particularly if it is not accompanied by knowledge of how an organization has evolved its structures and fit with the environment. Furthermore, it is important to connect the vision about future developments back to the history of an organization, as organizations will not sustain large changes from the past without a means to cross the chasms between new and old structures. This knowledge and vision can be supplied by an evolutionary view of organizational development. Thus, an evolutionary view of management adds the knowledge of the past as the force shaping the relations between modules and determining *how* easily they may be cut apart and reassembled. That is, development paths, historical constraints, adaptation, constrain systems in their development paths, and options—which may be used to change them so as adapt to the requirements of specific situations, including meta-rules for when to start to change and adapt again.

Complexity perspectives based on physics, often tend to share a strategy of cutting up problems into simple problems. Therefore, they should be accompanied by an evolutionary view to deal with situations on the lowest possible level of complexity, following the rules of requisite variety and subsidiarity, as otherwise complexity perspectives may be used as arguments to justify falling back into the traps of linear thinking and managing aggravated by the power of dealing with large data sets.

Conclusion

Future Issues

From the point of view of a complexity perspective, the issue for management is how to adapt on moving/co-evolving fitness landscapes and when and where to move across larger troughs in fitness. The Eigen-Schuster model tries to answer this question for biology by having adaptive variations and fitness landscapes moving in concert (or waiting for changes until fitness landscape has changed). The systemic evolutionary school tries to answer it by stressing the hierarchical organization of the codification of adaptive traits that allow larger jumps through structures space. One can argue that the similar processes as in the Eigen-Schuster model happen in large business organizations: Decisions are not made until advantages are clearly proven, which means that the gap in fitness has closed. However, at that point it is often too late to gain many rewards from the new technology, product, and organization form. This waiting period between emergence of a technology and its acceptance into the mainstream, offers advantages, windows of opportunity for smaller or more agile visionaries who believe in the value of approaches before they are proven (Moore, 2005)—and explains a lot of their risk. This in turn explains the dynamics of the process of industrial evolution, which can be captured in configurations (Harms et al., in press; Miller & Friesen, 1980) that should correspond to hills on fitness landscapes. Thus an accurate representation of the fitness landscape and its future changes can be used for risk assessment and management as well as planning and strategic management.

For instance, strategic management and industrial evolution can be conceived of as process of movements of competing and/or each other sustaining organizations along stable paths of configurations of variables that describe internal and external relations of the organization, its elements and environment. These configurations conform to the attractors of nonlinear systems (or local optima in economics). Often they need to change only incrementally, however sometimes also radically in order to maintain fit between organizations to environmental conditions. The process of economic industrial/organizational adaptation leads to local optima, if movements to optima are faster than shifts in the underlying fitness landscape; otherwise the process of social development tracks these optima in certain distances, which underlies Schumpeter's (1993) dynamic view of competition (Andersen, 1996) and may lead to a conceptual framework for historical development processes (cf. Reschke, 2005b).

One of the major problems in such evolutionary, complex development process is finding an orientation for managers and politicians alike. This often leads to a focus on idealized versions of past configurations, optima, and attractors that seem to have worked until new optima/attractors emerge. These new attractors may or may not conform to some degree to old ones. In cases of self-fulfilling prophecies the new attractors may resemble the old. However, specific configurations of forces may favor feeble and visionary, entrepreneurially-minded actors may use these to establish new attractors, as cases such as FedEx, South-West Airlines, or Dell suggest. The point of switching to a new path of adaptation, that is, changing radically depends on their ability to change, that is, the political and economic situation in an organization, the forces that are favored and the perception of actors' (vision) particularly of the "resource patch" that is available at both alternatives over time.

This view suggests starting a research program into developing a transition matrix between configurations of organizations. This matrix would tell researchers how likely the transition from one configuration of interactions to other types of configurations was historically given specific environmental conditions. This would be as desirable for entrepreneurial ventures (Harms et al., in press) as for established ones. Managers would be provided with a structure for building a map into their future based on a typology of past situations. Since "the future is open" (Popper, 1985), this map should not be used as a guide to seeing the future through the past but as a tool to prepare for the future, particularly when developments do not match the map anymore, as "luck favours the prepared mind" (Pasteur, 1854).

Conclusion

We have argued that a theory of economic processes informed by complexity and systemic evolutionary concepts may be able to better deal with the tension between tradition and innovation than any of these schools alone. Complexity perspectives provide the capability for data analysis, rigorous model building, and simulation of large systems. Systemic evolutionary theory argues that there must be a sufficient degree of variability of biological (sub) systems to ensure evolutionary change and that there must be sufficient traditionalizing forces in order to prevent drifting apart of a species' characteristics, which resembles theory and observations in organizational and innovation studies. Thus, this theory can be used to inform strategy making.

Obviously the story sketched here still has many limitations: The framework presented needs to be developed further and has to be tested empirically in its application to organizations. This requires research into the historical formation of constraints and opportunities for change in organizations. This research can be informed by systemic evolutionary biology and sociological theories on the evolution of modern society and requires data analysis tools from complexity research.

The research and particularly the results flowing from systemic evolutionary and complexity views may thus be employed in politics and management. The realization that linear models do not carry as far as we expected them to may not be surprising anymore. However, this still leaves the question unanswered what to do and how to do it if the world is a complex aggregation of evolving interactions. Even if we believe that "plus ça change, plus c'est la même chose" (Alphonse Karr in *Les Guelpes*, 1849, p. 305), there are still changes that need to be placed in the proper context of dynamical developments. And if history tends to repeat first as tragedy then as farce, as Karl Marx stated—we can learn from the past, but we need to be aware of the changes from the past at the same time. The internal "contents" and external conditions of change, the resulting developments, the intensity, and particularly the speed of required change are new and unprecedented. This correlates with a decrease in certainty about the direction of change and the right choices. Much of what was real, machine-like, determined, and objective became unpredictable, indefinable, and subjective in the middle of the last century (Arthur, 1999). If seen "systemically," the conditions for economic actors in a changing environment are doubly uncertain as trends in the environment cannot be identified and inabilities to calculate and predict developments increase. The knowledge required for identifying the best alternative is beyond the possibilities of actors (Hayek, 1945). Dealing with uncertainty, complexity, and the search for novelty are becoming increasingly important. Positioning advice and value chain analysis, re-engineering and "foresight" perspectives may be a short-term help to managers facing new competitors, new technologies, and cost pressures, but do not convey information on where to go and how to get there in dynamic, uncertain environments that nevertheless seem to follow historic patterns (Reschke, 2005a, 2005b).

These requirements can be fulfilled potentially by combining the power of historical analysis based on an evolutionary framework with the power of complexity tools to test specific hypotheses by researching data in large sets of information.

References

Alchian, A. (1950). Uncertainty, evolution, and economic theory. *Journal of Political Economy, 58,* 211-221.

Andersen, E. S. (1996). *Evolutionary economics: Post-Schumpeterian contributions.* London: Pinter.

Anderson, P. W., Arrow, K. J., & Pines, D. (Eds.). (1988). *The economy as an evolving complex system.* SFI Studies in the Sciences of Complexity. Redwood City, CA: Addison-Wesley.

Arthur, W. B. (1989). Competing technologies, increasing returns, and lock-in by historical events. *Economic Journal, 99,* 116-131.

Arthur, W. B. (1999). The end of economic certainty. In J. H. Clippinger (Ed.), *The biology of business—Decoding the natural laws of enterprise* (pp. 31-46). San Francisco: Jossey-Bass.

Arthur, W. B., Durlauf, S., & Lane, D. (Eds.). (1997). *The economy as an evolving complex system II.* Reading, MA: Addison-Wesley.

Bandura, A. (1986). *Social foundations of thought and action: A social cognitive theory.* Englewood Cliffs, NJ: Prentice Hall.

Banzhaf, W., Nordin, P., Keller, R. E., & Francone, F. D. (1998). *Genetic programming. An introduction.* San Francisco: Morgan Kaufmann.

Beinhocker, E. (2006). *The origin of wealth, evolution, complexity and the radical remaking of economics.* London: Random House.

Berger, P. L., & Luckmann, T. (1966). *The social construction of reality: A treatise its the sociology of knowledge.* Garden City, NY: Anchor Books.

Berndt, R. (1998). *Unternehmungen im Wandel.* Berlin, Germany.

Brown, S. L., & Eisenhardt, K. M., (1997). The art of continuous change: Linking complexity theory and time-paced evolution in relentlessly shifting organizations. *Administrative Science Quarterly, 42,* 1-34.

Camerer, C. F., & Loewenstein, G. (2004). Behavioral economics: Past, present, future. In C. F. Camerer, G. Loewenstein, & R. Matthew (Eds.), *Advances in behavioral economics* (pp. 3-51). Princeton and Oxford: Princeton University Press.

Cloak, F. T. (1975). Is a cultural ethology possible? *Human Ecology, 3,* 161-182.

Coase, R. (1937). The nature of the firm. *Economica, 4*(16), 386-405.

Cohen, W., & Levinthal, D. (1990). Innovation and learning: The two faces of R&D. *The Economic Journal, 99,* 569-596.

Crutchfield, J. P. (2001). When evolution is revolution—Origins of innovation. In J. P. Crutchfield & P. Schuster (Eds.), *Evolutionary dynamics—Exploring the interplay of selection, neutrality, accident and function.* Oxford, UK: Oxford University Press.

D'Aveni, R. A. (1994). *Hypercompetition: Managing the dynamics of strategic maneuvering.* New York: Free Press.

Daft, R. L., & Weick, K. E. (1984). Toward a model of organizations as interpretation systems. *Academy of Management Review, 9,* 284-295.

David, P. A. (1985). Clio and the economics of QWERTY. *American Economic Review, 75* (2), 332-337.

David, P. A. (1992). Heroes, herds, and hysteresis in technological history: Thomas Edison and "The Battle of the Systems" reconsidered. *Industrial and Corporate Change, 1,* 129-180.

Dawkins, R. (1989). *The extended phenotype: The long reach of the gene* (Rev. and extended ed.). Oxford, UK: Oxford University Press.

Dopfer, K. (2001). *Evolutionary economics. Program and scope.* Dordrecht, The Netherlands: Kluwer.

Edmonds, B. (2005). The revealed poverty of the gene-meme analogy—Why memetics per se has failed to produce substantive results. *Journal of Memetics—Evolutionary Models of Information Transmission, 9.*

Eigen, M., & Schuster, P. (1977). *The hypercycle. A principle of natural self-organization.* Berlin, Germany: Springer.

Gavetti, G. (2005). Cognition and hierarchy: Rethinking the microfoundations of capabilities' development. *Organization Science, 16*(6), 599-617.

Gavetti, G., & Levinthal, D. E. (2000). Looking forward and looking backward: Cognitive and experiential search. *Administrative Science Quarterly, 45*(1), 113-137.

Goertzel, B. (1992). Self-organizing evolution. *Journal of Social and Evolutionary Systems, 15,* 7-54.

Gold, B. (1989). On the adoption of technological innovations in industry: Superficial models and complex decision processes. *Omega, 8*(5), 505-516.

Goldschmidt, R. (1940). *The material basis of evolution.* New Haven, CT: Yale University Press.

Gould, S. J., & Eldredge, N. (1977). Punctuated equilibria: The tempo and mode of evolution reconsidered. *Paleobiology, 3,* 115-151.

Hamel, G., & Prahalad, C. K. (1994). *Competing for the future.* Boston: Harvard University Business Press.

Hannan, M. T., & Freeman, J. (1989). *Organizational ecology.* Cambridge, MA: Harvard University Press.

Harms, R., Kraus, S., & Reschke, C. H. (in press). Configurations of new ventures in entrepreneurship research—Contributions and research gaps. *Management Research News.*

Hayek, F. A. (1945). The use of knowledge in society. *American Economic Review, 35*(4), 519-530.

Hodgson, G. M., & Knudsen, T. (2006). Dismantling Lamarckism: Why descriptions of socio-economic evolution as Lamarckian are misleading. *Journal of Evolutionary Economics, 16,* 343-366.

Hunt, S. D., & Morgan, R. M. (1995). The comparative advantage theory of competition. *Journal of Marketing, 59,* 1-15.

Javidan, M. (1984). The impact of environmental uncertainty on long-range planning practices of the U.S. savings and loan industry. *Strategic Management Journal, 5,* 381-392.

Kane, D. (1996). Local hillclimbing on an economic landscape. In L. J. Fogel, P. J. Angeline, & T. Bäck (Eds.), *Evolutionary programming V: Proceedings of the Fifth Annual Conference on Evolutionary Programming.* Cambridge, MA: MIT Press.

Karr, A. (1849). *Les Guepes*, p. 305. January 31, 1849.

Kauffman, S. A. (1993). *The origins of order. Self-organization and selection in evolution.* Oxford: Oxford University Press.

Kelly, G. A. (1955). *The psychology of personal constructs* (2 Vols.). New York: Norton.

Kirsch, W. (1997). *Strategisches management. Die geplante evolution von Unternehmungen.* Munich, Germany: Kirsch.

Kirzner, I. (1997). Entrepreneurial discovery and the competitive market process: An Austrian approach. *Journal of Economic Literature, 35,* 60-85.

Kuhn, T. (1970). *The structure of scientific revolutions* (2nd, enlarged ed.). Chicago: UOC Press. (Original work published 1962)

Lambkin, M., & Day, G. S. (1989). Evolutionary processes in competitive markets: Beyond the product life cycle. *Journal of Marketing, 53,* 4-20.

Lane, D. A., & Maxfield, R. (1997). Foresight, complexity and strategy. In W. B. Arthur, S. Durlauf, & D. A. Lane (Eds.), *The economy as an evolving complex system II: Proceedings, Santa Fe Institute Studies in the Sciences of Complexity, 27.* Reading, MA: Addison Wesley.

Levinthal, D. (1997). Adaptation on rugged landscapes. *Management Science, 43,* 934-950.

Lorenz, K. (1977). *Behind the mirror: A search for the natural history of human knowledge.* New York: Harcourt Brace Jovanovich.

MacKay, D. M. (1956). The epistemological problem for automata. In C. E. Shannon & J. McCarthy (Eds.), *Automata studies.* NJ: Princeton University Press.

Malik, F. (1993). *Systemisches management, evolution, selbstorganisation. Grundprobleme, funktionsmechanismen und lösungsansätze für komplexe systeme.* Berne: Haupt.

Mansfield, E. (1961). Technical change and the rate of imitation. *Econometrica, 29,* 741-66.

March, J. G. (1991). Exploration and exploitation in organizational learning. *Organization Science, 2,* 71-87.

March, J. G., & Simon, H. (1958). *Organizations.* New York: Wiley.

Mayr, E. 1982. *The growth of biological thought: Diversity, evolution and inheritance.* Cambridge, MA: Harvard University Press.

McGahan, A. M. (2000). How industries evolve. *Business Strategy Review, 11*(3), 1-16.

McKelvey, B. (1982). *Organizational systematics—Taxonomy, evolution, classification.* Berkeley, CA: University of California Press.

McKelvey, B. (1999). Avoiding complexity catastrophe in coevolutionary pockets: Strategies for rugged landscapes. *Organization Science, 10*(3), 249-321.

Miller, D. (1996). Configurations revisited. *Strategic Management Journal, 17*(7), 505-512.

Miller, D., & Friesen, P. H. (1980). Momentum and revolution in organizational adaptation. *Academy of Management Journal, 23,* 591-614.

Mintzberg, H. (1994). The fall and rise of strategic planning. *Harvard Business Review, 72*(1), 107-114.

Mirowski, P. (1989). *More heat than light. Economics as social physics, physics as nature's economics.* Cambridge, UK: Cambridge University Press.

Mittleton-Kelly, E. (Ed.). (2003). *Complex systems and evolutionary perspectives on organisations: The application of complexity theory to organisations.* Kidlington, UK: Elsevier.

Mokyr, J. (2002, February 11). *Useful knowledge as an evolving system: The view from economic history.* Evanston, IL: Northwestern University, Departments of Economics and History, and the Center for Advanced Studies in the Behavioral Sciences.

Moore, G.A. (2005). *Dealing with Darwin: How great companies innovate at every phase of their evolution.* New York: Portfolio.

Nash, J. (1953). Two-person cooperative games. *Econometrica, 21,* 128-140.

Nelson, R. R., & Winter, S. G. (1982). *An evolutionary theory of economic change.* Cambridge, MA: Harvard University Press.

Pasteur, L. (1854). Lecture, University of Lille, France, December 7, 1854.

Phelan, S. (2005). *The BCG matrix revisited: A computational approach.* Paper presented at the Academy of Management Meeting, 2005. Retrieved December 7, from http://www.unlv.edu/faculty/phelan/Research/BCG.pdf

Popper, K.R. (1985). *The future is open.* Altenberg talk with K. Lorenz. Munich: Piper.

Rechenberg, I. (1973). *Evolutionsstrategie—Optimierung technischer systeme nach prinzipien der biologischen evolution.* Stuttgart, Germany: Fommann-Holzboog.

Reschke, C. H. (2003). *Routines, economic selection and economic evolution: Critique and possibilities.* Paper presented at the DRUID Tenth Anniversary Summer Conference on Dynamics of Industry and Innovation: Organizations, Networks and Systems, Copenhagen, Denmark: CBS.

Reschke, C. H. (2005a). *Evolutionary processes in economics. The examples of strategy and research in the biopharmaceutical industry.* Unpublished doctoral dissertation, University of Witten/Herdecke, Germany.

Reschke, C. H. (2005b). *Strategy, the path of history and social evolution.* Paper presented at the Critical Management Studies Conference, CMS 04, Oxford, UK. Retrieved October 25, 2006, from www.mngt.waikato.ac.nz/ejrot/cmsconference/2005/abstracts/strategy/Reschke.pdf

Reschke, C. H., & Kraus, S. (2007). Strategy, innovation and entrepreneurship—An evolutionary learning perspective. In H. Hannappi & W. Elsner (Eds.), *Advances in evolutionary institutional economics.* London: Edward Elgar.

Riedl, R. (1978). *Order in living systems: A systems analysis of evolution.* New York: Wiley.

Riedl, R. (2000). *Strukturen der Komplexität. Eine Morphologie des Erkennens und Erklärens.* Berlin, Germany: Springer.

Rivkin, J. W. (2000). Imitation of complex strategies. *Management Science, 46*(6) 824-844.

Rivkin, J. W., & Siggelkow, N. (2003). Balancing search and stability: Interdependencies among elements of organizational design. *Management Science, 49,* 290-311.

Rogers, E. M. (2003). *Diffusion of innovations* (5th ed.). New York: Free Press.

Schilling, M. A. (2000). Toward a general modular systems theory and its application to interfirm product modularity. *Academy of Management Review, 25*(2), 312-334.

Schumpeter, J. A. (1993). *The theory of economic development*. (Original work published 1934). New Brunswick: Transaction Publishers.

Siggelkow, N. (2002). Evolution toward fit administrative. *Science Quarterly, 47*(1), 125-159.

Simon, H., & March, J.G. (1958). *Organizations*. New York: Wiley.

Smith, J. M., & Szathmary, E. (1995). *The major transitions in evolution*. Oxford, UK: Freeman.

Smith, W. K., & Tushman, M. L. (2005). Managing strategic contradictions: A top management model for managing innovations streams. *Organization Science, 16,* 522-536.

Stacey, R. D. (1993). *Strategic management and organisational dynamics*. London: Pitman.

Standish, R. K. (2000). The role of innovation within economics. In W. Barnett et al. (Eds.), *Commerce, complexity and evolution* (pp. 61-79). New York: Cambridge University Press.

Steinbrecher, M. (1990). *Systemisch-evolutionäres management—Von der Notwendigkeit ganzheitlichen Denkens und Handelns*. Berlin, Germany: Research Institute of the Daimler-Benz AG.

Tellis, G. J., & Crawford, M. (1981). An evolutionary approach to product growth theory. *Journal of Marketing, 45,* 125-132.

Tooby, J., & Cosmides, L. (1989). Evolutionary psychology and the generation of culture, part I, theoretical considerations. *Ethology and Sociobiology, 10,* 29-49.

Tung, R. L. (1979). Dimensions of organizational environments: An exploratory study of their impact on organization structure. *Academy of Management Journal, 22*(4), 672-693.

Tushman, M. L., & Rosenkopf, L. (1992). Organizational determinants of technological change. *Research in Organizational Behavior, 14,* 311- 347.

Veblen, T. (1898). Why is economics not an evolutionary science? *Quarterly Journal of Economics, 12,* 373-397.

Volberda, H. W., & Lewin, A. Y. (2003). Co-evolutionary dynamics within and between firms: From evolution to co-evolution. *Journal of Management Studies, 40,* 2105-30.

Von Neumann, J. (1945). A model of general economic equilibrium. *Review of Economic Studies, 13,* 1-9.

Warglien, M. (1995). Organizational adaptation and hierarchies. *Industrial and Corporate Change, 4,* 161-186.

Weick, K. E. (1987). Substitutes for strategy. In D. T. Teece (Ed.), *Competitive challenge strategies for industrial innovation and renewal* (pp. 221-233). Cambridge, UK: Ballinger.

Williamson, O. (1981). The economies of organization: The transaction cost approach. *American Journal of Sociology, 87,* 548-577.

Chapter IX

Building Complex Adaptive Systems:
On Engineering Self-Organizing Multi-Agent Systems

Jan Sudeikat[1], Hamburg University of Applied Sciences, Germany

Wolfgang Renz, Hamburg University of Applied Sciences, Germany

Abstract

Agent oriented software engineering (AOSE) proposes the design of distributed software systems as collections of autonomous and pro-active actors, so-called agents. Since software applications results from agent interplay in multi-agent systems (MASs), this design approach facilitates the construction of software applications that exhibit self-organizing and emergent dynamics. In this chapter, we examine the relation between self-organizing MASs (SO-MASs) and complex adaptive systems (CASs), highlighting the resulting challenges for engineering approaches. We argue that AOSE developers need to be aware of the possible causes of complex system dynamics, which result from underlying feedback loops. In this respect current approaches to develop SO-MASs are analyzed, leading to a novel classification scheme of typically applied computational techniques. To relieve development ef-

forts and bridge the gap between top-down engineering and bottom-up emerging phenomena, we discuss how multi-level analysis, so-called mesoscopic modeling, can be used to comprehend MAS dynamics and guide agent design, respectively iterative redesign.

Introduction

AOSE (Weiß, 2002) is a prominent approach to the development of complicated distributed software systems. *Agents*, that is, autonomous and pro-active entities, are proposed as a basic design and development metaphor. Since highly dynamic and distributed application domains lend themselves to be understood as collections of collaborating actors, the agent metaphor provides appropriate design abstractions (Jennings, 2001). As the actual software applications result from agent interplay, they allow *decentralized* coordination mechanisms that promise the purposeful construction of systems that self-organize, that is, establish and maintain structures without external control, justifying intensive research activities (e.g., Kephart & Chess, 2003; Müller-Schloer, 2004). Awareness is rising that MAS implementations comprise the inherent potential to exhibit complex systems dynamics, for example, *criticality, phase transitions* (Parunak, Brueckner, & Savit, 2004) and *emergent* phenomena (Serugendo, Gleizes, & Karageorgos, 2006) have been observed.

The need to handle complex system dynamics in MASs is attracting increasing attention in AOSE research, as the rising phenomena complicate and challenge conventional top-down development efforts. So state Henderson-Sellers and Giorgini (2005):

...To alleviate this concern of an uncontrolled and uncontrollable agent system wreaking havoc, clearly emergent behavior has to be considered and planned for at the system level using top-down analysis and design techniques. This is still an area that is largely unknown in MAS methodologies... (p. 4)

It has been found that these dynamics can be embedded implicitly in top-down designs, leading to unexpected synchronizations and oscillations that impair system performance of MASs, composed of agents that individually perform as intended (Mogul, 2005; Moore & Wright, 2003; Parunak, & VanderBok, 1997). Simulations are required to identify these phenomena and empiric practices dominate development approaches (e.g., De Wolf & Holvoet 2006; Edmonds, 2004).

In this chapter, sources for CAS phenomena in MASs are discussed. Particularly, we give an overview on current best practices for the development of self-organizing dynamics in MASs, leading to a novel classification of implementation approaches. While these practices have been classified phenomenological, insights in underlying mechanisms are required (Maes, 1994) to guide the utilization of emergent dynamics in software.

Current approaches to the construction of MASs can be distinguished between top-down development *methodologies* and bottom-up, *experimentation-based* prototyping procedures. Engineering procedures address the purpose-, cost- and time-oriented construction of applications and typically rely on iterative, top-down procedures that start from system requirements, which are agreed with stakeholders, and refine these to implementable system designs (cf. *Toward Development Methodologies* and *Summary* sub-sections). When engineering efforts target complex system dynamics, the design of applications that reliably exhibit the nonlinear system behaviors is inherently intricate (Edmonds, 2004), forcing elaborate simulation cycles conducted by experts. In order to mediate between both development paradigms a CAS inspired multi-level, *mesoscopic* modeling approach is presented and demonstrated that can be used to *redesign* MASs, enforcing the intended dynamics. Complex systems and complexity scientists as well as AOSE practitioners find a discussion of the particular challenges that MAS development efforts face established solutions.

This chapter is structured as follows. In the next section software-engineering approaches for agent-based systems are briefly introduced, followed by a discussion of relationships between MASs and CASs. Afterwards, engineering approaches to self-organizing dynamics in MASs are discussed. In the fifth section, these are classified and in the sixth section a multi-level modeling approach is presented, supporting iterative cycles of bottom-up analysis and top-down (re-)design. Finally, conclusions and prospects for future work are given.

Agent-Oriented Software Engineering

AOSE proposes agents as a basic design and implementation metaphor for complicated distributed software systems. Agents are understood as autonomous and pro-active entities that are situated in an environment and collaborate with each other in so-called MASs, that is, sets of agents (Jennings, 2001). Different notions of agency exist that are supported by dedicated agent architectures, guiding agent implementation. These range from purely *reactive* mechanisms (e.g., Brooks, 1986), to *cognitive* models inspired by psychology and philosophy that address rational agent behaviors (e.g., Rao & Georgeff, 1991).

Agent-based application development is facilitated by dedicated programming languages and middleware platforms (recently reviewed by Bordini et al., 2006; Braubach, Pokahr, & Lamersdorf, 2006), directly supporting different theories of agency for application programmers. Agent platforms provide dedicated middleware platforms that offer specific services, for example, agent communication and coordination, to MAS developers utilize to construct MASs in general-purpose programming languages.

Three general software-engineering approaches to MASs can be distinguished (Müller, 2004), which comprise *agent-oriented, organizational,* and *emergentist* approaches. Agent-oriented approaches focus on the design of individual agents, typically biased towards certain agent architectures and organizational approaches that facilitate the specification of static organizational structures in the MAS. Corresponding methodologies guide MAS development from the initial examination of system requirements to the actual agent implementation. They commonly provide tailored development *processes* and modeling *notations,* supported by design *tools* (Henderson-Sellers & Giorgini, 2005; Sudeikat, Braubach, Pokahr, & Lamersdorf, 2004). These top-down approaches are opposed by bottom-up emergentist procedures that particularly focus on self-organizing dynamics. They distinguish carefully between *micro*-level agent implementations and *macroscopic* observable system-wide phenomena, providing heuristic design guidelines (Brueckner & Czap, 2006) and MAS analysis techniques (e.g., De Wolf, Holvoet, & Samaey, 2005).

Self-Organization: Complex System Dynamics in MAS

Industrial as well as academic research initiatives intend to utilize self-organizing dynamics for the construction of robust and scalable applications. Both properties require purely *decentralized* coordination of entities, so that the absence of single points of failure (robustness) as well as the coordination of increasing numbers of entities (scalability) is ensured. The terms *autonomic computing* (Kephart & Chess, 2003) and *organic computing* (Müller-Schloer, 2004) have been coined to express visions of future adaptive IT systems that configure and maintain themselves according to high-level policies.

To enable these properties IT research targets the construction of adaptive processes that give rise to and maintain configurations without external control. This *self-organizing* behavior is distinct from *emergent* phenomena, that is, novel artifacts that rise from microscopic interactions (De Wolf & Holvoet, 2004). Since development efforts aim at these two complex system phenomena via *modular* and *hierarchical* structures of artificial *autonomous* entities, the resulting software systems have the potential to exhibit CAS dynamics, for example, *criticality* and *phase transitions* (Parunak et al., 2004). However, they are distinguishable from CASs observed in nature, as *self-organized criticality* and *edge of chaos* phenomena are typically absent.[2] These phenomena result from *critical* points—configurations where system properties change suddenly—that are approached and maintained by the system itself. In MASs, critical points can be identified but are commonly controlled via fixed, tunable parameters (Parunak et al., 2004).

CASs are typically defined in terms of sets of autonomous actors that interact (Bar-Yam, 2002), and computational tools have been proven valuable to give insights in their intricate dynamics (e.g., Rauch, 2002). The typically applied simulation tools need to be distinguished from general-purpose AOSE technologies (Drogoul, Vanbergue, & Meurisse, 2002). While simulation tools allow the interleaved execution of simple program models in observable environment models, AOSE provides tools to the decomposition of computational systems in truly distributed and autonomous actors.

Figure 1 presents a canonical view on MASs. A number of agents execute concurrently and interact (act/sense) with an environment that exhibits its own dynamic. Abstracting from the applied agent architectures, agents maintain execution states that are altered by environment perception and reasoning dynamics inside individuals, that is, stochastic processes in adaptive agents or reasoning processes in cognitive agent architectures. The exhibited microscopic dynamics give rise to macroscopic phenomena, that is, self-organization and emergence.

Bonabeau, Dorigo, and Theraulaz (1999) identified four basic principles for the design of *swarm* intelligent systems: (1) *multiple interactions* among the individuals, (2) *positive feedback,* (3) *negative feedback,* and an (4) *increase of behavior*

Figure 1. A canonical view on multi-agent systems. Agents sense and modify (act) their environment. In addition, agents and their environment exhibit their own dynamics, leading to macroscopic system dynamics.

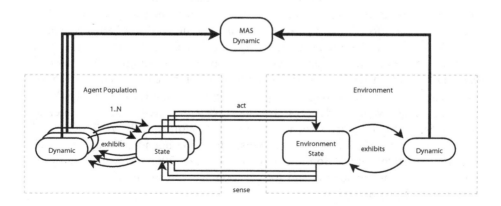

modification. Multiple interactions as well as positive and negative feedback generate nonlinearities responsible for complex system behaviors. Furthermore, increase of behavior modification introduces, for the systems under consideration, a *slaving* principle proposed in the 1970s by Haken (2004). The presence of feedback loops enforces that results of agent actions continuously influence agent behavior, leading to collective adaptation. According to our canonical MAS model, self-organization results from two basic ingredients. First, agents sense their (local) environment; and secondly, they adjust their behaviors to adapt to perceptions. From the abstract view on MASs in Figure 1, it becomes apparent that MASs inherently allow for these two components. It depends on the application domain and implementation details if agent interdependencies result in feedback loops that steer the system. Top-down development approaches have to either prevent their occurrence by restricting agent behaviors or to anticipate their rise from MAS designs.

When self-organizing properties are *intended* in MASs, system design forms a paradox in itself, that is, design requires developers to revise agent and environment implementations in a way that ensures the rise of the intended macroscopic artifacts (Sudeikat & Renz, 2006). Assuming that the constituent agents are properly implemented, that is, behave according to predefined rules, developers need to ensure that these rules actually lead to the intended dynamics. Due to nonlinearities and the complexity of the intended phenomena, it is a major challenge how to break the intended phenomena down into individual, microscopic agent models. Tools are needed to bridge the gap between the micro- and macro-scales of MAS implementations. In the following section, we examine current AOSE best practices to address this challenge.

Engineering Self-Organizing MAS

After numerous successful applications of self-organization in MASs have been reported (Brueckner & Czap, 2006; Serugendo, Gleizes, & Karageorgos, 2006), there are notable efforts to compare and classify the utilized mechanisms. These provide MAS models that guide collective agent behavior adjustment. Adjustment design can be used to create adaptive system behaviors, for example, *phase transitions*, finally leading to self-organizing structures and emergents. Mechanisms have been categorized according to (1) the applied computational techniques (De Wolf & Holvoet, 2006; Mamei, Menezes, Tolksdorf, & Zambonelli, 2006; Serugendo et al., 2006), (2) the intended system properties (De Wolf & Holvoet, 2006a); and (3) their sources of inspiration (e.g., Hassas, Marzo-Serugendo, Karageorgos, & Castelfranchi, 2006; Mano, Bourjot, Lopardo, & Glize, 2006). Development processes support their application and formal tools have been proposed to analyze and anticipate MAS behaviors.

Template Architectures

Following Serugendo et al. (2006), five coordination mechanisms, based on *direct interactions, stigmergy, reinforcement, cooperation,* and *generic architectures* are currently utilized for the construction of self-organizing MASs. Mechanisms based on *direct interactions* rely on environments that allow agents to directly sense information of other individuals and environment objects. A prominent example is the adaptive configuration of structural and/or spatial aspects in MASs via *gradient-fields* or *co-fields* (Mamei, Zambonelli, & Leonardi, 2004). Spatial and contextual information is represented by computational fields originating from agents and/or environment objects. Fields are propagated by the environment, allowing agents to directly sense field gradients and infer information to act coherently, for example, to arrange themselves in spatial formations.

Stigmergy-based coordination is particularly inspired by biological systems where individual efforts stimulate corresponding actions of other agents (Grasse, 1959). Numerous insect species rely on so-called *pheromones*, chemical substances that denote specific insect behaviors, sensible to population members and gradually evaporating when released to the environment. When insects exhibit specific behaviors they distribute corresponding pheromones, therefore communicating their behavior. For example, when a termite builds a wall its building brick is distributing a dedicated pheromone that stimulates other termites to drop bricks nearby, leading to unique nest structures. Corresponding MAS implementations utilize *digital pheromones* (Parunak, 1997). Their evaporation provides a means of inter-agent communication and ensures that obsolete stimuli disappear gradually when their reinforcement stops.

Adaptive behavior of whole MASs can also be achieved by mechanisms that use *reinforcement* of individual adaptive behaviors. Corresponding agent implementations adapt agent behaviors based on individual stochastic processes (e.g., Weyns, Schelfthout, Holvoet, & Glorieux, 2004). Perceived environment states provided feedback on the success or failure of agent actions. This feedback is used to enforce the usage of behaviors that have been successfully applied, commonly supplemented with stochastic perturbations allowing agents to try less common behaviors.

Collective coherent MAS behaviors can also rise from agent *cooperation*. These mechanisms design agent implementations to agree on cooperative scenarios with other individuals. The sum of the local cooperative behaviors leads to the globally observed system functionality. Examples include the *organization self-design* approach from Ishida, Gasser, and Yokoo (1992) and the *adaptive multi-agent systems* (AMASs) theory (Gleizes, Camps, & Glize, (1999), which lead to the ADELFE development methodology (Bernon, Gleizes, Peyruqueou, & Picard, 2003). The methodology and corresponding tool support (Bernon, Camps, Gleizes, & Picard, 2003) guide agent design in terms of *cooperative* and particularly *noncooperative* scenarios. Agents are designed to perceive and resolve the latter ones in order to ensure that the system itself maintains the intended functionality.

Finally, *generic agent architectures* have been developed to allow modification of the MAS structure at run time. Agents can change the MAS structure directly, for example, in *holons* and *holarchies* (Koestler, 1967) or reason about and modify MAS *meta-models* at run-time (e.g., Dowling & Cahill, 2001), resulting in MAS architectures that can adjust themselves according to environmental influences.

Independent from the previous classification, De Wolf and Holvoet (2006) have examined and cataloged decentralized coordination mechanisms. They distinguish between *stigmergy, co-fields, market-based, tag-based,* and *token-based* coordination. *Stigmergy* (digital pheromones) and *co-field* (gradient fields) mechanisms correspond to the aforementioned outlined classification by Serugendo et al. (2006). *Market-based* coordination denotes agent collaboration in virtual markets where agents negotiate prices of resource access and/or service offers. This coordination scheme is established to control MAS resource allocation, since market dynamics adapt to demand and supply changes, typically leading to equilibrium states. *Tag-based* coordination is typically used for team formation and relies on tags attached to individuals. These can be viewed and modified by population members, indicating trust and reputation information. Based on this information, agents can decide team formations and role adoptions. Finally, *tokens* can be used to represent special conditions, roles, or permissions, for example, resource access. Agents need to possess the corresponding token to adopt roles or use resources and pass the token to other individuals. The rules for token distribution control MAS configuration and adaptation.

Toward Development Methodologies

The basic principles that enable self-organizing processes in *stigmergic* MASs are well understood and lead to heuristic development guidelines. Early design principles have been given by Parunak (1997), were expanded and revised by Parunak and Brueckner (2004), leading to a classification of basic principles given by Brueckner and Czap (2006), regarding the design of suitable *agent populations*, appropriate *agent interactions* that ensure information flows, leading to positive and negative feedback loops and the *emergence of desired function* via behavioral diversity inside agents and local fitness measures.

The coordination mechanisms described in the previous section provide means to implement MASs according to these guidelines. Due to the well understood dynamics, a trend towards their *reconstruction* in self-organizing MASs can be observed (discussed by Sudeikat & Renz, 2006). Development teams (1) identify a well understood coordination mechanism and (2) map its constituent parts to the actual application domain. Finally, the (3) behavior of prototype implementations is examined and parameters—controlling agent and/or environment properties—are adjusted. In this respect, the usage of coordination mechanisms as *design patterns*, that is, reusable design examples (Gamma, Helm, Johnson, & Vlissides, 1995), has been proposed by De Wolf and Holvoet (2006b). Initial guidelines on the selection of these patterns based on system requirements have been given (De Wolf & Holvoet, 2006a), in terms of a look-up table relating intended system properties to suitable coordination mechanisms. While this methodological stance reflects current development trends, it raises concerns similar to the application of traditional design patterns, that is, how to combine patterns properly, leading to quality architectures.

General-purpose methodologies usually do not consider the rise of emergent and self-organized structures (Henderson-Sellers & Giorgini, 2005). An exception is the ADELFE methodology that provides an extended version of the *rational unified process* (Kruchten, 2003), tailored to the design of adaptive MASs composed of cooperative agents. ADELFE provides tool support guiding the development process (Bernon, Camps, 2003) and a development life-cycle that stresses the identification of cooperation failures (noncooperative situations) and the equipment of agents with procedures to recover from these. Accordingly, MASs provide the intended, adequate functionality when all constituent agents provide their designated (sub-) functionalities, that is, *cooperate*. The inherent focus on cooperative mechanisms impairs support for other coordination schemes.

Since the inherent nonlinearities in self-organizing MAS dynamics impair formal specifications and subsequently render reductionist, top-down development approaches, impractical (Edmonds & Bryson, 2004), typical development procedures adopt an empirical stance and regard development as iterations of experiments. Therefore, Edmonds (2004) proposes a tailored combination of *engineering* and *adaptation* procedures for MAS development. While engineering procedures address the construction of systems by design and implementation activities, examine adaptation procedures the available (prototype) implementations and fine-tune system parameters. Edmonds (2004) argued that complicated dynamics require the adaptation phase to revise the *theory* developers have about the system behavior. The theory leads to testable hypotheses that can be checked by scientific experiments. Only when the theory is thoroughly validated developers can make assumptions about system reliability.

Another example for an experimental approach to MAS design has been given by De Wolf and Holvoet (2005). They adjusted the incremental and reductionist *unified process* (Jacobson, Booch, & Rumbaugh, 1999) in order to revise MAS implementations. In their approach architectural design concerns the selection of an appropriate coordination mechanism for the identified system requirements. Testing is adjusted to address macroscopic properties via system simulations.

Gershenson (2006) proposes a conceptual framework for the description of self-organizing systems. In concordance to ADELFE, his approach provides a measurement of the *satisfaction* of the system under consideration, in terms of a weighted sum of the goal satisfaction of individual agents. The weights have to be evaluated via experiment. The aim of corresponding design efforts is to construct systems that autonomously maximize agent satisfaction, leading to maximal system satisfaction. MAS designs rely on the introduction of so-called *mediators* (Heylighen, 2003) that arbitrate among individuals, therefore minimizing *interferences* and *frictions* (Gershenson, 2006). The conceptual framework facilitates the identification of suitable domain entities and strategies, supporting system designs that intend equilibrium states via mediating agents.

Formal Methods

Since development practices depend on experimentation procedures to analyze (nonlinear) system behaviors, formal computer science tools promise to speed up MAS simulations. Formal specifications can be used to simulate abstract models of agent implementations. Two usages can be distinguished. First, formal models can be derived from actual MAS implementations (e.g., described by Sudeikat & Renz, 2006). The derived models then allow predicting system behaviors that are expected to emerge under different parameter values and initial conditions. Secondly, abstract specifications of MAS designs can be used as *proof-of-concept* allowing validating that an initial design allows the rise of the intended dynamics.

Applied models utilize mathematics, particularly systems of *differential equations* and transition systems, that is, *process algebra* (Viroli & Omicini, 2005). Most work on formal specifications of self-organizing processes addresses *swarm robotic* systems, mathematical approaches for these systems were reviewed by Lerman, Martinoli, and Galstyan (2004) and formal specification languages were examined by Rouff, Hinchey, Truszkowski, and Rash (2006).

Mathematical treatment of complex, nonlinear system dynamics typically models the rate of change of macroscopic observables (see e.g., Haken, 2004). Temporal development of discrete systems is represented by difference equations, but typically continuous functions can be assumed, leading to sets of coupled and nonlinear, first-order differential equations. These are well established to describe self-organizing system dynamics in various disciplines (Haken, 2004), for example, chemical reaction systems or population dynamics of biological ecologies. Lerman and Galstyan (2001) established these equations to model homogenous MASs composed of reactive agents and presented a structured process to derive these equations from microscopic agent modes (Lerman & Galstyan, 2004). Assuming an underlying time-continuous Markov processes, MAS dynamics can be modeled by rate equations, describing in quantitative terms mean occupation numbers of individual agent states. Sudeikat and Renz (2006a) exemplified how similar, phenomenologic models can be derived for MASs composed of cognitive agent when an underlying stochastic process can be assumed to govern MAS dynamics.

Process algebra is a prominent formal tool to describe, model, and verify concurrent and reactive systems (Milner, 1989). Subjects are described as *transition systems,* that is, as sets of states, actions, and transition relations (S → S'), caused by actions. Stochastic extensions to this algebra have been given (e.g., by Priami, 1995) that annotate activity rates to channel definitions and make process activities subject to delays. These extensions transfer the underlying transition systems to Markov transition systems (Brinksma & Hermanns, 2001). Activity rates define how the probability of state transitions increases in time. Interpreter implementations are available for large-scale simulations (e.g., Phillips, 2006).

Rouff et al. (2006) examined conventional and stochastic process algebra as well as logic-based approaches, concluding that stochastic process algebras are suitable to model concurrent system dynamics while the latter formalisms are more suitable to verify agent internal reasoning. Stochastic algebras have been applied to model complex biological and chemical processes, for example, ant colonies (Sumpter, Blanchard, & Broomhead, 2001) and have been applied to self-organizing MAS dynamics (Gardelli, Viroli, & Omicini, 2005, 2006). Gardelli et al. (2006) utilized stochastic algebra specifications for quantitative, large scale simulations of abstract MAS designs. These allowed illustrating, that intended MAS designs enable the rise of intended system dynamics and facilitate the examination of system parameters and macroscopic behavioral regimes. Having examined these regimes in abstract MAS designs, developers face the challenge to enforce similar macroscopic system parameters in the MAS to-be. While the relation between stochastic algebras and MAS implementations has not been examined yet, Sudeikat and Renz (2006a) provided an initial tool support to derive process terms semi-automatically from annotated implementations.

Summary

Development efforts for self-organizing systems intend complex system dynamics which in turn complicate top-down development procedures. Therefore, current development efforts rely on template architectures and prototype/simulation approaches. While experience and heuristics guide the MAS design, methodologies support application development, for example, via enforcing the distinction between *engineering* and *adaption* (Edmonds, 2004), the promotion of a certain coordination scheme (Gershenson, 2006), or the identification of suitable template architectures (Serugendo et al., 2006). Open research questions concern how the applied coordination schemes influence each other and how they can be combined without interferences in real-world scenarios. In order to relieve simulation procedures, formal tools have been proposed. These promise computationally cheap

Figure 2. The relation between the discussed techniques for MAS development and general software engineering phases. Design and implementation relate mainly to established coordination mechanisms; requirements engineering and testing are merely unsupported.

SO-MAS-Oriented Techniques	Software-Engineering Phases				
	Requirements	Analysis	Design	Implementation	Test
SO-Mechanisms (cf. section 4.1)	-	O	X	X	-
Formal Tools (cf. section 4.3)	O	X	-	-	O
SO-Processes (section 4.2; Edmonds; deWolf et al.)	-	X	X	-	O
Specific Methodologies (section 4.2; ADELFE)	O	X	X	X	O

X : Supported   O : Minor Support   - : Not Supported

simulations of large numbers of autonomous processes on a macroscopic scale. Therefore, they can be applied to both facilitate the analysis of available systems (Lerman & Galstyan, 2004) as well as to examine abstract MAS designs and their support for the intended dynamics (Gardelli et al., 2006). The abstract nature of these models facilitates examinations of distributed coordination mechanisms and self-organizing dynamics, but gives developers limited insight into the intended agent designs. Instead the derived models form a kind of requirements engineering for self-organizing MASs since the identified parameter ranges define properties that final agent designs have to bring by. For example, the simulation parameters for an intrusion detection system from Gardelli et al. (2006) comprise the probabilities that certain agent types interact. While simulations can ensure that a MAS composed of accordingly behaving agents will perform well, it is up to the developers to ensure consistent behavioral regimes in MAS implementations.

Software projects are commonly carried out in interactive sequences of development phases, comprising the analysis of system *requirements*, system *analysis*, *design*, *implementation*, and *testing* of the resulting software (Kruchten, 2003). System requirements express the intended functionality of the software system to-be. A detailed examination of the intended functionality guides system analysis, defining the system architecture, which is refined in the design phase until the implementation is enabled. In the last phase resulting implementations are tested. Figure 2 shows the support of these development phases by the here discussed techniques and procedures. The classified coordination mechanisms (SO-Mechanisms, cf.

Template Architectures sub-section) reduce requirements and system analysis to the identification of an appropriate pattern, mapping this template architecture to the application domains guides MAS design and implementation. Formal tools (cf. *Formal Methods* sub-section) have been applied to simulate abstract MAS models and derive mathematical models from MAS implementations. This allows examining behavioral regimes of intended MAS designs (analysis) and implementations (test). The available methodic development approaches (SO-process, cf. *Toward Development Methodologies* sub-section) focus mainly on system analysis and design in simulation-based procedures, broadening test to simulation. The specific ADELFE methodologies is considered separately (cf. *Toward Development Methodologies* sub-section), since it provides a complete development cycle supported with notation and tools, but focusing on the *cooperation* coordination mechanism.

This examination highlights the lack of *requirements engineering* and *testing approaches* to self-organizing MASs. While simulation-based development procedures are currently revised, testing refers to the automated validation of specification that defines how the system under development should behave. It is a major challenge for general-purpose AOSE research to move from experimentation to testing procedures. This transition will be possibly supported by suitable means to describe and analyze the requirements for self-organizing systems.

A CAS-Based Classification of Coordination Mechanisms

In the *Self-organization—Complex System Dynamics in MAS* section it has been found that complex system dynamics originate from entities that (inter-) act autonomously, but are correlated by positive and negative feedback from their environment. Agent reasoning, adjusting agent behaviors according to the available local information and the spread of this information in the MAS are two basic ingredients to self-organizing dynamics (cf. *Self-organization—Complex System Dynamics in MAS* section). The here discussed mechanisms are field tested and well understood, but their support for both of these ingredients has not been examined yet. Therefore, we differentiate in the following between interdependency- and behavior adaption-level mechanisms. While the former ones describe how information propagates to individuals from the environment and other agents, the latter ones provide blueprints for agent implementation, specifying how agents use the provided local information to select appropriate behaviors. Figure 3 displays this classification. It turns out to be that the identified coordination mechanisms form disjoint sets, supporting either feedback loops or behavior selection.

Figure 3. Coordination mechanisms for self-organizing MAS. These provide techniques to implement agent interdependencies and selection between different agent internal behaviors.

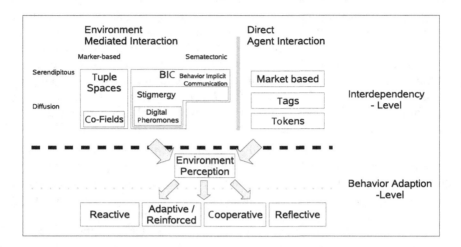

Interdependency-level mechanisms are distinguished between *direct* interactions of agents (right) and indirect interactions that are *mediated* by a (virtual) environment. The prominent stigmergy and co-field approaches are both examples for mediated interactions, since agents communicate implicitly via environment changes and virtual fields. The *environment* propagates information from anonymous individuals, and agents use these for behavior adjustment. Mamei et al. (2006) provide a fine-grained classification scheme of mediating mechanisms that inter alia concern the propagation of information and the introduction of dedicated representations. Information propagation can either rely on *diffusion* or on agents that wander a shared data space where they encounter *serendipitously* novel information. Coordination mechanisms require the introduction of explicit data items (*marker-based*) or agents infer implicit information from the perceived environment (*sematectonic*). *Behavior implicit communications* (BICs), introduced by Omicini, Ricci, Viroli, Castelfranchi, and Tummolini (2004) relates to the fact that agents do not necessarily need to engage in communication to spread information. Sole observation of other agents' behavior can be used by individuals to infer their states, enabling coherent agent coordination, similarly enforced and degraded as in stigmergy systems. BICs describe both marker-based and sematectonic coordination and stigmergy can be regarded as specialization. Co-field implementations rely on specific *tuple spaces* (e.g., reviewed by Mamei et al., 2006), that is, a standard coordination model, based on tokens that explicitly represent the distributed information. As tuple spaces and BICs support serendipitous mechanisms, specific frameworks support the spatial diffusion of markers (e.g., digital pheromones and tuples) in virtual environments. Diffusing tuples are used to construct co-fields (Mamei, Zambonelli & Leonardi, 2004) while stigmergy denotes mediated communications between individuals via the modification of either serendipitous or diffusing environment elements. Evaporating digital pheromones are a prominent example (Brueckner & Czap, 2006). It is to note that sematectonic data spaces contradict diffusing approaches.

Direct agent interactions take place between distinguishable agents, either exchanging messages/tokens or modifying tags. Message exchange enables negotiations for *market-based* coordination and transmitted *tokens* represent permissions to play certain roles, for example, access resources. *Tag*-based coordination also provides a direct interaction approach, since their modification requires direct interaction with a known individual (cf. *Template Architectures* sub-section).

Individual *behavior adaption* is controlled by the employed agent architectures, ranging from purely *reactive* mechanisms to, *adaptive, cooperative,* and *reflective* architectures. Reactive agent models respond directly, knee-jerk to sensor perceptions, possibly deciding between behaviors categorized in priorities (Brooks, 1986; cf. *Agent-oriented Software Engineering* section). Adaptive, cooperative, and reflective agent models correspond respectively to *reinforcement, cooperative* mechanisms and *generic* architectures, as identified by Serugendo et al. (2006) which support run time (re-)configuration (cf. *Template Architectures* sub-section). The term *reflective* is introduced to replace the term *generic,* characterizing the general feature of these systems that they explicitly enable MAS reconfiguration to be triggered by individual agents.

In principle, all combinations of interdependency and behavior adaption mechanisms are conceivable, however only specific combinations of agent architectures and interaction schemes are utilized. Figure 4 presents employed best practices. In

Figure 4. Established combinations of interdependency and behavior adaption mechanisms. Sophisticated information propagation schemes rely on simple agents, while complex agent models utilize generic platform message services.

Behavior Selection Level	Information Level					
	Stigmergy	Co-Fields	Tokens	Tags	Market-Based	Platform Service
Reactive	X	X	X	X	X	
Adaptive			X		X	X
Cooperative						X
Reflective						X

X : Established Best Practice

Figure 5. The distinction between interdependency-based (left) and adaption-based self-organizing architectures. Interdependency-based coordination focus on environment dynamics to coordinate rather simple agents. Adaption-based mechanisms control system dynamics via collective adaption of individuals.

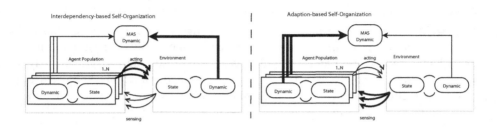

this matrix the previously discussed interdependency-level mechanisms are supplemented with *platform* (communication) *services*, since some agent architectures do not require dedicated information propagation techniques, but can be implemented using generic message services.

The literature review revealed a trend that these practices focus either on environmental dynamics, steering simple reactive agent models or on more sophisticated agent designs (adaptive, cooperative, and reflective), revised to emerge collective, adaptive system behaviors (cf. Figure 5). Exceptions are token- and market-based coordination that applies adaptive agent implementations as well. This observation indicates that the combination of coordination mechanisms in MAS applications is unexplored and agrees to the previously described focus of methodologies and heuristics on specific mechanisms.

CAS-Inspired MAS Analysis: Towards Multi-Level Modeling of MASs

Complex system dynamics are inherently nonlinear and it has been argued that their complexity impairs top-down design procedures (Edmonds, 2004). Therefore, intended system dynamics are typically anticipated, utilizing the established coordination mechanisms (cf. *Template Architectures* to *Formal Methods* sub-sections). In the following, a CAS-inspired, multi-level modeling approach to MASs is presented, showing how self-organizing processes can be explained by examining coarse-grained agent contributions to macroscopic phenomena. When constructing self-organizing MASs, developers typically have to understand and catalogue exhibited agent behaviors, forming ontologies of agent contributions to system-wide phenomena. So-called *mesoscopic* modeling, introduced by Renz and Sudeikat (2005a, 2006), aims to aid these efforts. This analysis view does not replace but supplement the available software engineering methodologies and toolsets (cf. *Engineering Self-organizing MAS* section).

Mesoscopic Modeling

Multi-level descriptions are appropriate tools to study CASs. Taking inspiration from established efforts to understand CAS behaviors (e.g., Haken, 2004), we propose intermediate—mesoscopic—description levels to mediate between top-down and bottom-up development. This modeling notion allows relating system behaviors to individual agent behaviors, facilitating bottom-up analysis of prototype implementations and their topdown (re-)design (cf. *Applying Mesoscopic Models—MAS Redesign Support* sub-section).

Macroscopic models describe the systems behavior space. Points in this space denote MAS configurations, in terms of behaviors observable in the sense of functional system requirements. Trajectories in this space represent system reconfigurations and their corresponding dynamics. Since designers intend specific macroscopic phenomena when conceptualizing MASs, it is necessary to foresee the principally possible system configurations. This helps to distinguish *intended* structures and/or emergents from *unintended* ones and the possible transitions between them. Since developers typically can not anticipate the complete MAS behavior space at design time, this model is subject to incremental revision and requirements engineering activities (Sudeikat & Renz, 2007).

The purpose of a *microscopic* modeling level is to provide sufficient details to guide agent implementation. Resulting models describe the available behaviors and the selection process that underlies agent adjustment, typically biased towards the applied agent architecture.

Transitions between qualitatively different macroscopic configurations can be explained by mesoscopic models (Renz & Sudeikat, 2005a, 2006) that introduce intermediate artifacts, abstracting from microscopic agent behaviors (cf. Figure 6). Abstraction is done by merging multiple microscopic agent behaviors and replacing them by a few abstract states, so-called *hidden* agent states, which are not directly observable in the behavior of the individual agents but average out short time fluctuations of the microscopic agent actions. This approach is inspired by similar modeling methods developed in physics to describe phase transitions in equilibrium as well as in far-from-equilibrium systems, see for example, Haken (2004).

Figure 6. The relation of MAS implementations (right) and mesoscopic modeling (following Sudeikat & Renz, 2006)

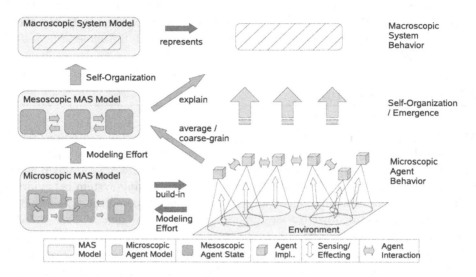

Appropriate abstraction is a considerable modeling effort, requiring classifying and merging agent states that contribute to macroscopic dynamics in similar ways. The introduced mesoscopic states resemble *roles* agents play in respect to the exhibited macroscopic system dynamics. The resulting models are distinct from macroscopic models since they still include the underlying mechanisms causing the short-time behavior of the self-organization process (Renz & Sudeikat, 2006). It has been found that these models are useful to mathematically describe these processes that result from distributed coordination mechanisms in MASs. When appropriate agent states have been identified, system reconfiguration can be expressed by rate equations (Sudeikat & Renz, 2006a) and process algebra (Sudeikat & Renz, 2006b), requiring estimation or measurement of relevant transition rates for typical environmental conditions.

Figure 6 relates the three description levels to each other (left) and the MAS implementation they model (right). Microscopic agent (inter-) actions (bottom) give rise to macroscopic MAS configurations (top). Mesoscopic descriptions capture averaged agent behaviors. These exhibited behaviors explain how agents contribute to rising structures.

Applying Mesoscopic Models: MAS Redesign Support

In bottom-up development procedures MAS prototype implementations are tuned by simulation. This typically focuses on parameter adjustment (cf. *Toward Development Methodologies* sub-section), a non-trivial task that requires extensive simulation (De Wolf et al., 2005). Procedures for the purposeful adjustment of prototypes and mechanisms have yet found minor attention (e.g., by Gershenson, 2006) but could relieve developers from costly simulation cycles. In addition these procedures provide vocabulary and tools to bridge the gap between bottom-up and top-down engineering. Sudeikat and Renz (2006) showed how the identification of agent contributions to the observable macroscopic structures (mesoscopic roles) can guide MAS redesign, that is, the purposeful modification of agent and environment implementations to enforce intended macroscopic structures. Here, two redesigns are exemplified, namely, reimplementation of adaptive minority game players and collectively clustering ants.

Case Study I: Minority Games

The so-called *minority game* (MG) (Challet & Zhang, 1997) is a socio-economically inspired setting to examine inductive reasoning in populations of adaptive agents. In a round-based game, an odd number of agents have to make repeatedly binary decisions (1 or 0) and agents in the *minority* group get rewarded. In order to increase their reward, agents need to conform to the next minority decision, while their only source of information is a limited memory of the past round results.

Renz and Sudeikat (2005, 2005a) redesigned a stochastic adaptive agent population, where agents adjust their probability to alternate their previous selection. Successful agents increase their likelihood to change, while unsuccessful agents tend to stick to their previous selection. It turned out that these agents—in specific parameter regimes—can play *optimal* and *fair*, that is, enter a behavioral regime where population reward is maximized and agents get awarded in turn.

A mesoscopic model classifies three behavioral regimes, namely, supplier *loyal, alternating,* and *undecided* agents. Optimal behavior occurs when agents synchronize into two distinct alternating groups. In this case the agent with the smallest alternation probability adopts a so-called *emergent role* (Renz & Sudeikat, 2006). Its selection determines which group will win and loose respectively, since the alternating groups are equal sized. This role was named *Schwarzer Peter* (get the short straw in German speaking countries) and solely arises from game dynamics. Since *Schwarzer Peter* agents force other individuals to loose, eventually this role will be adopted by other (less successful) agents.

Besides a mathematical treatment, the mesoscopic model guided agent *reimplementation*. The continuously changing strategies of the stochastic MG were replaced by deterministic transitions between three agent states, representing the mesoscopic behaviors. By means of self-organization, deterministic state transitions lead to similar, optimal behavior in a controlled and predictable way (Renz & Sudeikat, 2005a, 2006).

Case Study II: Collective (Ant) Sorting

Ants achieve global structures of grouped items (eggs, larvae, etc.) by continuously transporting items to similar ones nearby (Parunak, 1997). These *brood-sorting* mechanisms are well studied and have been applied to sort and cluster large scale data in open environments with streams of incoming items (Parunak, Weinstein, Chiusano, & Brueckner, 2005). A naive implementation comprises reactive agents that walk an environment (torus) in Brownian motion, inhabited by a number of randomly distributed items. Agents execute a searching behavior either to find items to pick up (when unbound) or to drop at another item (when bound to an item).

Figure 7 denotes the mesoscopic system description. Ants contribute to cluster formations in three distinct ways. They move items from the grid to a cluster after (1) a comparatively short walk, (2) they carry a comparatively long walk, or (3) they pick up items and release them on the same cluster. The length of a walk is related to the environment size and item density. From the mesoscopic system description (Figure 7), it was inferred that the short walk behavior (1) is to be amplified to enhance clustering efficiency. This increase is achieved by two redesigns, focusing on agent movement and the inhabited environment.

Figure 7. The transportation behaviors of sorting ants (left). Agent movement can be (1) comparatively direct (2), indirect, or (3) may also let agents pick up and drop items at the same cluster. These behaviors correspond to mesoscopic transportation velocities (right; from Sudeikat & Renz, 2006).

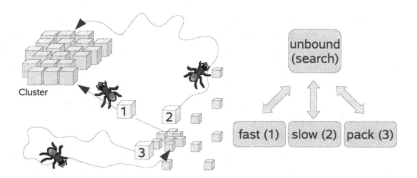

A first redesign replaced the Brownian motion with a stiffened random walk behavior. When agents have gained a high velocity, the average deviation to their current heading is reduced. Therefore, the trajectories of individual agents stiffen over time, resulting in a mean velocity increase. The second redesign increases agent's probability to drop items. It is enforced that items are dropped on top of encountered items. Released items adopt the heading of the encountered item and move (fall) till they reach an empty grid cell. What results are *elongated structures* of aligned items. The elongated shape increases the cluster surface, therefore increasing the probability to be encountered by stiffened walking agents. The obtained improvement has been quantified by Sudeikat and Renz (2006).

Mesoscopic models provide a novel vocabulary that depends on the application domain and allows us to reason about MAS behaviors. Their application poses a non-trivial modeling effort, but the resulting system abstraction can be formally specified, allowing developers to anticipate the effects of changes. Mesoscopic models describe how agents contribute to the globally observable structures. Mesoscopic states describe roles agents play in relation to the system structure, for example, fast and slow moving agents are *roles* agent play in relation to the global transport behavior toward a cluster. Therefore, the derivation of mesoscopic models relies inherently on the identification of contributions to global artifacts and different views on the same MAS are possible. Based on these models are two redesign strategies principally possible. (1) The MG case study exemplifies how intended system behavior can be controlled and adjusted by resembling the identified mesoscopic states directly in agent implementations. The wanted, emergent system behavior observed in the stochastic MG can now be obtained by self-organization in the mesoscopic model (Renz & Sudeikat, 2006). (2) In the case of collective (ant) sorting (Sudeikat & Renz, 2006) an increase in sorting efficiency was achieved solely by identifying an agent behavior to be amplified and corresponding adjustment of reactive agent models and environment objects representing the mesoscopic states explicitly. During these redesign efforts the mesoscopic models do only change when analysts gain novel insights in the agent contributions to structures. The estimation of transition rates between identified roles, that is, mesoscopic states, relies on environmental changes.

Conclusion

In this chapter we justified that AOSE research has to address the possible rise of emergent and self-organized phenomena in MASs. Design efforts may introduce them unintended, or revise agent and environment interactions to ensure their rise. In addition, we argued that the development of MASs—particularly ones with self-organizing properties—can be regarded as the challenge to construct CASs, leading to the question how both research areas can endorse each other. While MASs, that is, agent-based modeling, is an established tool for CAS research, corresponding analysis techniques only play a minor role in AOSE research.

Established techniques and methodologies to design and implement self-organizing MASs have been reviewed and classified according to their focus on collective *agent behavior adjustment* or *agent interdependency propagation*. Both are suitable to design self-organizing MASs and are currently applied rather independently from each other. In order to mediate between top-down development approaches and bottom-up experimentation procedures, mesoscopic modeling—a CAS-inspired multi-level analysis approach—has been discussed and it has been exemplified how the gained insights in system dynamics can be used to redesign agent implementations, enforcing the rise of intended structures. While simulations of the final implementations are necessary, representations of mesoscopic models allow the anticipation of (re-)design results. We expect the proposed modeling approach, together with the novel classification of MAS designs to stimulate the analysis of MAS implementations, allowing developers to examine and compare underlying mechanisms. In order to combine design heuristics and simulation procedures and top-down engineering practices, tools, and models for the examination of self-organizing MASs are necessary. The typically applied computational techniques to the construction of self-organizing MASs are catalogued and have been classified in this chapter (cf. *A CAS-based Classification of Coordination Mechanisms* section). Commonly agreed taxonomies of self-organizing phenomena and their causes are essential to revise prediction techniques and (semi-) automated analysis tools in order to move from MAS *simulation* to *testing* MASs for intended phenomena. This transition is crucial for purposeful engineering practices.

We expect the rising awareness that self-organization is a generic, inherent feature of MAS implementations (cf. *Self-organization—Complex System Dynamics in MAS* section) and that it will affect general-purpose AOSE practices. Tool support for MAS *analysis* by simulation and *construction* by adjusting template architectures will become more and more crucial. Since mesoscopic modeling facilitates the anticipation of system behaviors, it is a topic of future research how these can be introduced in structured development processes.

References

Bar-Yam, Y. (2002). *General features of complex system*. Encyclopedia of Life Support Systems (EOLSS) Publishers.

Bernon, C., Camps, V., Gleizes, M., & Picard, G. (2003). Tools for self-organizing applications engineering. In *Engineering Self-Organizing Applications—First International Workshop (ESOA)* (pp. 283-298).

Bernon, C., Gleizes, M.-P., Peyruqueou, S., & Picard, G. (2003). Adelfe: A methodology for adaptive multi-agent systems engineering. (LNCS 2577, 156-169).

Bonabeau, E., Dorigo, M., & Theraulaz, G. (1999). *Swarm intelligence: From natural to artificial systems. Oxford University Press.*

Bordini, R., Braubach, L., Dastani, M., Seghrouchni, A. E. F., Gomez-Sanz, J., Leite, J., et al. (2006). A survey of programming languages and platforms for multi-agent systems. *Informatica, 30,* 33-44.

Braubach, L., Pokahr, A., & Lamersdorf, W. (2006). Tools and standards. In *Multiagent engineering—Theory and applications in enterprises. International Handbooks on Information Systems. Springer.*

Brinksma, E., & Hermanns, H. (2001). Process algebra and markov chains. (LNCS 2090, pp. 183-231).

Brooks, R. (1986). A robust layered control system for a mobile robot. *IEEE Journal of Robotics and Automation, 2,* 14-32.

Brueckner, S., & Czap, H. (2006). Organization, self-organization, autonomy and emergence: Status and challenges. *International Transactions on Systems Science and Applications, 2*(1), 1-9.

Challet, D., & Zhang, Y. C. (1997). Emergence of cooperation and organization in an evolutionary game. *Physica* A, *246,* 407.

De Wolf, T., & Holvoet, T. (2004). Emergence and self-organisation: A statement of similarities and differences. In *Proceedings of Engineering Self-Organizing Applications '04 (pp.* 96-110). Springer.

De Wolf, T., & Holvoet, T. (2005). Towards a methodlgy for engineering self-organising emergent systems. In *Proceedings of the International Conference on Self-Organization and Adaptation of Multi-agent and Grid Systems* (SOAS 2005).

De Wolf, T. D., Holvoet, T., & Samaey, G. (2005). Engineering self-organising emergent systems with simulation-based scientific analysis. In *Proceedings of the International Workshop on Engineering Self-Organising Applications. Springer.*

De Wolf, T., & Holvoet, T. (2006). *A catalogue of decentralised coordination mechanisms for designing self-organising emergent applications* (Tech. Rep. CW 548). *K.U., Leuven, Department of Computer Science..*

De Wolf, T., & Holvoet, T. (2006a). A taxonomy for self-* properties in decentralised autonomic computing. In *Autonomic computing: Concepts, infrastructure, and applications.* CRC Press.

De Wolf, T., & Holvoet, T. (2006b). Decentralised coordination mechanisms as design patterns for self-organising emergent applications. In *Proceedings of the Fourth International Workshop on Engineering Self-Organising Applications (pp.* 40-61). Springer.

Dowling, J., & Cahill, V. (2001) The K-component architecture meta-model for self-adaptive software. In *Proceedings of Reflection 2001* (LNCS 2192, pp. 81-88). Springer.

Drogoul, A., Vanbergue, D., & Meurisse, T. (2002). Multi-agent based simulation: Where are the agents? In *Proceedings of MABS'02 (Multi-Agent Based Simulation).* Springer.

Edmonds, B. (2004). Using the experimental method to produce reliable self-organised systems. In *Engineering self organising sytems: Methodologiesand applications* (LNAI 3464, pp. 84-99). Springer.

Edmonds, B., & Bryson, J. J. (2004). The insufficiency of formal design methods—The necessity of an experimental approach for the understanding and control of complex MAS. In *Proceedings of the Third International Joint Conference on Autonomous Agents and Multiagent Systems. IEEE Computer Society.*

Gamma, E., Helm, R., Johnson, R., & Vlissides, J. (1995). *Design patterns—Elements of reusable object-oriented software. Addison-Wesley.*

Gardelli, L., Viroli, M., & Omicini, A. (2005). On the role of simulation in the engineering of self-organising systems: Detecting abnormal behavior in MAS. In *AI*IA/TABOO Joint Workshop (WOA 2005)* (pp. 85-90).

Gardelli, L., Viroli, M., & Omicini, A. (2006). On the role of simulations in engineering self-organising MAS: The case of an intrusion detection system in Tucson. In *Engineering self-organising systems* (pp. 153-166). Springer.

Gershenson, C. (2006). *A general methodology for designing self-organizing systems. ArXiv Nonlinear Sciences e-prints,* nlin/0505009.

Gleizes, M., Camps, V., & Glize, P. (1999). A theory of emergent computation based on cooperative self-organization for adaptive artificial systems. In *Fourth European Congress of Systems Science.*

Grasse, P. (1959). La reconstruction du nid et les coordinations inter-individuelles chez bellicostitermes natalensis et cubitermes.sp. la theorie de la stigmergie: essai d'interpretation du comportement des termites constructeurs. *Insectes Sociaux, 6,* 41-83.

Haken, H. (2004). *SYNERGETICS. Introduction and advanced topics. Springer.*

Hassas, S., Marzo-Serugendo, G. D., Karageorgos, A., & Castelfranchi, C. (2006). On self-organized mechanisms from social, business and economic domains. *Informatica, 30,* 62-71.

Henderson-Sellers, B., & Giorgini, P. (2005). *Agent-oriented methodologies. Idea Group.*

Heylighen, F. (2003). *Mediator evolution* (Tech. Rep.). Principia Cybernetica. Retrieved December 13, 2006, from http://pcp.vub.ac.be/Papers/Mediator-Evolution.pdf

Ishida, T., Gasser, L., & Yokoo, M. (1992). Organization self-design of distributed production systems. *IEEE Transactions on Knowledge and Data Engineering, 123-134.*

Jacobson, I., Booch, G., & Rumbaugh, J. (1999). *The unified software development process.* Addison-Wesley.

Jennings, N. R. (2001). Building complex, distributed systems: The case for an agent-based approach. *Communications of the ACM, 44*(4), 35-41.

Kephart, J. O., & Chess, D. M. (2003). The vision of autonomic computing, *Computer, 36(1), 41-50.*

Koestler, A. (1967). *The ghost in the machine.* Arkana.

Kruchten, P. (2003). *The rational unified process: An introduction. Addison-Wesley.*

Lerman, K., & Galstyan, A. (2001). *A general methodology for mathematical analysis of multiagent systems* (Tech. Rep. ISI-TR-529). Marina del Rey, CA: University of California, Information Sciences Institute.

Lerman, K., & Galstyan, A. (2004). Automatically modeling group behavior of simple agents. In *Agent Modeling Workshop.* New York: *IEEE Computer Society.*

Lerman, K., Martinoli, A., & Galstyan, A. (2004). A review of probabilistic macroscopic models for swarm robotic systems. *ISAB-04, 3342.*

Maes, P. (1994). Modeling adaptive autonomous agents. *Artificial Life, 1,* 135-162.

Mamei, M., Menezes, R., Tolksdorf, R., & Zambonelli, F. (2006). Case studies for self-organization in computer science. *Journal of Systems Architecture, 52,* 443-460.

Mamei, M., Zambonelli, F., & Leonardi, L. (2004). Co-fields: A physically inspired approach to motion coordination. *IEEE Pervasive Computing, 3*(2), 52-61.

Mano, J. P., Bourjot, C., Lopardo, G., & Glize, P. (2006). Bioinspired mechanisms for artificial self-organized systems. *Informatica, 30,* 55-62.

Milner, R. (1989). *Communication and concurrency.* Prentice Hall.

Mogul, J. C. (2005). *Emergent (mis)behavior vs. complex software systems* (HPL-2006-2). Palo Alto, CA: *HP Laboratories.*

Moore, D., & Wright, W. (2003). Emergent behaviours considered harmful. In *AAMAS '03: Proceedings of the Second International Joint Conference on Autonomous Agents and Multiagent Systems* (pp. 1070-1071).

Müller, J. (2004). Emergence of collective behaviour and problem solving. *Engineering Societies in the Agents World, 3071,* 1-21.

Müller-Schloer, C. (2004). Organic computing: On the feasibility of controlled emergence. *In Proceedings of the 2nd IEEE/ACM/IFIP international conference on Hardware/software codesign and system synthesis (pp. 2-5) ACM Press.*

Omicini, A., Ricci, A., Viroli, M., Castelfranchi, C., & Tummolini, L. (2004). A conceptual framework for self-organising mas. In *5th AI*IA/TABOO Joint Workshop "From Objects to Agents": Complex Systems and Rational Agents (pp.* 100-109).

Parunak, H., & Vander Bok, R. (1997). Managing emergent behavior in distributed control systems. In *Proceedings of ISA Tech '97.* Instrument Society of America.

Parunak, H. V. D. (1997). Go to the ant: Engineering principles from natural multi-agent systems. *Annals of Operations Research, 75*(1), 69-101.

Parunak, H. V. D., & Brueckner, S. (2004). Engineering swarming systems. In *Methodologies and software engineering for agent systems (pp.* 341-376*). Kluwer.*

Parunak, H. V. D., Brueckner, S., & Savit, R. (2004). Universality in multi-agent systems. In *Proceedings of the Third International Joint Conference on Autonomous Agents and Multiagent Systems (pp. 939-93). IEEE Computer Society.*

Parunak, H. V. D., Weinstein, P., Chiusano, P., & Brueckner, S. (2005). Sift and sort: Climbing the semantic pyramid. In *Engineering self-organising systems* (pp. 212-221). Springer.

Phillips, A. (2006). *The stochastic pi machine (SPIM)* [Version 0.042]. Microsoft Research. Retrieved December 13, 2006, from http://research.microsoft.com/~aphillip/spim/

Priami, C. (1995). Stochastic π–calculus. *Computer Journal, 6,* 578-589.

Rao, A. S., & Georgeff, M. P. (1991). Modeling rational agents within a BDI-architecture. In *Proceedings of the 2nd International Conference on Principles of Knowledge Representation and Reasoning (pp.* 473-484*). Morgan Kaufmann.*

Rauch, J. (2002). Seeing around corners. *The Atlantic Monthly,* 35-48.

Renz, W., & Sudeikat, J. (2005). Modeling minority games with BDI agents—A case study. In *Multiagent System Technologies (LNAI 3550, pp. 71-81). Springer.*

Renz, W., & Sudeikat, J. (2005a). Mesoscopic modeling of emergent behavior—A self-organizing deliberative minority game. In *Engineering Self-Organising Systems* (LNCS 3910, pp. 167-181). Springer.

Renz, W., & Sudeikat, J. (2006). Emergent roles in multi agent systems—A case study in minority games. In *KI - Zeitschrift fuer Kuenstliche Intelligen, Böttcher IT Verlag*.

Rouff, C. A., Hinchey, M. G., Truszkowski, W. F., & Rash, J. L. (2006). Experiences applying formal approaches in the development of swarm-based space exploration systems. *International Journal on Software Tools for Technolgy Transfer, 8*, 587-603.

Serugendo, G. D. M., Gleizes, M. P., & Karageorgos, A. (2006). Self-organisation and emergence in MAS: An overview. *Informatica, 30*, 45-54.

Sudeikat, J., Braubach, L., Pokahr, A., & Lamersdorf, W. (2004). Evaluation of agent-oriented software methodologies—Examination of the gap between modeling and platform. In *Agent-oriented software engineering V* (pp. 126-141). Springer.

Sudeikat, J., & Renz, W. (2006). On the redesign of self-organizing multi-agent systems. *International Transactions on Systems Science and Applications, 2*, 81-89.

Sudeikat, J., & Renz, W. (2006a). Monitoring group behavior in goal-directed agents using co-efficient plan observation. In *Proceedings of the 7th International Workshop on Agent Oriented Software Engineering*. Springer.

Sudeikat, J., & Renz, W. (2006b). On simulations in MAS development—Deriving stochastic models from agent implementations to examine self-organizing dynamics. In *Kommunikation in Verteilten Systemen* (pp. 279-290). VDE-Verlag.

Sudeikat, J., & Renz, W. (2007). Toward requirements engineering for self-organizing multi-agent systems. In *Proceedings of the First International Conference on Self-Adaptive and Self-Organizing Systems*. IEEE Computer Society.

Sumpter, D., Blanchard, G. B., & Broomhead, D. (2001). Ants and agents: A process algebra approach to modelling ant colony. *Bulletin of Mathematical Biology, 63*, 951-980.

Viroli, M., & Omicini, A. (2005). Process-algebraic approaches for multi-agent systems: An overview. *Applicable Algebra in Engineering, Communication and Computing, 16*, 69-75.

Weiß. G. (2002). Agent orientation in software engineering. *Knowledge Engineering Review, 16*(4), 349-373.

Weyns, D., Schelfthout, K., Holvoet, T., & Glorieux, O. (2004). A role based model for adaptive agents. In *Proceedings of the Fourth Symposium on Adaptive Agents and Multi-Agent Systems* (pp. 75-86).

Endnotes

[1]   Jan Sudeikat is doctoral candidate at: Distributed Systems and Information Systems (VSIS), Computer Science Department, University of Hamburg, Vogt–Kölln–Str. 30, 22527 Hamburg, Germany 4sudeika@informatik.uni-hamburg.de

[2]   See the SOS FAQ v.2.99 http://www.calresco.org/sos/sosfaq.html for references and a readable introduction

Chapter X

FinSim:
A Framework for Modeling Financial System Interdependencies[1,2]

Alexander Outkin, Los Alamos National Laboratory, USA

Silvio Flaim, Los Alamos National Laboratory, USA

Andy Seirp, Los Alamos National Laboratory, USA

Julia Gavrilov, Los Alamos National Laboratory, USA

The size and complexity of financial markets in the United States have created significant payment and settlement interdependencies involving the banking system, money and capital markets, and associated derivative markets. Market participants and the Federal Reserve have for many years pursued measures to strengthen major US payment mechanisms, to increase processing efficiency, and to reduce payment system risks.

BIS/CPSS - Red Book - 2003

Abstract

We present in this chapter an overview of a financial system model (FinSim) created by the authors at the Los Alamos National Laboratory. The purpose of this model is to understand the impacts of external disruptions to the financial system, in particular disruptions to telecommunication networks and electric power systems; and to model how those impacts are affected by the interactions between different components of the financial system, for example, markets and payment systems, and by individual agents' actions and regulatory interventions. We use agent-based modeling to represent the interactions within the financial system and the decision-making processes of banks and traders. We model explicitly message passing necessary for execution of financial transactions, which allows a realistic representation of the financial system dependency on telecommunications. We describe implementation of the payment system, securities market, and liquidity market components and present a sample telecommunications disruption scenario and its preliminary results.

Introduction

The global financial system is one of the most complex systems created by mankind. It includes hundreds of different markets around the world, thousands of large institutions and vast numbers of participants. Different components of the financial system are required for other parts of the system to function: For example, stock market operations require the ability to make payments and transfer money in the banking system. The ability to execute transactions on any part of the financial system depends crucially on electric power and telecommunications services and to a lesser degree upon other underlying infrastructures—such as transportation and water. These complex interactions and interdependencies may exacerbate the impacts of natural disasters or terrorist events and are important to understand during crises where parts of the system are entirely disabled or function in a diminished capacity. Although there is a substantial body of research dedicated to modeling of individual components of the financial system, for example, the equity and bond markets, what is lacking is an understanding of how interaction between these components affects the dynamics of the entire system and how this dynamic depends on the state of underlying infrastructures, such as telecommunications.

The global financial system and its subcomponents—financial markets, payment systems, and so forth—are dynamic, nonlinear, evolving systems. New financial products and services are constantly introduced, new strategies for making money are constantly invented, certain players go bust, and others prosper. Money flows among different types of accounts, in different markets around the world at the touch of a button. A key aspect of these systems is that they are composed of multiple interacting autonomous parts, diverse markets, complex rules of engagement, and agents who act for their own benefit and sometimes to the detriment of others. Each agent has goals; rules for action and interaction; and decision-making strategies. The global financial system is the environment where different agents and institutions interact. This interaction produces global system dynamics, generates equilibrium, or disequilibrium prices of various assets and affects the stability or fragility of the global financial system. The end result—asset prices, wealth allocation—are influenced by strategies employed by individual agents or groups of agents and by the rules governing those interactions. Those strategies and rules can affect the dynamics of the system purposefully or inadvertently in non-trivial and sometimes detrimental ways.

On the other hand, the majority of existing tools for the financial markets are based on the foundations of the general equilibrium theory that originated in the 1950s and are not suitable for handling the complexity and variety of agents and strategies observed in real world markets. Additionally, those tools operate under a range of rather unrealistic assumptions: equilibrium; perfect information and rationality; profit maximizing behavior; absence of market power; and so forth. Interactions normally are assumed to be non-local and non-evolutionary—thus the system magically arrives at the equilibrium by the means of unspecified tatonnement process. With tools available today, it is possible to relax some of these restrictive assumptions and develop more realistic and practical models of the financial system.

Our approach employs agent-based modeling to represent behaviors of individual traders, banks, and other financial system participants and to characterize overall system dynamics. More information on agent-based modeling can be found in Epstein and Axtell (1996), Schelling (1978); or in application to financial markets in Axtell (2003, 2005), Darley and Outkin (2007), Darley, Outkin, Plate, and Gao (2000, 2001), Lux and Marchesi (1999), Rust, Miller, and Palmer (1993), Shubik and Smith (2004). A part of our approach, where actions of agents and the system-level processing of those actions are modeled explicitly, is related to the area of casual models, and is described in King (2002). Shafer and Vovk (2001) describe an exciting new approach to finance, where game theory, rather than the measure theory serves as a foundation for probability theory. This approach may apply to agent-based modeling as well—for agent-based models can be considered an extension of game-theoretic models—they share the concepts of agents, strategies, and interaction structures but differ in analytical tractability, modeling goals, and other important characteristics.

The goal of this chapter is to present a conceptual and simulation framework for modeling disruptions to the financial system that arise due to external events and for development of rules and policies that may promote the financial system stability and enable quicker recovery from crises. We present a model, developed by the authors at the Los Alamos National Laboratory (LANL)—FinSim—that incorporates a number of generic financial system elements: a payment and settlements system model (similar to Fedwire), an equity market, and a market for liquidity (modeled after the Federal Funds market). FinSim models interaction between these components either through individual participant actions (when for example a bank participates in a payment system, handles accounts of equity market traders, and manages its liquidity positions using a liquidity market) or through explicit connections between those systems (when liquidity market transactions are settled over the payment system). FinSim includes a messaging framework, which enables modeling the financial system's dependency on the telecommunications system explicitly. The state of agents and institutions in the model includes the electric power availability—thus allowing explicit dependency on the electric power system. Because of those features, FinSim has an ability to address a broad set of questions related to the financial system policies and effects of disruptions. However, our goal in this chapter is limited to understanding the financial system impacts caused by telecommunications and electric power systems disruptions. The rest of this chapter presents an overview of the financial system and its interdependencies, a description of possible disruption scenarios, an overview of the FinSim model, and preliminary simulation results from several computer experiments representing a telecommunications disruptions scenario.

Overview of the Financial System and Its Interdependencies

The U.S. financial system encompasses an intricate combination of financial markets, institutions, and instruments. Businesses, governments, and individuals invest and borrow funds using a large array of financial and derivative instruments. Financial services are provided by banks; mutual funds; pension funds; insurance companies; security brokers and dealers; credit unions; and other financial institutions. Financial transactions among banks are enabled by payment systems, such as Fedwire and the Clearing House Inter-bank Payments System (CHIPS). A number of different financial markets exist and provide opportunities to find the best match for various investment objectives. The overview (see next section) does not attempt to even list all the components of the financial system, but instead concentrates on the parts represented in our model—payment systems, securities markets, and markets for central bank reserves (liquidity). The purpose of this section is to briefly outline the main features of the systems and interactions modeled in FinSim. Specific implementation details and an overview of dependencies on telecommunications can be found in the *Simulation Specification and Implementation* section.

Markets

U.S. equity markets are by far the largest and most visible to the public. Equity markets provide companies with access to capital and the trading public with the ability to invest, among other functions they perform. The New York Stock Exchange and NASDAQ are the largest and most important U.S. equity markets. Both have changed significantly over the last decade and still continue changing due to a number of factors: various regulatory changes (decimalization for example); the advent of Electronic Communications Networks (ECNs); market structure changes; globalization and international acquisitions; and changes in the business models of market participants. A description of the current state of those markets is outside of the scope of this chapter. NASDAQ, the New York Stock Exchange, Chicago Stock Exchange, American Stock Exchange, and other major U.S. exchanges list over 8,000 stocks. Few however, are traded actively. Overall, stocks represent only 20% of capital wealth. Greater capital wealth is concentrated in real estate (50%) and various bonds (35%) (see Harris, 2003).

Operations on the Federal funds, money markets, repo markets, foreign exchange, and so forth are not visible to the public, and yet they move trillions of dollars in daily transactions. These are mostly informal "telephone" markets with low transaction costs. Their market instruments include U.S. Treasury bills, short-term Federal agency securities, commercial paper, federal funds, large-denomination certificates of deposit, and spot and forward foreign-exchange contracts.

The Federal funds market is a core component of the U.S. financial system. It is a driver for payment system activity and allows banks to alleviate temporary reserve shortfalls or to receive interest income on their excess reserves. The Federal funds market transactions are settled through the exchange of funds via Fedwire—both the funds borrowed and the funds repaid are sent via Fedwire.

Central counterparties (CCPs) are critical to efficient market operation. Their key functions are:

- Trade match/clearance
- Trade settlement/guarantee of performance

Trade matching is a front-end operation involving the capture of trade data and verification that the specific terms of buyers' and sellers' trade records match exactly. Trade settlement involves procedures of novation, when a CCP becomes a central buyer for all sellers and a central seller for all buyers, so that each trade is substituted by two new trades. This way, a CCP assumes all outstanding obligations for contract performance and absorbs risks of settlement default. To manage the risk, a CCP employs risk management policies including deposits of performance collateral by clearing participants (original margin), revaluation of derivatives, and collecting incremental unrealized losses (variation margin). "A CCP has the potential to reduce significantly risks to market participants by imposing more robust risk controls on all participants and, in many cases, by achieving multilateral netting of trades" (Bank for International Settlements/Committee on Payment and Settlement Systems [BIS/CPSS], 2004, see also McPartland, 2005 for more information).

Payment Systems

Payment systems are categorized as retail or large-value payment systems. Retail payment systems generally process small payments and are settled with simple algorithms. These include check clearing, automated clearinghouse (ACH), and credit/debit card systems. The liquidity impact and settlement risks are generally low. The opposite is true for large-value payment systems. The two large value payment systems in the United States, which handle the greatest dollar value of payments, are Fedwire (supported by FEDNET, the underlying telecommunications network which connects the Federal Reserve and its depository institution customers) and CHIPS (see BIS/CPSS, 2003). The users of the payments system are the financial institutions active in wholesale financial markets such as the repo markets, the Federal funds market, money markets, foreign exchange markets, and securities markets.

Fedwire is owned and operated by the Federal Reserve. It has approximately 9,500 participants that can initiate or receive transfers. In 2006, the system processed on average 532,292 payments per day and the total value of transfers was approximately $573 trillion per year. Intra-day credit is permitted, subject to net debit caps. Those caps are enforced ex ante for only about 2% of the banks. Positions are monitored for all banks on an ex post basis.

CHIPS is privately owned and operated. In 2006, the system had 46 participants, processed on average 310,265 payments per day, and the total annual value of transfers was approximately $395 trillion. Intra-day credit is not permitted (BIS/CPSS, 2003).

Payment systems have several different approaches to settlement. The two large value systems mentioned previously, Fedwire and CHIPS, typically process payments in real time. With CHIPS, payments that are not processed during the day are processed as a part of a multilateral net settlement at the end of the day. If a CHIPS participant is left with a debit balance at the end of the day, that balance is paid by a transfer to an account held by CHIPS with the Federal Reserve Bank of New York.

In another contrast to Fedwire, which settles payments on a "gross" basis (each one is processed separately, see Murphy, 2004), CHIPS continuously matches, nets, and settles queued orders during the day. This involves bilateral offsetting and multilateral netting of payments. The process of netting queued payments between banks with opposing queued payment flows helps to preserve and optimize the use of liquidity, although this will sometimes prevent instantaneous processing.

Steps in Payment Processing

All payment settlement transactions consist of a debit and a credit. Funds are moved from one inter-bank settlement account to another. Each participant sees a flow of outgoing and incoming transactions that produce a settlement balance.

The process of payment settlement includes the following steps. First, payment requests from the institution's customers and internal departments accumulate in an internal transaction queue within a particular financial institution. An institution typically releases these payment requests into the inter-bank payment system after determining that its customer has sufficient funds or available credit on hand to cover the payment, and the institution in the aggregate has sufficient liquidity. At this point, payments released into the payment system are either immediately settled through the transfer of funds from the sender to the receiver, or rejected back to the sender. Depending on the algorithms employed by a payment system, payments that can not be processed immediately because of insufficient money balances or available credit in the sending institution's account, can by queued by the payment system, rather than rejected back to the sender (CHIPS is one example). Queued payments will remain as such until additional liquidity (in the form of incoming funds transfers or available credit) becomes available or a gridlock resolution algorithm is employed by the payment system that permits the payment to be released from the queue and settled. A payment left unprocessed for a certain period of time expires.

Payment systems attempt to optimize the following conditions when settling payments: finality, quick throughput, low liquidity consumption, and low settlement costs (see Leinonen & Soramäki, 2003).

Gridlock and Gridlock Resolution

Payment system gridlock occurs when the payment processing slows or stops altogether. This occurs primarily because of the lack of liquidity on the system level (when the total liquidity is insufficient to settle all the payments) or at an individual key institution level (when for example a payment system participant holds a significant portion of the overall system liquidity, but is not sending out fund transfers). Theoretically, at least for the Fedwire system, intra-day credit from the Federal Reserve should prevent gridlock from occurring. However, anecdotal evidence suggests that very large payment outflows (without offsetting inflows) that surpass bank's internal thresholds plus significant uncertainty about future receipts may prompt a bank to delay sending payments, thus potentially causing a system-level gridlock.

In the event of insufficient liquidity, banks have the ability to slow down scheduled payments. This permits their settlement account to be replenished with incoming payments. Further, the Federal Reserve has at times injected huge amounts of liquidity into the system (9/11/01 for instance) and can temporarily waive certain fees in an attempt to stimulate payment activity (see Cumming, 2002 for example). As mentioned previously, complex algorithms are also employed (as with CHIPS) in an attempt to make the most efficient use of available liquidity.

The Role of the Federal Reserve

The Federal Reserve (Fed) is perhaps the most critical government institution involved in the financial system. Its purpose (or more specifically the purpose of The Board of Governors of the Federal Reserve System and the Federal Open Market Committee) is "…to promote effectively the goals of maximum employment, stable prices, and moderate long-term interest rates."[3] The tools at its disposal include the tools of monetary policy, bank supervision, and promoting a safe, sound, and efficient payment system. The Fed steps in times of financial distress "to ensure and safeguard against bank panics," and to be the "lender of last resort."

There are numerous examples of the Fed acting as financial stabilizer, including the temporary $5 billion loan to the Continental Illinois National Bank when it failed in 1984, providing liquidity during the 1987 stock market crash, or, more recently, following the September 11 terrorist attack. After the 9/11 attack, the Fed maintained public confidence in the financial system by announcing that it was "open and operating." It provided over $425 million in cash to the New York banks located near the place of the attacks, so there were enough funds to cover any increased demand for cash. Most importantly, the Fed took measures to prevent liquidity shortages in the overall financial system by making it easier for the banks to get overnight loans through the discount window (on September 12, 2001, it lent through this channel a record $46 billion (source: Federal Reserve Bank of New York [FRBNY], "The Discount Window, " n.d.) compared to a the daily average for the preceding six weeks of $21 million (see Lenain, Bonturi, & Koen, 2002) and by lowering the overnight Fed funds rate. It also infused the system with cash by buying $38 billion, $70 billion, and $81 billion in U.S. treasury securities on September 12, 13, and 14 respectively (source: FRBNY, "Temporary Open Market Operations Historical Search," n.d.).

Crisis Scenarios and Crisis Modeling

In this chapter, our goal is limited to understanding the financial system impacts caused by telecommunications and electric power system disruptions. While this does not address many risks attributable to the financial system, disruptions to telecom and energy infrastructures can produce severe disruptions to the financial system as illustrated later on. Furthermore, FinSim is capable of addressing other risks, such as defaults of banks or traders; excessive risk concentration and high leverage levels; operational disruptions; and certain policy changes.

In general, risks can arise from a number of causes and manifest themselves in a number of ways: defaults of economic agents or financial intermediaries, excessive risk concentration, poorly understood risks, macro-economic imbalances, high leverage levels, operational disruptions, and regulatory/policy shifts. Of particular concern are the situations where the financial crisis propagates into the rest of the economy and negatively affects such observable variables as GDP, unemployment, and consumption.

Property and communication systems damage caused by the September 11, 2001, terrorist attacks rendered some banks unable to execute large-value payments through Fedwire. That significantly disturbed payment coordination—a strategy when banks use incoming payments to fund their outgoing payments. McAndrews and Potter (2002) show that payment timing variability in the aftermath of 9/11 almost doubled, and banks, denied an opportunity to synchronize incoming and outgoing transactions, reacted to the uncertainty by drastically increasing precautionary demand for liquidity. As mentioned earlier, the Fed met the demand through discount window loans and open market operations, pumping an unprecedented amount of cash into the financial system. See also Zimmerman and Horan (2004) for impact of telecommunications disruptions on the financial system functions following 9/11.

During the August 14-15, 2003 power outage that affected the Northeast and Midwest U.S. and Ontario, Canada, the financial system maintained its critical operations by quickly switching to back-up power. The Fedwire fund transfer service, relying on back-up generators, worked without interruption and even extended operating hours to accommodate affected participants.

However, from the congressional testimony of Federal Reserve Governor M.W. Olson,[4] it becomes apparent that had the outage lasted for longer than 48 hours and spanned several business days, the impact on the financial system would have been much more profound. The batteries used for power generators have a limited lifetime. Increased demand for fuel for the power generators becomes an issue very soon due to competing demand, delivery priorities, and transportation problems. Personnel of financial institutions located in Manhattan could not get to work on the second day of the outage because the transportation system was shut down. In Detroit, financial institutions had to close due to interrupted water supply. Yet other organizations discovered that, although backup power supported their outside telecommunication lines, the in-house voice and data telecommunications were down. Many cell phone towers turned out to be on buildings without backup power. All ATMs in the affected areas were down. Consumers were not significantly inconvenienced by that due to the availability of alternative methods of payment like checks, debit, and credit cards—those networks remained operational. No unusual demand for cash or signs of the public loosing confidence in the financial system were observed. This event demonstrated how interdependent our critical infrastructures are, and how failure of one cascades into others. The short duration of the outage and the ability of the financial system to continue with critical operations played a role in mitigating the effects of the outage. Moreover, according to Federal Reserve Governor M.W. Olson (ibid) the government's immediate announcement that the outage was not a result of a terrorist attack was crucial in preventing panic

Existing Modeling Approaches

While there are many market models available—see for example Axtell (2005), Darley and Outkin (2007), Darley et al. (2000, 2001), Farmer and Joshi (2002), Lux and Marchesi (1999), and Rust et al. (1993)—there are just a few payment system models available. Two of those models are briefly described later on. Additional work in payment systems and disruptions modeling includes Bech and Garratt (2006) and Soramäki, Bech, Arnold, Glass, and Beyeler (2006).

Bank of Finland Model

The Bank of Finland (BoF) Payment and Settlement System Simulator is a tool used for payment and settlement system simulations. The simulator is designed for analyzing liquidity needs and risks in payment and settlement systems. Users can study how behavioral patterns and changes in policy and conventions impact the payment and settlement systems and participants. The efficiency of gridlock-resolution and liquidity-saving measures can also be analyzed.

The execution process is separated into algorithms and processing steps which can be used to construct a large number of current and potential settlement conventions and structures. The simulator allows three modes for processing transaction flows: (1) real-time gross settlement system (RTGS), (2) continuous net settlement system (CNS), and (3) deferred net settlement system (DNS). It also offers multi-currency and securities settlement features (see Leinonen & Soramäki, 2003).

Bank of England/University of Essex Model

This simulator is similar to the BoF simulator. It, however, has the capability of handling stochastic simulations, which enable the inter-bank system properties such as size, arrival time, and distribution of payment flows to be varied. Further, strategic behavior of banks can be modeled (see Alentorn, Markose, Millard, & Yang, 2005).

FinSim Specification and Implementation

In our approach, we model the financial system as a complex decentralized system with multiple interacting autonomous decision nodes, such as agents (banks, traders), markets, and limit order books. Our model addresses the key components of the financial system—the payments system, markets (securities and liquidity/central bank reserves markets), their participants (banks and traders), and their interaction. As a novel part of our approach, the telecommunication system plays a central role—all the communications between financial system participants are intermediated through the messaging mechanism enabled by the telecommunication system. Agents and financial system entities pass messages (payment requests, orders, processed trades...) between themselves by using the telecommunication system to transmit and deliver those messages. This section provides an overview of how the parts of the financial system described previously were implemented in our simulation. Building a model, whether theoretical or in software, means necessarily departures from reality—not all features or aspects of the real world can be implemented. The art of building a model includes deciding what is important enough to include and what can be left out. This section, therefore, describes the parts of the financial system, not in their full complexity, but how they were actually implemented.

The simulation was implemented in Java. We used RePast[5] as an underlying agent-based framework. Figures 1 and 2 outline the objects in the simulation and their interactions while running the simulation.

Overview of the Market Design

Financial markets have various structures that define when, where, and how trades are executed. There are quote-driven markets, in which dealers provide liquidity at the prices they quote for traders. There are order-driven markets, in which traders trade without intermediation of dealers, and market rules define trade arrangement and pricing. And there are brokered markets, in which brokers arrange deals for

Figure 1. A list of top-level software and data objects in the simulation

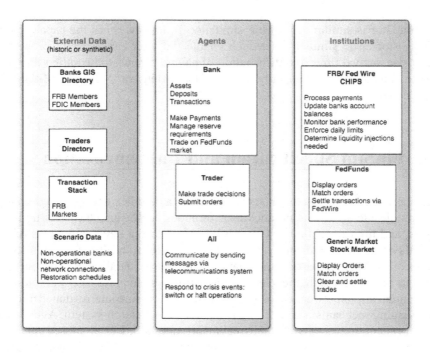

Figure 2. Top-level interactions during the simulation run

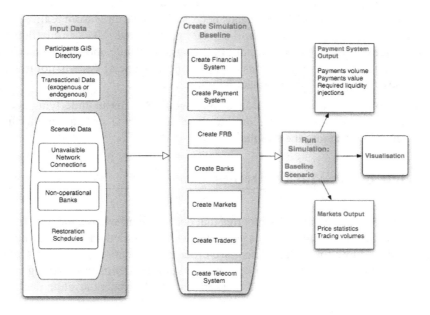

their clients, who usually want to trade privately and in large blocks of stocks or bonds.

We chose to model a continuous order-driven market with a rule-based order matching system that involves discriminatory pricing rule. While this is a departure from reality—for example NASDAQ uses market makers and NYSE uses specialists to provide liquidity—many exchanges, some brokerages, and almost all electronic communications networks use rule-based order-matching systems to arrange at least some of their trades.

In this market, public traders trade with each other anonymously via an electronic system. The system has a formalized and coded set of trade matching and trade pricing rules and accepts only limit orders. Orders flow in continuously, and trades are executed as soon as matches are found. Order matching is based on order precedence rules: the highest-priced bid and the lowest-priced offers have the highest priority and are matched. The precedence of orders with equal limit prices is determined based on their time of arrival. In the case of the Federal funds market, interest rates are used instead of prices.

An order book is maintained for each trading instrument to keep track of standing orders. In the book, buy and sell orders are separated and sorted by their precedence. When a new order comes in, its terms are compared with the terms of the highest-ranking standing order on the opposite side of the book. If the new order meets the terms of the standing order, the trade is executed; otherwise, the newly arrived order is placed in the book in accordance with its precedence and becomes a standing order.

Each trade price is determined by the limit price of the standing order. When a large new order arrives and is filled by several standing orders, each trade is executed potentially at a different price in accordance with the standing limit orders it is matched to. Such arrangement is called the discriminatory pricing rule.

The Federal funds market is also implemented as an order-driven market with a central broker. Duration of Fed funds contracts in one day. Banks submit their buy or sell orders for reserves. The orders are continuously matched by the broker, who sends notifications to the banks involved when a match has occurred. Subsequently, the seller of funds makes a transfer using the payment system. The borrower of funds repays the principal and interest the next day, also using the payment system.

To facilitate the implementation of a number of different markets, the Federal funds market and stock market, for example, we created a generic market template that defines common market components. A part of this template was implemented as a generic market in Java and is adaptable to specific markets.

Overview of the Payment System Design

The payment system main function is to move money from one agent to another. This typically involves the movement of money from the bank of one trading agent to the bank of another trading agent. To initiate this process, the agent sending the payment must send a message to its bank indicating its desire to send a payment to a specific counterparty. The sending agent's bank, upon receiving this message, must decide if and when to send this message (and other messages in its internal queue) to the payment system.

We have implemented algorithms for real-time gross settlement system (similar to Fedwire) and real-time multilateral net settlement system (similar to CHIPS, only preliminary implementation of the CHIPS algorithms is available). These two systems are most widely used in the United States for processing large-value payments. The simulation can be run with either Fedwire or CHIPS algorithms, but not both.

Once the payment(s) are sent to the payment system, they are processed as liquidity is available. In the case of real-time gross settlement (Fedwire), intra-day credit is available but must be paid back at the end of the day. Banks that fail to pay back end-of-day settlement account debt or exceed an intra-day credit limit will have their payment requests rejected or queued and must wait for additional liquidity before any more payments are processed. After each successfully processed payment, the payment queue is searched for any payments that can now be processed because of the increase in liquidity. In the case of multilateral net settlement, intra-day credit is not permitted, but smaller amounts of liquidity are required to process payments because of bilateral offsetting and multilateral netting techniques. At the end of the day, any payments, which have not yet been processed, are tallied and funded on a multilateral net basis prior to releasing these payments. Any bank failing to pay this daily obligation will no longer be permitted to submit payments for processing. Gridlock in the payment systems described previously will be measured in the simulation by the number of queued (unprocessed) transactions.

Interactions

Everything in the simulation is connected to each other: Traders receive information about prices from markets, request their available cash balances from banks, and submit their trades using the telecommunications system. In our implementation, any agent or financial entity can send or receive messages in order to perform their functions in the payment system or in the markets. The telecommunications system passes the messages independently of the message content, so that it is the sender and receiver's responsibility to understand the meaning of the message.

Figure 3. Market—Payment system interaction

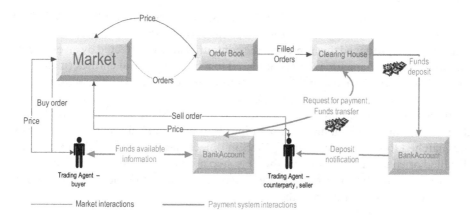

Banks provide services for traders and other agents and send payments via the payment system. Figure 3 provides an example of such interactions: It illustrates the interaction of an order-driven market and the payment system. The process begins when trading agents, buyers, and sellers submit orders to the market. In the case of buyers, they must first verify that their bank balance is greater than or equal to the order purchase price. As buy and sell orders flow in, an attempt is made to match and execute them based on a set of trading rules. New orders that come in and are not executed become standing orders and are placed in an order book based on precedence rules. Once orders are filled (executed), they are sent to a clearinghouse for recording-keeping and transfer of assets. Both the transfer of funds and securities must take place. The *clearing house* acts as a buyer to all sellers and a seller to all buyers. In particular, the clearing house (acting through a clearing house bank) transfers the funds to the seller's account using the payment system and requests the buyer's bank to transfer the funds to the clearing house bank also using the payment system.

Results: Interdependencies Between Financial System, Telecommunications, and Energy

At the time of simulation, financial entities are created as objects within FinSim. During object creation, various characteristics (geographic, financial, organizational, etc.) of actual, real-world financial entities are read from a database record and applied to this newly created object.

Using the National Infrastructure Simulation Assessment Center (NISAC) tools such as Interdependent Energy Infrastructure Simulation System (IEISS) and MIITS,[6] shape files are produced that represent the contour of an area affected by an electrical disruption. That shape file is then compared to a list of financial entities (using GIS tools such as ArcMap) to identify which entities are affected by the disruption. This process works the same to identify which entities have been restored at a particular time. The relevant entities are then listed in a file (with the times of both their disablement and enablement) and read into FinSim during simulation. Next, they are matched to their corresponding FinSim object and the FinSim object is either disabled or enabled depending on the time step of the simulation. This process will effectively shutdown or turn on these objects with respect to their ability to communicate with other entities in the simulation.

FinSim Scenario with Electrical Power/Telecommunications Failure

A crisis scenario mentioned earlier involved simulating damage to Fedwire or the underlying FEDNET infrastructure. A similar scenario (in terms of effect) would be one where numerous banks lose electrical power and then telecommunication capabilities such that they are not able to use Fedwire even though Fedwire is still functional. The goal of this simulation would be to discover the point at which the system (Fed-member banks, Federal Reserve, and Fedwire interacting) cannot quickly recover from disablement as well as understanding the Fed intervention required to system recovery. Fed intervention could take the form of reducing or eliminating charges for intra-day overdrafts and penalty fees for overnight overdrafts, increased "discount window" lending, injecting liquidity into the payment system through the *open market operations*. The primary measure of system breakdown/recovery will be the percentage of transactions failing to reach the Federal Reserve for processing as well as the percentage of transactions failing to be processed once they have reached the payment system. Further, the time required to recover from a position of gridlock will be estimated.

This simulation will have both a stock market and a Fed funds market component operating and generating payment requests that will ultimately be sent to the Fedwire system for processing. The stock market transactions will be produced by trading agents and routed through a clearinghouse and the Fed funds transactions will be produced by banks and routed through the Fed funds broker. The activity in the stock market will be the primary driver of transactions reaching the payment system. The Fed funds activity will largely be in response to varying bank balances at the

Federal Reserve due to customer stock trading. Each bank must maintain "reserve requirements" at the Federal Reserve and Fed funds trading, it is presumed, will ensure that this requirement is met.

In the first two scenarios (Table 1—TRF, TRN) all system components are operating as they should in an environment with no electrical/telecommunication problems. In the second two scenarios (IRF, IRN), electrical/telecommunication problems are introduced. The simulations will be run with a restricted amount of intra-day credit as well as with and without the operation of the Fed funds market, which serves as a source of liquidity. It is anticipated the Fed funds market liquidity (in addition to intra-day credit provided by the Fed) will support system recovery during times of gridlock. These results are preliminary and cannot be taken in quantitative fashion;

Table 1. Simulation run results

Scenarios	TRF	TRN	IRF	IRN
Simulation Parameters				
Completed Federal funds transactions sent to banks	3	0	0	0
Transactions sent by CH bank	24908	7312	24908	7312
Total transactions sent to PS	24712	7312	24706	7312
Transactions reaching PSS	24712	7312	24706	7312
Transactions processed in PSS	24712	7312	24706	7312
Transactions not reaching PSS-telecom failure	0	0	0	0
Queued transactions in banks	20	20	20	20
Queued transactions in PSS	0	0	0	0
Combined negative FRB balance (liquidity need)	0	0	0	0

Table 2. Scenario keys for Table 1

No telecom failure	(T)
Telecom failure	(I)
Restricted intra-day credit	(R)
Fed Funds Used	(F)
No Fed Funds	(N)

however, in a qualitative fashion they appear to be valid. However, our results for scenarios with unlimited banking credit are counterintuitive and need to be further verified prior to being reported.

The previous four scenarios were run with five banks and 200 different stock trading agents. Each of these agents used one of five different banks for holding their cash and making payments. For those simulations that involved telecom failure, two particular banks were disabled each time. The label "Transactions sent by CH bank" indicates the number of completed stock orders that were forwarded to the payment system by the clearinghouse bank.

The results derived are following:

- with no telecom failure and restricted bank credit (how much a bank can borrow intra-day from the Federal Reserve), 20 transactions were never sent to the payment system;
- with telecom failure there are numerous banks with negative ending balances; and
- when the Fed funds market is enabled in the simulation, there is a significantly greater number of trades being processed than without its availability.

Conclusion

This chapter outlines the entire FinSim framework and its individual components, such as payments systems and markets models, and their interactions with each other and with the telecommunications and energy infrastructures. We present implementation of models of Fedwire, Federal funds market, and outline an implementation of a stock market model. We further outline the process for populating the model with real-world entities, using GIS-level data, and a process for generating crisis scenarios. We conclude with an overview of crisis scenario runs; however, those results are provisional and will be improved and revised in the future.

The most important future improvement for FinSim is to obtain more extensive data sets for markets and payment systems to enable better model calibration and validation. Our future plans for FinSim also include implementation of different types of payment system settlement algorithms, such as the more complex "netting" techniques that were described earlier in the chapter and the inclusion of multiple payment systems or messaging frameworks to have the capacity to simulate international activity.

References

Alentorn, A., Markose, S., Millard, S., & Yang, J. (2005). *Designing large value payment system—An agent-based approach.* Retrieved from privatewww.essex.ac.uk/~aalent/IPSS

Axtell, R. (2003). Economics as distributed computation. In H. Deguchi et al. (Eds.), *Meeting the challenge of social problems via agent-based simulation.* Springer-Verlag.

Axtell, R. (2005). The complexity of exchange. *Economic Journal, 115*(504), F193-F210.

Bank for International Settlements/Committee on Payment and Settlement Systems (BIS/CPSS). (2003). *Payment and settlement systems in selected countries (read book)* (5th ed.). Basel, Switzerland: Author.

Bank for International Settlements/Committee on Payment and Settlement Systems. (2004). *Recommendations for central counterparties: Consultative report.* Basel, Switzerland: Author.

Bech, M. L., & Garratt, R. (2006). *Illiquidity in the interbank payment system following wide-scale disruptions* (Staff Report, No. 239). FRB of NY.

Board of Governors of the Federal Reserve System. (2005). *The Federal Reserve System purposes & functions.* Washington, DC: Author.

Cumming, C. M. (2002). September 11 and the U.S. payment system. *Finance and Development magazine, 39*(1).

Darley, V., & Outkin, A. (2007). *A NASDAQ market simulation: Insights on a major market from the science of complex adaptive systems.* Singapore: World Scientific.

Darley, V., Outkin, A., Plate, T., & Gao, F. (2000). Sixteenths or pennies? Observations from a simulation of the Nasdaq stock market. In *Proceeding of IEEE/IAFE/INFORMS 2000 Conference on Computational Intelligence for Financial Engineering (CIFEr).*

Darley, V., Outkin, A., Plate, T., & Gao, F. (2001). Learning, evolution and tick size effects in a simulation of the NASDAQ stock market. In *Proceedings of the 5th World Multi-Conference on Systemics, Cybernetics and Informatics.* Orlando, FL.

Eidenbenz, S. J. (2006). *MIITS: Multi-scale integrated information and telecommunication system* (LA-UR-06-1472). Los Alamos, NM: Los Alamos National Laboratory.

Epstein, J. M., & Axtell, R. (1996). *Growing artificial societies: Social science from the bottom up.* Washington, DC: The Brookings Institution.

Farmer, J. D., & Joshi, S. (2002). The price dynamics of common trading strategies. *Journal of Economic Behavior & Organization, 49.*

Federal Reserve Bank of New York. (n.d.). *Temporary open market operations historical search.* Retrieved May 31, 2007, from http://www.newyorkfed.org/markets/omo/dmm/historical/tomo/search.cfm

Federal Reserve Bank of New York. (n.d.). *The discount window.* Retrieved May 31, 2007, from http://www.newyorkfed.org/aboutthefed/fedpoint/fed18.html

Harris, L. (2003). *Trading and exchanges: Market microstructure for practitioners.* Oxford University Press.

King, J. (2002). *Operational risk: Measurement and modelling.* Wiley.

Leinonen, H., & Soramäki, K. (2003). *Simulating interbank payment and securities settlement mechanisms with the BoF-PSS2 simulator.* Bank of Finland Discussion Papers.

Lenain, P., Bonturi, M., & Koen, V. (2002). *The economic consequences of terrorism.* Paris: Organization for Economic Co-operation and Development.

Lux, T., & Marchesi, M. (1999). Scaling and criticality in a stochastic multi-agent model of a financial market. *Nature, 397.*

McAndrews, J. J., & Potter, S. M. (2002). Liquidity effects of the events of September 11, 2001. *Economic Policy Review, 8*(2).

McPartland, J. (2005). Clearing and settlement demystified. *Chicago Fed Letter,* Number 210.

Murphy, N. B. (2004). The effect on U.S. banking of payment system changes. *FDIC Banking Review, 16*(2).

Rust, J., Miller, J., & Palmer, R. (1993). Behavior of trading automata in a computerized double auction market. In *The double auction market: Institutions, theories, and evidence.* Westview Press.

Schelling, T. (1978). *Micromotives and macrobehavior.* W. W. Norton.

Shafer, G., & Vovk, V. (2001). *Probability and finance: It's only a game!* Wiley-Interscience.

Shubik, M., & Smith, E. (2004). The physics of time and dimension in the economics of financial control. *Physica A: Statistical mechanics and its applications, 340*(4), 656-667.

Soramäki, K., Bech, M. L., Arnold, J., Glass, R. J., & Beyeler, W. (2006). The topology of interbank payment flows (Staff Report, No 243). FRB of NY.

Zimmerman, R., & Horan, T. (2004). *Digital infrastructures.* New York: Routlege.

Endnotes

[1] We would like to thank the anonymous reviewers as well as Brian Edwards, Hari Khalsa, and Daniel Shevitz for valuable suggestions and comments. We thank Jeff Stehm, James McAndrews, Morten Bech, Kimmo Soramäki, Jeffrey Arnold, and other members of FRB staff for valuable discussions that helped to improve our understanding of the Federal Reserve roles and operations. We thank Mary Ewers for information and insight into the workings of the Federal Funds market. All errors that remain are ours. This work has been performed as a part of National Infrastructure Simulation Assessment Center program funded by the Department of Homeland Security.

[2] Emails: outkin@vt.edu, sflaim@lanl.gov, aseirp@lanl.gov, julia@lanl.gov.

[3] See Federal Reserve Act of 1913 and subsequent amendments (1977, 1978, 2000), also Board of Governors of the Federal Reserve System (2005).

[4] Testimony of Governor Mark W. Olson "Power outages and the financial system" before the Subcommittee on Oversight and Investigations of the Committee on Financial Services, U.S. House of Representatives, October 20, 2003.

[5] See http://repast.sourceforge.net/ for more information.

[6] **Multi-scale integrated information and telecommunications system (MIITS)** is a tool developed at LANL for modeling the telecommunications networks and disruptions to them. See Eidenbenz (2006) for more information.

Chapter XI

Complex Adaptive Systems Theory and Military Transformation

Kimberly Holloman, Science Applications International Corporation, USA

Abstract

The United States and many of its coalition partners have initiated a broad program of reform aimed at transforming their defensive capabilities to take advantage of recent advances in technologies and to meet emerging security challenges. Progress to date, however, has been mixed in terms of the ability of the U.S. Department of Defense (DoD) to redefine itself as an information age organization and in terms of the DoD's capacity to deliver transformational capabilities to war fighters. This chapter examines questions regarding our ability to guide, direct, and control large scale organizational change. I suggest that transformational efforts can be viewed through the lens of the agent structure debate, which posits that social change is the outcome of a complex dialectic between human agents and social structures. I argue that our understanding of this dialectic may be significantly enhanced if we examine the theoretical and empirical insights gained from the study of complex adaptive systems (CASs).

Introduction[1]

The United States and many of its coalition partners have initiated a broad program of reform aimed at transforming their defensive capabilities to take advantage of recent advances in information and communications technologies and to meet emerging security challenges. Transformation entails dramatic and sometimes disruptive changes in the way the U.S. DoD prepares for and conducts military operations. A critical component of this transformation is the theory of network-centric warfare (NCW). It posits that information sharing across traditionally separated organizational boundaries will lead to dramatic improvements in military effectiveness. In order to develop NCW capabilities, the DoD is sponsoring multiple programs, efforts, and initiatives aimed at harnessing new and emerging technologies that meet present and anticipated future war fighter needs.

Progress to date, however, has been mixed in terms of the ability of the DoD redefine itself as an information age organization and in terms of the DoD's capacity to deliver transformational capabilities to war fighters. The reasons for the limited success of transformation efforts are numerous, including the strain of two wars. However, this chapter focuses on difficulties associated with transforming large and complex bureaucracies such as the DoD. It addresses questions regarding our ability to guide, direct, and control large scale organizational change. I suggest that transformational efforts can be viewed through the lens of the agent-structure debate that examines questions of large scale social change. Social constructivists argue that social change, such as the transformation of the DoD, is the outcome of a complex dialectic between human agents and social structures. I argue that our understanding of this dialectic may be enhanced if we examine the theoretical and empirical insights gained from the study of CASs. I conclude by making recommendations for a program of research aimed at furthering our understanding of large scale social change efforts exemplified by military transformation.

U.S. Military Transformation

Although the U.S. military is continually evolving and developing new capabilities, in recent years military leaders have vigorously pursued a policy of transformation aimed at dramatically changing the way that the U.S. prepares for and conducts warfare. The current transformation effort formally began in January 2001 when President George W. Bush selected Donald Rumsfeld as the Secretary of Defense (SecDef). SecDef Rumsfeld was given considerable freedom to pursue his agenda of transforming the military into an information age institution. The impetus to move forward on transformation was dramatically accelerated following the September

11, 2001 terrorists attacks. Rumsfeld's first major formal policy statement on transformation was the *Quadrennial Defense Review,* or QDR, released September 30, 2001. The QDR placed transformation at the center of this new strategy.

... the defense strategy calls for the transformation of the U.S. military and Defense establishment over time. Transformation is at the heart of this new strategic approach. The Department's leadership recognizes that continuing "business as usual" within the Department is not a viable option given the new strategic era and the internal and external challenges facing the U.S. military. Without change, the current defense program will only become more expensive to maintain over time, and it will forfeit many of the opportunities available to the United States today. Without transformation, the U.S. military will not be prepared to meet emerging challenges. (DoD "Quadrennial Defense Review Report," 2001, p. 16)

While the QDR sets the goals and objectives of transformation, it was criticized for not providing details about how transformation was to be implemented (Schrader, Lewis, & Brown, 2003). There was little agreement in the defense community about what the term meant or what it implied for the U.S. military. In an effort to provide the broad DoD community information and a coherent story about transformation, the DoD's Office of the Secretary of Defense published the *Transformation Planning Guidance* (TPG) (DoD, 2003; Else, 2004). The TPG stated that the need for transformation was driven by the following assumptions:

* U.S. military superiority cannot be assumed in the future. As Information Age technologies proliferate, U.S. dominance will increasingly be challenged in novel ways.

* Growing asymmetric threats require new ways of thinking about conflict that require creative approaches.

* Force-on-force challenges are likely to increase as adversaries seek to take advantage of changes in global power relations resulting from the transition to the Information Age.

* Technological changes make transformation of the military imperative; there is a window of opportunity to leverage U.S. competitive advantage into the future.

The TPG called for transformation of three areas: "how we fight, how we do business inside the Department and how we work with our interagency and multinational partners" (DoD, 2003, p. 6). The TPG also provided a view of transformation as a long-term process rather than a short term policy. It defined transformation as:

...a process that shapes the changing nature of military competition and cooperation through new combinations of concepts, capabilities, people, and organizations that exploit our nation's advantages and protect against our asymmetric vulnerabilities to sustain our strategic position, which helps underpin peace and stability in the world (DoD, 2003, p. 3).

This conception of transformation was further elaborated in a DoD document, *Elements of Defense Transformation,* written in 2003:

[t]ransformation should be thought of as a process, not an end state. Hence there is no foreseeable point in the future when the Secretary of Defense will be able to declare that the transformation of the Department has been completed. Instead, the transformation process will continue indefinitely. Those responsible for defense transformation must anticipate the future and wherever possible help create it (DoD, Office of Force Transformation [OFT], 2003, p. 2).

Over the next few years, the SecDef led efforts aimed at clarifying the emerging transformational concepts and doctrine. In 2005, the U.S. National Defense Strategy (NDS) (DoD, 2005) was published. It refined the operational necessity for transformation, stating that transformation was driven by four changes in the strategic environment that present significant threats to national interests:

- Traditional challenges are posed by states employing recognized military capabilities and forces in well understood forms of military competition and conflict.

- Irregular challenges come from those employing unconventional methods to counter the traditional advantages of stronger opponents.

- Catastrophic challenges involve the acquisition, possession, and use of weapons of mass destruction (WMD) or methods producing WMD-like effects.

- Disruptive challenges may come from adversaries who develop and use breakthrough technologies to negate current U.S. advantages in key operational domains.

The NDS strategy for meeting these threats reiterated the goals of the 2001 DoD QDR, calling for an active, layered defense, continuous transformation, development of a capability-based approach to acquisition, and a strategy for managing risk (DoD, 2005). It reiterated that transformation was more than just about technology:

...[c]ontinuous defense transformation is part of a wider governmental effort to transform America's national security institutions to meet 21st century challenges and opportunities. Just as our challenges change continuously, so too must our military capabilities.The purpose of transformation is to extend key advantages and reduce vulnerabilities. We are now in a long-term struggle against persistent, adaptive adversaries and must transform to prevail. Transformation is not only about technology, it is also about changing the way we think about challenges and opportunities; adapting the defense establishment to that new perspective; and, refocusing capabilities to meet future challenges, not those we are already most prepared to meet (DoD, 2005).

A recent Congressional Research Report describes transformation as "large-scale, discontinuous, and possibly disruptive changes in military weapons, concepts of operations (i.e., approaches to warfighting), and organization" (O'Rourke, 2006, p. 3). Military transformation is fundamentally about changing the way that we prepare for, plan, conduct, and hopefully learn from military operations. Additionally, with transformation, military effectiveness is no longer to be measured using kinetic metrics such as traditional battle damage assessment reports (kill ratios, number of tanks, buildings, bridges, etc. destroyed, disabled, etc.). Rather the concept of effects-based operations (EBO) or the more broadly defined term *effects-based approach* encapsulates the notion that military effectiveness is achieved when we are able to successfully coordinate actions directed at shaping the behavior of friend, foe, and neutral in peace, crisis, and war so as to achieve our objectives (Smith, 2006, p. x).

A central element of transformation strategy is the theory of NCW.[2] While originally conceived in the context of major combat operations (Alberts, Garstka, & Stein, 2000; DoD, "NCW Report to Congress," 2001;), the concepts behind NCW have broad applicability to many military operations besides combat. Therefore, the term *network-centric operations* (NCO) is often used to denote this broader usage (Garstka & Alberts, 2004). The theory of NCO hypothesizes that when Information Age technologies are paired with transformational changes in organizations and processes, dramatic improvements in effectiveness can be achieved. These improvements can be experienced in any operational environment and across different levels of operation (tactical, operational, or strategic). The mechanisms by which these improvements are expected to be realized are illustrated by the following hypotheses/tenets:

- A robustly networked force improves information sharing.
- Information sharing and collaboration enhances the quality of information and shared situational awareness.

- Shared situational awareness enables collaboration and self-synchronization, and enhances sustainability and speed of command.

- Enhanced sustainability and speed of command, in turn, dramatically increase mission effectiveness.

The focus is on empowering the "pointy end of the spear" to be as effective as possible by providing the "right" information to the "right" people at the "right" time. However, providing the right information to the "edge" of military organizations requires not only sophisticated communications and information systems, importantly, it entails significant changes in military doctrine and command and control processes and practices (Alberts & Hayes, 2003).

Transformation Efforts

The U.S. DoD has initiated multiple efforts to implement transformational strategies. The OFT was established in October 2001 under the leadership of Rear Admiral (Retired) Cebrowski and charged to provide insight and guidance to the DoD on transformation related issues. The OFT conducted research on NCO via a series of case studies, developed an educational out-reach initiative aimed at providing the military service academies and senior service schools with up-to-date information on transformation, and issued guidance to the Services which were developing individual plans for how to achieve transformation objectives. [3] The OFT also sponsored an innovative experimentation effort aimed at rapidly developing and delivering advanced net-centric capabilities to war fighters. [4] In addition to the OFT, many other DoD organizations support transformation initiatives. The Office of the Assistant Secretary of Defense, Networks and Information Integration (ASD, NII) is a key player in implementing transformational strategies. The ASD NII developed a net-centric data strategy aimed at establishing DoD wide standards for data sharing and dissemination. The Defense Information Systems Agency (DISA) is responsible for developing and managing the infrastructure necessary for net-centric information technologies to operate effectively. The Global Information Grid (GIG):

...will be a net-centric system operating in a global context to provide processing, storage, management, and transport of information to support all Department of Defense (DoD), national security, and related Intelligence Community missions and functions-strategic, operational, tactical, and business-in war, in crisis, and in peace...The overarching objective of the GIG vision is to provide the National Command Authority (NCA), warfighters, DoD personnel, Intelligence Community,

business, policy-makers, and non-DoD users with information superiority, decision superiority, and full-spectrum dominance (National Security Agency, n.d.).

As stated, each of the Services has developed and is implementing its own trans-formation strategy (U.S. Air Force, 2004; U.S. Army, 2004; U.S. Navy, 2003). The Navy's approach, termed FORCENet, is defined as:

...[t]he operational construct and architectural framework for Naval Warfare in the Information Age, to integrate warriors, sensors, networks, command and control, platforms, and weapons into a networked, distributed combat force, scalable across the spectrum of conflict from seabed to space and sea to land (U.S. Navy, n.d.).

The Air Force is developing Command and Control (C2) Constellation, while the Army is moving forward with the Future Combat System (FCS) as its transitional instantiation of NCO. In addition, U.S. Joint Forces Command (USJFCOM) is designated as the military's top "transformation laboratory" empowered:

...to enhance the combatant commanders' capabilities to implement the president's [transformation] strategy. USJFCOM develops joint operational concepts, tests these concepts through rigorous experimentation, educates joint leaders, trains joint task force commanders and staffs, and recommends joint solutions to the Army, Navy, Air Force and Marines to better integrate their warfighting capabili-ties (USJFCOM, n.d.).

From the initiation of transformation, SecDef Rumsfeld acknowledged that signifi-cant changes were needed within the DoD bureaucracy if the broader objectives of force transformation were to be realized. He maintained that while developing new technologies to meet emerging war fighter needs was a daunting but tractable challenge, what was more difficult was developing new military doctrine; organi-zational structures; processes; and tactics, techniques, and procedures (TTPs) that take advantage of the information and communications capabilities provided by the new systems. Consequently, transformation entailed:

...making changes in DOD business policies, practices, and procedures, particu-larly with an eye toward streamlining operations and achieving efficiencies so as to reduce costs and move new weapon technologies from the laboratory to the field more quickly. The Administration has also used the term transformation to refer to proposed changes in matters such as the budget process and environmental matters affecting military training (O'Rourke, 2006, p. 4).

As a result, the DoD introduced broad reform of its business practices in order to implement transformational strategies. A center piece of this reform is the movement toward capabilities-based planning and away from threat-based planning. In the past, the U.S. military prepared and trained for a well known threat: the Soviet Union. With the collapse of the Soviet Empire and the terrorist attacks of September 11, 2001, the U.S. military now faced threats that were more difficult to predict and therefore more challenging to prepare and train for. As a solution, the DoD adopted a capabilities-based planning (CBP) approach that focuses on obtaining fundamental competencies that can be applied in a broad range of operational contexts, from humanitarian assistance to major combat operations. A recent experimental initiative, the Capabilities Portfolio Management Test Case, is focused on developing and implementing joint capability areas in an effort to streamline and integrate DoD governance across policy, requirements, acquisition, budgeting and planning processes (U.S. Defense Acquisition University, 2006).

Challenges to Transformation

Despite the strong commitment of U.S. military leaders to transformation, NCO, and an effects-based approach, questions exist regarding the desirability and feasibility of these efforts. With the resignation of SecDef Rumsfeld in December 2006, uncertainty over the future of transformation efforts increased. While officially adopted by the U.S. military, transformation has been harshly criticized by many inside and outside of the DoD (Else, 2004). While case studies examining the role of network-centric capabilities in the war in Iraq demonstrate the promise of network-enabled capabilities at the tactical level (DoD, "Transformation," 2007), the limited abilities of advanced technologies to support the counterinsurgency has raised questions about the applicability of NCW and the transformational agenda of the Bush administration.

In addition, many critics point to the lack of a theoretical and empirical foundation for transformation, arguing that NCO and EBO are undeveloped and untested theories (Barnett, 1999; Borgu, 2003; Echevarria, 2006; Giffin & Reid, 2003; Lambeth, 2006). Some criticize the U.S. for adopting a "if you build it they will come" approach, that is, building the GIG without an adequate understanding of how people will use the network and what impact it will have on military performance and effectiveness.

Concurrently, there is an emerging debate regarding the feasibility of developing a coherent DoD-wide transformation strategy. The challenge of ensuring that the various military systems are technically interoperable and able to share information is huge. Traditional engineering approaches treat each system as a complete and closed system. However, this approach is ineffective when dealing with the complex interdependencies implied by NCO and effects-based approaches (Anderson, Brown, & Flowe, 2006). As Kuras (2006) notes:

[t]he notion of a system is central to system engineering. In fact, it is the sine qua non of system engineering. System engineering has been successfully applied to a wide range of systems. Increasingly, however, system engineering has been seen to be les effective when applied to such systems as the Health Care System, the Internal Revenue System, and a Missile Defense System. It has also been found to be ineffective when applied to the introduction of new capabilities into such a system (for example, the introduction of net centric capability into the DOD). (p. 1)

Perhaps more challenging than integrating technologies is the desire to coordinate system development, acquisition, program management, and planning efforts across the myriad of organizations that comprise the DoD industry and other defense-related institutions. The DoD is often characterized as an industrial age institution which is hierarchical and "stove-piped," meaning that information flows up and down the chain of command within specific DoD organizations and Services but does not flow across. Despite efforts to transform the DoD bureaucracy, a recent assessment of the defense acquisition process found that:

...the Acquisition System is believed to be a simple construct that efficiently integrates the three interdependent processes of budget, acquisition and requirements termed—"Big A." Little "a" is the acquisition process that tells us "how to buy" but does not include requirements and budget, creating competing values and objectives. Actually, our observations showed the system to be a highly complex mechanism that is fragmented in its operation. Further, the findings we developed indicated that differences in the theory and practice of acquisition, divergent values among the acquisition community, and changes in the security environment have driven the requirements, acquisition and budget processes further apart and have inserted significant instability into the Acquisition System (Defense Acquisition Performance Assessment [DAPA] Project, 2006, p. 4).

The challenges of orchestrating transformation of the DoD were highlighted in a review of DoD transformation performed by the U.S. Government Accountability Office (GAO). It reported that transformation efforts were hampered by a lack of leadership. It stated that:

[a]lthough the Secretary of Defense has assigned responsibility for managing key aspects of transformation, DOD has not established clear leadership and accountability for achieving transformation results, nor has it established a formal

mechanism to coordinate and integrate the various transformation efforts within the department...Although the Secretary of Defense has provided the vision for transformation and set the tone for accomplishing it, the responsibility for various parts of the transformation strategy for military capabilities is spread among several organizations ... and no single individual or organization has been given the overarching leadership responsibilities, authority, or the accountability for achieving transformation results (U.S. GAO, 2004, pp. 3-4).

While the purpose of this chapter is not to systematically review the pros and cons of the transformation debate (see Else, 2004), the history of recent military transformation clearly illustrates that changing the way an organization, as large and complex as the DoD, operates and does business is an exceedingly difficult endeavor. Despite the commitment of top U.S. officials to guide and direct military transformation and billions of dollars spent on transformational initiatives, current transformation efforts are a cacophony of different, sometimes conflicting approaches. There is no guarantee that transformation objectives will be realized in the near or far term. This raises the question of whether any purposeful large scale policy change on the scale of military transformation is possible. I suggest in the next section that the history of military transformation highlights fundamental limitations in our ability to orchestrate and control large scale change. I then explore the extent to which these limitations can be mitigated by examining insights gained from theories and empirical analysis of CASs. First, however, it is useful to briefly discuss theories that may inform our understanding of large scale social change.

Theories of Social Change

While there are many competing theories and explanations of social change (Olson, 1982; Tilly, 1978; Wallerstein, 1974 are considered foundational), few explicitly incorporate what I consider to be the necessary, if not sufficient, components of a theory of social change. In order to understand and explain large scale social change, I suggest a theory of social change must include the following elements.

First, a theory of social change must account for the continuities and changes in the historical circumstances that all actors confront. By historic circumstances, I refer to the structural factors that constrain as well as enable certain actions—for instance, distribution of material power capabilities, identities, or normative understandings (Lloyd, 1989). Second, it must incorporate a definition of people as purposeful actors who reflexively evaluate circumstances and are capable of effecting change by their actions—it must explicitly incorporate a theory of agency. Third, a theory of change must account for the social construction of historic structures: "Structures cannot produce or reproduce themselves," (p. 465) people do so by their actions (Lloyd,

1989). Finally, the most important requirement of theory is that it must explicitly acknowledge the role and distribution of power which pervades all human—and hence all social—interaction.

While no extant theory of social change adequately accounts for all of the previous requirements, some do partially address these concerns. Specifically, structuration theory, as presented by Giddens (1976, 1984) and Onuf (1989), provides a starting place. Structuration theory begins by addressing what is known as the "agent-structure debate," that is, do people act as purposeful agents, making their own history, or do social structures determine history (Dessler, 1989; Klotz, 2006; Wendt, 1987). Structuration suggests that agents and structures are co-constituted in a dynamic process. An important question emerges: By what means does structuration occur? The sociologist Anthony Giddens explains this process in terms of the recursive behavior of human beings. Nicholas Onuf, in a constructivist explanation of international relations, explains the process in terms of social rules: rules are both the medium and outcome of social interaction.

Giddens (1984) suggests that a resolution to the agent-structure debate can only be obtained in an ontology that does not privilege agents at the expense of structures or structures at the expense of agents. Structuration theory maintains that the dualities of subject and object, agent and structure, can be reconciled if they are reconceptualized as a duality instead of a dualism, a duality of structure. What ties together agent, structure, and system is recursion. Giddens argues that power is embedded in the process of recursion. Individuals have the power to create, reproduce, and transform social structures by their actions. He defines power as the capability, not necessarily always manifested, to "make a difference" (1984, p. 16). This conception suggests that power is inherent in human activity—power is not a resource to be utilized. Instead, "resources are media through which power is exercised" by knowledgeable and reflexive agents (1984, p. 16). While Giddens' structuration theory addresses each of the necessary components of a theory of social action, it does not go far enough in providing a theoretical foundation for explaining the dynamics of large scale social change. Structuration is best understood as a "metatheory," in that it identifies the ontological assumptions necessary to explain the complexity of human behavior. However, it does not provide, by itself, a theory of social change. What is needed is an explicit account of how recursion actually works in the co-constitution of agents and social structures. I suggest that insights from CAS theory can shed insight into the process by which social structures, such as the U.S. DoD, are created, maintained, and sometimes transformed by the actions of individuals, or agents, in a dynamic and complex process.

Complex Adaptive Systems Theory

Increasingly, researchers are using the theory of CASs to understand and describe phenomena in the physical and social world. The study of CASs is interdisciplinary and very diverse, however, Holland (1995) and Gell-Mann (1995) are often cited as foundational thinkers in the evolution of CAS theory. Holland utilizes the concept of CAS to explain the coherence found in seemingly complex phenomena such as the human immune system and supply chains. Holland (1995) defines CASs to be:

...systems composed of interacting agents described in terms of rules. These agents adapt by changing their rules as experience accumulates. In CAS, a major part of the environment of any given adaptive agent consists of other adaptive agents, so that a portion of any agent's efforts at adaptation is spent adapting to other adaptive agents. This one feature is a major source of the complex temporal patterns that CAS generate. To understand CAS we must understand these ever-changing patterns. (p. 10)

Gell-Mann (1995) considers CASs to be ones that adapt by obtaining information about their environment, identifying regularities or patterns in the information, consolidating these patterns into rules or "schema," and then taking actions based on this information. While complex physical systems can change over time, only CASs can "learn."

Although relatively new, CAS-related research has resulted in a wealth of academic and popular books and articles that reflect different assumptions about the underlying principles of CASs and to date, there is no universally accepted definition of what constitutes a CAS. There does seem, however, to be general agreement that CASs are complex, meaning they are composed of a large number of parts whose interactions are nonlinear, and therefore non-deterministic, and that system-level behavior emerges from these interactions. A recent working paper published by the Santa Fe Institute (Mitchell, 2006) addresses the challenges of defining complexity and emergence. It states that:

[t]here is no generally accepted formal definition of "complex system." Informally, a complex system is a large network of relatively simple components with no central control, in which emergent complex behavior is exhibited. Of course, the terms in this definition are not rigorously defined. "Relatively simple components" means that the individual components, or at least their functional roles in the system's collective behavior, are simple with respect to that collective behavior. (p. 2)

Mitchell (2006) next addresses the notion of emergence.

'Emergent complex behavior' is tougher to define. Roughly, the notion of emergence refers to the fact that the system's global behavior is not only complex but arises from the collective actions of the simple components, and that the mapping from individual actions to collective behavior is non-trivial. The notion of nonlinearity is important here: the whole is more than the sum of the parts. The complexity of the system's global behavior is typically characterized in terms of the patterns it forms, the information processing that it accomplishes, and the degree to which this pattern formation and information processing are adaptive for the system |that is, increase its success in some evolutionary or competitive context. (p. 2)

An additional defining characteristic of CASs is that the units (cells, individuals, firms, nations, etc.) have the ability to act. These units are therefore commonly referred to as "agents" (Harrison, 2006, p. 3). This "agency" enables them to make "choices" that impact others in the system and the environment. Agents are typically conceptualized and modeled as truly simple entities, with very simple rules governing their behavior. The use of agent-based models to explore the emergence of complex behavior from the interaction of agents following relatively simple rules has dramatically expanded researchers' ability to simulate and study complex and adaptive systems. Researchers have "grown" artificial societies using simple agents that follow basic rules (Agent-based Computational Economics [ACE], 2007; Epstein & Axtell, 1996; Tesfatsion & Judd, 2006). These societies demonstrate characteristics strikingly similar to real societies.

However, some scholars question the utility of assuming that agents are simple elements and are exploring the ramifications of conceptualizations agents as complex systems in their own right (Atay & Jost, 2004). If we consider agents as complex systems, a central question is: how does coordination and coherence of systems of complex agents, such as social institutions comprised of complex human agents, emerge? Jost (2005) argues that social institutions "in the sense of stable patterns of interactions or implicit conventions obeyed by the actors emerge as unintended consequences of individual actions at the group level" (p. 3). He further states that social institutions "...emerge on the basis of the human cognitive ability to integrate an evaluation of the behavior and performances of other group members over long periods of time" (Jost, 2005, p. 1). Jost contrasts this notion of emergence with the more mechanistic concept of "self-organization" typically used to describe adaptation of CASs. He argues that while social institutions often result in restrictions or limitations to the range of available actions, that individuals gain from institutions benefits unavailable to them individually. Jost (2005) states:

[h]uman individuals are themselves very complex ... That means that the coordination of intrinsically complex elements reduces the individual degrees of freedom, but can lead to emergent behavior at some higher level that the individuals are not capable of. (p.7)

Social institutions, as emergent structures created by the interaction of complex human agents, are successful because they shift complexity and therefore uncertainty to different scales. For example, individual hunters may mitigate the effects of random fluctuations in food supply by sharing food because "fluctuations and randomness at one scale can average out to produce regular patterns at some higher scale" (Jost, 2005, p. 5). Food sharing requires coordination which over time can become institutionalized as social structures (rules, roles, and relations).

In summary, intelligent agents can "make a difference" by making choices and taking actions, even if the consequences of those actions are not immediately evident. Social institutions emerge over time as the accumulated emergent result of agent's behaviors. These structures present agents with both constraints and opportunities. This conceptualization of the interactions of structures and agents is remarkably similar to the one described previously in the discussion of structuration theory, which pre-dated CAS theory by at least two decades. Both are concerned with social structures, agency, and the nature of stability and change. Both identify social rules (both formal rules such as laws and informal rules such as conventions and norms) to be a central mechanism of stability and change. What is still missing, however, is a theory that helps explain the process by which some rules are accepted and end up becoming institutionalized while others fail, that is, how does structuration occur? I argue elsewhere that competition over rules, that is, competition over who has the authority to create, define, and enforce the rules that govern social interactions, is the primary mechanism by which social institutions are created, maintained, and sometimes transformed or destroyed. Importantly, competition over social rules is the mechanism by which human agents establish relations of authority and power over others (Holloman, 2000). Following this logic, social institutions, as the manifestations of this competition, reinforce patterns of power, that is, relations of authority and control that are not random. Politics, traditionally defined as the allocation of scare resources, is conceptualized here as the competition over social rules that result in patterns of authority, that have consequences in terms of allocation of scarce resources.

This discussion raises an important question: how can we reconcile the notion that control in CASs is decentralized and distributed with our understanding of social institutions as instruments of authority and control? Some argue that this is impossible, and therefore, CAS theory is an inappropriate framework for understanding social and political institutions and behaviors. Earnest and Rosenau (2006) assert that:

...the pattern of authority in a complex adaptive system is one of its distinctive features: it has none. Authority is perfectly decentralized; each agent decides and acts on the basis of internal rules that evolve in response to environmental feedback. This is the logical antithesis of social authority, in which a privileged agent makes allocative decisions for a group of other actors. (p. 153)

They conclude that CAS theory is "inconsistent with our conventional understanding of what an authoritative system is" (Earnest & Rosenau, 2006, p. 153). Rather than dismiss the potential that CAS theory can provide insights regarding social phenomena, I suggest that we consider the implications of introducing the concepts of power, that is, structures or patterns of authority, and politics or competition over authority, into CAS theory. What effect will this have on our core understanding of CASs? While I agree with Earnest and Rosenau that if CAS theory cannot explain non-random authority patterns that its utility is questionable, I do not concur that authority is perfectly decentralized in CASs. I suggest that power and politics are not anathema to CAS theory, but rather, they can be considered uniquely human (i.e., intelligent) manifestations of processes that have analogs in non-intelligent CASs. To some extent, all agents (both intelligent and other) confront an environment that has been shaped by countless interactions in the past and whose rules of action are shaped by "environmental feedback." While the differences between any two environments may be governed by random events, the evolution of a particular environment is influenced by its own history. The concept of "path dependency" in CAS theory captures the notion that an agent's decision space in any particular environment is bounded by past decisions of the agent as well as all other agents interacting across time. If we are discussing social systems, it seems reasonable to assume that we can describe the environment that confronts agents in terms of authority structures (rules, roles and relations) that have emerged over time. It is also conceivable that rules may emerge in intelligent CASs that result in individual agents sacrificing decision making autonomy on one scale, say willingness to adhere to some of the rules of central authority, for benefits on another scale, say security from external threats. When viewed at a distance, institutional governance patterns of all social institutions vary across time. If viewed narrowly, however, governance patterns have the appearance of permanence. I suggest that CAS theory can accommodate the notion of differential social authority if we consider the evolution of social institutions and governance structures across time and space.

Further, Jost (2005) makes the point that coordination in complex social institutions need not be decentralized when he states, "[t]his coordination can be achieved by a central commander, but, more interestingly, also from local interactions" (p. 7). Jost (2005) goes on to argue that:

[i]ndividual members of human groups or societies are never completely equal. Besides differences of their physical or cognitive abilities, they are usually distinguished by their position in the network of social interactions. Social rank, expressed and enforced by power, is a more formal distinction, but the informal one of social status that is based on respect received instead of power exerted may often be even more powerful. Social status reflects the standing of an individual within a group, leads to some unsymmetries in the interactions with other individuals of different status, and may regulate the access to scarce items ... (pp. 7-8)

While Jost (2005) argues that social status is a mechanism that facilitates emergence of institutions that result in benefits to individuals, it is equally possible that social institutions may result in negative consequences to specific individuals, thus creating tensions within the system and the desire on the part of some agents to change. It is these tensions that contribute to the continuous evolution and adaptation of social institutions.

The preceding discussion, although preliminary and tentative, is needed if we wish to consider how CAS theory may inform our understanding of current military transformation efforts. The DoD is arguably one of the most hierarchical organizations ever created. Power is not decentralized nor distributed randomly; rather, it is distributed across a complex structure of organizations and individuals via formal and informal ranking systems. Command and control is a central, perhaps the central objective of military organizations. It is defined as:

[t]he exercise of authority and direction by a properly designated commander over assigned and attached forces in the accomplishment of the mission. Command and control functions are performed through an arrangement of personnel, equipment, communications, facilities, and procedures employed by a commander in planning, directing, coordinating, and controlling forces and operations in the accomplishment of the mission (DoD, "Joint Publication 1-02," 2007).

In order to effectively execute missions in complex environments, commanders have traditionally relied on a strategy that decomposes and de-conflicts the battlefield into smaller and simpler units. The concepts associated with command and control of the battles space have parallels within the organization of the DoD, which is structured to decompose problems and de-conflict actions into clearly differentiated sub-organizations, such as the U.S. Air Force, Navy, and Army, for instance. This process of differentiation continues within each sub-organization ad infinitum, resulting in "stove piped" structures that limit cross-organizational conflict, the original goal of the structure, but which also stifle cross-organizational collaboration, a goal of transformation.

While this description captures the formal structure of the DoD, it does not fully describe the scale, complexity, and dynamics of the institution. The DoD is a very large bureaucracy with many elements. As of late 2006, over 1.3 million active duty military personnel, over 800,000 reservists, and over 670,000 civilians were employed by the DoD (Women Research and Education Institute [WREI], 2007). The defense department's base budget for 2007 is $439.3 billion (DoD, "Budget Request," 2007), which is larger than the GDP for the majority of the countries in the world. Given the scale of the DoD, the ability of a centralized authority to exercise effective control over all of the elements is unlikely. Additionally, despite a plethora of rules and regulations; standard operating procedures; and TTPs, outcomes on the battlefield and within the DoD bureaucracy are often unpredictable. As an organization created by and maintained by human beings, the DoD is a social institution that reflects fundamental characteristics of social interactions and perhaps some of the characteristics of complex adaptive social systems.

I argue that we can apply the concept of systems of CASs to defense in at least two ways. First, military operations, especially those in counter-terrorism and urban environments, have many of the defining characteristics of CASs. The U.S. Marine Corps' (USMC) concept of the "three block war" encapsulates many of the aspects of CASs (Krulak, 1999).

Modern crisis responses are exceedingly complex endeavors. In Bosnia, Haiti, and Somalia the unique challenges of military operations other-than-war (MOOTW) were combined with the disparate challenges of mid-intensity conflict. The Corps has described such amorphous conflicts as—the three block war—contingencies in which Marines may be confronted by the entire spectrum of tactical challenges in the span of a few hours and within the space of three contiguous city blocks.

While military operations are often complex, they are not always conducted in environments that are also as rapidly adaptable as we find today and expect to encounter in the future. In the modern battle space, it is much more likely that actions taken at the tactical level will have unintended operational or strategic effects. The USMC's notion of the "strategic corporal" is based on the premise that local actions can have larger unanticipated effects.

The inescapable lesson of Somalia and of other recent operations, whether humanitarian assistance, peacekeeping, or traditional war fighting, is that their outcome may hinge on decisions made by small unit leaders, and by actions taken at the lowest level … Success or failure will rest, increasingly, with the rifleman and with his/her ability to make the right decision at the right time at the point of contact…. In many cases, the individual Marine will be the most conspicuous symbol of American foreign policy and will potentially influence not only the immediate tactical situation, but the operational and strategic levels as well. His/her actions, therefore, will directly impact the outcome of the larger operation; and he will become, as the title of this article suggests—Tthe Strategic Corporal (Krulak, 1999).

When viewed through the perspective of CAS theory, network centric operations can be considered an attempt to change system level behavior (military effectiveness) by changing the behavior of the individual units (sharing information). Another way of stating the tenets of NCO is as follows: if individual agents change their behavior (i.e., they share more information), then desirable system level changes will result (improved mission effectiveness across the tactical, operational, and strategic levels). The tenets of NCO are in effect postulating "simple rules" that can be used to guide agent's behaviors. The theory suggests that the more agents follow these rules, the more likely are the desirable system level effects to emerge. If we examine how the U.S. National Defense Strategy (DoD, 2005) describes NCO, we clearly see elements of CASs:

The foundation of our operations proceeds from a simple proposition: the whole of an integrated and networked force is far more capable than the sum of its parts. Continuing advances in information and communications technologies hold promise for networking highly distributed joint and combined forces. Network centric operational capability is achieved by linking compatible information systems with usable data. The functions of sensing, decision making, and acting which often in the past were built into a single platform now can work closely even if they are geographically distributed across the battlespace.

Similarly, EBO explicitly recognizes what military operators have long known: waging war and maintaining peace are complex endeavors.

The strength of an effects-based approach to operations is that it squarely addresses these complexities by concentrating on their most nonlinear aspects: humans, their institutions, and their actions. Indeed, the entire effects-based approach can be characterized by four things: a focus on the human dimension of competition and conflict; the consideration of a full spectrum of actions whether in peace, crisis, or hostilities; a multifaceted, whole-of-nation concept of power; and the recognition of the complex interconnected nature of the actors and challenges involved (Smith, 2006, p. ix).

The second way in which the DoD can be conceived as a CAS involves understanding the DoD as a bureaucracy charged with providing war fighting capabilities. This bureaucracy is comprised of multiple internal organizations that interact in a complex larger external environment of local, federal, and multi-national organizations, both governmental and non-governmental. Traditional approaches to understanding defense organizations and processes tend to simplify and decompose them to make them tractable. Current approaches to military planning exemplify this methodology. For instance, the Planning, Programming, Budget and Execution System (PPBES), originally initiated by SecDef McNamara in the 1960s, is intended to decompose the entire process of acquiring military capabilities into few manageable steps. However, in practice, the PPBES process is enormously complex and inefficient (McCaffery & Jones, 2005). As Davis (2002) has argued, traditional defense planning has limited utility due to the inherent complexity and adaptability of the systems involved. He states:

Ultimately, planning is about control: we seek, by decisions that we make today, to improve future circumstances. The enemy of planning, of course, is uncertainty. Although this fact is sometimes suppressed, strategic planners are often faced with massive and ubiquitous uncertainty in many dimensions. Moreover, many of the uncertainties involve people and organizations, some of them in competition. That is, the relevant systems are not only complex, but also adaptive. (Davis, 2002)

Rear Admiral (Retired) Cebrowski, recognized as one of the leading thinkers on transformation, explicitly linked the need for military transformation to the complexity of the operating environment. He also believed that increasing the capability of the military to be complex (agile, responsive, maneuverable, etc.) was a strategy for countering the complexity of the environment (Else, 2004; Mullen, 2004).

Several military researchers and practitioners have begun to systematically explore the implications of conceptualizing transformation through the lens of CAS theory. For instance, Moffat (2003) provides a detailed technical description of several applications of complexity theory to NCW. Grisogono (2006) and Grisogono and Ryan (2003) discuss lessons learned from studying defense systems in the context of CAS theory (discussed in the next section). Increasingly, defense researchers are utilizing methods and models developed to study CASs to understand military issues and problems. To date, most applications of CAS theory to defense involve utilization of agent-based models to simulate tactical military operations (Cioppa, Lucas, & Sanchez, 2004; Yang, Curtis, Abbass, & Sarker, 2006). Agent-based modeling is uniquely suited to explore possible outcomes in CASs are beginning to be widely used in the social sciences (Axelrod & Tesfatsion, 2006). Although not with out its critics (Earnest & Rosenau, 2006), agent-based simulation is one of the primary methodologies utilized to explore and evaluate CASs (Hazy & Tivnan, 2003, 2004; Kewley, 2004; Kilicay, Dagli, Enke, & Meteoglu, 2006; Samuelson & Macal, 2006).

Implications for Transformation Related Experimentation and Research

By conceptualizing transformation in the context of CASs, we can better understand the challenges of implementing transformational reform. Military transformation is a catch all term for a wide variety of purposeful actions intended to direct and control the co-evolutionary development of new defense-related capabilities. Transformation in essence is a top-down attempt to change the nature of the DoD from an institution characterized by hierarchically structured organizations or "stovepipes" with central-ized control and limited cross-organizational interactions to an institution with the potential for decentralized control and multiple cross-organizational interactions. The challenge is that if the DoD is a complex and adaptive system, top-down directives are not likely to be effective at inducing the desired system level changes. From what researchers have learned about CASs, changing the behavior of individual elements within specific systems is the only mechanism for introducing large scale systemic change. However, it is difficult if not impossible to know exactly what behavioral changes will result in the desired system level changes. Also, because of the interconnectedness of the systems, behavioral changes always have second-ary and tertiary effects that are difficult or impossible to predict. Additionally, path dependencies that develop based on previous choices can seriously constrain the opportunities for change in the present and future. The DoD's struggle to integrate new technologies, organizations, and processes with "legacy" systems, organizations and processes illustrate the significance of path dependencies. Importantly, the DoD, as a social institution, maintains a specific distribution of power and authority whose benefits and costs are not evenly distributed. One of the challenges of implementing military transformation stems from the fact that it threatens the current distribution of power and influence within the DoD. Without an appreciation of the politics of transformation, efforts are unlikely to be successful.

The complexity of the problem appears to be overwhelming, making purposeful ac-tions in support of transformation impossible. However, research on CASs in other fields can be used to illuminate a transformation strategy that provides guidelines for how to proceed.

If we explicitly consider military transformation as a purposeful endeavor aimed at changing the structure of the DoD by implementing unit level changes in behavior, an important question is: what can be done? Since efforts to force transformation from the top down have had limited success, what can be done to establish the conditions from the bottom up to foster transformation? Based on her CAS research, Grisogono (2006) posits that we have several options for dealing with CASs:

- Observation without intervention
- Shaping behavior via indirect influences
- More direct influence via interventions altering the systems components, interactions, and/or resources
- Destruction of the system. (p. 11)

Grisogono argues (2006) that we can improve our chances of achieving our desired objectives by:

- Finding and identifying existing adaptive mechanisms that contribute to the outcomes we desire
- Selecting those adaptive mechanisms that are the best targets for intervention
- Shaping perceptions of the system's agents so as to induce them to take the actions expected to achieve the desired outcomes. (p. 13)

In order to make informed decisions about what actions to take, however, requires that we have some knowledge of the systems of interest we are attempting to influence. A critical strategy for gaining this knowledge is a campaign of experimentation and research aimed at improving our understanding of adaptation and dynamics within modern military environments and complex adaptive organizations like the DoD.

The need for a rigorous campaign of experimentation and research is based on the premise that CASs evolve by a complex process of actions, feedback, and reactions, that is, through learning (Axelrod & Cohen, 2001; Garcia-Lorenzo Mitleton-Kelly, & Galliers, 2003). While in theory we have the option of letting the systems of interest evolve and learn on their own (the do nothing but observe option, cited previously), in practice, our actions, and importantly our inactions, have effects. As participants and observers of transformation, military decision makers are inevitably caught up in the defense systems they operate within. The choice is not between doing nothing and doing something; rather it is about choosing what to do based on what we expect to occur as a result from our actions.

While complexity and adaptation limit our ability to make point predictions, CASs are not necessarily chaotic or random. It is possible to identify patterns in outcomes and systematically evaluate tendencies. Formal experimentation and research efforts should focus on discovering observable patterns of behavior that provide insight into what works and what does not work in terms of moving the DoD to the desired direction. A campaign of experimentation and research is needed to identify critical patterns and tendencies within the DoD and the modern military operating environment. Experimentation should be augmented with modeling and simulation using agent-based models that explore how social institutions, and the structures of power and authority that characterize them, adapt and change.

Conclusion

Transformation of the DoD, either guided by strategies or by chance, is likely to proceed and accelerate as new technologies develop and new security challenges arise. The operating environment encountered by the U.S. military will also continue to become more complex, adaptive, and challenging. Therefore, gaining a better understanding of CASs makes sense for those interested in military transformation if we wish to take advantage of the opportunities provided by information age technologies and practices and avoid failures.

This paper is intended to introduce the communities of defense policy makers and practitioners to a theoretical framework that may inform transformational research efforts. It is also intended to inform the CAS communities of researchers of transformation-related efforts and to encourage a dialogue between the various communities. It proposes that a campaign of experimentation and research be conducted to systematically explore the intersection of CASs and defense transformation. In actuality, this campaign is already underway, as researchers across the different communities are actively exploring CASs and defense-related issues. This effort, like most human endeavors, itself can be thought of as a CAS comprised of a myriad of organizations and individuals. What is needed is a way to enhance collaboration and learning among the various researchers so that the "sum of the whole will be greater than the parts." Like any CAS, it is unlikely that top-down directives aimed at uniting the efforts of these disparate researchers will succeed. Rather, we should look to influence mechanisms so as to create learning opportunities that cut across disciplines. This paper is intended to be part of this effort. Hopefully they will spawn additional opportunities for cross-disciplinary learning across the divergent communities of researchers concerned about defense issues and those intrigued by the challenges of CASs.

References

Agent-Based Computational Economics (ACE). (2007). *Introductory materials.* Retrieved April 1, 2007, from http://www.econ.iastate.edu/tesfatsi/aintro.htm

Alberts, D. S., Garstka, J. G., & Stein, F. P. (2000). *Network centric warfare: Developing and leveraging information superiority* (2nd rev. ed.) Washington, DC: Command and Control Research Program (CCRP) Publication Series.

Alberts, D. S., & Hayes, R. E. (2003). *Power to the edge.* Washington, DC: Command and Control Research Program (CCRP).

Anderson, W. B., Brown, M. M., & Flowe, R. (2006) *Joint capabilities and system-of-systems solutions: A case for crossing solution domains.* (Technical Note CMU/SEI-2006-TN-029). Pittsburgh, PA: Carnegie Mellon University. Retrieved October 10, 2006, from http://www.sei.cmu.edu/pub/documents/06. reports/pdf/06tn029.pdf

Atay, F., & Jost, J. (2004). *On the emergence of complex systems on the basis of the coordination of complex behaviors of their elements.* Retrieved April 10, 2007, from http://www.santafe.edu/research/publications/workingpapers/04-02-005.pdf

Axelrod, R., & Cohen, M. D. (2001). *Harnessing complexity: Organizational implications of a scientific frontier.* New York: Free Press.

Axelrod, R., & Tesfatsion, L. (2006). *On-line guide to agent-based modeling in the social sciences.* Retrieved December 10, 2006, from http://www.econ.iastate.edu/tesfatsi/abmread.htm

Barnett, T. (1999, January). The seven deadly sins of network centric warfare. The U.S. Naval Institute (pp. 36-39).

Borgu, A. (2003, September 17). *The challenges and limitations of network centric warfare—The initial views of an NCW skeptic.* Paper presented to the conference: Network Centric Warfare: Improving ADF capabilities through Network Enabled Operations.

Cioppa, T. M., Lucas, T. W., & Sanchez, S. (2004). Military applications of agent-based simulations. In R. G. Ingalls, M. D. Rossetti, J. S. Smith, & B. A. Peters, (Eds.), *Proceedings of the 2004 Winter Simulation Conference* (pp. 171-180).

Davis, P. (2002). RAND Strategic planning amidst massive uncertainty in complex adaptive systems: The case of defense planning. *InterJournal, 375.*

Defense Acquisition Performance Assessment Project (DAPA). (2006, January). *Defense acquisition performance assessment report.* Retrieved December 10, 2006, from http://www.acq.osd.mil/dapaproject/documents/DAPA-Report-web/DAPA-Report-web-feb21.pdf

Department of Defense. (2001, July). *Network centric warfare report to congress.*

Department of Defense. (2001, September 30). *Quadrennial defense review report.* Retrieved February 1, 2007, from http://www.defenselink.mil/pubs/pdfs/qdr2001.pdf

Department of Defense. (2003, April). *Transformation planning guidance.* Retrieved February 1, 2007, from http://www.oft.osd.mil/library/library_files/document_129_Transformation_Planning_Guidance_April_2003_1.pdf

Department of Defense. (2005, March) *National defense strategy of the United States of America.* Retrieved July 11, 2006, from http://www.globalsecurity.org/military/library/policy/dod/nds-usa_mar2005.htm

Department of Defense. (2007). *Budget request.* Retrieved March 15, 2007, from http://www.defenselink.mil/comptroller/defbudget/fy2007/2007_Budget_Rollout_Release.pdf

Department of Defense. (2007). *Transformation.* Retrieved February 1, 2007, from http://www.defenselink.mil/transformation/documents/

Department of Defense. (2007, March). *Joint Publication 1-02. Department of Defense dictionary of military and associated terms.* Retrieved March 15, 2007, from http://www.dtic.mil/doctrine/jel/new_pubs/jp1_02.pdf

Department of Defense, Office of Force Transformation (OFT). (2003). *Elements of defense transformation.* Retrieved August 16, 2006, from http://www.oft.osd.mil/library/library_files/document_383_ElementsOfTransformation_LR.pdf

Dessler, D. (1989). What's at stake in the agent-structure debate? *International Organization, 43.3,* 441-473.

Earnest, D., & Rosenau, J. (2006). Signifying nothing? What complex systems theory can and cannot tell us about global politics. In N. Harrison (Ed.), *Complexity in world politics: Concepts and methods of a new paradigm* (pp. 143-163). Albany, NY: State University of New York Press.

Echevarria, A. (2006). *Challenging transformation's cliches.* Retrieved March 15, 2007, from http://www.StrategicStudiesInstitute.army.mil/

Else, S. E. (2004). *Organization theory and the transformation of large, complex organizations: Donald H. Rumsfeld and the U.S. Department of Defense, 2001-04.* Unpublished doctoral dissertation, University of Denver, CO.

Epstein, J., & Axtell, R. (1996). *Growing artificial societies: Social science from the bottom up.* MIT Press/Brookings, MA.

Garcia-Lorenzo, L., Mitleton-Kelly, E., & Galliers, R. D. (2003). Organisational complexity: Organizing through the generation and sharing of knowledge. *International Journal of Knowledge, Culture and Change Management, vol. 3,* MC 03-0023.

Garstka, J. G., & Alberts, D. S. (2004). *Network centric operations conceptual framework* [Version 2.0]. Retrieved August 16, 2006, from http://www.oft.osd.mil/library/library_files/ConceptualFramework.pdf

Gell-Mann, M. (1995). What is complexity? *Complexity, 1*(1). Retrieved April 1, 2007, from http://www.santafe.edu/~mgm/complexity.html

Giddens, A. (1976). *New rules of sociological method: A positive critique of inter-pretative sociologies.* New York: Harper & Row.

Giddens, A. (1984). *The constitution of society; Outline of the theory of structuration.* Los Angeles: University of California Press.

Giffin, R. E., & Reid, D. J. (2003, June 17-19). A woven web of guesses, canto two: Network centric warfare and the myth of inductivism. In *Proceedings of the 8th ICCRTS,* Washington, DC.

Grisogono, A. (2006). *The implications of complex adaptive systems theory for C2.* Retrieved October 10, 2006, from http://www.dodccrp.org/events/2006_CCRTS/html/papers/202.pdf

Grisogono, A., & Ryan, A. (2003). *Designing complex adaptive systems for defense.* Retrieved July 14, 2006, from http://www.seecforum.unisa.edu.au/sete2003/papers%20&%20presos/Ryan_Alex%20and%20Grisogono_Anne-Marie_PA-PER.pdf

Harrison, N. E. (2006). Thinking about the world we make. In N. Harrison (Ed.), *Complexity in world politics: Concepts and methods of a new paradigm* (pp. 1-23). Albany, NY: State University of New York Press.

Hazy, J. K., & Tivnan, B. F. (2003). Simulating agent intelligence as local network dynamics and emergent organizational outcomes. In S. Chick, P. J. Sanchez, D. Ferrin, & D. J. Morrice (Eds.), *Proceedings of the 2003 Winter Simulation Conference* (pp. 1774-1778).

Hazy, J. K., Tivnan, B. F., & Schwandt, D. R. (n.d.). *Permeable boundaries in organizational learning.* Washington, DC: George Washington University.

Holland, J. (1995). *Hidden order: How adaptation builds order.* Basic Books.

Holloman, K. (2000, March). *Constructivist international relations theory: Reflections, critical evaluation, and suggestions for future research.* Paper presented to the International Studies Association Annual Convention, Los Angeles, CA.

Jost, J. (2005). *Formal aspects of the emergence institutions.* Retrieved December 10, 2006, from http://www.mis.mpg.de/jjost/interest/inst-stov05-03-20.pdf

Kewley, R. H., Jr. (2004). *Agent-based model of AUFTRAGSAKTIK:* Self organization in command and control of future combat forces. In R. G. Ingalls, M. D. Rossetti, J. S. Smith, & B. A. Peters (Eds.), *Proceedings of the 2004 Winter Simulation Conference* (pp. 926-930).

Kilicay, N. H., Dagli, C. H., Enke, D., & Meteoglu, E. (2006). *Methodologies for understanding behavior of system of systems.* Retrieved December 10, 2006, from http://www.sosece.org/pdfs/2ndConference/Presentations/SoSECE%20Howell%20Day%20One/Meteoglu.pdf

Klotz, A. (2006). Moving beyond the agent-structure debate. *International Studies Review, 8*(2), 355-381.

Krulak, C. C. (1999, January). The strategic corporal: Leadership in the three block war. *Marines Magazine*. Retrieved July 10, 2006, from http://www.au.af. mil/au/awcgate/usmc/strategic_corporal.htm

Kuras, M. L. (2006). *A multi scale definition of a system* (MITRE Report MTR 06B000060). Retrieved October 10, 2006 from http://www.mitre.org/work/ tech_papers/tech_papers_06/06_1058/06_1058.pdf

Lambeth, B. (2006, January 2). The downside of network-centric warfare. *Aviation Week & Space Technology*.

Lloyd, C. (1989). Realism, structurism, and history: Foundations for a transformative science of society. *Theory and Society, 18,* 481.

McCaffery, J. L., & Jones, L. R. (2005). Reform of the program budgeting in the department of defense. *International Public Management Review, 6*(2), 141-176.

Mitchell, M. (2006). *Complex systems: Network thinking.* Retrieved April 1, 2007, from http://www.santafe.edu/research/publications/workingpapers/06-10-036. pdf

Moffat, J. (2003). *Complexity theory and network centric warfare.* Washington, DC: Command and Control Research Program (CCRP) Publication Series.

Mullen, R. (2004, June 15). Cebrowski: More complexity essential to defense. *Defense Today.* Retrieved December 10, 2006, from http://www.oft.osd.mil/ library/library_files/article_381_Defense%20Today.doc

National Security Agency. (n.d.). *Global information grid.* Retrieved December 12, 2006 from http://www.nsa.gov/ia/industry/gig.cfm?MenuID=10.3.2.2

Olson, M. (1982). The rise and decline of nations. New Haven, CT: Yale University Press.

Onuf, N. (1989). *World of our making: Rules and rule in social theory and international relations.* Columbia, SC: University of South Carolina.

O'Rourke, R. (2006). *Defense transformation: Background and oversight issues for Congress.* Retrieved January 15, 2007, from http://www.fas.org/sgp/crs/ natsec/RL32238.pdf

Samuelson, D. A., & Macal, C. M. (2006, August). Agent-based simulation comes of age. *OR/MS Today.* Retrieved December 12, 2006, from http://www.lionhrtpub. com/orms/orms-8-06/fragent.html

Schrader, J., Lewis, L., & Brown, R. A. (2003). *Quadrennial defense review 2001: Lessons on managing change in the Department of Defense.* Retrieved January 21, 2007, from http://www.oft.osd.mil/library/library_files/document_133_R AND%20QDR%20Lessons%20Learned%20Report.pdf

Smith, E. (2006). *Complexity, networking, and effects based approaches to operations.* Washington, DC: Command and Control Research Program (CCRP) Publication Series.

Tesfatsion, L., & Judd, K. L. (Eds.). (2006). *Handbook of computational economics, Volume 2: Agent-based computational economics.* Handbooks in Economics Series. North Holland, The Netherlands: Elsevier.

Tilly, C. (1978). *From mobilization to revolution.* Addison-Wesley.

U.S. Air Force. (2004). *Transformation flight plan 2004.* Retrieved December 5, 2006, from http://www.oft.osd.mil/library/library_files/document_385_2004_USAF_Transformation_Flight_Plan.pdf

U.S. Army (2004, July). *2004 Army transformation road map.* Retrieved December 5, 2006, from http://www.oft.osd.mil/library/library_files/document_386_ATR_2004_Final.pdf

U.S. Defense Acquisition University. (2006, September). *OSD memo capability portfolio management test case roles, responsibilties, authorities, and approaches (Dtd 14).* Retrieved December 5, 2006 from https://acc.dau.mil/CommunityBrowser.aspx?id=117813

U.S. General Accountability Office (GAO). (2004, December). *Military transformation: Clear leadership, accountability, and management tools are needed to enhance DOD's efforts to transform military capabilities.* Retrieved March 15, 2007, from http://www.gao.gov/new.items/d0570.pdf

U.S. Joint Forces Command. (n.d.). *About us.* Retrieved December 10, 2006, from http://www.jfcom.mil/about/about1.htm

U.S. Navy. (n.d.). *FORCENet.* Retrieved December 10, 2006, from http://forcenet.navy.mil/fn-definition.htm

U.S. Navy. (2003). *Transformation road map.* Retrieved December 5, 2006 from http://www.oft.osd.mil/library/library_files/document_358_NTR_Final_2003.pdf

Wallerstein, I. (1974). The rise and future demise of the world capitalist system. *Comparative Studies in Society and History, 14*(4), 387-415.

Wendt, A. (1987). The agent-structure problem in international relations theory. *International Organization, 41.2,* 335-370.

Women Research and Education Institute (WREI). (2007). Retrieved March 15, 2007, from http://www.wrei.org/Women%20in%20the%20Military/2006SeptNumbers.pdf

Yang, A., Curtis, N. J, Abbass, H. A., & Sarker, R. (2006). *NCMAA: A network centric multi-agent architecture for modelling complex adaptive systems.* Retrieved December 10, 2006, from http://www.itee.adfa.edu.au/~alar/techreps/200605012.pdf

Endnotes

[1] A previous draft of this chapter was presented at the *48th International Studies Association Annual Convention,* February 28-March 3, 2007, Chicago, IL.

[2] Network Centric Warfare (NCW), also referred to as Network Centric Operations (NCO), is the term utilized in the U.S. and Australia. The term Network Enabled Capabilities (NEC) is used by NATO and Great Britain. Although there are some differences between the different approaches, all share a desire to empower war fighters by improving information sharing, and enhancing shared situational awareness and collaboration.

[3] Note that the author was contracted by the OFT from 2004 until 2006 to support NCO-related research and educational efforts; contract #W74V8H-04-D-0051. This chapter reflects the author's personal views and is not representative of the OFT or the DoD.

[4] Citing the fact that the need for transformation of the U.S. military has largely become accepted, the Bush administration realigned the OFT in October 2006, transferring its functions to other DoD offices. The OFT Web page was still maintained, however, as of April 11, 2007. See http://www.oft.osd.mil/index.cfm.

Chapter XII

Insights into the Impact of Social Networks on Evolutionary Games

Katia Sycara, Carnegie Mellon University, USA

Paul Scerri, Carnegie Mellon University, USA

Anton Chechetka, Carnegie Mellon University, USA

Abstract

In this chapter, we explore the use of evolutionary game theory (EGT) (Nowak & May, 1993; Taylor & Jonker, 1978; Weibull, 1995) to model the dynamics of adaptive opponent strategies for a large population of players. In particular, we explore effects of information propagation through social networks in evolutionary games. The key underlying phenomenon that the information diffusion aims to capture is that reasoning about the experiences of acquaintances can dramatically impact the dynamics of a society. We present experimental results from agent-based simulations that show the impact of diffusion through social networks on the player strategies of an evolutionary game and the sensitivity of the dynamics to features of the social network.

Introduction

We use EGT (Cabrales, 2000; Hofbauer & Sigmund, 2003; Weibull, 1995) to model the dynamics of adaptive opponent strategies for a large population of players. Previous EGT work has produced interesting, and sometimes counter-intuitive results about how populations of self-interested agents will evolve over time (d'Artigues & Vignolo, 2003; Frey & Luechinger, 2002).

In our model, at each stage of the game, boundedly rational players observe the strategies and payoffs of a subset of others and use this information to choose their strategies for the next stage of the interaction. Building on EGT, we introduce a model of interaction where, unlike the standard EGT setting, the basic stage game changes over time depending on the global state of the population (state here means the strategies chosen by the players). More precisely, each player has three strategies available (cooperate C, defect D, and do-nothing N), and the payoffs of the basic stage game are re-sampled when the proportion of the players playing D crosses a certain threshold from above. This feature requires long-term reasoning by the players that is not needed in the standard EGT setting. A possible example of a similar real-world situation is a power struggle between different groups. When cooperation drops sufficiently and there are many defections—the situation turns to chaos. When order is restored, that is, when cooperation resumes, the power structure and thus, the payoffs, will likely be different than before the chaos. The payoffs are kept constant while most of the players Cooperate (support the status quo) or do-Nothing, but when enough players are unhappy and choose to Defect, the power balance breaks and a radically different one may emerge afterwards.

The available strategies were chosen to abstractly capture and model violent uprisings in a society. Players playing C cooperate with the current regime and receive reward when interacting with others playing C. If a player has a good position in a regime, it has a large incentive to continue playing C. D is a strategy played to change the payoffs over a long term, but at an unavoidable immediate cost. Intuitively, it resembles resorting to insurgency or other violent tactics to overthrow a regime. When many players play D, playing C can lead to very low payoffs. For example, one can imagine a person trying to run a small business during a violent uprising. If these costs are too high, but the player has no incentive to change the regime, playing N can limit payoffs—both negative and positive, until the situation stabilizes. Intuitively, this might correspond to going into hiding or temporarily leaving the conflicted area.

Similar to Nowak and May (1993) and Killingback and Doebeli (1996), we investigate the spatial aspect of the interaction. Previous work has shown that spatial interaction can change which strategies are most effective, for example, in Brauchli, Killingback, and Doebeli (1999) an interaction lattice changed which strategies were most effective in an iterative prisoner's dilemma game. In our model, the players are connected into a *social network*, through which the rewards are propagated (Travers & Milgram, 1969; D. J. Watts, Dodds, & Newman, 2002). Thus the players can benefit (or suffer) indirectly depending on how well off their friends in the network are. We show empirically that the connectivity pattern of the network, as well as the amount of information available to the players, have significant influence on the outcome of the interaction. In particular, the presence of a dense scale-free network or small-world network led to far higher proportions of players playing C than other social network types.

Game Details

We consider a finite population X of players. At each stage all the players are randomly matched in triples to play the basic stage game. Each player thus participates in every stage. Each player has three strategies available: cooperate (C), defect (D), and do-nothing (N) (one can interpret these choices as participating in democratic process, resorting to insurgency, and minimizing interactions with the outer world correspondingly). The payoff $p_i(k)$ of the stage k game to player x_i is ($\#_i(N)$ means the number of agents playing N)

		0 opponents play D	1 or 2 opponents play D
	C	$cc_i - \#_i(N)$	cd
x_i's strategy	D	dc	dd
	N	n	

where $cc_i - 2 > n > dc > dd > cd$. Here is a simple rule for distinguishing between these four variables: the first letter corresponds to x_i's strategy, the second letter is c if both of the x_i's opponents play C and d otherwise. For example, cd is the payoff of playing C given that at least one of the opponents plays D. Note that the payoff matrices for different players can only differ in the value of cc_i. All the other payoffs are constant across the population.

Denote $SD(k)$ the proportion of the population that defected during stage k:

$$SD(k) = \frac{\text{number of players that played } D \text{ during stage } k}{|X|},$$

Figure 1. An example trace of an individual run of the system. x-axis is the stage number ("time step"), y-axis is the proportion SD of the population playing D. The level of threshold T is also plotted for a reference.

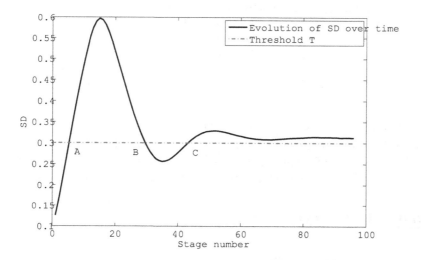

Before the start of the first stage, c_i are sampled uniformly from an interval $[CC_{min}, CC_{max}]$. If during stage k^* the series $SD(k)$ crosses a fixed threshold (see the end of this section for the interpretation of the threshold) $T \in (0,1)$ from above, that is,

$$SD(k^* - 1) > T \text{ and } SD(k^*) < T,$$

then all cc_i are re-sampled. Otherwise they stay the same as for previous stage. For example, in an individual run plotted in Figure 1, the values of cc_i would be re-sampled only at point B.

One can interpret the previous interaction as a power struggle: If the proportion of players supporting status quo (i.e., cooperating or doing nothing) is high enough, the payoffs for each individual players do not change. When enough players defect, the system "falls into chaos" and after it emerges back from this state, a new power balance is formed and the payoffs change correspondingly. Threshold T in this interpretation is the minimum number of defectors that brings the system into chaos.

Impact of Social Networks

A social network for finite population X is an undirected graph $<X,E>$. Two players i and j are neighbors in the network if and only if $(x_i, x_j) \in E$. We investigate the effect of reward sharing in social networks. After each stage k every player x_i obtains in addition to its own payoff p_i a shared payoff ps_i:

$$ps_i(k) = a \sum_{x_j \in \text{neighbors}(x_i)} p_j(k),$$

where $\alpha \in [0,1]$ is a parameter of the system.

Notice that this does not incur payoff redistribution: The shared payoff is not subtracted from payoffs of the players that cause it. One can interpret this phenomenon as players being more happy when their friends are happy.

Social Network Type

The *small-world property* of the network means that the average distance between two nodes in the network is small. It has been shown (D. Watts & Strogatz, 1998) that regular non-small-world networks, such as grids, may be transformed to small-world ones by changing only a small fractions of edges. We followed the algorithm from D. Watts and Strogatz to generate the networks with probability 0.1 of rewiring any edge of the regular structure.

In scale-free networks (Barabási & Albert, 1999) the number of neighbors of a vertex is distributed according to a scale-free power law, therefore few highly connected vertices dominate the connectivity. Many real-world networks possess the small-world and/or scale-free properties (Barabási & Albert, 1999; D. Watts & Strogatz, 1998).

The impact of both small-world and scale-free networks are explored next.

Player Reasoning

Information Available to Players

Before describing the player reasoning algorithm one has to define what information is available to the player, that is, define an observation model. We assume that the players are aware of the overall behavior of the game, but may not be aware of the true values of parameters, such as the proportion $SD(k)$ of the population that played D at stage k. The players only observe the actions of their opponents for the given stage, as opposed to observing the whole population. Therefore, the observations available to i after stage k are its payoff $p_i(k)$, shared payoff $ps_i(k)$, and proportion $SC_i^{obs}(k), SD_i^{obs}(k), SN_i^{obs}(k) \in \{0, 0.5, 1\}$ of its direct opponents playing C, D and N during the kth stage.

Note that the information about the global properties of social network connectivity, such as density or whether the network is small worlds or scale free, is not available to players. Therefore, this global information is not used in the reasoning algorithm.

The Reasoning Algorithm

It is easy to see that for any triple of players, a single-stage game has 2 Nash equilibria in pure strategies: everybody cooperating and everybody defecting. The cooperative equilibrium Pareto-dominates the "all-defect" equilibrium. Therefore, if the "all-cooperate" payoffs cc_i were always held constant across the stages, one would expect a population of rational players to always play C. However, the payoffs are re-sampled once the proportion of players playing C drops below T and then grows above T again. This provides an incentive for the players that happened to receive relatively low values of cc_i, to play D for some period of time in order to try and cause the re-sampling of payoffs. On the other hand, if a significant share of the players play D, some of the players may decide to play N, which guarantees a fixed payoff and provides an opportunity to "wait until the violence ends."

A natural way for a player to choose a strategy for the next stage is to compare the (approximate) cumulative future expected payoffs resulting from different strategies. Denote $EP_i(X)$ the approximate cumulative future expected payoff for player i and strategy X. Let $SX_i(k)$ be i's estimate of the share of population playing X on time step k. Then the action selection for step $k+1$ is as follows. If $SD_i(k) > T$, player i chooses action $\arg\max_{X=C,N} EP_i(X)$. Otherwise it chooses $\arg\max_{X=C,D,N} EP_i(X)$. The reason for treating situation $SD_i(k) > T$ specially is that once the share of defectors reaches the threshold, reducing the share of players below T is in common interest of all the players, and the approximate computations of expected utilities do not always capture this feature.

The previous paragraph assumed $EP_i(X)$ to be known. We now turn to their approximate computation.

First consider $EP_i(D)$. The only incentive for a player i to play D is to try to bring the system into chaos in hopes that, when the system emerges from chaos, the re-sampled all-cooperate payoff cc_i for that player will be higher than it is now. Denote TTC_i the i's estimate of the number of stages that it will need to play D before the share of those playing D is higher than T, TC_i—estimate of the number of stages that the system will spend above the threshold and finally, TS_i the length of the following "stability period." Then

$$
\begin{aligned}
EP_i(D) &\approx (TTC_i + TC_i)E\big[p_i(D)\big] + TS_i E[cc_i^{new}] \\
&= TTR_i E[p_i(D)] + TS_i \frac{CC_{min} + CC_{max}}{2},
\end{aligned}
\tag{1}
$$

where $TTR_i \equiv TTC_i + TC_i$ is "time to re-sampling" and

$$
E\big[p_i(D)\big] = P(\#_i(D) = 0)dc + P(\#_i(D) > 0)dd.
$$

Expected payoff for action C over the time period is approximated as

$$
\begin{aligned}
EP(C) &\approx TS_i(p_i(C) + ps_i) + TTC_i E\big[p_i(c)\big] \\
&\quad + TC_i\big(P(\#_i(D) > 0)cd + P(\#_i(D) = 0)(p_i(C) + ps_i)\big)
\end{aligned}
\tag{2}
$$

where $P(\#_i(D) > 0) = 1 - (1 - T)^2$ and

$$
\begin{aligned}
E\big[p_i(C)\big] &= P(\#_i(C) = 2)cc_i + P(\#_i(C) = 1, \#_i(N) = 1)(cc_i - 1) \\
&\quad + P(\#_i(N) = 2)(cc_i - 2) + P(\#_i(D) > 0)cd
\end{aligned}
$$

(note that the probabilities here sum to one).

Finally, expected payoff for N over the same time interval is

$$
EP(H) = (TTC_i + TC_i + TS_i)n.
$$

One can see that a player only expects to get the shared payoff in case of all-cooperative outcomes.

In our model, time of stability TS_i and time in chaos TC_i are system constants that do not differ across the population.

The belief $SX_i(k)$ about the proportion of players playing X at stage k is maintained by each player individually. After each stage each player learns about the strategies of its opponents for that stage. SX_i is then updated according to

$$SX_i(k+1) = \gamma SX_i^{obs}(k+1) + (1-\gamma)SX_i(k) \tag{3}$$

where $\gamma \in (0,1]$ is learning rate. Each player also maintains $\delta SX_i(k)$, an estimate of

$$\delta SX(k) \equiv SX(k) - SX(k-1),$$

using an expression analogous to Equation 3 to update it. In the expressions (1-2) $P(\#_i(X))$ are approximated straightforwardly using SX_i, for example

$$P(\#_i(C) = 2) \approx SC_i^2(k)$$

Having SX_i and dSX_i, each player can estimate TTC_i using a linear approximation. For $SD_i < T$, we have (TTC is a system-wide constant)

$$TTC_i = \begin{cases} TTC, & \delta SD_i \leq 0 \\ \dfrac{T - SD_i}{\delta SD_i}, & \delta SD_i > 0 \end{cases}$$

For $SD_i^3 T$, $TTC_i = 0$.

Experimental Results

In our experiments the population size was fixed to 1,000 players. The numerical values of payoff constants were

$$dc = -1, \, dd = -3, \, cd = -5, \, CC_{min} = 3, \, CC_{max} = 10$$

Estimated time of stability was fixed to $TS_i = TS = 50$ stages, "chaos threshold" $T=0.3$. Initial player-specific values were $SC_i(0) = 1$, $\delta SC_i = -0.02$. For each set of specific parameter values the results were averaged over 500 runs. Unless otherwise noted, the players were connected via a scale-free network with average density of 8.

We were primarily interested in how different parameters of the model affect the evolution of proportion of players playing C over time. On all graphs x-axis denotes the stage of the interaction, y-axis denotes SC, SD, and SN. In a previous work (Sycara, Scerri, & Chechetka, 2006), we presented results for the case where action N was not available to the players. In each of the following figures we contrast the results when N is and is not available to the players.

Note that because the plotted results are averages over 100 runs, averages provide more meaningful information about the influence of the parameters values on the system, than do individual runs which can vary distinctly from run to run. Most parameter values allow the SC to fall below T on some occasions, but what varies is how often this occurs, how rapidly changes happen, and how quickly cooperation resumes. These effects are more clearly seen on graphs of averages than many individual runs superimposed on a single graph. Notice that the fact that the value of SD on the plots rarely rises above T does not mean that payoffs are almost never re-sampled—individual runs have much more variance and re-sampling happens quite often. It simply means that on average SD is below T.

Figure 2 shows the baseline configuration, with 2(a) showing the case where N is available and 2(b) showing the case where it is not. In both cases, early in the game many players choose D to either try to change the payoffs or protect against losses. When N is available to the players, many choose this action in response to others

Figure 2. Baseline configuration (scale-free network with density 8) with available action N (a) and with N not available (b).

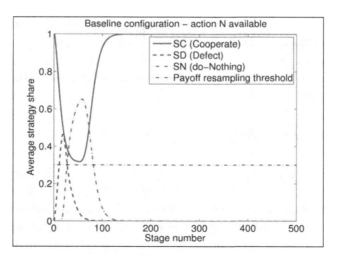

(a)

Figure 2. continued

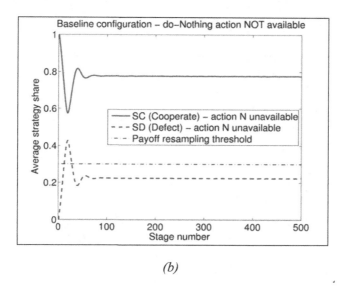

(b)

playing *D*. Eventually this discourages the use of *D* and an equilibrium settles in. While the initial dynamics in both cases are similar, notice that over time the proportion of *C* is far higher in the case where *N* is available than when it is not. This may indicate that if players are able to avoid spasms of violence without getting hurt, the outcome for all will be better.

Figure 3 shows the impact of setting the network density to 2, 4, 8, and 16. In general, the higher the average network degree, the more players played *C* and the more quickly players stopped playing *D*. For the less dense networks, players often chose *D* early on, but in the most dense network, the lure of shared rewards was too high for players to have incentive to try to move the system towards chaos. In the less dense networks, the availability of the *N* action allowed the system to move toward all playing *C*, but as in the baseline case, without the *N* action, some level of *SD* persisted. When the average network density was 4, the system moved back towards *SC*=1 faster than when the network density was 2. This result may indicate that dense social networks are critical to stable societies.

Figure 4 shows what happens when there is no sharing across the social network. The sharp early peak in *SD* is similar to the sparse network shown above. This is one of the few cases where the availability of the *N* action leads to a lower *SC* over

Figure 3. Impact of network density on the players' strategies. In the top row, the share of players playing cooperate, in the bottom—defect. On the left, the action N is available to the players, on the right—not available.

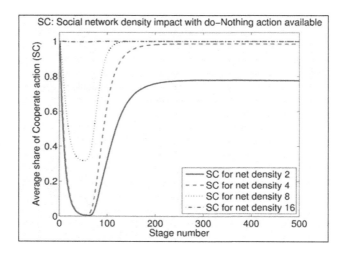

(a)

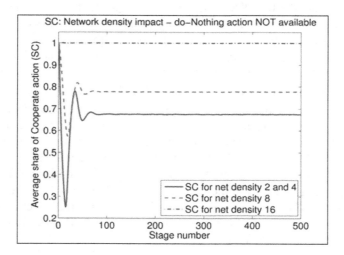

·(b)

Figure 3. continued

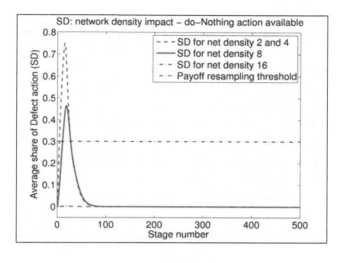

(c)

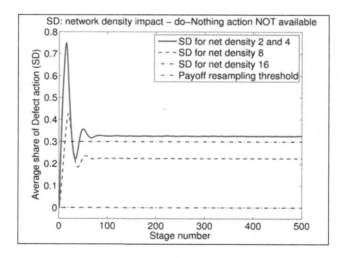

(d)

Figure 4. Results with reward sharing disabled with available action N (a) and with N not available (b)

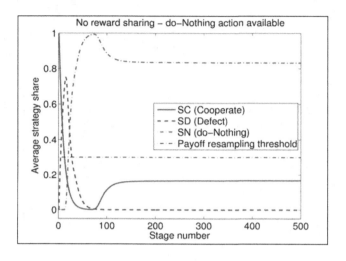

(a)

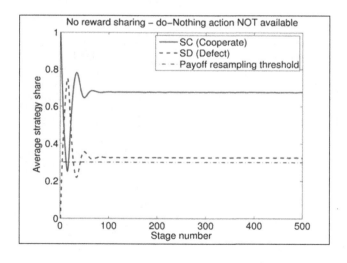

(b)

the course of the game. However, the option to play N is extensively used and SD is reduced to 0. Over an extended period of time, SC does rise to 1, but N dominates for a long time.

If the type of the network is set to small-world instead of scale-free (with the average of four neighbors), SC stays very close to 1 regardless of the availability of N to the players (there is no plot for this case, because the results are so trivial). This remarkable relative stability is likely due to the very even sharing of reward across all members of the team, reducing the possibility of a cascade towards chaos. This result may suggest that human societies that have a more scale-free nature will be more likely to descend into chaos.

Figure 5 shows the result as the learning rate is set to 0.05, 0.1, 0.4, and 0.8. Smaller learning rate means that the players are reluctant to change their estimates of the parameters; the closer the learning rate to 1, the more importance is attributed to the most recent observations.

Several interesting effects occur due to the learning rate. Firstly, an intermediate

Figure 5. Impact of learning rate on the players' strategies. In the top row, the share of players playing cooperate, in the bottom—defect. On the left, the action N is available to the players, on the right—not available.

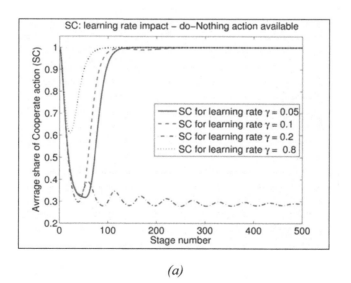

(a)

Figure 5. continued

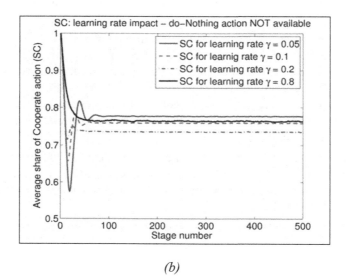

(b)

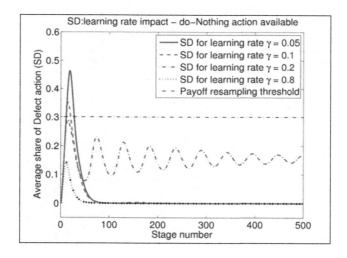

(c)

Figure 5. continued

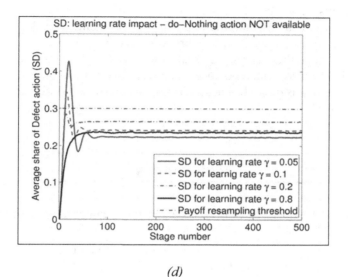

(d)

learning rate induces an oscillation in behavior with increasing and decreasing *SD*. Higher or lower learning rates induce different behavior. A high learning rate quickly settles the population down to playing *C*, because the players are better able to estimate future rewards which are maximized by a stable society. A low learning rate eventually allows a stable society but not before a large *SD* has occurred. Interestingly, none of these effects were observed when the *N* action was not available to the players. With learning eventual behavior (except for the intermediate learning rate) *SC* was higher when *N* was available.

Conclusions and Future Work

This chapter presented an evolutionary game with players connected into a social network, sharing payoffs with their neighbors in that network. If individual players reason that increased long-term payoffs might be higher if the whole society can be forced into chaos, they will accept significant short-term costs and risk, to bring that situation about. The key conclusion from this game is that a society of *rational* agents who will all gain if they all play cooperative strategies can easily be induced to play strategies that are guaranteed to lead to a negative payoff.

Our experiments show that the existence and nature of a social network makes a dramatic difference to the evolution and conclusion of the game. Very dense networks or small-world networks had far higher proportions of players playing cooperative strategies than when there is a sparse scale-free network. This result has implications for all EGT where interaction occurs between players, but only simple social networks are used. It is possible that such results will change if different interaction networks are used.

References

Barabási, A.-L., & Albert, R. (1999). Emergence of scaling in random networks. *Science, 286*.

Brauchli, K., Killingback, T., & Doebeli, M. (1999). Evolution of cooperation in spatially structured populations. *Journal of Theoretical Biology*.

Cabrales, A. (2000). Stochastic replicator dynamics. *International Economic Review, 41*(2).

d'Artigues, A., & Vignolo, T. (2003). Why global integration may lead to terrorism: An evolutionary theory of mimetic rivalry. *Economics Bulletin, 6*(11).

Frey, B. S., & Luechinger, S. (2002). Terrorism: Deterrence may backfire. *European Journal of Political Economy, 20*(2).

Hofbauer, J., & Sigmund, K. (2003). Evolutionary game dynamics. *Bulletin of the American Mathematical Society, 40*(4).

Killingback, T., & Doebeli, M. (1996). Spatial evolutionary game theory: Hawks and doves revisited. In *Proceedings of The Royal Society (Biological Sciences)*.

Nowak, M., & May, R. (1993). The spatial dilemmas of evolution. *International Journal of Bifurcation and Chaos, 3*.

Sycara, K., Scerri, P., & Chechetka, A. (2006). Evolutionary games and social networks in adversary reasoning. In *Proceedings of the international conference on complex systems*. Boston.

Taylor, P., & Jonker, L. (1978). Evolutionary stable strategies and game dynamics. *Mathematical Biosciences, 40*.

Travers, J., & Milgram, S. (1969). An experimental study of the small world problem. *Sociometry, 32*, 425-443.

Watts, D., & Strogatz, S. (1998). Collective dynamics of small-world networks. *Nature, 393*.

Watts, D. J., Dodds, P. S., & Newman, M. E. J. (2002). Identity and search in social networks. *Science, 296*(5571), 1302-1305.

Weibull, J. (1995). *Evolutionary game theory*. Cambridge, MA: MIT Press.

About the Contributors

Yin Shan is with Medicare Australia as a senior review assessment officer, working on data mining and machine learning applications on medical data. He previously worked as a scientific programmer in the Australian National University and a postdoctoral research fellow at the University of New South Wales, Australia. He received his PhD in computer science from the University of New South Wales, in 2005 and his MSc and BSc in computer science from Wuhan University, China in 1999 and 1996, respectively. His main interests are evolutionary computation, in particular genetic programming and its applications.

Ang Yang joined the Division of Land and Water at the Commonwealth Scientific and Industrial Research Organization (CSIRO) in 2007. Yang holds a PhD in computer science (UNSW, Australia), an MInfoSc in information systems (Massey University, New Zealand), an MSc in environmental geography (Nanjing University, China), and a BSc in ecology and environmental biology (Ocean University of China, China). His current research interests include complex adaptive systems; multi-agent systems; modeling and simulation; evolutionary computation; network theory; and Web-based intelligent systems.

* * *

Terry Bossomaier is the director of the Centre for Research in Complex Systems at Charles Sturt University. He co-chaired the inaugural Asia-Pacific Complex Systems conference in Canberra 1992 and was a founding editor of the electronic journal *Complexity International*. He is the co-author/editor of several books on complexity, including *Complex Systems* published by Cambridge University Press. His research interests range from parallel and distributed computing to the use of neuroscience models for advanced pattern recognition and computation.

Anton Chechetka is a doctoral student at the Robotics Institute at Carnegie Mellon University. He received his BS in applied mathematics and physics from Moscow Institute of Physics and Technology in Russia, and an MS in robotics from the Robotics Institute. His research interests are mostly in machine learning and probabilistic inference.

Raymond Chiong obtained his MSc in advanced computer science from the University of Birmingham, and a first class bachelor of computer science with honors from University Malaysia Sarawak. He is a lecturer at Swinburne University of Technology (Sarawak Campus), Malaysia. He is also a member of IEEE, ACM, and BCS. His research interest mainly lies in the field of artificial intelligence, and he is directed at investigating the principles and dynamic behavior of game theory.

Rosaria Conte is responsible for the Laboratory of Agent Based Social Simulation (LABSS) at the Institute for Cognitive Science and Technology (ISTC) and teaches social psychology at the University of Siena. She is a cognitive and social scientist, with a special interest for the study of positive social action (altruism, cooperation, and social norms), and reputation-based social regulation. Quite active in the multi-agent system (MAS) field, she contributed to launch the field of social simulation in Europe by organizing among the main events held in the last 10 years or so, editing collective volumes, and coordinating an EU-funded special interest group on agent-based social simulation. She has been a member of several European research projects and networks of excellence. She has published about 120 scientific articles and books on cognitive social agents; norms representation and reasoning; and agent-based simulation. Her research interests range from agent theory to MAS, from agent-based social simulation and cultural evolution to info-societies and virtual markets.

Stefano De Luca received the degree in philosophy from the University -Y´La Sapienzai of Rome, with specialization in mathematical logic and philosophy of science. He works as research and development manager for information and computer technology companies, where he realized products such as a logic-based middleware, a semantic Web-enabled content manager, and agent-based hazard simulators. He teaches artificial intelligence and multi-agent systems at University ´Tor Vergatai of Rome. He has published books on agent-based modeling, process optimization in health care, and several papers on intelligent adaptive systems. He is interested in nature inspired computing, evolutionary computation, and distributed artificial intelligence.

Anne Dray is a research fellow at the Australian National University (ANU). Part of her work aims at developing a negotiation support tool based on agent-based modeling and role-playing games to facilitate equitable water allocation in Tarawa

(Republic of Kiribati). She is also teaching agent-based modeling techniques at ANU and developing new tools for policy makers to deal with issues related to the harm of illegal drugs in Australia.

Silvio Flaim has 30 years experience leading large economic and environmental assessments of the energy industries and 5 years experience modeling financial system infrastructure. Flaim has substantial experience providing testimony before judicial, regulatory, and administrative authorities in national and international forums including various state courts, U.S. District Courts, and the U.S. Supreme Court.

John Foster is fellow of the Academy of Social Science in Australia (2001-present); vice president of the International J.A. Schumpeter Society (2004-present); member of the Social Behavioral and Economic Panel of the ARC College of Experts (2005-2007); member of the Australian Federal Treasury Academic Consultative Panel (2007-present); member of the Australian Federal Department of Employment and Workplace Relations Economic Research Advisory Group (2007-present); life member of Clare Hall College, Cambridge (1995-present); and honorary fellow of the ESRC Centre for Research on Innovation and Competition, University of Manchester (1997-present). Foster has served as a member of the following editorial boards: *Journal of Evolutionary Economics, Review of Political Economy, Scottish Journal of Politifal Economy, Journal of Institutional Economics, and Economic Analysis and Policy.* Foster's research fields include: modelling the macroeconomy as a complex adaptive system; the application of self-organization theory to statistical and econometric modeling in the presence of structural transition; legal and regulatory interactions with the process of economic evolution; energy systems; and economic growth.

Julia Gavrilov has 7 years experience in network modeling and analysis, and in international studies at the Los Alamos National Laboratory. An economist by training, Gavrilov has participated in numerous projects related to national infrastructure protection and nonproliferation.

R. Quentin Grafton is professor of economics and director of economic development, growth economics and sustainability, Asia-Pacific School for Economics and Government at the Australian National University (ANU). His research interests include social networks and network theory; fisheries management (especially marine reserves); productivity and efficiency analysis; property rights (especially quantitative instruments in resource and environmental management); and economic growth and environmental performance.

Kimberly Holloman is director of Advanced Transformational Initiatives for Science Applications International Corporation (SAIC). At SAIC Holloman supports U.S. Department of Defense (DoD) research efforts related to military transformation and network-centric operations. From 2004 until 2006, she served as lead integrator of the Office of Force Transformation's Network Centric Operations Conceptual Framework Initiative. Prior to her work supporting the DoD, Holloman was an assistant professor at the School of International Service, The American University in Washington, DC. Holloman holds a PhD in international relations from The American University, an MA in economics, and a BA in political science, both from Virginia Tech.

Martin Huelse has been working in the field of embodied artificial intelligence, evolutionary robotics, and artificial neural networks since 2000. Within these areas, his work was focused on the design and analysis of recurrent neural networks for behavior control of autonomous mobile robots. Before he started to work at the Computer Science Department of the University of Wales, Aberystwyth (UK) in 2007, Huelse worked for 5 years at the former Fraunhofer Institute for Autonomous Intelligent Systems (AIS) in Sankt Augustin (Germany). During his time at AIS, Huelse received his PhD in computer science from the University of Osnabrueck, Germany.

Lubo Jankovic obtained his PhD in mechanical engineering from the University of Birmingham. He is the founding director of InteSys Ltd, honorary lecturer at the University of Birmingham, senior lecturer at the UCE, and fellow of the Institution of Analysts and Programmers. His research interests are in the field of science of complexity and application of its principles to dynamic modeling and analysis of behavior of complex systems.

Tom Kompas is director of the International and Development Economics Program and senior research economist at the Australian Bureau of Agricultural and Resource Economics (ABARE). He specializes in economic growth and dynamics, the economics of fisheries, agricultural economics, and productivity. He is currently an associate editor of the *Australian Journal of Agricultural and Resource Economics*.

Sascha Kraus is an assistant professor at the University of Oldenburg, Germany, and lecturer at the University of Klagenfurt, Austria, where he also received his doctorate in business administration. He holds several university degrees in business administration and management from business schools in Germany, the Netherlands, and Australia. Besides, he has spent 3 months as a visiting researcher at the University of Edinburgh, UK. He is also the founder of a new business venture in the media industry, and member of the board of two German small and medium-sized enterprises (SMEs). His main research interests are strategic management and entrepreneurship.

Mario Negrello studied mechanical engineering at the Federal University of Paraná in Brazil, Diploma (1997). To that followed a career in research and development with companies such as VW A.G., Delphi A.G., and Siemens A.G. (1998-2004). With interests in cognitive science, especially dynamical systems theory, he pursued a masters course at the University of Osnabrueck. He received his MSc in cognitive science (2006), with work on applications of computer vision. Currently he does research on neurodynamics and robotics for his PhD at the Fraunhofer Institute for Intelligent Analysis and Information Systems, Department of Autonomous Robots.

Alexander Outkin received his MS in theoretical physics from Moscow State University in 1991 and a PhD in economics from Virginia Tech in 1998. He has long been fascinated with emergent behaviors in socioeconomic and financial systems and with using agent-based and game-theoretic approaches to understand those behaviors. The results of his research into the NASDAQ stock market have been published in a book titled *-Y'A NASDAQ Market Simulation: Insights on a Major Market from the Science of Complex Adaptive Systems*¡. At present, Outkin works as a scientist at the Los Alamos National Laboratory, where he leads a multi-year effort to build a model of the financial system that incorporates individual agents' behaviors, payment systems, markets, telecommunications systems, and interactions between them. He lives in Los Alamos, NM with his wife and two daughters.

Mario Paolucci is technology expert at Laboratory of Agent Based Social Simulation (LABSS) (http://www.istc.cnr.it/lss/) in the Institute for Cognitive Science and Technology (IST/CNR), Rome. He has been teaching Fundamentals of Computer Science II at University of Perugia and data bases at the University of Rome 1. His research interests include social artifacts, norms, reputation, responsibility, and the cultural evolutionary mechanisms that support them. He has been studying and applying agent theory and multi-agent-based social simulation to understand social artifacts. He has chaired the RASTA '02 and '03 workshops, the RAS '04 workshop, and has participated in the program committee of conferences and workshops, including the MABS series. His publications include a book on reputation with Rosaria Conte and articles on JASSS and adaptive behavior.

Frank Pasemann studied physics and mathematics at Universities Marburg and Würzburg, and at the International Center for Theoretical Physics (ICTP), Trieste. Diploma (1971), Dr. rer.nat. (1977), and Habilitation (1985) in theoretical physics. Since 1985 Pasemann has been a professor for theoretical physics at Technical University Clausthal; since 2004 honor professor, Institute of Cognitive Science, University Osnabrück, Germany; Pasemann has headed research groups at the Research Centre Jülich, Jülich (1993-1996); the Max-Planck-Institute for mathematics in the sciences, Leipzig (1997-1999); the University Jena (2000-2001); and at the Fraunhofer Institute of Intelligent Analysis and Information Systems, Sankt Augustin (since 2002).

Pascal Perez is currently seconded by his French research agency CIRAD to the Australian National University (ANU) in Canberra (Australia). He is the gonvenor of the Human Ecosystems Modeling with Agents (HEMA) international network. An agronomist by training, his most recent work focuses on human ecosystems modeling. He has developed projects in northern Thailand, Indonesia, and Micronesia. He is currently teaching agent-based modeling at the ANU.

Walter Quattrociocchi is currently attending the last year of his masters degree in computer science at the University of Pisa, with a specialization in spatio-temporal classification in data mining. He is a member of the bioinformatics group at the University of Siena and member of Isti-KDD Lab at the National Council of Research. He has published works on theoretical model for knowledge extraction. He is currently having lectures in the field of data mining and knowledge extraction in complex systems. He is interested in data mining, complex systems, and cognition.

Nazmun N. Ratna is a PhD candidate at Asia Pacific School of Economics and Government (APSEG), The Australian National University (ANU). Before starting her PhD program she was working as an assistant professor in the Department of Economics, University of Dhaka, Bangladesh. In her thesis she focuses on the impact of social networks on diffusion processes and economic outcomes and the policy implications. Currently, she is working on an agent-based model for developing optimal marketing strategies with two competing pharmaceutical companies under a game theoretic framework.

Wolfgang Renz studied physics and mathematics at Stuttgart University. He received his degree in theoretical physics from the founder of Synergetics, Hermann Haken, and was awarded a doctoral degree by the RWTH Aachen in 1983. His primary research interests were the theory, modeling, and simulation of self-organization and cooperative phenomena. After research stays in Cambridge (UK) and the Rutherford Lab (UK) he worked at the Jülich Research Center, the FhG Bonn/St. Augustin (former GMD). Currently he is a professor at Hamburg University of Applied Sciences, where he founded the Multimedia Systems Lab. Research interests are self-organizing, multi-agent systems and virtual/augmented environments.

Carl Henning Reschke is a co-founder of the Institute for Management Research Cologne. He holds a doctorate in economics and business administration from the University of Witten/Herdecke, Germany. His dissertation analyzes evolutionary processes in the biopharmaceutical industry. He was as a researcher at MERIT, Maastricht, and participated in two startup projects. He has studied business and international economics at the Universities of Passau, Maastricht, Strasbourg, and Santa Cruz and taken courses in sociology at the University of Cologne. His research interests focus on strategy, innovation, and entrepreneurship as evolutionary learning processes.

Teresa Satterfield is an associate professor of romance linguistics and a faculty affiliate of the Center for the Study of Complex Systems at the University of Michigan. Her research incorporates notions of complex adaptive systems in the study of language acquisition and language contact phenomena, particularly with an eye toward providing greater socio- and psycho-linguistic explanations for the emergence of bilingualism and creole languages. She is the author of *Bilingual Selection of Syntactic Knowledge: Extending the Principles and Parameters Approach.*

Paul Scerri is a system scientist at the Robotics Institute at Carnegie Mellon University. He holds a BS in applied science (honors) from RMIT University in Australia and a PhD from Linkoping University in Sweden. He has been a research associate at the Information Sciences Institute at the University of Southern California. His research focuses on multi-agent coordination and human interaction with intelligent systems. He has contributed to the areas of adjustable autonomy, multi-agent systems, and team work. He has authored over 70 technical publications and has made contributions to several research programs including Defense Advanced Research Projects Agency (DARPA) programs software for distributed robotics, robot-agent-person teams, and autonomous negotiating teams.

Andy Seirp has a BBA and MA in economics from New Mexico State University and earned the Series 7 (registered rep) and Series 65 (registered investment advisor) securities licenses. He worked for 9 years in the securities industry with emphasis given to equity research and trading strategies. Following this, he worked for the state of New Mexico as a senior economist. Currently, he is employed by the Los Alamos National Laboratory where he has participated in projects such as NISAC's Financial Markets Modeling and JGI's genome sequencing. Seirp enjoys living in Los Alamos, NM with his wife, Jennifer, their two dogs and soon-to-be-home adopted son, Nathan.

Jan Sudeikat received a diploma degree in software engineering from the Hamburg University of Applied Sciences (HAW) in 2004. During his studies he spent one semester at the University of Shanghai for Science and Technology (USST). Currently, he is doctoral candidate at the Distributed Systems and Information Systems (VSIS) group at Hamburg University, research assistant at the HAW Multimedia Systems Lab, and lecturer at the Faculty of Engineering and Computer Science at HAW. He focuses on engineering methodologies for cognitive agent models and approaches to self-organizing, that is, decentralized coordinated, multi-agent systems.

Katia Sycara is a professor in the School of Computer Science at Carnegie Mellon University and the Sixth Century Chair in Computing at the University of Aberdeen.

She holds a PhD in computer science from Georgia Institute of Technology and an honorary doctorate from the University of the Aegean. She has authored more than 300 technical papers on Semantic Web services, multi-agent systems, and human-agent interaction. She is a lead developer of the OWL-S language for Semantic Web services. She is a fellow of IEEE, Fellow of AAAI, and the recipient of the 2002 ACM/SIGART Agents Research Award. She is a founding editor-in-chief of the journal *Autonomous Agents and Multi Agent Systems* and on the editorial board of six additional journals.

Paolo Turrini is a PhD student in cognitive science at the University of Siena. His research topics concern the mechanisms of regulation of multi-agent systems, such as norm enforcement, reputation dynamics, and organization emergence. He uses formal methods for modeling such mechanisms.

Index